Brussels,
Bruges & Antwerp

Leanne Logan
Geert Cole

LONELY PLANET PUBLICATIONS
Melbourne • Oakland • London • Paris

MAP 1 FLANDERS (VLAANDEREN)

Middelburg

Vlissingen

To Hull (UK)

NORTH SEA

To Dover (UK)

Het Zoute
Heist
Zeebrugge Knokke
Blankenberge

Het Zwin
Nature Reserve

De Haan

Damme

Leopoldkanaal

Ostend
(Oostende)

A10

E40

N9

Bruges
(Brugge)

N49

Eeklo

A18 E40

Nieuwpoort

To St Idesbald (1km)
& De Panne (2km)

Veurne

A17
E403

A10   E40

Ghent
(Gent)

Esen

Diksmuide

Tielt

Lije

Roeselare

E17

Vleteren

A14

Westvleteren

WEST-VLAANDEREN

Poperinge

Ypres
(Ieper)

A19

Waregem

Oudenaarde   Mater

Schelde (Schelde)

Kortrijk

Menen

Ronse

E42

Tourcoing

Armentières

Roubaix

A17
E403

A8   E429

Lille

FRANCE

Tournai

Pipaix   Tourpes

E17

To Paris
(175km)

0   5   10km
0   3   6mi

FLANDERS (VLAANDEREN) MAP 1

Brussels, Bruges & Antwerp
2nd edition – September 2001
First published – November 1999

Published by
Lonely Planet Publications Pty Ltd ABN 36 005 607 983
90 Maribyrnong St, Footscray, Victoria 3011, Australia

Lonely Planet Offices
Australia Locked Bag 1, Footscray, Victoria 3011
USA 150 Linden St, Oakland, CA 94607
UK 10a Spring Place, London NW5 3BH
France 1 rue du Dahomey, 75011 Paris

Photographs
Many of the images in this guide are available for licensing from
Lonely Planet Images:
Web site: www.lonelyplanetimages.com

Front cover photograph
Beer labels of Belgium (Leanne Logan)

ISBN 1 86450 314 9

Printed through Colorcraft Ltd, Hong Kong
Printed in China

**Although the authors
and Lonely Planet try
to make the informa-
tion as accurate as
possible, we accept
no responsibility for
any loss, injury or
inconvenience sus-
tained by anyone
using this book.**

Contents – Text

1

2 Contents – Text

The Authors

Leanne Logan

Leanne has been a regular visitor to Belgium since she got hooked on Belgian beers and a Flemish man while researching Lonely Planet's *Western Europe* guide a decade ago. Since then she has learnt to laugh with the locals at strange Belgian jokes, tallied up 188 of the country's hundreds of beers, managed not to become a raving chocoholic and has found out what it's like to be pummelled with dried pigs' bladders during Belgium's Carnival celebrations.

A journalist by trade, Leanne spent much of the 1990s researching and writing for Lonely Planet in places as diverse as Burkina Faso and New Caledonia. When she's not on the road, she can be found tending veggies and watching wallabies at the rural retreat she shares with her partner, Geert, in northern New South Wales, Australia.

Geert Cole

The Flemish love sayings and one of their favourite expressions is: *met een baksteen in de maag geboren* – 'born with a brick in the stomach'. It's their way of explaining why Belgians are not big on travel.

Geert must have dipped out when the bricks were handed out, for this Belgian has been travelling the world for almost as long as he can remember. Initially he set off to discover broader horizons and later, throughout the 1990s and beyond, to work on many Lonely Planet guides.

Life outside Belgium, however, has its drawbacks, not least the dearth of good beers. So when it came to working on a guide to Belgium's three best cities, including his home town of Antwerp, this brickless Belgian was more than ready to return. After all, someone had to test the beers and roam the best pubs.

FROM THE AUTHORS

As always, we had a ball in all three cities. Thanks in particular to Dirk Mertens and Els Maes at Toerisme Vlaanderen, Sabine Rosen at the OPT, Vera Verschooren (Antwerp), Anne De Meerleer (Bruges) and Anousjka Schmidt (Brussels).

We enlisted and were offered the support of many other people. We'd like to thank the travellers we met in the various pubs and bars, as well as Alain Hije from ARAU, John Miller and Tony Mallet at the *Bulletin* magazine and Olivier Guilbaud at the Album Museum.

Our warmest *bedankt* to the Cole family for lighting a candle and ordering snow on Christmas Day; to the Van Roey family for braving frostbite while exploring parks; the Werders for risking life and limb at Mebbin, and Sandy Thompson for keeping a watchful eye on things; and to our best mates, Sixy and Bluey, for knowing life was meant to be one big Delirium Tremens.

And last but not least, *dank U wel* to all those at Lonely Planet's UK office who were involved with the production of this book.

This Book

The 1st edition of *Brussels, Bruges & Antwerp* was written by Leanne Logan, Geert Cole and Renée Cordes.

This 2nd edition was written and updated by Leanne and Geert.

From the Publisher

This edition of *Brussels, Bruges & Antwerp* was edited and proofed in Lonely Planet's London office by Michala Green, with help from Arabella Shepherd and Helen Parry. James Timmins was responsible for mapping, design and layout. James Ellis drew the climate chart, David Wenk drew the map legend, Andrew Weatherill designed the cover with help from Adam McCrow and Lachlan Ross drew the back-cover map. Quentin Frayne and Emma Koch produced the language chapter. Lonely Planet Images provided photographs, and illustrations were drawn by Albert Cole and Asa Andersson.

Thanks to Leanne and Geert for their enthusiasm and ideas.

Thanks

Many thanks to the travellers who used the last edition and contacted us with helpful hints, advice and interesting anecdotes:

Dirk Bruynee, Michael Clinch, Lison Dekkers, Colette Dollin, Bruno Geoffrion, Mr J Glover, M Grant, Tom Horton, Jo Lane, Ashton P Morris, Glenn Proctor, Alex Tomlin.

Foreword

ABOUT LONELY PLANET GUIDEBOOKS

The story begins with a classic travel adventure: Tony and Maureen Wheeler's 1972 journey across Europe and Asia to Australia. Useful information about the overland trail did not exist at that time, so Tony and Maureen published the first Lonely Planet guidebook to meet a growing need.

From a kitchen table, then from a tiny office in Melbourne (Australia), Lonely Planet has become the largest independent travel publisher in the world, an international company with offices in Melbourne, Oakland (USA), London (UK) and Paris (France).

Today Lonely Planet guidebooks cover the globe. There is an ever-growing list of books and there's information in a variety of forms and media. Some things haven't changed. The main aim is still to help make it possible for adventurous travellers to get out there – to explore and better understand the world.

At Lonely Planet we believe travellers can make a positive contribution to the countries they visit – if they respect their host communities and spend their money wisely. Since 1986 a percentage of the income from each book has been donated to aid projects and human rights campaigns.

Updates Lonely Planet thoroughly updates each guidebook as often as possible. This usually means there are around two years between editions, although for more unusual or more stable destinations the gap can be longer. Check the imprint page (following the colour map at the beginning of the book) for publication dates.

Between editions up-to-date information is available in two free newsletters – the paper *Planet Talk* and email *Comet* (to subscribe, contact any Lonely Planet office) – and on our Web site at www.lonelyplanet.com. The *Upgrades* section of the Web site covers a number of important and volatile destinations and is regularly updated by Lonely Planet authors. *Scoop* covers news and current affairs relevant to travellers. And, lastly, the *Thorn Tree* bulletin board and *Postcards* section of the site carry unverified, but fascinating, reports from travellers.

Correspondence The process of creating new editions begins with the letters, postcards and emails received from travellers. This correspondence often includes suggestions, criticisms and comments about the current editions. Interesting excerpts are immediately passed on via newsletters and the Web site, and everything goes to our authors to be verified when they're researching on the road. We're keen to get more feedback from organisations or individuals who represent communities visited by travellers.

Lonely Planet gathers information for everyone who's curious about the planet – and especially for those who explore it first-hand. Through guidebooks, phrasebooks, activity guides, maps, literature, newsletters, image library, TV series and Web site we act as an information exchange for a worldwide community of travellers.

Research Authors aim to gather sufficient practical information to enable travellers to make informed choices and to make the mechanics of a journey run smoothly. They also research historical and cultural background to help enrich the travel experience and allow travellers to understand and respond appropriately to cultural and environmental issues.

Authors don't stay in every hotel because that would mean spending a couple of months in each medium-sized city and, no, they don't eat at every restaurant because that would mean stretching belts beyond capacity. They do visit hotels and restaurants to check standards and prices, but feedback based on readers' direct experiences can be very helpful.

Many of our authors work undercover, others aren't so secretive. None of them accept freebies in exchange for positive write-ups. And none of our guidebooks contain any advertising.

Production Authors submit their raw manuscripts and maps to offices in Australia, USA, UK or France. Editors and cartographers – all experienced travellers themselves – then begin the process of assembling the pieces. When the book finally hits the shops, some things are already out of date, we start getting feedback from readers and the process begins again ...

WARNING & REQUEST

Things change – prices go up, schedules change, good places go bad and bad places go bankrupt – nothing stays the same. So, if you find things better or worse, recently opened or long since closed, please tell us and help make the next edition even more accurate and useful. We genuinely value all the feedback we receive. A well-travelled team reads and acknowledges every letter, postcard and email and ensures that every morsel of information finds its way to the appropriate authors, editors and cartographers for verification.

Everyone who writes to us will find their name in the next edition of the appropriate guidebook. They will also receive the latest issue of *Planet Talk*, our quarterly printed newsletter, or *Comet*, our monthly email newsletter. Subscriptions to both newsletters are free. The very best contributions will be rewarded with a free guidebook.

Excerpts from your correspondence may appear in new editions of Lonely Planet guidebooks, the Lonely Planet Web site, *Planet Talk* or *Comet*, so please let us know if you *don't* want your letter published or your name acknowledged.

Send all correspondence to the Lonely Planet office closest to you:

Australia: Locked Bag 1, Footscray, Victoria 3011
USA: 150 Linden St, Oakland, CA 94607
UK: 10a Spring Place, London NW5 3BH
France: 1 rue du Dahomey, 75011 Paris

Or email us at: talk2us@lonelyplanet.com.au

For news, views and updates see our Web site: www.lonelyplanet.com

HOW TO USE A LONELY PLANET GUIDEBOOK

The best way to use a Lonely Planet guidebook is any way you choose. At Lonely Planet we believe the most memorable travel experiences are often those that are unexpected, and the finest discoveries are those you make yourself. Guidebooks are not intended to be used as if they provide a detailed set of infallible instructions!

Contents All Lonely Planet guidebooks follow roughly the same format. The Facts about the Destination chapters or sections give background information ranging from history to weather. Facts for the Visitor gives practical information on issues like visas and health. Getting There & Away gives a brief starting point for researching travel to and from the destination. Getting Around gives an overview of the transport options when you arrive.

The peculiar demands of each destination determine how subsequent chapters are broken up, but some things remain constant. We always start with background, then proceed to sights, places to stay, places to eat, entertainment, getting there and away, and getting around information – in that order.

Heading Hierarchy Lonely Planet headings are used in a strict hierarchical structure that can be visualised as a set of Russian dolls. Each heading (and its following text) is encompassed by any preceding heading that is higher on the hierarchical ladder.

Entry Points We do not assume guidebooks will be read from beginning to end, but that people will dip into them. The traditional entry points are the list of contents and the index. In addition, however, some books have a complete list of maps and an index map illustrating map coverage.

There may also be a colour map that shows highlights. These highlights are dealt with in greater detail in the Facts for the Visitor chapter, along with planning questions and suggested itineraries. Each chapter covering a geographical region usually begins with a locator map and another list of highlights. Once you find something of interest in a list of highlights, turn to the index.

Maps Maps play a crucial role in Lonely Planet guidebooks and include a huge amount of information. A legend is printed on the back page. We seek to have complete consistency between maps and text, and to have every important place in the text captured on a map. Map key numbers usually start in the top left corner.

Although inclusion in a guidebook usually implies a recommendation we cannot list every good place. Exclusion does not necessarily imply criticism. In fact there are a number of reasons why we might exclude a place – sometimes it is simply inappropriate to encourage an influx of travellers.

Introduction

Think of Belgium, and it's probably not Brussels, Bruges and Antwerp that spring to mind. More likely word associations might be the EU and Hercule Poirot, or – depending on your view of life – chocolate, beer and chips. Brussels, Bruges and Antwerp are the keys to Belgium, as different from each other as it gets yet inextricably linked.

It's surprising how little is generally known about Belgium (België in Flemish, Belgique in French) or its three most popular cities. Brussels, Bruges and Antwerp were among medieval Europe's greatest centres, home to famous painters like Van Eyck, Breugel and Rubens, and at the forefront of many of Europe's most decisive battles. At one time quaint little Bruges – now Western Europe's best-preserved medieval city – was one of the world's most prosperous trading centres. By the 16th century Antwerp – Rubens' home – was Europe's undisputed economic hub. A century ago Brussels, the capital, led the way in Art Nouveau, a movement that influenced modern art and architecture around the world.

As well as a dynamic and often troubled history, the three cities share a vibrant culture that, from a visitor's point of view, is all the more rich for its diversity. Many Belgians, however, don't see it quite that way, and the two main linguistic groups – the Flemish and the Walloons – are often at loggerheads over economics, politics and, indeed, the future of the country.

At the heart of all of this is Brussels, the 'capital of Europe'. It is not a teeming metropolis like New York or a giant like London; instead it's a city of human proportions. The exquisite Grand Place, Brussels' famous central square, is a magnet for visitors during the day and is romantically lit up at night. The splendid Musées Royaux des Beaux-Arts is home to a superb array of paintings by old masters and Surrealists. At the Centre Belge de la Bande Dessinée, a gorgeous Art Nouveau building, you can revel in Belgium's wonderful comic-strip culture. 'Boring' is the word used by some Europeans who see Brussels as the artificial centre of Europe, the home of Eurocrats and businesspeople who jet off every weekend leaving behind a deserted city. Those in the know tell a different story, a tale of fabulous restaurants, the best beers, and cafes where you can drink until dawn (or later).

In Bruges you step back in time. This picture-postcard city has gabled houses lining serene canals, a mighty belfry rising from the centuries-old Markt, and the Groeningemuseum, a marvellous showcase of Flemish Primitive art. At the other extreme is Antwerp, one of Europe's designer capitals which manages to successfully mix the hip, the hedonistic and the historical. It boasts acclaimed works by Rubens, architectural delights in the celebrated Cogels-Osylei area and some of the best nightlife to be enjoyed anywhere in this corner of Europe.

Brussels and Antwerp – the two largest cities – sit less than 50km apart in the north of Belgium. Bruges is an hour's drive from either, near the coast. The trio's proximity to each other is a boon for visitors.

At the end of the day, Belgium's restaurants await. Cuisine here is among Europe's best, with traditional fare served alongside innovative contemporary dishes. Belgium also has the world's most mind-boggling array of beers (and most of them are excellent) as well as an enviable array of great drinking places.

So what does excellent food, great beer and a diverse mix of enticing museums, old masterpieces and architectural gems in one tiny area all add up to? Three of Western Europe's best-kept secrets: Brussels, Bruges and Antwerp.

Facts about the Cities

HISTORY

Although Brussels, Bruges and Antwerp evolved quite independently from each other, their histories are, of course, linked. The wealth of one affected the prosperity of the other; as one fell another rose.

Similarly, Belgium's history as a whole is largely intertwined with that of neighbouring Luxembourg and the Netherlands. The current borders of these three countries – known throughout much of their history as the Low Countries – were only realised in the 19th century. The development of this little corner of Europe reflects some of the major events in Western European history, and the fortunes and misfortunes of the three cities has been largely shaped by Europe's ever-changing balance of power.

Early Settlements

Neolithic settlers were the first inhabitants of the Low Countries. They are believed to have lived in the Brussels districts of Schaerbeek, Boitsfort and Uccle from around 2250 BC, though there are now no traces of their civilisation. In Bruges, historical records begin in AD 850; however, archaeologists have unearthed evidence of a settlement from 3000 BC.

The arrival of the Romans in 57 BC heralded Belgium's long history of invasion. During his conquest of Gaul (roughly current-day France, Belgium and a part of Germany), Julius Caesar made mention of the Belgae, from which the 19th-century name Belgium was derived. Belgium's tribal people, mainly of Gallo-Celtic stock, steadfastly opposed Caesar's armies but were eventually defeated. The Romans remained in the region, which became known as Gallia Belgica, for the next 500 years. Compared with other places in Gaul, Gallia Belgica was never a vital cog in their wheel and, these days, there is very little to show of the Romans' presence.

By the 3rd century, with the Roman Empire on the verge of collapse, Germanic

Franks took control. This change in power is the basis of Belgium's current language division as the northern region gradually became German-speaking while the southern portion remained Latin-based. The Franks ousted sailors from the north-Germanic Frisian tribe who had first settled in Antwerp around the 2nd century.

In 695, St Géry, bishop of Cambrai and Arras, built a chapel on one of the islands in the swampy River Senne (Zenne) in the area now known as Brussels. A settlement developed, though the name Bruocsella (from *bruoc*, marsh or swamp, and *sella*, dwelling) was not recorded before 966.

The Franks' successors were the Carolingians whose most celebrated king, Charlemagne, ruled for nearly half a century from 768 and extended the kingdom from Denmark to Italy. In 800, Charlemagne was crowned the first Holy Roman Emperor by the pope. At around this time, a fort was built in Antwerp and it was visited by noted Christian missionaries such as St Amand and St Bavo.

After Charlemagne's death in 814, the Treaty of Verdun (843) cut his mighty empire into three portions corresponding roughly to Germany, France and the Low Countries. The River Scheldt was the dividing line between the French and German regions; this was the first division of Belgian lands into what would become modern-day French-speaking Wallonia and Flemish-speaking Flanders.

The Rise of Flanders

The arrival of raiding parties of Vikings in the 9th and 10th centuries promoted the growth of feudal domains and authority. Although the kings of France and emperors in Germany took overall control of most of the Low Countries, the real power was held by local counts who ruled over fiefdoms.

One of the most powerful courts during feudal times was that of the counts of Flanders. Its instigator was Baldwin the Iron

Arm who kidnapped the daughter of a French king in 867, married her and constructed a fortress in Ghent. Baldwin also built a castle in Bruges and gradually a town grew up there, based on the trade that came via the nearby town of Damme and the Zwin, an estuary that led to the North Sea. Baldwin's successors expanded the territory and influence of Flanders over the next three centuries beyond the Scheldt and as far south as the River Somme in northern France. One of his successors, Robert the Frisian, made Bruges the capital of the Duchy of Flanders in 1093.

With the decline of feudalism in the 12th and 13th centuries came the rise of the first towns. Flanders had been producing cloth since about the 10th century but its manufacture took off with the growth of cities such as Ypres, Ghent and Bruges, which blossomed with the expansion of trade across northern Europe. Merchant ships from all over Europe docked in Bruges to trade Flemish cloth for cheese, wool, lead, tin and coal from England; pigs from Denmark; wine from Spain and Germany; silks and oriental spices from Venice and Genoa; and furs from as far away as Russia and Bulgaria. When Philip the Fair, king of France, visited Bruges in 1301 his wife, Joanna of Navarre, was so surprised by the inhabitants' wealth and luxurious clothes that she purportedly claimed: 'I thought I alone was queen, but I see that I have 600 rivals here.'

This flurry of activity bred a new class of rich merchants who gained increasing political power. At the same time, craftsmen and traders joined forces and established guilds (see the boxed text 'Guilds').

But it wasn't long before the aspirations of the burgeoning burghers and weavers clashed with those of the local counts. The Flemish weavers relied for trade on a steady supply of high-quality wool from England and for this purpose they sided with the English during conflicts between England and France. The local counts, on the other hand, were vassals of the king of France, and their dynastic ambitions were steadfastly tied to France's territorial gains. In addition, merchants and townspeople were starting to demand greater powers and more rights, demands that the local counts quelled by calling in the French army. The result of all this disharmony came to a head in 1302 in two bloody confrontations.

The first, known as the Brugse Matin, was sparked by the guildsmen's refusal to pay a new round of taxes. Philip sent a 2000-strong army to Bruges to restore order and garrison the town. On 18 May Pieter De Coninck, dean of the Guild of Weavers, and Jan Breydel, dean of the Guild of Butchers, led a revolt against the army. The guildsmen crept into the town early in the morning and murdered anyone who could not correctly pronounce the Flemish phrase *schild en vriend* (shield and friend). The revolt sparked a widespread rebellion and led, just six weeks later, to the guildsmen's victory over the French at the Battle of the Golden Spurs near Kortrijk south of Bruges. This battle has become a celebrated landmark in Flemish resistance to the French, though at the time it kept the French overlords off the doorstep for a short time only.

Guilds

In medieval Belgium, traders and craftsmen formed groups known as guilds, setting standards for their craft and establishing a trade monopoly in their geographic area. But the guilds, run mainly by wealthy families, also sought to exert political influence and control town or city governments to further their own economic interests, particularly in Brussels.

During the 16th century they began building headquarters, first in wood and then in stone. In Brussels and Antwerp these guildhalls border the old market square (the Grand Place and Grote Markt, respectively), which emerged as the gathering place and centre of public life.

The Burgundian Empire

By the 14th century Bruges, Ghent, Ypres, Brussels, Leuven and Mechelen were all prosperous towns. In fact, by 1340, Ghent had grown to become the largest city in

Europe after Paris. Bruges became a key member of the Hanseatic League of Seventeen Cities, a powerful association of northern European trading cities, and Italian cities such as Genoa, Florence and Venice built trade houses here (see the boxed text 'The First Bourse'). However, much of the remainder of the Low Countries was still largely a rural society.

During the Hundred Years' War (1337–1453), a conflict between France and England over the French throne, the dukes of Burgundy came to power. This series of four dukes ruled for less than a century but the cultural changes that took place during their reigns were profound.

Philip the Good (ruled 1419–67) presided over a vast empire that included the Burgundian region of eastern France and the area covering most of modern Belgium and the Netherlands. The court had a palace in Dijon (France) but Philip ruled the kingdom from Brussels and Bruges, earning the title Conditor Belgii, Belgium's founder. Philip was the richest man in Europe and his court was the height of culture and fashion. Belgium's first university was founded in Leuven, Brussels' magnificent Grand Place was constructed, Bruges' population ballooned to 200,000 (double that of London), and the arts, particularly painting and tapestry-making, flourished. Philip employed Jan Van Eyck (c1390–1441) of Bruges as court painter, and so rose a group of artists – known as the Flemish Primitives – who perfected a style of painting in bold colours that are still vivid today.

On his death, Philip was succeeded by his son Charles the Bold (known as Karel de Stoute in Flanders) who ruled from 1467 to 1477 and, for a time, used the town of Mechelen as his administrative base. Charles tried to expand his empire but was killed at the Battle of Nancy. This prompted Louis XI of France to seize the French part of Burgundy for himself; Charles' daughter, Mary, was then left ruling only the Low Countries. Mary's mother, Margaret of York (sister of Edward IV of England), arranged a marriage between Mary and Maximilian I, a member of the ruling Austrian Hapsburg family.

Hapsburg Rule

When Mary was killed in a riding accident in 1482, Maximilian became ruler. He acted as regent until their son, Philip the Handsome, who was four at the time of his mother's death, assumed power in 1494. Two years later the houses of Burgundy and Hapsburg were united when Philip married Jeanne of Aragon and Castile. Their son, Charles V, was born in Ghent in 1500 and became duke of Brabant and ruler of the Low Countries at the ripe old age of 15. The next year he became king of Spain and later of Naples, Sardinia, Sicily and the Spanish territories in the New World (Mexico, Peru and the Caribbean). He was crowned king of Germany and Holy Roman Emperor in 1519, thus becoming Europe's most powerful ruler.

Charles grew up in Mechelen in the court of his guardian, Margaret of Austria and, after being crowned, initially ruled from Brussels. He was advised by the great humanist Desiderius Erasmus (see the boxed text 'Erasmus – Renaissance Man' for more details). Charles always considered the Low Countries his home and returned often; however, much of his life was spent travelling in far-flung parts of the Empire and, later, ruling from Spain. His sister, Mary of Hungary, was responsible for the region for

The First Bourse

When Hanseatic merchants from all over Europe passed through Bruges in the 14th century, many stayed a while. Some bought or rented houses, while others sought accommodation in taverns such as the one owned by the Van der Beurs, a leading merchant family, at Grauwwerkersstraat 35. The family met with merchants from Italy, Spain and Portugal on the little square in front of the house, fixing prices and laying the foundation for the first stock exchange – or *beurs*. Some say that this is the origin of the word Bourse, still used today to denote stock exchanges.

Erasmus – Renaissance Man

Desiderius Erasmus (1469–1536), a humanist philosopher considered the greatest Renaissance scholar, became advisor to the young duke of Brabant, later Emperor Charles V, in 1516.

That year he wrote *The Education of a Young Prince* for Charles and published his Latin translation of the Greek version of the New Testament. Although he was religious, he believed human beings had control over their destinies and should be nurtured through secular education. After helping to establish the College of Three Languages at Leuven between 1517 and 1521, Erasmus spent five months at the home of Canon Wijkman in nearby Anderlecht in Brussels recuperating from illness – the 16th-century gabled house is now a museum.

most of his reign, during which the Low Countries as a whole experienced unprecedented commercial and cultural growth.

But it wasn't all prosperity. The great Flemish cloth towns were in decline due to competition from cloth manufacturers in England and to the silting of the Zwin, which connected Bruges to the sea. In addition Charles, like Maximilian before him (who'd actually been imprisoned in Bruges when he attempted to restrict the city's privileges), favoured the rising city of Antwerp over the old cloth towns as the principal centre for trade and commerce. His choice was fuelled by frustration with the rebellious burghers of Flanders – in 1540 he personally repressed an uprising by townsfolk in Ghent against heavy taxes imposed to

help finance the wars of their absent leader. This was just one of many such revolts. Eventually tired of facing opposition for the high taxes and after spending a lifetime fighting wars, Charles returned to Brussels where he abdicated in 1555 in favour of his son, Philip. By this time, the Hanseatic League headquarters had moved from Bruges to Antwerp and the latter became the Empire's greatest port. Bruges, meanwhile, entered a 400-year slumber.

Religious Revolt

During Charles' reign, Protestantism had been sweeping through much of Europe. This religious and political rethink of the world according to the Roman Catholic elite became known as the Reformation. Theologians and humanists such as Erasmus, Martin Luther, the German leader of the Reformation and John Calvin, his French counterpart, brought different interpretations to traditional religious thought.

The Reformation met with severe repercussions in the Low Countries. In 1550 Charles ordered the Edict of Blood, which decreed the death penalty to those convicted of heresy. When his son, Philip II, came to the throne, he took a more zealous approach. Philip was born in Spain and ruled from there; he had little interest in his subjects in the Low Countries and was largely unpopular in the region.

Determined to defend the Catholic faith, he quashed any resistance by implementing a string of anti-Protestant edicts and garrisoning towns in the Low Countries with Spanish mercenaries.

In 1566, the Protestants revolted, running riot and ransacking churches in a wave of violence that has become known as the 'Iconoclastic Fury'. Philip retaliated with a force of 10,000 troops lead by the duke of Alva who immediately set up the 'Council of Blood' that handed out thousands of death sentences to those involved in the rioting. Count Egmont and Count Hoorn, vocal protesters against Spanish rule, were executed on Brussels' Grand Place in front of the Maison du Roi. In the following years, rebellions broke out in many cities, including Brussels and Antwerp, but the Spanish held firm.

By the end of the Revolt of the Netherlands, as this whole period became known, the Low Countries' present borders were roughly established. Holland and its allied northern regions, known as the United Provinces, victoriously expelled the Spaniards while Belgium and Luxembourg, or the Spanish Netherlands, stayed under their rule.

This episode of history was particularly debilitating for Antwerp. Its mighty cathedral was plundered during the Iconoclastic Fury. Then, 10 years later, the unpaid Spanish garrison based in Antwerp mutinied, pillaging the city and in three nights massacred 8000 people in what has become known as the 'Spanish fury'. To top it all off, Philip II demanded that Antwerp become a Catholic city. Protestants were forced to head north to the relative safety of the United Provinces (today's Netherlands) and, by 1589, Antwerp's population had nosedived to 42,000. The United Provinces, in particular Amsterdam, would soon benefit from this influx of skilled and independent-minded people.

The Spanish Netherlands

Brussels was proclaimed capital of the Spanish Netherlands in 1585. In 1598 Philip II handed the Spanish Netherlands to his daughter, Infanta Isabella, and her husband, Archduke Albert of Austria. The pair signed a peace deal with the United Provinces in 1609 that lasted for 12 years but, other than that, their 40-year reign is most noted for its flamboyant court, which gave rise to new industries such as lacemaking and diamond processing. In turn this brief economic boom boosted cultural life and brought to the fore Antwerp-based painters such as Pieter Paul Rubens (see the boxed text 'Pieter Paul Rubens' in the Antwerp chapter for more details), Antoon (Anthony) Van Dyck and Jacob Jordaens.

The Treaty of Westphalia in 1648 brought to an end the religious-based Thirty Years' War which had involved much of Western Europe since 1618. This treaty recognised the United Provinces as an independent republic and closed part of the Scheldt to all non-Dutch ships. This act guaranteed the rise of Amsterdam as the region's premier port and heralded its Golden Age; in contrast, the port city of Antwerp was ruined.

Antwerp was not alone in its predicament. With the loss of many of its most skilled workers, bankers and merchants, much of the Spanish Netherlands sunk into poverty and life became an exercise in religious piety. During this Catholic Counter-Reformation, the newly-formed Jesuit order prospered and multiplied, and elaborate baroque churches were built. Filled with magnificent statues, huge wooden pulpits and glorified paintings of Christ's suffering executed by artists such as Rubens, the churches symbolised the Catholic Church's power and the magical redemption that awaited the faithful.

A new round of European wars broke out in the 17th century. In 1695 Louis XIV's French army under Marshal De Villeroy bombarded Brussels for two days in retaliation for Dutch and English attacks on French ports. They destroyed 4000 houses and much of Grand Place, although this was restored to its full glory within five years. The fighting came to a head with the War of Spanish Succession (1701–13), which involved much of Europe and ended with the Treaty of Utrecht. This treaty saw the Spanish Netherlands handed over to the Austrians.

The Austrian Netherlands

The mighty Austrian Hapsburgs ruled from 1713 to 1794. Although there was some initial unrest as the citizens of Brussels rebelled against their new leaders, the century as a whole was a peaceful change to what had come before. Austrian rule fostered a surge in urban development in Brussels, with the construction of squares such as Place Royale and completion of the royal palace at Laeken (1784). Most of the architectural gems of Brussels' Upper Town were built during the reigns of three successive Austrian rulers: Charles VI (ruled 1711–40), Maria-Theresa (ruled 1740–80) and Joseph II (ruled 1780–90).

When Joseph II came to the throne he tried to bring about radical change, such as taxing the Church and recognising religious freedom, which alienated the privileged and working classes equally. Austrian troops were forced out of Brussels and, in 1790, the United Belgian States were proclaimed. But fighting within the rebels' two main factions lead to anarchy and, by the end of the year, the Austrians regained control.

French Occupation

After easily defeating the Austrians at the Battle of Fleurus in 1794, the French took over the Austrian Netherlands. Initially the locals welcomed the French, thinking they would create a modern state based on merit not wealth. But the French sought to suppress the people and, in 1795, absorbed the area into France. Old provinces were abolished, French laws were ushered in, the Catholic Church was repressed (many churches were ransacked and monasteries closed) and conscription was introduced. The latter was widely unpopular and a passionate Peasants' Revolt in 1798 was cruelly put down.

In 1815 Napoleon Bonaparte, leader of the new French state, was defeated by British, Dutch and Prussian forces at the Battle of Waterloo near Brussels (see the boxed text 'The Battle of Waterloo' in the Brussels chapter for details). This resulted in the creation of the United Kingdom of the Netherlands, incorporating Holland, Belgium and Luxembourg.

The United Kingdom of the Netherlands

The Congress of Vienna created the United Kingdom of the Netherlands largely to preserve the balance of power in Europe and to create a buffer state to inhibit any plans the French might have had of northwards expansion. The fact that people of different religions and customs were being forced together was of little consequence.

William, Prince of Orange, crowned King William I in Brussels, was given the throne and he divided his time equally between Brussels and its twin capital, The Hague. But William made enemies quickly after refusing to give southern Belgium fair

A Revolutionary Performance

ALBERT COLE

An opera performance at the Théâtre de la Monnaie in Brussels on 25 August 1830 started a revolution. That night marked the Brussels premiere of a new opera called *La Muette de Portici* (The Dumb Girl of Portici) by French composer Daniel-François-Esprit Auber. The story, which centres on a 1647 Naples uprising against the Spanish, features large crowd scenes and dramatic effects.

But the opera was nothing compared with the encore that followed on Brussels' streets. Patriotic cries such as 'far better to die than to live a wretched life in slavery and shame!' and 'away with the yoke before which we tremble, away with the foreigner who laughs at our torment!' incited an instant rebellion, with the mainly bourgeois audience pouring into the streets to join workers already demonstrating outside the theatre against their Dutch rulers.

Together they stormed the Palais de Justice, chased out the Dutch troops and in a glorious crowning moment raised the flag of Brabant over the Hôtel de Ville.

Demonstrations continued for days, culminating in a skirmish between the Dutch and Belgians in the Parc de Bruxelles, with the Dutch giving up their fight by September.

Belgian independence was recognised at the Conference of London in January 1831 and Léopold of Saxe-Coburg Gotha became Belgium's first king.

political representation and trying to impose Dutch as the national language. The latter angered not only the French-speaking Walloons in the south of Belgium but also Flemish speakers in the north who regard their language as distinct from Dutch.

The inevitable Belgian revolution against the Dutch began on 25 August 1830 during an opera performance in Brussels (see the earlier boxed text 'A Revolutionary Performance'). William I sent in his troops but they were defeated. And so a new nation was born.

Belgian Independence

At the Conference of London in January 1831, the European powers recognised Belgian independence and the country was officially declared a neutral state. On 21 July 1831 Léopold of Saxe-Coburg Gotha, uncle of the future British monarch Queen Victoria, took the constitutional oath and became King Léopold I of Belgium. Brussels, which had 100,000 inhabitants, was declared the capital.

During Léopold's reign Belgium was caught between Franco-German rivalry, although it remained neutral during the Franco-Prussian War (1870–1). The ensuing years saw the start of Flemish nationalism, with tension growing between Flemish and French speakers that would eventually lead to a language partition dividing the country to this day (see the boxed text 'The Linguistic Divide' later in the chapter).

After his death in 1865 Léopold I was succeeded by his son Léopold II (ruled 1865–1909) who was committed to transforming the tiny country into a strong nation, both through colonial conquests and the development of Brussels and Antwerp. Brussels was bolstered by the construction of monumental buildings such as the Palais des Beaux-Arts (1876) and a new Palais de Justice (1879). New railway lines meant Antwerp's port, interest in which had been rekindled during the French occupation, was further developed and it soon became the world's third-largest port after London and New York. This boom culminated in the 1880 golden jubilee exhibition celebrating the founding of the Belgian state.

However, Léopold II had wider aspirations and in 1878 he sought a territory to colonise. By 1885, mainly through a series of dubious treaties and contracts, Léopold came to personally control a huge slice of central Africa – an area 70 times larger than Belgium itself. But he was forced to relinquish it to the state in 1908 amid mounting international criticism at the way the colony was being run (see the boxed text 'Léopold II & the Congo' in the Brussels chapter). Belgium held onto the Congo until 1960.

The 20th Century

In 1909 Léopold died and was succeeded by his 21-year-old nephew, Albert I (ruled 1909–34), who was nicknamed the 'Soldier King' due to his hugely popular actions during World War I. When war broke out in 1914, Germany violated Belgian neutrality and occupied the country. Albert moved his administration to the seaside town of De Panne, part of a small triangle of land that remained unoccupied throughout the war. From here he led the Belgian army's efforts to man the northern end of the frontline which separated the Allies and the strategic French coastal towns around Calais from the advancing German army. The former cloth town of Ypres bore the brunt of the battles on Belgian soil and when the war ended in 1918 Ypres was reduced to rubble.

After the war the Treaty of Versailles abolished Belgium's neutral status and the country was given reparations from Germany including a chunk of land around the towns of Eupen and St Vith in the east of the country (home these days to Belgium's small German-speaking community) as well as the colonies of Burundi and Rwanda in central Africa. In 1934 Albert I died in a rock-climbing accident near Namur and was succeeded by his son, Léopold III (ruled 1934–51).

On 10 May 1940, the Germans launched a surprise air attack on the Netherlands, Belgium and Luxembourg and within eight days Belgium was occupied. Unlike his father, Léopold III put up little resistance and quickly surrendered, leaving the Allies in a precarious state. The Belgian government opposed the king's decision and fled to London where it operated in exile throughout WWII. A strong resistance movement developed during Nazi occupation but there was also collaboration from fascist elements of Belgian society and from within the Flemish movement. Belgium's Jewish population fared terribly and the country's small Gypsy minority was all but wiped out. Belgium was liberated in September 1944.

After WWII, the country was caught up in a constitutional crisis over Léopold III's wartime actions. While some accused him of collaborating with the Germans, others said the early surrender saved the country. In 1951, under pressure from Walloon socialists, he abdicated in favour of his son, Baudouin I (ruled 1951–93).

Although only 21 when he took the throne, Baudouin succeeded in bringing the nation together (see the boxed text 'A King for All Times'). He died childless and was succeeded by his younger brother, Albert II, who is king today. Albert reluctantly accepted the throne after the government rejected his eldest son Prince Philippe as king, largely because he was unmarried at the time.

Like a phoenix rising from the ashes, Belgium emerged as a key player in international politics after WWII. In 1958 Brussels became the provisional seat of the European Commission and the Council of Ministers (see the boxed text 'The EU in Brussels' in the Brussels chapter). In 1967 the North Atlantic Treaty Organisation (NATO) moved to Brussels from France a year after the French withdrew from NATO's military wing. In 1999, to celebrate its 50th anniversary, NATO leaders agreed to close the existing base and build a new headquarters at Haren on the north-eastern outskirts of the capital. It's expected to be finished in 2006.

In the past decade, Belgium has had to cope with a series of shocking crimes that has blighted the nation's reputation. At the heart of this is the case of paedophile, convicted rapist and suspected child murderer Marc Dutroux, which involved the murder of four girls and kidnapping of another two. Due to Belgium's complex legal system, Dutroux has not yet faced court.

In a nation already heartily disillusioned with politicians, government and workable democracy, the public revelations about incompetence during the investigation of the Dutroux case were intolerable. In October 1996, some 300,000 Belgians marched through the streets of Brussels in the 'White March' to protest against the nation's malfunctioning police and judicial systems.

Reform has been slow if almost nonexistent and many Belgians remain pessimistic about the future of their country. One of the

A King for All Times

King Baudouin I (ruled 1951–93) was the first leader to truly unite Belgium.

The son of Léopold III and Queen Astrid, Baudouin (Boudewijn in Flemish) was both interned with his father by the Germans during WWII and exiled to Switzerland following the war. After Léopold abdicated in August 1950, Baudouin acted as head of state until 16 July 1951. The next day, he became Belgium's fifth king.

His first act was to take a fact-finding tour to war-torn Congo in 1959; he declared it independent that same year. At home, his fair treatment of the Flemish and the Walloons earned him the respect – and even love – of the nation. Most importantly, he could fluently speak both Flemish and French.

When Baudouin unexpectedly died in 1993, the entire nation mourned, gathering in front of the royal palace to show their support for the royal family whose image had blossomed under his reign.

ALBERT COLE

main unifying forces is the royal family, and the wedding in December 1999 of Prince Philippe, the 39-year-old heir to the Belgian throne, and Mathilde d'Udekem d'Acoz, a speech therapist whose family has both Flemish and Walloon roots, was a high note to end the 20th century.

GEOGRAPHY

Belgium, with a surface area of 30,000 sq km, is one of Europe's smallest countries. It is bordered by the Netherlands to the north and north-east, Germany and Luxembourg to the east, France to the south and south-west, and the 66km-long North Sea coastline to the north-west. It is about 240km at its widest from east to west and 193km from north to south.

The north of Belgium is Flanders, a flat, topographically uninteresting countryside broken by the slender steeples of churches. Into this landscape rose the spires and belfries of the medieval cloth towns – tall symbols of wealth and power that acted as reminders of territorial boundaries and which could – and still can – be seen from miles around. The country's North Sea coastline is monopolised by largely unattractive resort towns between which a few patches of windswept – and now highly prized – dunes have been spared from the developer's bulldozer.

In stark contrast to the north is the hilly countryside of the Ardennes in Belgium's south-eastern corner.

Brussels, Bruges and Antwerp all lie within Flanders. Brussels is in the valley of the Senne, a tributary of the Scheldt, Belgium's most important river. Antwerp, nestled against the Scheldt, is 45km north of Brussels and 88km upriver from the North Sea. Bruges is about 100km north-west of the capital and 16km south of Zeebrugge, the closest North Sea port.

CLIMATE

Belgium has a generally mild, maritime climate characterised by many days of grey and/or rainy weather. July and August are the warmest months but can also be the wettest, though precipitation is spread rela-

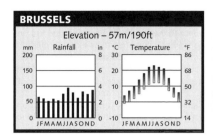

tively evenly over the year. The sunniest months are May to August, but April and September can be pretty nice as well. Winters tend to be mild and heavy snow is rare. The average winter temperature in Brussels is 6°C in the day and 3°C at night, though it has been known to drop well below zero when the wind blows from the east. There is little difference in temperatures between the three cities.

ECOLOGY & ENVIRONMENT

This densely populated, tiny country has been at the heart of European development and destruction for centuries...Belgium's ecological and environmental story is not a pretty one. National passions don't include the environment and the dearth of grassroots environmental consciousness means that this pitiful situation has improved little in recent decades. In 1993 Belgium was dubbed the 'dirty child of Europe' by Greenpeace International, and the European Parliament recently criticised Flanders for having the highest levels of groundwater nitrate pollution in the European Union (EU).

Water and noise pollution, urbanisation and waste management are some of the most pressing environmental issues. The high population density and a good standard of living have resulted in high energy consumption, the production of large quantities of waste and the intensive use of land for agriculture. About 25% of Belgium's land area is cultivated; forest and pasture each make up an additional 20% of the country's surface area. The remainder includes industry and urban living space, and a small area of wetlands.

Electricity is primarily generated by nuclear power plants. Belgium's largest rivers, the Scheldt and Meuse, are heavily polluted and in the capital, Brussels, untreated sewage goes straight into the Senne, just as it has done for centuries. Water taken from these rivers is, of course, treated and tap water can be drunk.

Belgium was a late-starter in recycling, beginning with selective household rubbish collection as late as mid-1998, but both rubbish and household glass recycling are now in full swing.

Local environmental groups have been around since the 1970s but the movement has only gained recognition in recent years due to the rising power of green political parties such as Agalev and Ecolo in the 1980s and '90s. Their success, however, has been hampered by tensions relating to the language divide.

More than 30 European environmental groups have offices in Brussels, where they seek to put pressure on EU policy-makers.

FLORA & FAUNA

The native forests that once covered much of Belgium have been destroyed by centuries of clearing for agriculture and pasture. Today's forests – concentrated in the Ardennes – are largely coniferous monocultures used for logging and are unable to sustain the diversity of plant and animal species that once lived in this region. Other isolated patches of forest, mainly beech, birch and oak, are dotted around the countryside, such as the Forêt de Soignes (Zoniënwoud in Flemish) close to Brussels (for details, see Excursions in the Brussels chapter).

Belgium has very few nature parks and reserves, and those that do exist are the *last* refuge for many indigenous bird, plant and insect species.

The Het Zwin nature reserve, on the coast north-east of Bruges, protects a wetland ecosystem maintained by North Sea flooding. The area silted up in the 16th century, transforming Bruges from a busy medieval port to a small provincial city. It is now the largest salt marsh in Belgium. For

more on Het Zwin see The Belgian Coast under Excursions in the Bruges chapter.

The Kalmthoutse Heide nature reserve, north of Antwerp on the Dutch-Belgian border, features important remnants of the area's original heath and dune landscape; its vegetation includes wet and dry heath as well as active and inactive sand dunes. The conservation area contains important roost sites for several species of bird, including the whimbrel, and over 90% of the dragonfly species found in Belgium.

About 400 species of flora exist in Belgium and one in five is threatened. The Nationale Plantentuin van België (National Botanic Garden of Belgium) in Meise boasts one of the largest collections of plants in Europe, housed in a vast complex of greenhouses (for details see under Meise in the Excursions section of the Brussels chapter).

GOVERNMENT & POLITICS

Belgium is a constitutional hereditary monarchy, led by King Albert II and a parliament. The parliament consists of the Senate and a Chamber of Representatives, which have responsibility for policy areas affecting the country as a whole, such as finance, defence and foreign affairs.

In 1993 the government was decentralised via the signing of the St Michel Accords, which saw the creation of three regional governments representing the Flemish and French-speaking communities (Flanders and Wallonia, respectively) and the Brussels-Capital region. This was the most recent step in a long string of constitutional reforms dating back to the 1970s when the Flemish, Walloon and German-speaking communities started demanding linguistic, territorial and cultural autonomy.

The overall political scene is now very complex with municipal, provincial and regional governments as well as the centralised state government. Brussels is the national capital and the capital of the Flemish region. The Ardennes town of Namur holds the seat of the Walloon regional government. The regional governments have legislative authority in matters of economic

policy, regional development, urban re-
newal, housing and the environment.

To date, the 1993 accords have managed
to keep the more radical Flemish separatist
movement at bay, though talk of secession
from the south is always in the wind.

The overall political scene has long been
dominated by the (Catholic) Christian Democrats, Socialists and Liberals, though
support for the green parties, Agalev (in
Flanders) and Ecolo (in Wallonia) is increasing. The extreme right-wing Vlaams
Blok (Flemish Bloc) has gained considerable ground, primarily in Antwerp, since
the mid-1990s. At the municipal election in
October 2000 it won a third of the votes in
Antwerp.

Throughout the 1990s, Belgium was lead
by a seemingly ever-changing coalition
government headed by former prime minister Jean-Luc Dehaene from the Christian
Democrats. But his government was
plagued with political and judicial scandals
that have left Belgium with the nickname of
the 'Italy of the north'. One such scandal
was the Agusta affair, in which bribes of
US$1.7 million were allegedly paid to the

Socialists to sweeten the sale of Italian
helicopters to the Belgian government. The
scandal forced Willy Claes, a Socialist minister at that time, to resign as Secretary-
General of NATO.

Then came the Dutroux affair, in which
police and judicial incompetence was held
partly to blame for the crimes of Marc
Dutroux (see under History earlier in the
chapter for details).

The government's mishandling of a crisis
over dioxin-contaminated chicken in May
1999 was the straw that broke the camel's
back – Dehaene's government was trounced
in national elections held the following
month.

The Liberals emerged from that latest
election as the leading political force and
formed a coalition government (known as
the purple-green or 'rainbow' coalition)
with the Socialists and Greens. These unusual bed partners joined forces in order to
exclude the extreme right-wing Vlaams
Blok, which rose spectacularly at the 1999
federal election. The prime minister, Guy
Verhofstadt, is the country's first Liberal
leader in more than 50 years.

The Linguistic Divide

Magazine articles debate the country's future, newspaper polls question the likelihood of a split, the
king calls for regional harmony…nearly four decades after the Linguistic Divide was drawn across
the country – cutting it almost equally in half between the Flemish and Walloon populations –
Belgium is still a divided land.

The roots of Belgium's divisive language issue can be traced back to Roman times; however, it
was the formation of the Belgian state in 1831 that crystallised it. The nation's first constitution was
drawn up in French – the country's official language at that time – by the ruling elite. A campaign
for the Flemish language started, but it wasn't until 1898 that Flemish was recognised as a second
language. Even then, it was another 30 years before it was used in schools.

In the 1950s and 1960s, Flemish assertiveness grew as Flanders became the country's modern-
day economic powerhouse. Soon after, Wallonia's steel and mining industries sank into decline, leaving French-speaking Belgians in an impoverished region. Their vulnerability led many of them to
believe that their northern counterpart's bid for equality was actually a fight for domination. Due to
these tensions, the country was split in 1962 by the invisible line known as the Linguistic Divide,
which created the regions of Flanders, Wallonia and bilingual Brussels. Each region has its own government and much autonomy, thanks to decentralisation of the national government during the
1980s and early 1990s.

The establishment of three regional governments was designed to appease the language commu-

Belgium is divided into 10 provinces. The Brabant region encircles Brussels and was one province until linguistic tensions boiled over and it was split in two – the Brabant-Wallon and Vlaams-Brabant. Bruges is the capital of the province of West-Vlaanderen (West Flanders), Ghent heads Oost-Vlaanderen (East Flanders) and Antwerp governs the Antwerpen province.

ECONOMY

Over the centuries, Belgium's economic prosperity has swung between one language community and the other, starting with Flanders' medieval textile wealth which was later supplanted by Wallonia's coal, iron and steel industries. The latter's decline has spurred Flanders to re-emerge as the engine propelling the country's economic growth, although Wallonia is now looking towards high-tech industries such as aeronautics and biotechnology.

The economy as a whole, however, is struggling with a huge public debt and high unemployment (12%). In 1998, the GDP was US$236 billion and it grew by only 1.8% in 1999 due largely to a considerable downturn in exports and other economic woes caused by the dioxin crisis. Economists predict annual growth to rise to 2.9% in 2002. The inflation rate of 1% in 1998–9 was slightly below the average for the 11-country euro-zone.

The country's main industries are engineering and metal products, chemicals, car manufacturing, iron and steel, textiles and food. Financial services, including banking and insurance, are also important as are agriculture (cereals), horticulture and stock breeding.

Brussels accounts for about 15% of the Belgian economy. In the early days the city's economic lifeline was agriculture but this has now been replaced by industrial, commercial and service activities. White-collar workers in Brussels far outnumber factory workers, with financial and service industries accounting for more than two-thirds of all jobs. More than 2000 foreign companies have offices in Brussels, due largely to the presence of the main EU institutions which themselves account for a sizeable workforce. In recent decades Brussels has also steadily emerged as a conference city, with

The Linguistic Divide

nities and to a certain degree it has, but it has not thwarted the inter-community squabbles or the 'them and us' mentality, particularly in some areas immediately around Brussels. The Walloons consider the Flemish to be arrogant and the Flemish think the Walloons are feckless. The massive increase in bureaucracy generated by the additional tier of government is a burden for taxpayers, and many in Flanders resent the fact that they are financially propping up their ailing southern counterpart.

As a visitor, much of the tension will go unnoticed. In Flanders, people will readily communicate in whatever language is needed, be it English, French or Flemish. In Brussels and Wallonia the story is slightly different, as the Walloons have been reluctant to learn or speak Flemish or English.

As for the future of Belgium? That question is moot. Some parts of Flemish society are vocal in their calls for independence but it's questionable whether the majority of Belgians would back such a move were it ever put to a vote. Those who think Belgium will stick together largely attribute this to three things: the country's huge public debt, Brussels and the monarchy.

The royal family, with its foreign origin, is linked to none of the language communities in particular and is therefore a unifying force. Late last century, King Albert II, in a speech to the nation, called for Belgians to 'live in harmony, and treat our cultural and regional differences not as problems but as riches'. Many also hope that the marriage in 1999 of Prince Philippe, the heir to the throne, and Mathilde d'Udekem d'Acoz, whose family has both Flemish and Walloon connections, will also strengthen unity.

more than 10,000 business conventions held here annually.

The country's other economic hub is Antwerp. The city's lifeline has always been its shipping link to the North Sea – what was once a medieval trading centre has reinvented itself as the world's third largest port. The 1920s and '30s marked the appearance of the first petroleum refineries in the port area, and these were soon followed by car assembly plants. After WWII heavy manufacturing flourished.

Since the 16th century, Antwerp has been one of the world's most important diamond centres, with about 85% of the international trade in uncut stones and 50% of its cut diamonds changing hands in an unassuming cluster of streets near the city's main train station. The 1600 diamond-related businesses had a turnover of €20 billion (roughly US$21.2 billion) in 1999. Diamonds account for about 7% of Belgium's export revenue.

POPULATION & PEOPLE

Belgium has a population of 10.2 million people. While spread over 10 provinces, the population is basically split in two: the Flemish and the Walloons. Language is the dividing factor, made official in 1962 when an invisible line – or Linguistic Divide as it's called – was drawn across the country, cutting it almost equally in half (see the earlier boxed text 'The Linguistic Divide').

To the north of the divide lies Flanders (Vlaanderen), whose Flemish speakers make up 62% of Belgium's population. This is one of the most densely populated corners of Europe, with 400 people per sq km, compared with 240 in Britain and just 100 in France. To the south sits Wallonia (La Wallonie) where French-speaking Walloons make up most – but not all – of the rest of the population. The German-speaking remainder (about 700,000 people) occupy a tiny enclave known as the Eastern Cantons in the country's far east.

Then there's Brussels. Officially bilingual but predominantly French speaking, it lies within the Flemish region but is governed separately. Brussels' population of 977,800 includes about 100 different nationalities (non-Belgian nationals make up about 30% of Brussels' population) and, while many other Belgian cities have large immigrant communities, none are as multicultural as the capital. This mix includes many European nationalities as well as Moroccans, Turks and Africans. The African population is largely made up of immigrants from the former Belgian colony of the Congo. Antwerp is the second-largest city with a population of 456,700. Bruges is home to around 119,000 people.

EDUCATION

School attendance is compulsory up to the age of 18 and the standard of education is high.

Brussels boasts a number of prestigious institutions of higher learning, such as Université Libre de Bruxelles and the Vrije Universiteit Brussel. Many other large towns and cities have their own universities including Antwerp, Ghent and Leuven. The Europacollege in Bruges is a highly regarded postgraduate college for students from around the world. Another renowned institution is the Royal Academy of Fine Arts (Koninklijke Academie voor Schone Kunsten) in Antwerp.

SCIENCE

Of the three cities, Brussels is the one that stands out, with pioneers in the fields of science and medicine.

Ernest Solvay (1838–1922), an industrialist and chemist, is best known for discovering a way to produce soda ash (ammonium carbonate), used to make glass, soap and other products, on a large-scale commercial basis. He and his brother, Alfred, founded their own company, built a factory in 1863 and by 1880 had factories around the world. He founded several international scientific research institutes and brought together the likes of Albert Einstein and Madame Curie for conferences.

The father of anatomy, Andreas Vesalius (1514–64), was born in Brussels and educated in Leuven. While teaching surgery at the University of Padua, Italy, Vesalius wrote the definitive work on human anatomy, *De Humani Corporis Fabrica Libri Septum* (The Seven Books on the Structure of the Human Body), published in 1543. He based his work on dissections of human bodies, boldly defying the Roman Catholic religion, which forbade this.

Bacteriologist Jules Bordet (1870–1961), founder and director of the Pasteur Institute in Brussels, developed the whooping cough vaccine and won the 1919 Nobel Prize for Medicine for his research into blood serum.

ARTS
Painting & Sculpture
Flemish Primitives Belgium's art history dates right back to the late Middle Ages when the medieval cloth towns of Bruges and Ghent were thriving, prosperous centres of trade and where art became a means of displaying this wealth. This was one of Belgium's most glorious artistic periods with painters commissioned to create religious artworks and to record momentous events, like marriage, in the lives of the local nobility. These painters are known nowadays as the Flemish Primitives. Their works are famous for their naturalism and vibrancy and for the intricate detail that brings their subjects and that period in history to life. Many of these artists became official town painters and they lived esteemed and rewarding lives. Superb collections of Flemish Primitive works are on display in both Bruges and Ghent, as well as in Brussels.

Jan Van Eyck (c1390–1441) is generally considered to be the first of this genre, and is widely credited as the artist who invented oil painting. This isn't strictly true – what Van Eyck did was use oil as a medium for mixing colours instead of using the traditional, less-resilient tempera (an egg-based substance). Van Eyck lived in Bruges but worked both there and in Ghent. His most celebrated artwork is *The Adoration of the Mystic Lamb* (1426–32), which he painted for the cathedral in Ghent, where it's displayed today. For more details see the boxed text 'Jan Van Eyck'.

Rogier Van der Weyden (c1400–64) succeeded Van Eyck as court painter to Philip the Good and his style followed very much in the line of his predecessor, blending religious emotion with sharp realism. Van der Weyden became the town painter for Brussels and executed several works for the Hôtel de Ville (town hall) there, though many of his paintings were destroyed during the French bombardment of 1695. He also designed for the famous tapestry workshops of Brussels.

Dirk Bouts (c1415–75), born in Haarlem

Jan Van Eyck

Jan Van Eyck (c1390–1441) is considered the father of Flemish painting.

Little is known of his early life. The first written mention of Van Eyck was in 1422 as *valet de chambre et peintre* (honorary equerry and painter) to John of Bavaria, count of Holland. He worked at the palace in The Hague until the count died in 1425 and then settled in Bruges, where he was recruited to be official painter to Philip the Good, duke of Burgundy.

Backed by this powerful ruler, a generous patron of the arts, Van Eyck perfected the technique of oil painting. One of the single greatest works in medieval art is his altarpiece *The Adoration of the Mystic Lamb* (1432) in St Baafskathedraal in Ghent. Although some historians claim the painting was designed by Jan and his brother, Hubert, it's not known for sure whether Hubert actually existed.

However, there is no question of the existence of Jan, who broke with the custom of the day and signed his paintings by name. Several bear his artistic motto, *Als ich chan* (As best I can). Some of his paintings can be seen at the Groeningemuseum in Bruges and the Koninklijk Museum voor Schone Kunsten in Antwerp.

(in what is now the Netherlands), studied in Brussels under Van der Weyden and worked mainly in Leuven where he became the town painter. Strictly controlled paintings with rich, broad landscapes and static, unmoving figures were his passion. His *Last Supper* triptych (1464–7) is one of the period's masterpieces and now hangs in Leuven's St Pieterskerk.

Hans Memling (c1440–94) was a disciple of Van der Weyden and worked most of his life in Bruges. For details, see the boxed text 'Hans Memling' in the Bruges chapter.

Gerard David (c1460–1523), who was born in the Netherlands and moved to Bruges in the 1480s, succeeded Memling as the city's premier painter but was in fact the last great artist of this era as Bruges' fortunes were in decline. At the end of the 15th century, trade and wealth moved to Antwerp, which became the focus of art in the next great artistic period.

Flemish Renaissance Towards the end of the 15th century, the increasingly prosperous port city of Antwerp replaced Bruges as the main art centre in the Low Countries. Flemish art proceeded along two courses: while some painters were influenced by Italian art, others developed a more independent Flemish style.

A Dutch painter worth mentioning here is Hieronymus (or Jeroen) Bosch (1450–1516). He worked mainly in the Netherlands but his style influenced Flemish artists later in this period and his works feature quite prominently in museums in Bruges, Ghent and Brussels. In any case, the distinction between Dutch and Flemish painting actually dates from the late 16th century – prior to that Belgium and the Netherlands were simply known as the Low Countries and artists moved from one royal court or town to another. Bosch's paintings are the stuff that nightmares are made of – scenes filled with gruesome beasts and devilish creatures devouring agonised humans and other such treats. Looking at his work it's easy to think he suffered bad karma, but Bosch's paintings are generally thought to illustrate parables told in those days.

Quinten Matsijs (1460–1530), spelt Matsys in English, founded the Antwerp school of painting. His works reflected a deep understanding of landscape perspective and featured the type of dreamy landscapes preferred and no doubt inspired by Leonardo da Vinci. Bernard Van Orley (c1499–1541) introduced the Renaissance to Brussels with his designs for tapestry and stained glass.

Perhaps the greatest Flemish painter of the 16th century was Pieter Breugel the Elder (c1525–69) who depicted, among other subjects, lively peasantry scenes filled with earthy enjoyment. For more on Breugel as well as his two sons, see the boxed text 'The Breugel Family' in the Brussels chapter.

Baroque Antwerp remained a cultural centre during the 17th century, mainly because of Flemish painter Pieter Paul Rubens (1577–1640). He served as official court painter to Archduke Albert and Infanta Isabella of the Spanish Netherlands and was allowed to reside in Antwerp rather than Brussels, where the court was based, because of his prestige. He worked steadily until he died, leaving behind more than 2000 major paintings. For more details on Rubens see the boxed text 'Pieter Paul Rubens' in the Antwerp chapter.

The Rubens studio nurtured artists such as Antoon (Anthony) Van Dyck (1599–1641) and his contemporary Jacob Jordaens (1593–1678). Van Dyck, who was probably the most prominent Flemish painter of the 17th century after Rubens, painted numerous portraits of European aristocrats as well as religious and mythical subjects. He was appointed court painter by Charles I of England in 1632 and also knighted. Jordaens was one of the few Flemish artists who did not go to Italy; he specialised in painting typically Flemish scenes of everyday life and merrymaking, but also did biblical and mythological works.

The 19th Century After a dull 18th century, Belgian art experienced a gradual revival in the 19th century, inspired by French Romanticism. Jacques-Louis David, who became Napoleon's official painter, fled from

France to Brussels in 1816 and influenced an entire generation of Belgian painters.

Antoine Wiertz (1806–65) was born in Dinant but moved to Brussels where he delighted in painting gruesome canvases of damnation, hell and other religious bents and whose house/workshop is now a museum devoted to his love-'em-or-hate-'em works.

At about the same time, Constantin Meunier (1831–1905), who studied in Brussels, emerged as the country's most important 19th-century sculptor. His emotive, larger-than-life bronzes generally depict working-class themes – muscular miners from Wallonia's rapidly-developing industrial areas, dockworkers from Antwerp and men reaping the fields. His old house and studio in the Brussels suburb of Ixelles is now a museum displaying his, at times, poignant artworks.

James Ensor (1860–1949) is Belgium's best-known painter from the late 19th century and is often considered a forerunner to the expressionists. Ensor, the son of an English father and Flemish mother, was born in Ostend and is most recognised for his macabre and sometimes quite savage images of skeletons, phantoms and garish masks.

His early works were quite traditional – portraits and seascapes – but in the early 1880s he abandoned these for clashing colours and carnavalesque scenes which often have a whiff of death and a distinctly unnerving effect. After his works were rejected by the Brussels Salon in 1883, Ensor joined a progressive band of artists who called themselves *Les XX* (The Twenty), but was eventually even expelled from that group.

René Magritte

René Magritte (1898–1967) was one of the world's most prominent Surrealist painters, blending ordinary images with those that could be conjured up only from the subconscious. His most famous motif, the man in the bowler hat whose face is hidden from view, exemplified Surrealism's main premise: a rebellion against European rationalism, which had deteriorated into the horrors of WWI. The motif, and a drawing of the painter, is featured on Belgium's f500 note introduced in early 1998 and destined for extinction when the euro notes arrive.

Born in Lessines, north of Mons, Magritte spent most of his working life in Brussels. His interest in Surrealism was sparked in 1922, when he saw a reproduction of Giorgio de Chirico's painting *The Song of Love* (1914), featuring the unlikely combination of a classical bust and a rubber glove. For the next few years, Magritte became active in the Belgian Surrealist movement and in 1926, with the support of a Brussels art gallery, he became a full-time painter. His paintings often confused space and time, as in *Time Transfixed* (1939), in which a steaming locomotive roars out of a living room mantelpiece as if it is just leaving a tunnel.

In 1927 he and his wife Georgette moved to Paris where he befriended several Parisian Surrealists, including poets André Breton and Paul Eluard. The couple returned to Brussels three years later and moved into a very ordinary house on an ordinary street in the ordinary Brussels' suburb of Jette – Magritte's thoughts and paintings may have been surreal but he was at the same time conventional to the hilt. Magritte painted most of his famous works here – he set up his easel in the dining room of the house, which is now a museum, and painted wearing a three-piece business suit. The dining room window offered a view of a wall; for Magritte it was a looking-glass into another world.

ÅSA ANDERSSON

The 20th Century The modern art movements of last century were all picked up by Belgian artists.

Rik Wouters (1882–1916) was born in Mechelen and was one of the prime figures of Brabant Fauvism. His sundrenched landscapes, light interiors and still life canvasses were a search for the vibration of light in pure colours.

From 1904, two groups of painters, first symbolists and then expressionists, set up in the village of St-Martens-Latem near Ghent. Of the first group, Valerius De Saedeleer (1867–1941) and Albert Servaes (1883–1952) are the best known; later came Gustave De Smet (1877–1943) and Constant Permeke (1886–1952). Permeke put out bold portraits of rural Flemish life that blended Cubism, expressionism and social realism.

In 1894 a new artistic circle, called La Libre Esthétique, was established in Brussels, aiming to foster cooperation among artists. From this group emerged Art Nouveau (see the Art Nouveau in Brussels special section later in the book for details).

Surrealism, a movement that developed in Paris in the 1920s, used images from the subconscious to revolt against rationalism and to define a new way of perceiving reality. Belgium's best-known Surrealists were René Magritte and Paul Delvaux. Magritte is considered one of the movement's masters (for more details see the earlier boxed text 'René Magritte'). Paul Delvaux (1897–1994) covered canvases with haunting images such as dreamy and erotic sleepwalkers in trams and stations, skeletons, moonlight, classical features and reclining nude women.

In the years that immediately followed WWII, a group of artists that called itself *La Jeune Peinture Belge* (1945–8) produced mainly abstract work. Among the most prominent artists in the group were Victor Sevranckx, Anne Bonnet and Louis Van Lint.

In 1948 an international group called COBRA (an acronym standing for Copenhagen, Brussels and Amsterdam) was formed as a reaction against formalism in art. The group sought to promote free artistic expression of the unconscious and used intense expressive colours. Belgium's most famous member is Pierre Alechinsky (born 1927), who has gained international prominence for his works (mainly in inks).

Architecture

As with painting, Belgium is endowed with a fine legacy of architectural delights. Some of the country's earliest buildings, though largely restored in later centuries, are now on UNESCO's World Heritage list. These include the belfries and *begijnhoven* (buildings of a Belgian Catholic order of women) in many Flemish cities (see the boxed text 'Begijnen & Begijnhoven' in the Brussels chapter), all of central Bruges and, in Brussels, the famous Grand Place together with several houses by Victor Horta.

The Middle Ages The ornate towers and churches that dominate the skylines of many Belgian cities are testimony to the rich heritage of pre-15th-century art. The main architectural achievements of the Middle Ages were ecclesiastical, built first in the Romanesque, then the Gothic style. The former is characterised by columns and semicircular arches; the latter by the pointed arch. During the 15th century secular buildings were also built in the increasingly flamboyant Gothic style, such as the Hôtel de Ville in Brussels (started in 1402). The most stunning tribute to secular Gothic architecture may be the town hall of Leuven. The cathedral in Antwerp is the largest Gothic cathedral in Belgium, towering 123m high.

Baroque Baroque was an artistic and architectural movement of the Counter-Reformation in the 16th and early 17th centuries, characterised by ornate and exuberant decoration. Flemish artists and architects of that time altered and added to it to come up with a style now called Flemish baroque. Although it has distinct Italian influences it's largely home-grown and is a style much flaunted in Antwerp. Indeed, the city is extremely proud of this heavy, distinct architecture; an excellent example is the house of artist Pieter Paul Rubens.

After the 1695 bombardment of Brussels, the guildhalls on Grand Place were rebuilt in baroque style, though many of the buildings retained Gothic features.

Neoclassical For most of the 18th century, while Brussels was under Austrian rule, architecture took on a rational neoclassical style. It is perhaps best reflected in the Palais des Nations, Belgium's parliament building in Brussels, not to mention the nearby cluster of stark white buildings surrounding Place Royale. The sombre Place des Martyrs in Brussels is another good example.

After Belgian independence in 1831, a number of extravagant buildings were constructed to allow Brussels to compete with the likes of Paris and London. One of the first was the 1847 construction by Jean-Pierre Cluysenaar of continental Europe's first covered shopping gallery, the glass-roofed Galeries St Hubert, which today retains its former glory.

Léopold II Throughout his reign, Léopold II (ruled 1865–1909) focused on the urban development of his country, realising that making a city more aesthetically appealing would boost its economic potential. He used the vast riches gained through exploitation of the Congo to fund the construction of gigantic public buildings and elaborate town-planning schemes. Almost everything that's big or ruler-straight in Brussels is due to him; it's a style that's sometimes admired but is largely unloved these days.

The jewel in his architectural crown was the Palais de Justice, Brussels' law courts. Designed by Joseph Poelaert and intended to evoke the temples of the Pharaohs, it necessitated the destruction of several streets and many homes in the Marolles, a working-class neighbourhood – as a result the Marolles dialect adopted the word *architek* as a derogatory term.

The industrial boom in the late 19th century resulted in the construction of several glass and iron buildings in Brussels. One

notable example is the Halles de Schaerbeek (1901).

Art Nouveau For details on the history of Art Nouveau and its leading figures, see the Art Nouveau in Brussels special section later in the book.

The Zurenborg neighbourhood of Antwerp is also renowned for its kaleidoscope of Art Nouveau buildings – for details see Zurenborg in the Antwerp chapter.

Art Deco The impassioned style of Art Nouveau cooled off with Art Deco, a movement that originated in the 1920s and developed into a major style in Western Europe and the USA in the 1930s. Victor Horta, a pioneer of the Art Nouveau movement in Belgium, abandoned it for the cleaner lines of Art Deco in his later works, which include the Gare Centrale and the Palais des Beaux-Arts in Brussels.

Brussels boasts many remarkable Art Deco apartment blocks; however, the style's most intimate example is the Musée David et Alice Van Buuren, a private house built in 1928 in the Brussels suburb of Uccle and now a museum. More grand is the 1930 Palais du Centenaire, an exhibition centre on the northern edge of the city featuring terraced tiers capped by statues.

Post-WWII Belgium's most unique architectural structure is the Atomium, an eye-catcher that sits in the suburb of Heysel to the north of central Brussels and is visible from the city centre on a clear day. Modelled on a molecule of iron, it was built by the powerful Belgian metal industry as the showpiece for the 1958 World Fair. For more details, see Atomium under Laeken in the Brussels chapter.

The establishment in 1958 of the European Economic Community, the predecessor of the EU, led to the frenzied construction of several ill-fated projects, such as the huge Manhattan office complex near the Gare du Nord, which was later abandoned after office demand slumped.

Brussels' most recent architectural coup has been the development of the somewhat controversial EU area – for details see the boxed text 'The EU in Brussels' in the Brussels chapter.

Literature

Belgium has a low literary profile. In the past, writers have relied on their more dominant neighbours in this sphere – the Flemish have aligned themselves with their Dutch-speaking counterparts in the Netherlands and the Walloons have gone under the umbrella of French literary fame.

The literature of the Middle Ages was mainly religious and written in Latin. Plays and fables in French began to emerge in the 16th century, penned by writers such as Jean Froissart and Georges Chastellain.

By the 18th century Willem Verhoeven and Jan Baptist Verlooy had started a reaction against the French influence in literature. Romanticism, closely linked to a revival of Flemish nationalist feelings, influenced the 19th century. Writers such as Frans Willems and Jan Baptist David and poets Karel Lodewijk Ledeganck and Prudens Van Duyse heralded the new age. This new pride in Flemish heritage also drew inspiration from the historical novel *De Leeuw van Vlaanderen* (The Lion of Flanders), written in 1838 by Antwerp novelist Hendrik Conscience (1812–83).

At the same time, Guido Gezelle (1830–99), considered the greatest Flemish poet of the 19th century, led a poetry revival in Flanders. His book *The Evening and the Rose* contains 30 poems that have been translated into English. For more on Gezelle, see the boxed text 'Guido Gezelle' in the Bruges chapter.

By about 1860 Romanticism, which emphasised emotions and sensitivity, had begun to fade out and a new style known as realism had become prominent. Realist writing was characterised by accurate description, humour and pessimism. Albrecht Rodenbach wrote militant songs and a tragic epic, *Gudrun* in 1882. A decade later, Georges Rodenbach (1855–98) wrote *Bruges-la-Morte*, the tale of a doomed love affair set in the dream-like 'dead city' of Bruges. It has been translated into English.

Major writers during and after WWII were novelists Louis-Paul Boon and Hugo Claus, who both wrote in Flemish. Boon (1912–79) had an anarchistic undertone; his most famous books are *De Kapellekesbaan* (Chapel Road; 1953) and *Pastoor Daens*. Claus was born in Bruges in 1929 and is one of the few Flemish writers who has succeeded in making a name for himself abroad. His best-known novel is *Het Verdriet van België* (The Sorrow of Belgium), published in 1983. It weaves a story of wartime Belgium seen through the eyes of a Flemish adolescent. The underlying theme, however, is the collaboration during WWII. Other novels by Claus to look out for are *Verlangen* (Desire; 1978) and *Zwaardvis* (Swordfish; 1989).

Liège novelist Georges Simenon (1903–89) is most famous for his books devoted to detective character Inspector Maigret but he also wrote serious literature.

Belgium's most famous female writer and one of the few novelists to gain an international reputation is Marguerite Yourcenar (1903–87). Born as Marguerite de Crayencour in Brussels, this poet and author became the first woman elected (in 1980) to the male-dominated Académie Française – an exclusive French literary institution – in its 350-year history. She was a prolific writer who visited Bruges many times. Her *L'Œuvre au Noir* is a classic, philosophical work about a boy who goes to school in Bruges and becomes a 'magical' doctor. The English translation is entitled *Zeno of Bruges*.

More contemporary is Flemish author Anne Provoost whose novel *Vallen* (Falling; 1994) examines racial tensions, intolerance and the appeal of extreme right-wing politics.

A handful of foreign artists have found inspiration while in Brussels, such as Charlotte Brontë, whose novels *The Professor* (1846) and *Villette* (1853) paint unflattering pictures of the city in the 1840s, and Victor Hugo, who worked on *Les Misérables* in Brussels between 1837 and 1871.

Music

The country's first collection of medieval folk songs was found in a 14th-century manuscript from Bruges. After 1450 the Netherlands became the main musical centre, and from there the polyphonists became known throughout the world. But Belgium regained its place in the 16th century as Antwerp printers such as Susato, Plantin and Phaleslus published scores making it possible for more musicians to perform and for large segments of society to hear music.

Carillons (*beiaarden* in Flemish, *carillons* in French), sets of bells attached to town clocks as a service to citizens, evolved in the early 16th century. Many international carillon players these days have studied at the renowned campanology (bell ringing) school in Mechelen near Brussels.

Belgian composer André-Modeste Grétry (1741–1813) was born in Liège and is known as the 'father of comic opera'. His compositions include *Richard Cœur de Lion* (Richard the Lionheart).

Music schools began taking over from church choir schools in the 19th century. In 1833, François Fétis became the first director of the Conservatoire Royal de Musique in Brussels. At about the same time, Peter Benoit founded the Royal Flemish Music Conservatory in Antwerp.

But it was not until the 20th century that Belgian musicians really made their mark on the world stage. Adolphe Sax (1814–94) gave his name to the musical instrument he invented while Jean 'Toots' Thielemans achieved fame in the USA for his harmonica playing. Jazz remains extremely popular today and both Brussels and Antwerp boast big jazz festivals (in May and August respectively – see under Special Events in the Facts for the Visitor chapter).

In the 1950s, Jacques Brel took the French-speaking world by storm and is still much-loved in his homeland (see the boxed text 'Jacques Brel').

Some contemporary home-grown Belgian bands that you might come across on the live music circuit include the well-established K's Choice and Front 242. There's a good range of alternative rock bands, whose lyrics are mostly in English, including dEUS (an Antwerp-based group that has a following in Belgium, the UK and

---

Jacques Brel

Raspy-voiced Jacques Brel (1929–78), a Brussels native, rose to stardom in Paris in the 1950s for his passionate songs that have transcended a generation. The legendary *chansonnier* was a transient troubadour who performed with intensity. Love, freedom, the spirit of revolt and the hypocrisy of the bourgeois were his cherished themes.

Brel's career started in 1952 in La Rose Noire, a Brussels cabaret. The following year he headed to Paris and mixed with songwriters and singers like Edith Piaf. His first record was cut in 1955 and within two years he was a national idol.

In the early 1960s he toured the USA and USSR, and became known as the singer 'from France'. Brel never denied his link with Belgium but he also cherished France, so much so his daughter is named France Brel. He died of cancer in 1978.

France); Zita Swoon and Dead Man Ray (both also from Antwerp), Venux (Brussels) and Hooverphonic (Ghent), a 100% electronic band.

The country's top classical event is the Concours Musical International Reine Élisabeth de Belgique held every May and June in Brussels (see under Special Events in the Facts for the Visitor chapter).

Opera Opera has always been important in Brussels, which is perhaps the only city in the world where an opera has sparked a revolution (see the boxed text 'A Revolutionary Performance' earlier in the chapter). The Théâtre de la Monnaie (better known by its Flemish/French abbreviations – De Munt/La Monnaie) has long been at the heart of Belgium's cultural scene and the theatre's eponymously named company is famous for the high quality of its productions and innovative staging. It's a training ground for future stars, preferring to nurture new talent rather than book big names. The company's most glorious era was between 1875 and 1889, marked by the premieres of

Massenet's *Hérodiade* (1881), Reyer's *Sigurd* (1884) and Godard's *Jocelyn* (1888).

Antwerp is home to the Royal Flemish Opera, founded in 1893 by bass Hendrik Fontaine and opened that year with *Der Freischütz*, by Carl Maria von Weber. Performances were originally in the Royal Dutch Theatre, but the company has had its own theatre since 1907. The Royal Flemish Opera benefits from subsidies from state, city and provincial authorities, and today all operas are sung in Flemish, involving more than 300 artists every season.

Dance
The Antwerp-based company, Royal Flanders Ballet, was founded in 1960 and has lead the nation's dance scene. Since the late 1980s it has been headed by artistic director Robert Denvers, who has shaped the company's image with a repertory that includes new works by young choreographers alongside the classics. He is a particularly enthusiastic fan of Russian choreographer George Balanchine, under whom he studied in New York for a year after leaving Maurice Béjart's Ballet of the 20th Century.

Rosas, a Flemish dance company in residence at De Munt (Théâtre de la Monnaie) in Brussels, is directed by internationally known Anne Teresa De Keersmaeker, who has managed to strike a winning balance between the traditional and the avant-garde.

Traditional Textiles
Flemish Tapestry Medieval Flanders thrived on a trade in woollen textiles, inspiring the art of weaving decorative designs into fabric known as tapestry.

Tapestry has always been a luxury product and was particularly prized by royalty and the upper classes throughout Europe in the Middle Ages. Weavers in Bruges, Antwerp and especially Brussels gained prominence in the 16th century. They preferred the Flemish method of tapestry, which involves passing threads that run horizontally across a textile (weft threads) over and under vertical threads (warp threads) so that the latter are completely covered by the former.

Weavers copied artistic designs such as Rubens' *Triumph of the Eucharist*, working from the reverse side of the image so the final result was a mirror version of the original. By far the best works resulted from close cooperation between weaver and artist.

During the 16th century Flemish weavers set up workshops throughout Europe and took the new art with them as far away as Spain, Italy and England.

Lace Known as *kant* in Flemish or *dentelle* in French, lace is an ornamental fabric formed by looping, braiding or twisting thread and was first made by women living in *begijnhoven* (for more details see the boxed text 'Begijnen & Begijnhoven' in the Brussels chapter).

Lace-making blossomed in Flanders in the 16th century. Needlepoint lace *(naaldkant)*, which developed in Italy, was predominantly made in Brussels. Bobbin lace *(kloskant)*, believed to have originated in Bruges, required thousands of painstaking and meticulous movements of bobbins and pins. Each lace maker had her own patterns, which stayed in the family and were handed down through generations.

Cinema
The first public film-screening in Belgium took place in 1896 in the Galeries St Hubert in Brussels. The nation's film industry was originally dominated by the French film-industrialist Charles Pathé, one of whose colleagues, Alfred Machin, set up a production studio in Brussels in 1910. Film buffs can still see a few of his films at the Musée du Cinema in Brussels.

Surrealist films such as André Delvaux's *L'Homme au Crâne Rasé* (1965) and *Un Soir, un Train* (1968) have had a following among art-house audiences for years. But it's the last decade that has really been productive internationally for the nation's filmmakers, with a steady stream of films – many of them decidedly provocative and addressing current social issues – reaping high praises from the critics.

In 1992 joint directors Rémy Belvaux, André Bonzel and Benoit Poelvoorde drew wide attention with their film *Man Bites Dog*.

Jaco Van Dormael presented his film *The Eighth Day* at the 1996 Cannes film festival; it was nominated for the Palme D'Or and Belgium's Pascal Duquenne shared the award for best actor. Van Dormael also directed the highly acclaimed *Toto le Héro* (1991).

Belgian directors have gained world acclaim for works such as *La Vie Sexuelle des Belges* (The Sexual Life of the Belgians; 1994) by Jan Bucquoy and *Left Luggage* (1998) starring Isabella Rossellini and Maximilian Schell. *Antonia's Line* and *Karakter* are Belgian-Dutch co-productions which have won recent Best Foreign Language Film prizes at the Oscars.

In 1999 *Rosetta*, starring teenager Émilie Dequenne, won the Palme D'Or at Cannes. It was made by brothers Luc and Jean-Pierre Dardenne and delves into the issue of immigrants and black (illegal) labour. *Une Liaison Pornographique* by Frédéric Fonteyne and starring Nathalie Baye was honoured at the 2000 Venice film festival.

Belgium's biggest export to Hollywood is the 'Muscles from Brussels', actor Jean-Claude Van Damme. Van Damme's career in the USA took off after he put on an impromptu display of his martial arts repertoire outside a posh restaurant for the startled head of a Hollywood studio. He made his film debut in *Bloodsport* (1987). Off screen he finds time to provide prime fodder for the British tabloids.

Theatre
Belgium does not have a great theatrical tradition. English-speakers will be able to find a range of amateur plays in Brussels and Antwerp, but to enjoy good local theatre will need to be fluent in French or Flemish. The most famous Brussels play, the comedy *Le Marriage de Mademoiselle Beulemans*, still performed today, was written in 1910 by Franz Fonson and Fernand Wicheler.

Puppets
Belgium has a long history of puppetry, which in Belgium is not specifically for kids. At Brussels' famous Théâtre de Toone, puppeteers put on works by Aristophanes and

Shakespeare (for details, see Theatre under Entertainment in the Brussels chapter).

Comics
For details on Belgium's thriving comic art, see the boxed text 'The Art of Belgian Comics' on the following page.

Fashion
Antwerp may not have the fashion shows to rival Paris or Milan, but it certainly has the designer talent, nurtured at the Koninklijke Acadamie voor Schone Kunsten. It all started with the 'Antwerp Six' who received international acclaim in the mid-1980s (see the boxed text 'At the Cutting Edge' in the Antwerp chapter for details).

Brussels designers Kaat Tilley, Nicolas Woit, Patrick Pitschon and Olivier Strelli have also made a contribution to fashion.

SOCIETY & CONDUCT
Belgians are well used to visitors and their different habits – there are few social taboos that travellers are likely to break.

It is customary to greet shopkeepers and cafe/pub owners when entering their premises. When invited to a home, it's polite to bring a gift – wine, flowers or chocolates will go down well. Belgians greet one another with two or three kisses on both cheeks and sometimes bestow the gesture on unsuspecting foreigners.

Cigarette smoke can be a problem for travellers who are used to nonsmoking sections in restaurants and bars. Few establishments – small or large – have separate areas and although ventilators are required by law, they're rare.

Red-light districts, similar but on a much smaller scale to Amsterdam's famous quarter, can be found around Gare du Nord in Brussels and the Schipperskwartier in Antwerp.

Belgians love pets, particularly dogs. Don't be surprised to find yourself sitting next to a dog in a restaurant (such behaviour flaunts the EU's health laws but it's still done) or to have Snoopy snoring in the hotel room next to you (top-end hotels generally charge between €4.95 and €12.40 per night for a dog).

The Art of Belgian Comics

Comic strips (*beeldverhalen* in Flemish, *bandes dessinées* in French) are a much-loved and highly regarded art in Belgium. And with 30 million cartoon books printed each year, colourful comic murals dotting the capital and even a national centre in Brussels devoted to this art form, you can be sure Belgians take their comics seriously.

Comic strips originally appeared in the USA in the late 19th century. Belgium published its first comic book in the 1920s. It was Hergé, the creator of Tintin, who set the ball rolling. Hergé's real name was Georges Remi – his pseudonym comes from his reversed initials (RG) pronounced in French. In 1929 the first adventure of his roving reporter, *Tintin au Pays des Soviets* (Tintin in the Land of the Soviets), was published. A further 22 books followed, and the series is still Belgium's top international seller. See the boxed text 'Tintin & Hergé' in the Brussels chapter for more information on the character and his creator.

The end of WWII saw a fresh spirit of creativity in comics around the world, but particularly in Belgium where a host of comic-strip authors emerged. One of the first was Antwerp artist Willy Vandersteen, who came up with the delightful *Suske en Wiske* (*Bob and Bobette* in English) in 1945. This is one of the nation's longest-running comic-book series and one of the biggest domestic sellers (with a print run of about 100,000 albums per year). In 1946 Maurice De Bevère, better known as Morris, created *Lucky Luke*, a classic Western parody, and Edgar P Jacobs brought out the exciting sci-fi exploits of *Blake en Mortimer*. The following year Marc Sleen invented *Nero* and in 1948 Pierre Culliford (aka Peyo) created the little blue characters known as *Les Schtroumpf* (The Smurfs).

The next decade saw Belgium's comic authors move into the adult realm and in 1968 one of the nation's biggest publishers, Casterman, printed *À Suivre*, a monthly magazine aimed at a mature audience. It ran until 1997.

Belgium's contemporary comic-strip scene is as alive as ever. Well known are the works of Brussels artist François Schuiten and author Benoit Peeters, who teamed up to produce the highly regarded *Les Cités Obscures*. The best-known title from this intellectual series is *Brüsel*, the exaggerated story of an old city destroyed by the new (a thin disguise of Brussels and the EU). *De Kat* (The Cat) by Philippe Geluck is long-running and still going strong.

Writer Jean Van Hamme has joined forces with various artists to publish several successful comic series: with William Vance he produces an espionage series called *XIII*, some of which are translated into English; with Philippe Francq he has put out a business thriller series entitled *L'Argo Winch*; and with Polish-born artist Rosinski has come the *Thorgal* series based on mythology and fantasy.

Kiekeboe (in Flemish) by Merhoand, *Yoko Tsuno* by Roger Leloup and *Alix* by Jacques Martin (both in French) are three of the most popular kids' comics, all tallying up about 100,000 copies per year. Leloup and Martin were both assistants of Hergé.

This bevy of comic-strip talent is easily admired in Brussels, where the Centre Belge de la Bande Dessinée showcases the nation's best, and where you can follow the Comic Strip Route (see the boxed text 'Murals of Brussels' in the Brussels chapter). Belgium is proof that comics are not just for kids.

Belgians are big meat-eaters and they're quite liberal when it comes to the flesh they consume. Rabbit and game are commonplace and horse (€11 per kilo) can be found in butcher shops and on restaurant menus around the country.

Bird lovers should be aware that *pâté de foie gras*, a delicacy produced primarily in Wallonia, is often made by force-feeding geese for a couple of weeks so that their livers expand.

In a survey carried out in 1999 by Gaia, an animal-rights pressure group, 80% of Belgians thought force-feeding (which is illegal in the UK and Germany) should be outlawed.

RELIGION

Christianity was established early in Belgium and today Catholicism reigns supreme. Roughly three-quarters of the population is Roman Catholic. Church attendance has dropped dramatically since the 1970s and 1980s, however, religious traditions remain strong and influence many aspects of daily life, including politics and education.

Other religious denominations include Protestants, Jews and Muslims.

Some of the country's best-known events are religious-based festivals such as the Heilig-Bloedprocessie in Bruges and Brussels' famous Ommegang procession (see under Special Events in the Facts for the Visitor chapter).

LANGUAGE

Belgium's three main languages are Flemish, French and German. Flemish speakers occupy Flanders, the northern half of the country, and French speakers live in Wallonia in the south. The small German-speaking region, known as the Eastern Cantons, is in the far east of the country. Brussels is officially bilingual though French has long been the city's dominant language.

Flemish, or Vlaams as it's known by most Belgians, is a form of Dutch; some people in Belgium do in fact prefer to call the language Dutch, or Nederlands as it's also known.

For details on the underlying tensions between the Flemish and French-speaking communities, see the boxed text 'The Linguistic Divide' earlier in the chapter.

If you're unsure of which language group someone comes from, it's probably best to stick to English until you've sussed it out – some Flemish take exception to being greeted in French and Walloons may feel insulted if addressed in Flemish. In all three cities, tourists can get by with English most of the time.

Belgium's Linguistic Divide may cause some confusion when you're travelling, particularly when crossing between Flanders and Wallonia. For example, when driving from Antwerp, the sign you're following to Bergen (the Flemish name) will disappear and Mons (French) will appear – you'll need to know both the Flemish and French names for a city in order to keep up with roadsigns. The same goes for reading timetables and signboards at train stations. With the exception of Brussels, these are written in the local language only, hence you may start your journey scanning a timetable to 'Ypres' and end up needing to look out for a station called 'Ieper'. A list of alternative place names is included in an appendix at the end of this book. For some helpful phrases and vocabulary in Flemish and French, see the Language chapter.

Facts for the Visitor

WHEN TO GO
The three cities are alluring at any time of the year. However, most visitors arrive between May and September and if you want any chance of decent weather these are the best months to visit. The disadvantages of this time of year are the considerable crowds at tourist sights and booked-out accommodation, especially in Bruges.

If you're considering a weekend visit, Brussels is a particularly attractive option (see the boxed text 'Weekend Deals' in the Brussels chapter for more details).

From November to March the weather is often wretched and tourist numbers fall dramatically. If you pack the right clothes and keep in mind that the daylight hours will be short, you can make the most of uncrowded museums and there's always a cosy cafe in which to escape from the cold and rain.

MAPS
Lonely Planet's fold out Brussels City Map contains five maps including central Brussels at a scale of 1:15,000. It also contains a transport map, walking tour and a complete index of street names and sights.

The tourist offices in each of the three cities have good, cheap maps. These, combined with the detailed maps at the back of this book, should suffice for most purposes. Remember that Brussels maps often have street names in both French and Flemish (see the boxed text 'What Street Is This?' in the Brussels chapter).

The Institut Géographique National (IGN; Map 3; ☎ 02-629 82 11, fax 02-629 82 83, ℮ sales@ngi.be), Abbaye de la Cambre 13 in Brussels, publishes topographical maps covering all of Belgium in scales ranging from 1:10,000 to 1:50,000. Its sales office in the abbey (door No 5) opens 9 am to 5 pm Monday to Friday. Many of these maps are also available in bookshops.

Geocart's Brussels map No 19 (scale 1:17,000) opens out to cover 44 communes in the region. It includes a street index and

is good for exploring the area around the city, but is not so great for the centre.

De Rouck publishes a map of the Forêt de Soignes near Brussels that shows walking and cycling paths.

The city map provided by Bruges tourist office is adequate for most purposes. Geocart's Super Plan No 69 (scales 1:17,500 and 1:10,000) of Antwerp and its environs also lists streets and useful addresses.

TOURIST OFFICES
All three cities have good, centrally located tourist offices. Staff are generally friendly and efficient, and will help with accommodation bookings and arranging guided tours.

Local Tourist Offices
Brussels The Flemish and Walloon tourist authorities (Toerisme Vlaanderen and Office de Promotion du Tourisme, respectively) have their head office (Map 5; ☎ 02-504 03 90, fax 02-504 02 70, ℮ info@toeimevlaan deren.be or ℮ info@opt.be) at Rue du Marché aux Herbes 63. It opens 9 am to 6 pm daily (until 1 pm on Sunday from 1 September to 30 June). This office is for national tourist information (as opposed to information on Brussels itself) and the staff are very helpful. Much of the tourist literature it supplies is free.

Tourist Information Brussels (Map 5; ☎ 02-513 89 40, fax 02-513 83 20) – better known as TIB – is in the town hall on Grand Place. It's a small office but has plenty of information; it opens 9 am to 6 pm daily (10 am to 2 pm on Sunday from October to December, and closed on Sunday from 1 January to Easter). TIB sells two discount booklets: the Tourist Passport (€7.45) includes two public transport one-day passes plus discounts for a range of museums and restaurants; the Must of Brussels (€14.87) is a voucher system allowing admission to some of the city's top sights. TIB also sells one-day passes (€3.47) for public transport.

Visitors arriving on the Eurostar and

Thalys trains can use the tourist office kiosk inside Gare du Midi (Map 6). It opens 8 am to 8 pm daily (until 9 pm on Friday).

The arrivals hall at Zaventem airport (Map 3) has an Info Tourism desk (☎ 02-725 52 75) where you can get information on Flanders, Wallonia and Brussels. It's open 6 am to 10 pm daily. This desk does not handle hotel bookings – for those you must go to the nearby Destination Belgium kiosk (☎ 02-720 51 61), open 7.45 am to 9.30 pm weekdays, 10 am to 5 pm Saturday and 2 to 9.30 pm Sunday.

The national tourist office, TIB and Destination Belgium will reserve accommodation for visitors. The service is free – you simply pay a deposit that's taken off the bill.

Bruges The main tourist office (Map 10; ☎ 050-44 86 86, fax 050-44 86 00, e toerisme@brugge.be), at Burg 11, occupies a large hall in the former palace of the Brugse Vrije. It opens 9.30 am to 6.30 pm on weekdays, 10 am to noon and 2 to 6.30 pm at the weekend from April to September. It opens 9.30 am to 5 pm on weekdays and 9.30 am to 1 pm and 2 to 5.30 pm on Saturday from October to March. The office at the train station (Map 9) opens 9.30 am to 1.15 pm and 2 to 5.30 pm Monday to Saturday. At the time of writing there was talk of a new Visitors Centre being set up on the Markt for 2002.

Antwerp The helpful tourist office (Map 12; ☎ 03-232 01 03, fax 03-231 19 37, e toerisme@antwerpen.be), Grote Markt 13, opens 9 am to 6 pm daily (until 5 pm on Sunday). A new office, handy for those arriving at Centraal Station, is due to open on Koningin Astridplein (Map 12) in mid-2001. The opening hours will be 9 am to 6 pm Monday to Saturday and until 5 pm Sunday.

The Stadswinkel (Map 12; ☎ 03-220 81 80), Grote Markt 40, is a good place to find out what's happening in Antwerp, and to book tickets for some cultural events.

Tourist Offices Abroad

In the UK and in the Netherlands, there are separate tourist offices for Flanders and

Wallonia. Australia, Ireland, Luxembourg and New Zealand do not have a Belgian tourist office – enquiries should be addressed to Toerisme Vlaanderen/Office de Promotion du Tourisme in Brussels (see the previous section).

Belgium has tourist offices in the following countries:

Austria
Tourismuswerbung Flandern-Brüssel (☎ 01-596 06 60, fax 596 06 95, e office@flandern .co.at) Mariahilferstrasse 121b/6St, A-1060 Vienna
Canada
Office Belge du Tourisme (☎ 514-484 3594, fax 489 8965, e wallonie_bruxelles@ yahoo.com) PO Box 760, Succursale NDG, Montreal, Quebec H4A 3S2
Denmark
Det Belgiske Turistbureau (☎ 033-93 01 30, fax 93 48 08, e info@belgien.dk) Vester Farimagsgade 1, 3rd floor, DK-1606 Copenhagen
France
Tourisme Belgique Flandre-Bruxelles and Office Belge du Tourisme Wallonie-Bruxelles (☎ 01 42 66 37 41, fax 01 43 12 59 09, e info@ tbfb.org) 21 Blvd des Capucines, F-75002 Paris
Germany
Belgisches Haus (☎ 0221-27 75 90, fax 27 75 91 00, e infobelgien@t-online.de) Cäcilien-strasse 46, D-50667 Köln
Italy
Ufficio Belga per il Turismo (☎ 02-86 05 66, fax 87 63 96, e pubblico@belgio.it) Piazza Velasca 5, I-20122, Milan
Netherlands
Flanders: Toerisme Vlaanderen-Brussel (☎ 070-416 81 10, fax 416 81 20, e verkeers bureau@toerisme-vlaanderen.nl) Koningin-negracht 86, NL-2514 AJ The Hague
Wallonia: Belgisch Verkeersbureau voor de Ardennen en Brussel (☎ 023-534 44 34, fax 534 20 50, e belgisch.verkeersbureau@ wxs.nl) Kennemerplein 3, NL-2011 MH Haarlem
UK
Flanders: Tourism Flanders-Brussels (☎ 020-7867 0311, fax 7458 0045, e info@ flanders-tourism.org) 31 Pepper St, London E14 9RW
Wallonia: Belgian Tourist Office Brussels-Ardennes (020-7531 0390, fax 7531 0393, e info@belgium-tourism.org) 225 Marsh

Wall, London E14 9FW. To order brochures call ☎ 0800 954 5245 (UK£0.60 per minute).
USA
Belgian Tourist Office (☎ 212-758 8130, fax 355 7675, ⓔ info@visitbelgium.com) 780 Third Ave, Suite 1501, New York, NY 10017

TRAVEL AGENCIES
The following are some of the more useful agencies:

AirStop/TaxiStop
Brussels: (Map 5; ☎ 070-23 31 88 for AirStop, ☎ 070-22 22 92 for TaxiStop, fax 02-223 22 32) Rue du Fossé aux Loups 28. This agency offers cheap charter flights and car transport (which costs €0.03 per kilometre) to other European cities.
Bruges: (Map 10; ☎ 070-23 31 88) Dweersstraat 2
Antwerp: (Map 12; ☎ 070-23 31 88, fax 03-226 39 48) St Jacobsmarkt 84

Reizen Wasteels
Bruges: (Map 10; ☎ 050-33 65 31) Geldmuntstraat 30a

usit Connections
Brussels: (Map 5; ☎ 02-550 01 00) Rue du Midi 19. This good, all-round travel shop opens 9.30 or 10 am to 6.30 pm Monday to Saturday.
Bruges: (Map 10; ☎ 050-34 10 11) St Jakobsstraat 30
Antwerp: (Map 12; ☎ 03-225 31 61) Melkmarkt 23

DOCUMENTS
Visas
There are no entry requirements or restrictions on European Union (EU) nationals. Citizens of Australia, Canada, Israel, Japan, New Zealand and the USA do not need visas to visit Belgium as tourists for up to three months. Except for people from a few other European countries (such as Switzerland), everyone else must have a Schengen Visa.

This visa is named after the Schengen Agreement that abolished passport controls between Austria, Belgium, France, Germany, Greece, Italy, Luxembourg, the Netherlands, Portugal and Spain – Denmark, Finland, Sweden, Norway and Iceland joined the agreement in early 2001. A visa for any of these countries should in theory be valid throughout the area, but it pays to double-check with the embassy or consulate

of each country you intend to visit. Residency status in any of the Schengen countries negates the need for a visa, whatever your nationality.

Three-month tourist visas are issued by Belgian embassies or consulates. You'll need a valid passport and sufficient funds to finance your stay. Fees vary depending on your nationality.

Travel Insurance
A travel insurance policy to cover theft, loss and medical problems is a good idea. Some policies offer lower and higher medical expense options; the higher ones are chiefly for countries such as the USA, which have extremely high medical costs. There is a wide variety of policies available, so check the small print.

Some policies specifically exclude 'dangerous activities', which can include scuba diving, motorcycling, and even trekking. A locally acquired motorcycle licence is not valid under some policies.

You may prefer a policy that pays doctors or hospitals directly rather than you having to pay on the spot and claim later. If you have to claim later make sure you keep all documentation. Some policies ask you to call back (reverse charges) to a centre in your home country where an immediate assessment of your problem is made.

Check that the policy covers ambulances or an emergency flight home.

Driving Licence
Visitors from non-EU countries officially need an International Driving Permit (IDP) to drive in Belgium. However, police will generally tolerate a valid licence from your home country. If you plan to hire a car or motorcycle it can make life easier to have an IDP. They are issued by your local motoring association – you'll need a passport, photo and valid licence. IDPs are usually inexpensive and valid for one year.

Useful Cards & Passes
In order to stay at hostels run by Les Auberges de Jeunesse (in Brussels and Wallonia) and Vlaamse Jeugdherbergcentrale (in

Brussels and Flanders) you must be a member of an organisation affiliated to Hostelling International (HI). Non-Belgians who don't have a HI card pay €2.47 extra per night for up to six nights, after which an International Guest Card, valid for one year, is issued.

The International Student Identity Card (ISIC) provides discounts on admission to many museums and sights and on train fares.

Travellers aged between 60 and 65 can buy a Golden Railpass, which gives six one-way train trips in one year. It costs €44.62 and is valid for 1st class only (for details on discounted 2nd-class travel see the Senior Travellers section later in the chapter).

If you intend to fish in rivers, public ponds or lakes during your visit, you must obtain a licence. They're available from post offices for a nominal fee.

Copies

All important documents (passport data page and visa page, credit cards, travel insurance policy, air/bus/train tickets, driving licence etc) should be photocopied before you leave home. Leave one copy with someone at home and keep another with you, separate from the originals.

There is another option for storing details of your vital travel documents before you leave – Lonely Planet's online Travel Vault. Storing details of your important documents in the vault is safer than carrying photocopies. It's the best option if you travel in a country with easy Internet access. Your password-protected travel vault is accessible online at any time. You can create your own travel vault for free at www.ekno .lonelyplanet.com. For details see eKno Communication Service later in the chapter.

EMBASSIES & CONSULATES
Belgian Embassies & Consulates
Diplomatic representation abroad includes:

Australia (☎ 02-6273 2501, fax 6273 3392) 19 Arkana St, Yarralumla, Canberra, ACT 2600
Canada (☎ 613-236 7267, fax 236 7882) 80 Elgin St, 4th floor, Ottawa, Ontario K1P 1B7
France (☎ 01 44 09 39 39, fax 01 47 54 07 64) Rue de Tilsitt 9, F-75840 Paris Cedex 17
Germany (☎ 030-203 520, fax 203 522 00)

Internationales Handelszentrum, 9–10 Etage, Friedrichstrasse 95, D-10117 Berlin
Ireland (☎ 01-269 2082, fax 283 8488) 2 Shrewsbury Rd, Ballsbridge, Dublin 4
Luxembourg (☎ 25 43 251, fax 45 42 82) Résidence Champagne, Rue des Girondins 4, L-1626 Luxembourg City
Netherlands (☎ 070-312 34 56, fax 364 55 79) Lange Vijverberg 12, NL-2513 AC The Hague
New Zealand (☎ 04-917 0237, fax 917 0239) Axon House, 12th floor, 1–3 Willeston St, Wellington
UK (☎ 020-7470 3700, fax 7259 6213) 103–5 Eaton Square, London SW1W 9AB
USA (☎ 202-333 6900, fax 333 3079) 3330 Garfield St, NW, Washington DC 20008

Embassies in Belgium

It's important to realise what your own embassy – the embassy of the country of which you are a citizen – can and can't do to help you if you get into trouble. Generally speaking, it won't be much help in emergencies if the trouble you're in is remotely your own fault. Remember that you are bound by the laws of the country you are in. Your embassy will not be sympathetic if you end up in jail after committing a crime locally, even if such actions are legal in your own country.

In genuine emergencies you might get some assistance, but only if other channels have been exhausted. For example, if you need to get home urgently, a free ticket home is exceedingly unlikely – the embassy would expect you to have insurance. If you have all your money and documents stolen, it might assist with getting a new passport, but a loan for onward travel is out of the question.

Some embassies used to keep letters for travellers or have a small reading room with home newspapers, but these days the mail holding service has usually been stopped and even newspapers tend to be out of date.

Foreign embassies in Brussels include:

Australia (Map 4; ☎ 02-231 05 00, fax 02-230 68 02) Rue Guimard 6, B-1040
Canada (Map 3; ☎ 02-741 06 11, fax 02-741 96 43) Ave de Tervuren 2, B-1040
France (Map 4; ☎ 02-548 87 11, fax 02-513 68 71) Rue Ducale 65, B-1000

Germany (Map 3; ☎ 02-774 19 11, fax 02-772 36 92) Ave de Tervuren 190, B-1150
Ireland (Map 7; ☎ 02-230 53 37, fax 02-230 53 12) Rue Froissart 89, B-1040
Luxembourg (Map 7; ☎ 02-735 57 00, fax 02-737 57 10) Ave de Cortenbergh 75, B-1000
Netherlands (Map 3; ☎ 02-679 17 11, fax 02-679 17 75) Ave Herrmann-Debroux 48, B-1160
New Zealand (Map 6; ☎ 02-512 10 40, fax 02-513 48 56) Square de Meeus 1, 7th floor, B-1100
UK (Map 7; ☎ 02-287 62 11, fax 02-287 63 55) Rue d'Arlon 85, B-1040
USA (Map 4; ☎ 02-508 21 11, fax 02-511 27 25) Blvd du Régent 27, B-1000

CUSTOMS

Since 1999 duty-free goods have no longer been sold to those travelling from one EU country to another. For goods purchased in airports or on ferries outside the EU, the usual allowances apply for tobacco (200 cigarettes, 50 cigars or 250g of loose tobacco), alcohol (1L of spirits or 2L of liquor with less than 22% alcohol by volume, plus 2L of wine), coffee (500g, or 200g of concentrate), perfume (50g of perfume and 0.25L of eau de toilette) and other goods to a value of €175.

Do not confuse these with duty-paid items (which include alcohol and tobacco) bought at normal shops and supermarkets in another EU country and brought into Belgium, where certain goods might be more expensive. The allowances for these goods are far more generous: 800 cigarettes, 200 cigars or 1kg of loose tobacco; 10L of spirits (more than 22% alcohol by volume), 20L of fortified wine or aperitif, 90L of wine and 110L of beer.

MONEY
Currency

The unit of currency is the Belgian franc, which can be written as franc, /-, bf, Bef, BF, FB or f, as in this book. There are coins of f1, f5, f20 and f50, and notes of f100, f200, f500, f1000, f2000 and f10,000. Along with most other EU nations, Belgium is in the process of converting to euros (see the boxed text 'Introducing the Euro' for details) and prices are given in euros throughout this book.

Exchange Rates

Country	unit	francs	euros
Australia	A$1	f23.05	€0.57
Canada	C$1	f28.97	€0.72
euro zone	€1	f40.34	€1.00
France	1FF	f6.14	€0.15
Germany	DM1	f20.62	€0.51
Japan	¥100	f36.67	€0.90
Netherlands	Dfl1	f18.30	€0.45
New Zealand	NZ$1	f18.46	€0.45
UK	UK£1	f64.60	€1.60
USA	US$1	f44.75	€1.10

Exchanging Money

Nothing beats cash for convenience, or risk. If you lose it, it's gone forever and very few insurers will come to your rescue. Since Belgium is still a cash-based society, you can't avoid having at least some cash in your pocket. Belgians generally use cash for small purchases (though local Proton cards are gradually taking over this market) and local direct debit cards – known as Bancontact and Mister Cash – for larger transactions. These debit cards are more common than credit cards, but all the major credit cards are readily accepted by top and mid-range hotels and restaurants, and in many shops and petrol stations. Eurocheques are widely accepted (up to €173).

The easiest places to change money are banks and foreign-exchange bureaux (*wisselkantoren* in Flemish, *bureau de change* in French) at airports or train stations. Banks charge about 1.25% commission on cash for EU currencies, €1.23 on other currencies, and €5.60 on travellers cheques. Out of hours there are exchange bureaux, which mostly (but not always) have lower rates and higher fees. Automated Teller Machines (ATMs) are not widespread but there are usually a few in the city centres, and a couple at Zaventem airport. They generally accept MasterCard (called EuroCard in Belgium) and Visa, as well as Bancontact and Mister Cash. A few banks have currency-exchange machines outside their main entrance but they don't give good rates.

Brussels Citibank (Map 5; ☎ 02-511 64 74), Carrefour de l'Europe 13, immedi-

Introducing the Euro

On 1 January 1999 a new currency, the euro, was introduced in Europe. It's all part of the harmonisation of the European Union (EU) countries. Along with national border controls, the currencies of various EU members are being phased out.

Not all EU members have agreed to adopt the euro, however: Denmark, Greece, Sweden and the UK rejected or postponed participation. The 11 countries which have participated from the beginning of the process are Austria, Belgium, Finland, France, Germany, Ireland, Italy, Luxembourg, the Netherlands, Portugal and Spain. The timetable for the introduction of the euro runs as follows:

- On 1 January 1999 the exchange rates of the participating countries were fixed to the euro. The euro came into force for non-cash transactions and prices could be displayed in both local currency and in euros.
- On 1 January 2002 euro banknotes and coins will be introduced. This ushers in a period of dual use of euros and existing local notes and coins.
- By 28 February 2002 local currencies will be withdrawn. Only euro notes and coins will remain in circulation and prices will be displayed in euros only.

The €5 note in Belgium will be the same €5 note you will use in Italy and Portugal. There will be seven euro notes in different colours and sizes; they come in denominations of 500, 200, 100, 50, 20, 10 and five euros. There are eight euro coins, in denominations of two and one euros, then 50, 20, 10, five, two and one cents. Each participating state will be able to decorate the reverse side of the coins with their own designs, but all euro coins can be used anywhere that accepts euros.

Until 2002, travellers will probably find differences in 'euro-readiness' between different countries, between different towns in the same country, or between different establishments in the same town.

Many shops, hotels and restaurants will list prices in both local currency and euros. Travellers may be given the option of paying in euros if they are using a credit card.

Thomas Cook, American Express and other banks have started issuing travellers cheques in euros. The usefulness of these is debatable, however: until cash euros come into circulation in 2002, travellers will still have to convert their euro travellers cheques into the local currency of each country.

After 2002, once the euro has been fully introduced, it should make travel within the euro zone easier.

One of the main benefits will be that prices in the 11 countries will be immediately comparable.

Also, once euro notes and coins are issued, you won't need to change money at all when travelling to other euro-zone members. Even EU countries not participating may price goods in euros and accept euros over shop counters.

The EU has a dedicated euro Web site, http://europa.eu.int/euro, and you can also check the currency converter at www.oanda.com for the latest rates.

---

ately opposite Gare Centrale, has a couple of ATMs in its 24-hour banking centre. It is good for Visa, MasterCard and Citibank card transactions and for the Cirrus network.

The handy Fortis Banque (Map 5; ☎ 02-289 05 70), just off Grand Place at Rue de la Colline 12, opens 9 am to 4 pm on weekdays.

A good central exchange agency is Basle (Map 5; ☎ 02-511 56 30), Rue au Beurre 23. It accepts only cash and charges 1% commission but the rates are competitive. It opens 9 am to 5 pm on weekdays.

euro currency converter f10 = €0.25

Thomas Cook (Map 5; ☎ 02-513 28 45), Grand Place 4, opens 9.15 am to 8 pm on weekdays and from 10 am at the weekend.

All three train stations have Camrail Exchange offices. The head office (☎ 02-556 36 00) is inside Gare du Midi (Map 6) and opens 7 am to 10 pm daily. They charge no fees for cashing travellers cheques but the rates are lower than those at the banks. They provide cash advances on Visa and MasterCard, and the Gare du Midi office also handles American Express (Amex) cards.

There's a BBL Bank (Map 6; ☎ 02-544 17 86) in the Upper Town at Place Louise 7. It opens 9 am to 4 pm weekdays.

At Zaventem airport there are exchange bureaux (open 6.30 am to 10 pm daily) and ATMs that accept all major cards.

American Express (☎ 02-676 21 11, or 02-676 21 21 for lost or stolen cards) has an administrative office way out of the centre at Blvd du Souverain 100 (Map 3).

Diners Club's 24-hour telephone number is ☎ 02-206 98 00. Visa and MasterCard use the same 24-hour number (☎ 070-34 43 44) and the same regular number (☎ 02-205 85 85).

Bruges Weghsteen & Driege Exchange (Map 10; ☎ 050-33 33 61), Oude Burg 6, offers competitive rates for cash (travellers cheques not accepted). It opens 9 am to noon and 2 to 4.30 pm weekdays.

The BBL Bank (Map 10; ☎ 050-44 22 12), at Markt 19, handles foreign exchange and also has an ATM.

The exchange bureau at the Bruges tourist office opens 9.15 am to 6 pm weekdays and 10 am to 6.30 pm at the weekend.

You can also change cash (but not US$ or Italian lira) at decent rates at the train station ticket counters from 5 am to 10.45 pm daily.

Antwerp Good rates are offered by the Leo Stevens exchange bureau (Map 12; ☎ 03-232 18 43), De Keyserlei 64, but it handles cash only. It opens 9 am to 5 pm weekdays (until 1 pm on Saturday).

Thomas Cook (Map 12; ☎ 03-226 29 53), Koningin Astridplein 33, opens 9 am to 8.45 pm daily. The KBC bank (Map 12;

☎ 078-15 21 53), at Eiermarkt 20, opens 9 am to 4 pm on weekdays.

ATMs are located at the post office branch (Map 12) at Pelikaanstraat 16, opposite Centraal Station, and at the Dexia Bank (Map 12), Grote Markt 25.

Goffin (Map 12; ☎ 03-232 28 56), Suikerrui 36, is an exchange bureau close to the Grote Markt and open 9 am to 9.30 pm daily.

Security

The rate of violent crime in Belgium is low compared with many European countries but petty theft does occur. Favoured haunts for pickpockets in Brussels include Grand Place, the narrow streets around Ilôt Sacré, Rue Neuve and the markets at Gare du Midi and Place du Jeu de Balle.

It's a good idea to split your money into different stashes, preferably keeping the bulk of it in a pouch that you can wear around your neck inside your clothing or in a money belt, which you can wrap firmly around your waist and under your shirt or sweater. It is highly inadvisable to carry a wallet in your back pocket – it is easy prey for pickpockets.

Costs

What with excellent restaurants, exciting fashions, great beers and sublime chocolates, it's easy to go overboard in Belgium. In general, Brussels is a slightly more expensive experience than either Bruges or Antwerp.

At the budget end, if you stay at a camp site or hostel and eat very cheaply, you can survive on about €40 a day. A cheap hotel, cafe meals and the occasional beer and sundries will take it up to about €90. Things start to become quite comfortable at €130 a day, and from there the sky's the limit.

Many museums offer concession prices for children, students and seniors.

Tipping & Bargaining

Tipping is not obligatory as service and value-added tax (VAT) are included in hotel and restaurant prices. However, if you're pleased with the service, by all means add something extra. Cinema and theatre attendants generally expect a €0.50 tip, and in public toilets it's usual to leave €0.25 for the attendant.

Bargaining is not customary, though you can always try at flea markets.

Taxes & Refunds

The tax system in Belgium is complicated and direct income taxes are high. VAT (*Belasting Toegevoegde Waarde*, or BTW in Flemish; *Taxe sur la Valeur Ajoutée*, or TVA in French) is calculated at 21% for most goods, except basic necessities such as food, which attract 6% only. High excise is levied on petrol and alcohol – petrol in Belgium is among the most expensive in Europe. Hotel accommodation is subject to a tourist tax, which is always included in the room rate.

Non-EU residents leaving the EU can have the VAT (minus a processing fee) refunded for goods (not services) that exceed €125 (per invoice) and that are exported within three months of purchase. This is definitely worth claiming for large purchases. Check that the shop where you're buying has the necessary Global Refund Cheques. It will issue you one for the amount of VAT to be refunded, which you can cash in at VAT Cash Refund Points when leaving the country. Before you get your money, the Global Refund Cheque, together with the invoice/receipt, must be stamped by customs when leaving the country.

If you're travelling on to another EU country, you must go through this procedure at the EU airport from which you depart for your non-EU destination. For more information contact Global Refund (☎ 02-479 94 61, fax 02-478 36 64, @ taxfree@be.globalrefund.com).

POST & COMMUNICATIONS
Post

Within Belgium, letters weighing less than 20g cost €0.42. There are two rates for sending international letters and packages – *prioritaire* (priority) and *non-prioritaire* (non-priority). Letters under 20g to EU countries cost €0.52/0.47 for priority/non-priority; to other European countries it's

€0.74/0.52 and for the rest of the world it's €0.84/0.57. Letters sent priority average a week to nine days to reach places outside Europe, two to three days inside; non-priority is, of course, slower.

Packages up to 2kg (up to 5kg for books and brochures) can be sent via normal airmail. The price of sending a 2kg parcel is €15/7 priority/non-priority within the EU; €17/11 for the rest of Europe; and €25/14 to the rest of the world. Parcels between 2kg and 30kg can be sent using the post office's Kilopost service. This service has six international tariff zones – as an example, a 10kg package will cost €23.50/66 to the UK/USA and €118/193 to Canada/Australia.

Major international courier services such as DHL, TNT and UPS are all present in Belgium. The Belgian postal service also offers an efficient national and international courier service called EMS-Taxipost (☎ 078-15 33 43). Depending on the destination, expect parcels using EMS to take between two and four days to arrive.

In Belgium, the street number generally follows the street name, though in Brussels the number is sometimes placed first. A four digit postal code is given in front of the city or town name (for example, B-1000 Brussels). The 'B' attached to the postal code stands for the country, ie, Belgium. The abbreviation for PO Box is 'PB' (*postbus* in Flemish or 'BP' *boîte postale* in French); 'bus' or 'bte' *(boîte)* in an address stands for 'box number'. Poste restante attracts a €0.34 fee and you'll need to show your passport. Useful poste restante addresses in the three cities are:

Poste Restante, Bureau de Poste Central, Centre Monnaie, B-1000 Brussels, Belgium
Poste Restante, Hoofdpostkantoor, Markt 5, B-8000 Bruges, Belgium
Poste Restante, Hoofdpostkantoor, Groenplaats, B-2000 Antwerp, Belgium

Brussels The main post office (Map 5; ☎ 02-226 20 57) is in the Centre Monnaie (1st floor) on Blvd Anspach and opens 8 am to 6 pm weekdays and 9.30 am to 3 pm Saturday. Poste restante is collected from counter Nos 1 and 2.

Other offices scattered around town include the 24-hour office outside Gare du Midi (Map 6; ☎ 02-538 33 98), Ave Fosny 1E; the office (Map 4; ☎ 02-211 40 50) in the basement of the City 2 shopping centre on Rue Neuve; and the branch (Map 6; ☎ 02-539 19 62) at Chaussée de Charleroi 31.

Bruges The main post office (Map 10; ☎ 050-33 14 11) is at Markt 5. It opens 9 am to 5 pm weekdays and 9.30 am to 12.30 pm Saturday.

Antwerp The main post office (Map 12; ☎ 03-202 69 95) is at Groenplaats 43 and opens 9 am to 6 pm weekdays and 9 am to noon Saturday. Useful branches include the post office (Map 12; ☎ 03-233 06 77) at Pelikaanstraat 16, opposite Centraal Station, and the office (Map 12; ☎ 03-233 94 05), at Jezusstraat 26.

Telephone
Belgium's international country code is ☎ 32. To telephone abroad, the international access code is ☎ 00.

Belgacom is the main telephone company, but privatisation and deregulation in the late 1990s has meant that a host of other companies (most offering discounted international calls) have entered the fray. The competition has forced Belgacom to improve its service substantially, and it now runs a number of modern shops *(teleboetiek/téléboutique)* servicing customers in most cities.

Calls to anywhere within Belgium cost €0.04/0.02 per minute in peak/off-peak times. Peak-hour rates operate 8 am to 7 pm Monday to Friday; it is off-peak the rest of the time.

Most telephone numbers prefixed with 0900 or 070 are pay-per-minute numbers – the usual charge is €0.44 per minute. Numbers prefixed with 0800 are free calls, and those prefixed with 0475 to 0479, 0486 and 0496 are mobile numbers. Note, directory enquiries are expensive with a fixed cost per call (see the boxed text 'Useful Telephone Numbers').

Call boxes will take f5, f10 and f50 coins until the euro takes over as well as €4.96, €12.39 and €24.78 Telecards (Belgacom phonecards), available from post offices and newsagents. Call boxes inside shopping centres and train stations cost a minimum of €0.50. International calls can be made using phonecards such as Belgacom's Telecom or XL-Call card and The Phonecard (available from post offices and newsagents).

For travellers with mobile phones, Belgium uses GSM 900/1800, which is compatible with the rest of Europe and Australia, but not with the North American GSM 1900 or the system used in Japan. If you have a GSM phone, check with your service provider about using it in Belgium, and beware of calls being routed internationally (very expensive for a 'local' call).

Belgium's three biggest mobile networks are Proximus (operated by Belgacom), Mobistar and Orange. Mobiles can be rented

Useful Telephone Numbers

Emergencies
Police	☎ 101
Ambulance/Fire	☎ 100

Operator Assistance
	French	Flemish	English
International Operator	☎ 1324	☎ 1224	☎ 1324/1224
Customer Service	☎ 0800-33800 (free)	☎ 0800-22800 (free)	☎ 0800-55800 (free)
Directory Enquiries (national)	☎ 1307 (€2.18)	☎ 1207 (€2.18)	☎ 1405 (€2.18)
Directory Enquiries (international)	☎ 1304 (€1.12)	☎ 1204 (€1.12)	☎ 1405 (€1.12)

Belgium's New Telephone System

Belgium's telephone system changed in a couple of ways in 2000. Under the new system, area codes have been incorporated into phone numbers and, as such, there are now no separate area codes. For example, if you're anywhere in Belgium (including in Brussels) and are phoning Brussels, the number must include the former '02' area code (eg, ☎ 02-555 55 55); however, if you're phoning Brussels from outside Belgium you must drop the leading zero. The same goes for phone numbers all over the country.

To help adjust to the new system, the Belgian telecommunication authorities decided to retain the old format for writing telephone numbers – thus the former area code is still separated from the number by either a slash or a hyphen. We've used hyphens throughout this book.

The other new development was the introduction of a single telephone zone for the entire country. This means it costs the same to make a telephone call within Brussels as to call, for example, Bruges from Brussels.

from Locaphone (☎ 02-652 14 14) in the arrivals hall at Zaventem airport in Brussels. Prices start at €9.05 per day for the first five days then drop to €3.22 per day (not including 21% VAT). Payment is by credit card only, and there's a one-off insurance payment of €10.66. Note, it's illegal to use hand-held mobile phones while driving a vehicle in Belgium.

The Yellow Pages (telephone guide) in Belgium's major cities has a handy English-language index.

eKno Communication Service

Lonely Planet's eKno global communication service provides low-cost international calls – for local calls you're usually better off with a local phonecard. eKno also offers free messaging services, email, travel information and an online travel vault, where you can securely store all your important documents. You can join online at www.eKno.lonelyplanet.com, where you will find the local-access numbers for the 24-hour customer-service centre. Once you have joined, always check the eKno Web site for the latest access numbers for each country and updates on new features.

Fax

Faxes can be sent and received from Belgacom shops and cost €1.98 for the first page plus €1.85 per subsequent page to the UK, the USA and Canada. To Australia and New

Zealand the rates are €8.67/4.95. Receiving a fax costs €0.61 per page.

Brussels Several Belgacom Téléboutiques are dotted around Brussels. The head office (Map 5; ☎ 0800-22 800, fax 02-540 67 85) is on Blvd de l'Impératrice and there's another handy branch (Map 5; ☎ 0800-22 800, fax 02-223 32 01) in the Centre Monnaie. Both will send and receive faxes and open 9 am to 6.30 pm Monday to Saturday.

Bruges Faxes can be sent and received at Varicopy (Map 10; ☎ 050-33 59 43, fax 050-34 61 92), at Oude Burg 22a, or Speedprint (Map 9; ☎ 050-33 04 58, fax 050-34 75 15), at Langestraat 5.

Antwerp The Belgacom Teleboetiek (Map 12; ☎ 0800-22 800, fax 03-232 51 51), at Jezusstraat 1, provides fax services.

Email & Internet Access

Travelling with a portable computer is a great way to stay in touch with life back home, but unless you know what you're doing it's fraught with potential problems. If you plan to carry your notebook or palmtop computer with you, remember that the power supply voltage in the countries you visit may vary from that at home, risking damage to your equipment. The best investment is a universal AC adapter for your appliance, which will enable you to plug it in anywhere without frying the innards. You'll also need a plug adapter for each country you visit – often it's easiest to buy these before you leave home.

Also, your PC-card modem may or may not work once you leave your home country – and you won't know for sure until you try. The safest option is to buy a reputable 'global' modem before you leave home, or buy a local PC-card modem if you're spending an extended time in any one country. Keep in mind that the telephone socket in each country you visit will probably be different from the one at home, so ensure that you have at least a US RJ-11 telephone adapter that works with your modem. You can almost always find an adapter that will convert from RJ-11 to the local variety. For more information on travelling with a portable computer see www.teleadapt.com or www.warrior.com.

Major Internet service providers such as AOL (www.aol.com), CompuServe (www .compuserve.com) and IBM Net (www.ibm .net) have dial-in nodes throughout Europe; it's best to download a list of the dial-in numbers before you leave home. If you access your Internet email account at home through a smaller ISP or your office or school network, your best option is either to open an account with a global ISP, like those mentioned above, or to rely on cyber-cafes and other public access points to collect your mail.

If you do intend to rely on cybercafes, you'll need to carry three pieces of information with you to enable you to access your Internet mail account: your incoming (POP or IMAP) mail server name, your account name and your password. Your ISP or network supervisor will be able to give you these. Armed with this information, you should be able to access your Internet mail account from any net-connected machine in the world, provided it runs some kind of email software (remember that Netscape and Internet Explorer both have mail modules). It pays to become familiar with the process for doing this before you leave home.

Belgium was initially slow to embrace the Internet, but its growth in the last few years has been phenomenal. The Yellow Pages in Belgium lists dozens of ISPs offering telephone dial-up connections. On top of these are cable service providers. These companies use Belgium's extensive TV cable network to access the Internet, thereby providing a vastly superior service to conventional telephone dial-up connections. It's much faster, you can stay online 24 hours at no extra cost and your telephone line is free at all times. Indeed, as Belgium is the most cabled country in Europe, its cable-service-provider potential is enormous. At the time of writing this system was available throughout much of Brussels and many parts of Flanders and Wallonia.

Belgium's largest service provider is Skynet (☎ 0800-98 640, ⓔ info@skynet .be) operated by Belgacom. Its Web site is www.skynet.be.

There are cybercafes where you can buy online time in all three cities. You may also find public net access in libraries, hostels and hotels. Check out www.netcafeguide .com for the most up-to-date list, or try the places listed here.

Brussels easyEverything (Map 5; ☎ 02-211 08 20), Place de Brouckère, opens 24 hours daily and has 450 terminals. The minimum charge is €1.23, however the amount of access time you get for this price varies with demand – count on somewhere between 30 and 90 minutes. Afternoon and early evening are the busiest and therefore most expensive times; pop in between 3 and

---

Where's the @?

Those unfamiliar with French keyboards may find shooting off a quick email while in Belgium frustratingly slow. Most, but not all, cybercafes use computers with French keyboards. Keys on these keyboards are positioned differently than on an English keyboard and some keys also contain three (rather than one or two) symbols. To access the third symbol – that is, to reach the all important '@' symbol – use the 'Alt Gr' key.

5 am for the best rate. Bring your passport when you register for the first time.

CyberTheatre (Map 6; ☎ 02-500 78 28), Ave de la Toison d'Or 4, is the city's original cybercafe. It charges €6.19 per hour (or you can buy a 10-hour surfing card for €49.57). It opens noon to 8 pm daily.

The hostels Sleep Well and Centre Vincent Van Gogh (see Places to Stay in the Brussels chapter) each have a computer for surfing.

Bruges The Coffee Link (Map 10; ☎ 050-34 99 73, e info@thecoffeelink.com), Mariastraat 38, is tucked away in the St Janshospitaal complex. It's arguably one of the nicest Internet cafes in Belgium – freshly-roasted coffee permeates the air and the ambience is smooth and relaxed. Best of all, it uses English-style keyboards (see the boxed text 'Where's the @?'). The charge is €0.07 per minute, with a minimum of €1.24. It opens 11 am to 9.30 pm Tuesday to Saturday and until 7 pm Sunday.

Cybercafe DNA (Map 9; ☎ 050-34 10 93), Langestraat 145, has 10 terminals and a cool, minimalist interior. Rates are the same as at The Coffee Link, but those staying at the nearby Bauhaus hostel get a 10% discount.

The hostel Snuffel Sleep In (Map 10; see Places to Stay in the Bruges chapter) has a terminal providing Internet access; it charges €2.47 per half hour.

The Openbare Bibliotheek (Map 10; see the Libraries section later in the chapter) has a bank of terminals. If you plan on spending much time on the Internet, it's the cheapest option. After paying a €4.95 one-off membership fee you can use the terminals for one hour every day (bookings are necessary).

Antwerp The city's biggest cybercafe is easyEverything (Map 12; ☎ 03-231 04 70), in the Century Shopping Centre on De Keyserlei, close to Centraal Station. Prices and opening hours are the same as in Brussels – see the Brussels section for details.

Much more personal and cosmic is 2Zones (Map 12; ☎ 03-232 24 00), Wolstraat 15. It opens 11.30 am to midnight daily and surfing costs €1.11 for 15 minutes.

The Centrale Openbare Bibliotheek (Map 12; see the Libraries section later in the chapter for details) has 10 terminals on the 3rd floor where you can surf the Internet free of charge for up to one hour. You'll need to book a day in advance. Travellers must get a day pass in order to use the terminals.

DIGITAL RESOURCES

The World Wide Web is a rich resource for travellers. You can research your trip, hunt down bargain air fares, book hotels, check on weather conditions or chat with locals and other travellers about the best places to visit (or avoid!).

There's no better place to start your Web explorations than the Lonely Planet Web site (www.lonelyplanet.com). Here you'll find succinct summaries on travelling to most places on earth, postcards from other travellers and the Thorn Tree bulletin board, where you can ask questions before you go or dispense advice when you get back. You can also find travel news and updates to many of our most popular guidebooks, and the subWWWay section links you to the most useful travel resources elsewhere on the Web.

Other useful sites (most of the following have English-language versions) include:

Belgian Tourist Office This excellent site includes listings of events and general information on the country.
www.visitbelgium.com
International Community in Belgium Run by and for expatriates in Belgium, this site provides general information and includes an expats club for exchanging news of events and activities.
www.xpats.com
Living in Belgium Online version of a popular annual publication that gives newcomers tips about settling in and setting up in Belgium.
www.expatica.com/belgium.asp
Belgacom Skynet Access to many Belgian Web sites and the white and yellow pages of the telephone guide among many other things.
www.skynet.be

BOOKS

Most books are published in different editions by different publishers in different countries. As a result, a book might be a hard-cover rarity in one country while it's readily available in paperback in another. Fortunately, bookshops and libraries search by title or author, so your local bookshop or library is best placed to advise you on the availability of the following recommendations.

For suggested books by Belgian authors see under Literature in the Facts about the Cities chapter.

Lonely Planet

For those travelling farther afield than Brussels, Bruges and Antwerp, Lonely Planet publishes *Belgium & Luxembourg*. *Europe on a Shoestring* and *Western Europe* also contain sections on Belgium. *Travel with Children* and the *Europe phrasebook* provide specialist advice and information.

Guidebooks

Live & Work in Belgium, the Netherlands & Luxembourg, by André de Vries. Good if you're planning to settle in Belgium.

Expats in Brussels, by Claire de Crayencour. A practical guide to living in Brussels.

Living in Belgium A glossy guide for diplomats and expats; it covers everything from legislation to relocation and education.

Travel

A Tall Man in a Low Land, by Harry Pearson. A runaway hit among foreigners living in Belgium since it was published in 1998. Full of hilarious accounts of everyday life and travel in Belgium, it firmly shines the spotlight on the country's many idiosyncrasies.

History & Politics

Brussels, by Claire Billen. A large, richly illustrated book that delves into the city's social, economic and linguistic history. An excellent newcomer.

Medieval Flanders, by David Nicolas. Gives insight into the historical and political events of that time.

Bruges – Two Thousand Years of History, by Noël Geirnaert & Ludo Vandamme. A local archivist and a researcher teamed up to produce this concise account.

King Léopold's Ghost, by Adam Hochschild. Investigates the atrocities committed in the Congo during Léopold II's reign and chronicles the small band of activists who fought his rule.

Outrageous Fortune, by Roger Keyes. Favourably recounts Léopold III's early surrender to the Germans in WWII. The author is the son of Lord Keyes who liaised between Churchill and Léopold III.

The Politics of Belgium, by John Fitzmaurice. Looks at the country's complex federal system including the vast changes in the last two or so decades.

Waterloo – The Hundred Days, by David Chandler. An illustrated account of this decisive battle.

In Flanders Fields, by Leon Wolff. Recounts the battles fought in Flanders, using them to illustrate the nature of war and political leadership.

Art

History of Painting in Belgium, introduced by Phillipe Robert-Jones. Details the country's rich artistic heritage from the 14th century to contemporary works.

Art Nouveau in Belgium, by Dierkens & Vanderbranden. A large illustrated book that would sit well on any coffee table.

Magritte, by Suzi Gablik. For Surrealist fans.

From Ensor to Magritte: Belgian Art 1880–1940, by Michael Palmer. A beautiful, large, soft-cover book with full-page, colour reproductions of works by the major figures during this time. It's informative and covers some of the overlooked artists of that era.

Tintin & the World of Hergé: An Illustrated History, by Benoit Peeters. Explores the differences between various editions of the stories and traces Tintin's development.

Flemish Tapestry, by Guy Delmarcel. Gives a thorough overview of the Flemish tapestry industry from the 15th century to the French Revolution. It's full of splendid colour reproductions of famous and little-known tapestries.

Food & Drink

Everybody Eats Well in Belgium, by Ruth Van Waerebeek and Maria Robbins. Lovely book containing 250 easily followed recipes including those for the crispest *frites*, the plumpest garlicky mussels and some beer-based concoctions.

The Belgo Cookbook, by Denis Blais and André Plisnier. The creators of a London-based Belgian restaurant chain have produced this zany, in-your-face cookbook with advice on good tunes to play while cooking guinea fowl in raspberry beer, among other things.

The Great Beers of Belgium, by Michael Jackson. Superb introduction to the country's rich beer culture.

General

The Folding Star, by Alan Hollinghurst. Shortlisted for the Booker Prize in 1994, this is a fictional account of an Englishman who comes to a city in Belgium (a thinly disguised Bruges) to tutor two boys and falls in love with one of them.

The Factory of Facts, by Luc Sante. Ruminations of an American who visits Belgium to trace his roots.

A Dog of Flanders, by Marie-Louise de la Ramée (alias Ouida). A sad children's tale about the life of an Antwerp boy and his dog. It's particularly popular in Japan.

NEWSPAPERS & MAGAZINES

The best national daily newspapers are *Le Soir* and *La Libre Belgique* (in French) and *De Standaard* and *De Morgan* (in Flemish). There are, of course, plenty of others available including tabloid-style papers such as *La Dernière Heure*, *Het Laatste Nieuws* and *De Gazet van Antwerpen*.

European Voice is published each Thursday by the *Economist* and looks at what's happening within the EU.

The Brussels-based English-language *Bulletin* magazine (€2.23) is published on Thursday; featuring national news and including a good entertainment guide covering major events around the country, it's readily available at newsstands.

The cosmopolitan nature of the populations of Brussels and Antwerp means that there's no shortage of international newspapers and magazines, including many from America and Britain.

RADIO & TV

Two state-owned radio and TV stations operate: the Flemish-language Vlaamse Radio & Televisie (VRT) and the French-language Radio Diffusion Télévision Belge (RTBF). In addition, there's a plethora of privately-owned radio and TV stations. Digital TV has been introduced in Belgium but it's still in its infancy.

The main Flemish-language radio stations are Radio 1, which covers news, politics and current events (its frequency varies depending on where you are in Flanders); Studio Brussel (100.9 kHz FM in Brussels), good for light entertainment; and Radio 3 (96.4 kHz FM in Antwerp), an excellent jazz and classical music station. The premier stations for French speakers are Radio 21 (93.2 kHz FM in Brussels), which is big on commercial pop; Radio Wallonie (92.8 and 101.1 kHz FM) does a dose of everything; and Musique 3 (91.2 kHz FM in Brussels), which spotlights classical music. None of these stations broadcast in English.

The BBC's World Service in English can be picked up on 648 kHz AM.

The main Flemish-language TV channels are TV1 (news and sport); VTM (sensational news, soaps and game shows); Ketnet /Canvas (screens kids' programs until 8 pm followed by documentaries/foreign films); and Kanaal 2 (usually has a good line-up of English-language soaps and movies). French-language stations include RTBF1 (general news and sport) and ARTE (a pan-European channel broadcasting cultural shows, non-mainstream films and international documentaries).

These stations, of course, are just the tip of the iceberg. Nearly every home in Belgium has long had access to numerous channels thanks to cable TV, which was installed in the 1960s. Viewers can access a myriad of international stations including BBC1, BBC2, CNN, MTV, Eurosport and NBC Superchannel, as well as most German, Dutch and French TV stations. If you're staying in a mid or top-end hotel, it's likely the TV in your room will pick up all of these.

Lurking behind several TV channels is Teletext, an information service that offers hundreds of pages of up-to-date information. English-language versions are available on BBC and CNN.

VIDEO SYSTEMS

Belgian video and television operate on the PAL (Phase Alternative Line) system that is predominant in most of Europe and Australia. It is not compatible with the US and Japanese NTSC or French SECAM systems; pre-recorded video tapes bought in countries using those systems won't play in Belgium, and vice-versa.

PHOTOGRAPHY & VIDEO

Film is widely available. In Belgium, a Kodak 100 ASA (36 exposure) Elitechrome slide film costs about €5.82, while 12/24/36-exposure 100 ASA print films are about €3.50/4.58/5.57.

Developing a 36-exposure slide film costs €3.96/5.94 for unmounted/mounted transparencies. For print films you'll be looking at about €0.54 per photo plus €2.72 for processing; thus developing and printing a 36-exposure film will cost about €22.30. A 90-minute standard/Hi8 8mm video cassette costs about €7.56/15.50.

High-speed film (200 ASA or higher) is generally called for due to relatively dark conditions – the skies are often overcast and buildings cast shadows.

Lonely Planet's *Travel Photography: A Guide to Taking Better Pictures* is written by the internationally renowned travel photographer Richard I'Anson. It's full colour throughout, designed to take on the road and might just help you capture the perfect city snapshot.

TIME
Belgium runs on Central European Time. At noon it's 3 am in San Francisco, 6 am in New York and Toronto, 11 am in London, 9 pm in Sydney and 11 pm in Auckland. Daylight-saving time comes into effect at 2 am on the last Sunday in March, when clocks are moved an hour forward; they're moved an hour back again at 2 am on the last Sunday in October. The 24-hour clock is commonly used.

ELECTRICITY
The current used in Belgium is 220V, 50Hz; the socket used is the two-round-pin variety.

WEIGHTS & MEASURES
Belgium uses the metric system. Like other continental Europeans, Belgians indicate decimals with commas and thousands with points (full stops). In Flemish shops, 250g is called a *half pond* and 500g a *pond*.

The chart on the inside back cover of this book can help with conversions.

LAUNDRY
Self-service laundrettes *(wassalon/laverie)* generally open 7 am to 10 pm daily and charges about €3 to €3.50 for a 5kg wash and €0.5 per dryer cycle. Service laundries charge between €4.95 and €9.90 (depending on their location and facilities) for 5kg, and will wash, dry and fold the lot.

Brussels
Salon Lavoir de la Chapelle (Map 4; ☎ 02-512 45 03), at Rue Haute 5, is an old-fashioned, full-service, well-priced laundry open 8 am to 6 pm weekdays.

The following are self-service laundrettes: Lavoir Friza (Map 6), Rue Haute; Wash Club (Map 5), Place St Géry 25; Ipsomat (Map 5), Rue de Flandre 51; and Randy Wash-matic (Map 4), Rue de Laeken 150a.

Bruges
The Ipsomat (Map 9), at Langestraat 151, and the Wassalon (Map 10), on Ezelstraat, are both self-service laundries, open 7 am to 10 pm daily.

Antwerp
The following are self-service laundries: Was-o-Was (Map 11), Plantin-Moretuslei 77; Wassalon (Map 12), Nationalestraat 18; and Wassalon (Map 11), Verschansingstraat 13.

TOILETS
Public toilets tend to be few and far between, which is why most people avail themselves of the facilities in pubs and cafes. If you're not actually buying something, it's polite to ask first; few pub owners will object. A €0.25 fee is commonly charged in public toilets, as well as in the toilets in some popular cafes and fast-food restaurants.

Facilities for the disabled are rarer still, but a toilet can usually be found at the major train stations and in some shopping centres.

Brussels
There are toilets at each of the three train stations as well as in most of the major shopping complexes such as Agora, City 2, Monnaie and Anspach. A toilet for the disabled is located in the Centre Anspach.

Bruges
Public toilets are located across the court-yard from the tourist office, in the Hallen at the base of the belfry, on 't Zand and at the train station. Wheelchair users can access toilets at the Hallen (attached to the belfry) and in the St Janshospitaal complex.

Antwerp
Toilets can be found at the Grand Bazar shopping centre, at Centraal Station and opposite the bike rental office on Steenplein. Toilets for the disabled are located in Café Leffe on the Grote Markt and next to Rubenshuis.

LEFT LUGGAGE
The major train stations have either luggage lockers (€1.48/1.98/2.47) per 24 hours depending on the size of the locker, with a maximum of 72 hours or left-luggage offices (generally open 5 am until midnight), which charge €1.48 per article. Youth hostels often have lockers or luggage rooms and charge about €1.48 per 24 hours. There are also lockers in the foyer at the Bruges tourist office (€0.37) and on level 0 at Zaventem airport (€2.47/4.95/7.43 per 24 hours).

HEALTH
Travel health depends on your predeparture preparations, your daily healthcare while travelling and how you handle any medical problem that does develop. Make sure you're healthy before you start travelling. If you wear glasses take a spare pair and your prescription. If you require a particular medication take an adequate supply, as it may not be available locally. Take part of the packaging showing the generic name rather than the brand, which will make getting replacements easier. It's a good idea to have a legible prescription or letter from your doctor to show that you legally use the medication to avoid any problems.

No jabs are required to travel to Belgium, but it's wise to make sure routine vaccinations such as polio (usually administered during childhood), tetanus and diphtheria (usually administered together during childhood and updated every 10 years) are up-to-date.

EU citizens are eligible for free emer-gency medical care (with an E111 certificate, which they must obtain from their local health authority before travelling), but other visitors should have medical insurance or be prepared to pay (see under Travel Insurance in the Documents section earlier in the chapter). Belgium has excellent and extensive healthcare systems, and most doctors speak English. For 24-hour medical emergencies including ambulance services, dial ☎ 100.

Medical Kit
It's always a good idea to travel with a basic medical kit, even when your destination is a country like Belgium where first-aid supplies are readily available; don't forget any medication you may already be taking.

Hospitals & Pharmacies
Hotels and tourist offices will be able to assist in finding a hospital (ziekenhuis/hôpital) with an English-speaking doctor.

Pharmacies (apotheek/pharmacie) usually sport a green cross or the symbol of Aesculapius (the Roman god of healing – the symbol shows a snake coiled around a staff) and open from about 8.30 am to 7 pm on weekdays and mostly on Saturday morning. In cities and major towns, pharmacies work on a weekend and late-night roster: look for the notice displayed in the window listing which pharmacy is on duty that weekend or late at night.

Brussels Several hospitals in Brussels provide 24-hour emergency assistance. Hôpital St Pierre (Map 6; ☎ 02-553 31 11 or emergency ☎ 02-535 40 51), on the corner of Rue Haute and Rue de l'Abricotier, is one of the most central.

A good contact is the Community Help Service's 24-hour Helpline (☎ 02-648 40 14), which can provide a list of English-speaking doctors, dentists and other health professionals.

Multipharma (Map 5; ☎ 02-511 35 90), Rue du Marché aux Poulets 37, is a big pharmacy close to Grand Place. It opens 8.30 am to 6.30 pm weekdays and 9.30 am to 6.30 pm Saturday.

Medical Kit Check List

Following is a list of items you should consider including in your medical kit – consult your pharmacist for brands available in your country.

- ☐ **Aspirin or paracetamol (acetaminophen in the USA)** – for pain or fever
- ☐ **Antihistamine** – for allergies, eg, hay fever; to ease the itch from insect bites or stings; and to prevent motion sickness
- ☐ **Cold and flu tablets, throat lozenges and nasal decongestant**
- ☐ **Multivitamins** – consider for long trips, when dietary vitamin intake may be inadequate
- ☐ **Loperamide or diphenoxylate** –'blockers' for diarrhoea
- ☐ **Prochlorperazine or metaclopramide** – for nausea and vomiting
- ☐ **Sunscreen, lip balm and eye drops**
- ☐ **Calamine lotion, sting relief spray or aloe vera** – to ease irritation from sunburn and insect bites or stings
- ☐ **Antifungal cream or powder** – for fungal skin infections and thrush
- ☐ **Antiseptic (such as povidone-iodine)** – for cuts and grazes
- ☐ **Bandages, Band-Aids (plasters) and other wound dressings**
- ☐ **Water purification tablets or iodine**
- ☐ **Scissors, tweezers and a thermometer** – note that mercury thermometers are prohibited by airlines

Bruges The main hospital is Akademisch Ziekenhuis St Jan (☎ 050-45 21 11, for emergencies ☎ 050-45 20 00), Ruddershove 10, 2km north-west of the city centre. At weekends call ☎ 050-81 38 99 for a doctor.

Apotheek Dryepondt (Map 10; ☎ 050-33 64 74), Wollestraat 7, is a modern pharmacy with an old facade.

Antwerp There are many hospitals in Antwerp but the most central one with 24-hour service is the St Elisabethgasthuis (Map 12; ☎ 03-234 41 11), Leopoldstraat 26.

Apotheek Lotry (Map 12; ☎ 03-233 01 86), Grote Markt 56, is a handy central pharmacy open 9 am to 12.30 pm and 2 to 7.30 pm weekdays.

WOMEN TRAVELLERS

Belgium is not a European leader when it comes to women's issues. Catholicism, together with the nation's cultural and linguistic rift, have kept women's issues firmly on the backburner. Women's centres are almost unheard of in Belgium and it wasn't until 1990 that abortion was legalised. Even then it caused a national drama as the former king Baudouin felt morally obliged to abdicate for a day in order to allow the abortion bill to pass through parliament. Only in 1991 was succession to the Belgian throne opened to women.

That said, women should encounter few problems while travelling in Belgium. Brussels is small by capital-city standards, but violent crime is on the increase so it's advisable not to wander alone late at night or to arrive late at the Gare du Midi or Gare du Nord. The metro is relatively safe at all times. In Antwerp the risks are fewer and in Bruges the chance of anything unpleasant happening is almost non-existent.

However, in the event of rape or attack, contact SOS Viol (☎ 02-534 36 36) or Community Help Service's 24-hour Helpline (☎ 02-648 40 14).

Amazone (Map 4; ☎ 02-229 38 00, fax 02-229 38 01, ⓔ info@amazone.be), Rue du Méridien 10, is a women's information and meeting centre open 9 am to 5 pm weekdays.

Red-light districts can be found in many cities and towns in Belgium. Unlike in neighbouring Amsterdam, these districts are not famous or promoted. They are usually small (a couple of narrow side streets) so you often don't realise it's a red-light district until you've turned into it and start passing red or blue neon-lit windows. If this sort of area disturbs you, steer clear of Rue Verte and nearby streets in St Josse (Map 4) in Brussels and the Schipperskwartier (Map 12) in Antwerp.

GAY & LESBIAN TRAVELLERS

Attitudes to homosexuality are becoming less conservative. In 1998 the national parliament gave the green light to a new law recognising all cohabiting couples regardless of sexual orientation, and in early 2000 the first legal marriage between two men took place in Brussels. The age of consent is 16.

Flanders' biggest gay and lesbian organisation is the Federatie Werkgroepen Homoseksualiteit (FWH), Kammerstraat 22, B-9000 Ghent. It runs an information and help hotline called Holebifoon (☎ 09-238 26 26) that operates 6 to 10 pm daily (from 2 pm on Wednesday). Its Web site is at www.fwh.be (the site is not in English).

In early 2000 FWH opened a new headquarters – Casa Rosa – which includes a cafe and information centre and is now Ghent's premier gay meeting place. Here you can pick up a good free guidebook (in Flemish) which lists organisations, bookshops and cafes throughout Flanders and Brussels, plus *Zizo*, a bimonthly, Flemish-language magazine (€2.97) which lists upcoming parties (*fuif* in Flemish) in Flanders and addresses of active gay groups. There are also organisations in Brussels and Antwerp (see the following sections for details).

The Festival du Film Gay & Lesbien de Bruxelles is now firmly established and runs for 10 days in late January. The Brussels Pride march/festival is held on the first weekend in May.

The *Spartacus International Gay Guide*, published annually by Bruno Gmünder, is a good, male-only directory of gay entertainment venues in Europe and elsewhere.

Brussels

Tels Quels (Map 5; ☎ 02-512 45 87, fax 02-511 31 48), Rue du Marché au Charbon 81, is the city's premier French-speaking gay and lesbian meeting place. It opens 5 pm to 2 am weekdays, from 2 pm on Saturday and from 6 am on Sunday. It publishes a monthly French-language magazine (€2.47), also called *Tels Quels*, which lists gay bars, restaurants and activities. It also runs Télégal (☎ 02-502 79 38), an anonymous helpline operating 8 pm to midnight daily.

The English-Speaking Gay Group (EGG; ☎ 02-537 47 04, 🖃 tomhoemig@skynet .be), BP 198, B-1060 Brussels, holds Sun-

day afternoon parties for gay people of all nationalities.

The city's lesbian scene is minimal. There are no exclusively lesbian cafes, and only one or two nightclubs that operate on Saturday night only. The best place to find out what's happening is Artemys (Map 5; ☎/fax 02-512 03 47, 🖃 artemys@multi mania.com), Galerie Bortier 8, a lesbian bookshop and information centre. It opens noon to 6 pm Tuesday to Thursday, until 7 pm Friday and 10 am to 7 pm Saturday (closed the last week of July and first week of August). Its Web site is at www.multi mania.com/artemys.

The English-Speaking Gay Organisation for Women (EGOW; 🖃 egow11@hotmail .com) started out as a group for English speakers but now has a multilingual face. It usually meets monthly and can be contacted at BP 9, B-1030 Schaerbeek.

Bruges

There is no homosexual scene to talk about in Bruges – gays and lesbians from here generally head to Ghent or Antwerp for a night out.

Antwerp

Antwerp's long-awaited gay and lesbian community centre, Het Roze Huis (the Pink House; Map 11; Draakplaats) opened in a beautifully restored building in the Zurenborg area in late 2000. The centre has a modern cafe, **Den Draak**, where you can pick up *Antwerpen Homo Gids*, a pamphlet listing gay or gay-friendly bars, restaurants and hotels.

The well-established GOC (Map 12; ☎ 03-233 10 71), at Dambruggestraat 204, is a long-standing information and meeting place, open 8 pm to midnight weekdays and 10.30 pm to 4 am Saturday. Atthis (Map 11; ☎ 03-216 37 37), Geuzenstraat 6, is a lesbian venue open on Friday and Saturday evenings.

For more on venues, see under Entertainment in the Antwerp chapter.

DISABLED TRAVELLERS

Belgium is not a terribly accessible country for those travellers with a mobility problem.

It's riddled with buildings that are centuries old and although an effort is being made to consider disabled needs when renovating, it's no small task. Some government buildings, museums, hotels, and arts venues have lifts and/or ramps, but many don't. Many restaurants and cafes are at street level but accessing them often involves a few steps. Wheelchair users will be up against rough, uneven pavements and cobblestones, and will need to give an hour's notice when travelling by train. Note, while most large train stations are equipped with ramps, there are none at Gare Centrale in Brussels.

New buildings are required by law to be fully accessible. In all three cities you'll find hotels (usually in the mid or top-end price range) that can accommodate travellers in wheelchairs, as can the official HI hostels in Brussels, Bruges and Antwerp. Some major museums – such as the Musées Royaux des Beaux-Arts in Brussels – also have access.

Braille plaques have been erected at the entrance to some metro stations in Brussels and there's a model of the belfry in Bruges with explanatory notes in Braille (it's located on the Markt).

Taxi Hendriks (☎ 02-752 98 00, fax 02-752 98 01) in Brussels offers taxi services for disabled people.

For more information in Belgium, contact Mobility International (☎ 02-201 56 08, fax 02-201 57 63, e mobint@acradis.be), Blvd Baudouin 18, B-1000 Brussels, or the Vlaamse Federatie voor Gehandicapten (☎ 02-515 02 60, fax 02-511 50 76), 31 Rue de l'Hôpital, Brussels.

A good source of travel information is the British Royal Association for Disability and Rehabilitation (RADAR; ☎ 020-7250 3222, fax 7250 0212, e radar@radar.org.uk), 12 City Forum, 250 City Rd, London EC1V 8AF, UK. Its Web site is at www.radar .org.uk.

In the USA, you can try Mobility International (☎ 541-343 1284, fax 343 6812, e info@miusa.org). Its Web site is at www .miusa.org.

In Australia, contact the National Information & Awareness Network (NICAN;

☎ 06-285 3713, fax 285 3714, e nican@ spirit.com.au), or visit its Web site at www.nican.com.au.

SENIOR TRAVELLERS

Belgium's population is ageing and the number of elderly people here is very noticeable. Older Belgians (particularly those in cities) tend to be immaculately dressed and highly fashion conscious – they might not be getting around in a Van Beirendonck label, but you can be sure they're *au fait* with top European designers, not to mention home-grown Olivier Strelli.

As a traveller, you'll find getting around poses few major problems, although at some train stations platforms are low, making it difficult to climb into carriages. Seniors over 65 (including visitors with appropriate identification such as a passport) pay only €2.47 for a return train trip (2nd class) to anywhere in Belgium.

Most museums and other attractions offer discounts for those aged over 65 – there's no standard rule, so check the tariffs to see if you are eligible for a reduction.

BELGIUM FOR CHILDREN

Successful travel with young children requires planning and effort. Don't try to overdo things, and make sure daily activities include the kids as well. For further general information see Lonely Planet's *Travel with Children*, by Maureen Wheeler.

Most car rental firms in Belgium have children's safety seats for hire at nominal cost, but it's essential to book them in advance. The same goes for cots in hotels and highchairs in restaurants if you want to be sure of getting one.

Dining out with the kids is fine in casual and touristy restaurants, but not in top-end establishments. Children are allowed in cafes and pubs but bear in mind that these places are generally full of smoke. Also remember that in Bruges there's a lot of open water – beware no-one takes an unexpected plunge. Kids under 12 years of age travel for free on Belgian trains when accompanied by an adult. In many cities, adult and children's bicycles are readily available for hire; remember adult bikes can be fitted front and rear with baby/toddler seats. There's nothing like a ride in the country-side against a stiff North Sea wind to give them (and you) a good night's sleep.

Babysitting can be arranged through Bond van Grote & Jonge Gezinnen, a family-oriented organisation with 800 cen-tres throughout Flanders. They charge €2.23/2.97 per hour in the day/evening for babysitters, or €12.39 for overnight ser-vice. You must book two days ahead – call during weekday working hours.

Brussels

Babysitting organisations include Bond van Grote & Jonge Gezinnen (☎ 02-507 89 66) and the ULB Job Service (☎ 02-650 21 71), whose babysitters tend to be stu-dents.

Brussels has a couple of museums aimed specifically at kids. The Musée du Jouet (Toy Museum; Map 4; ☎ 02-219 61 68), Rue de l'Association 24, has a good repu-tation. It opens 10 am to 1 pm and 2 to 6 pm daily; admission costs €2.47.

The Scientastic Museum (Map 5; ☎ 02-736 53 35), inside Bourse metro station, has interactive science-related exhibits. It opens 2 to 5.30 pm at weekends and daily during school holidays; admission costs €3.71 (children and seniors €3.22).

Parts of some adult museums are also attractive to kids. These include the Centre Belge de la Bande Dessinée, Album, the Musée des Sciences Naturelles de Belgique and Autoworld. The Koninklijk Museum voor Midden-Afrika at Tervuren also gen-erally appeals to kids.

Children usually enjoy the Atomium, the Théâtre Royal de Toone and ice-skating on Grand Place at Christmas, as well as a run around at the Mellaerts ponds (Map 3), Bois de la Cambre (Map 3) or Parc de Woluwé (Map 3). The Bruparck entertainment com-plex (Map 8) is also a winner.

Bruges

The Bond van Grote & Jonge Gezinnen (☎ 050-33 75 60), Jacob van Maerlantstraat 118, has babysitters.

Kids generally enjoy the sweet-making demonstrations at the Museum voor Volk-skunde, watching other children making lace at the Kantcentrum, exploring St Jan-shuismolen, playing on the frames and slip-pery slides next to Magdalenakerk in Koningin Astridpark (Maps 9 and 10) and, of course, taking a canal trip.

Children's bikes can be hired from Hotel 't Koffieboontje and if you cycle along the raised paths encircling the town there are few cobbles to contend with (cobblestones, by the way, are known as *kinderkopkes*, which literally means children's heads). A good cycling destination is Damme (Map 1).

Boudewijnpark (☎ 050-38 38 38), at St Michiels, is a theme park with ice-skating in winter, rollerblading rinks and an indoor 'dolphinarium' where dolphins and seals are put to work.

Antwerp

The Bond van Grote & Jonge Gezinnen (☎ 03-233 64 18), at Schermersstraat 32, organises babysitters.

Lancelot & Co (Map 12; ☎ 03-213 15 63, Meir 28) is a child-minding service (for kids aged between three and 12 years) on the 1st floor of the Meir Square shopping gallery. The charge is €1.23 per hour. It's well run, the staff speak English and there's plenty for kids to do. Opening hours are noon to 6 pm Wednesday and Saturday. During school holidays it opens 10 am to 6 pm Monday to Saturday.

Pirateneiland (Pirate Island; Map 11; ☎ 03-213 50 60), at Bordeauxstraat, is in a renovated warehouse. It's designed for kids aged between two and 12 and is basically an indoor fun park. It opens 10 am to 6 pm Wednesday to Sunday; admission costs €3.71. Kids usually enjoy Flandria boat trips, walking through the St Annatunnel underneath the River Scheldt and visiting Antwerp Zoo (Map 12). There's a play-ground in the Stadspark (Map 12).

USEFUL ORGANISATIONS

The *Bulletin* magazine, available at news-stands, publishes the contact details of, and events run by, many social and sporting clubs.

Other useful organisations in Brussels include:

Act Together (☎ 02-511 33 33) Rue d'Artois 5. An English-speaking AIDS/HIV support organisation. It has a helpline (☎ 02-512 05 05) open 7 to 9 pm daily.

American Women's Club (☎ 02-358 47 53) Ave des Érables 1.

British & Commonwealth Women's Club (Map 3; ☎ 02-772 53 13) Rue au Bois 509. One of the city's best-known expatriate women's social clubs.

Infor Jeunes (Map 5; ☎ 02-514 41 11) Rue Ste Cathérine 9a. A centre assisting young people in a broad range of areas, including housing, employment and legal advice. It opens noon to 5.30 pm weekdays.

Service for Foreign Students (Map 6; ☎/fax 02-511 69 43) Rue de la Prévoyance 60. A support agency for foreign students open 2 to 5 pm Monday to Thursday.

LIBRARIES
Brussels

Bibliothèque Royale Albert I (Map 4; ☎ 02-519 53 11), Blvd de l'Empereur 4, is the country's largest library. Borrowing is not allowed, and access to the reading rooms is for members only (€2.47 per week or €14.87/7.43 per year for adults/students). The reading rooms open from 9 am to 7.45 pm weekdays and until 4.45 pm on Saturday.

The Université Libre de Bruxelles (ULB) library (Map 3; ☎ 02-650 23 77), Ave Franklin Roosevelt 50, has a good English-language section and opens 8 am to 5 pm weekdays and 10 am to 4 pm Saturday. Yearly membership costs €26.64/14.25 for adults/students (a photograph and a passport are required).

The Centre Belge de la Bande Dessinée (Map 4; ☎ 02-219 19 80), Rue des Sables 20, has a specialised comic-strip library open noon to 5 pm Tuesday to Thursday, to 6 pm Friday, 10 am to 6 pm Saturday and noon to 6 pm Sunday. Admission to the reading room costs €0.50; access to the study section costs €1.23 (but is free if you have a ticket to visit the centre).

Bruges

The Openbare Bibliotheek (Map 10; ☎ 050-33 00 50), Kuipersstraat 3 in the Biekorf building, is the city's main public library. It opens daily except Sunday.

De Wegwijzer (Map 10; ☎ 050-33 75 88, **e** wegwijzer@unicall.be), Beenhouwersstraat 9, is a library and research centre specialising in travel worldwide. Annual membership costs €18.59.

Antwerp

The Centrale Openbare Bibliotheek (Map 12; ☎ 03-204 70 11), Lange Nieuwstraat 105, is Antwerp's main public library. Strictly speaking the library is open only to members (€7.43 per year) but visitors are generally allowed to use the 3rd floor reading room. It opens 8.30 am to 4.30 pm on weekdays (until 8 pm on Monday and Wednesday) and 9 am to noon on Saturday.

The Stadsbibliotheek (Map 12; ☎ 03-206 87 11), Hendrik Conscienceplein 4, is the city's main reference library.

UNIVERSITIES

Belgium has many universities and institutions of higher education, and a good number of these offer courses that are taught in English.

Brussels

Université Libre de Bruxelles (ULB; Map 3; ☎ 02-650 21 11), Ave Franklin Roosevelt 50, was founded in 1834 and is a well-regarded, French-speaking university with medicine and chemistry faculties; it has a high number of foreign students.

Vrije Universiteit Brussel (VUB; Map 3; ☎ 02-629 21 11), Blvd de la Plaine, is a Flemish-speaking university that runs many courses taught in English and is also home to the American-style Vesalius College.

Bruges

The nearest universities to Bruges are in Ghent and Antwerp. The city does, however, boast the prestigious Europacollege (College of Europe; Map 10; ☎ 050-44 99 11), Dijver 11. This postgraduate college for European studies was founded in 1950 to train future leaders of Europe. English and French are the languages of instruction for the 500 students.

Antwerp

Universitaire Faculteiten St Ignatius (UFSIA; Map 12; ☎ 03-220 41 11), Prinsstraat 13, is the city's premier university, with courses in politics, economics, social sciences, philosophy, history and literature.

Rijksuniversitair Centrum Antwerp (RUCA; ☎ 03-218 05 12), Groenenborgerlaan 171, in the suburb of Wilrijk, is a state university specialising in the sciences, economics and developing-world studies.

Universitaire Instelling Antwerp (UIA; ☎ 03-820 20 20), Universiteitsplein 1 in Wilrijk, has faculties of biochemistry, law and medicine.

CULTURAL CENTRES

The following cultural centres are all in Brussels:

Alliance Française (Map 3; ☎ 02-732 15 92, fax 02-736 47 00) Ave de l'Émeraude 59. This centre is dedicated to teaching the French language and culture.
Le Botanique (Map 4; ☎ 02-226 12 11, e info @botanique.be) Rue Royale 236. This is the main cultural centre of Belgium's French-speaking community.
Goethe Institut (Map 7; ☎ 02-230 39 70, fax 02-230 77 25) Rue Belliard 58. This institute offers day and evening courses ranging from German language to business.

DANGERS & ANNOYANCES

Belgium is, in general, very safe. The only danger you're likely to confront is a big night out on Belgian beer.

Racism has been on the increase in Belgium in the last decade. Hostility is mainly directed at the nation's immigrant populations, particularly Moroccans and Turks. Members of these communities are known to get a hard time from police in Brussels. Thankfully, there have so far been no fatal attacks against immigrants of the kind that have made headline news elsewhere in recent years.

An ongoing spate of car and house break-ins over the last couple of years has kept the nation talking. The thieves break into wealthy residences and demand the keys to the owners' expensive BMW 525 or Mercedes E series cars. If you're not driving one of these, you'll probably be safe.

In Antwerp, De Coninckplein, just north of Centraal Station (Map 12), is noted for its (hard) drugs scene.

Nonsmokers may find the cafe and restaurant scene trying at times. Although required by law to have adequate ventilation, few establishments do. Even fewer have sections for nonsmokers (niet rokers/non-fumeurs). In April 2000 the government threatened to impose a total ban on smoking in cafes where owners failed to provide a smoke-free area; however, the threat has yet to be carried out.

And lastly there's the subject of dog shit. Belgians' love of dogs unfortunately manifests itself in footpaths dotted with doggie doodles. Visitors generally find it very hard to wander along ogling architectural delights while at the same time trying to dodge these offensive donuts.

EMERGENCIES

The national emergency numbers in Belgium are police ☎ 101 and fire/ambulance ☎ 100. In the event of rape or attack, contact SOS Viol (☎ 02-534 36 36) or Community Help Service's 24-hour helpline (☎ 02-648 40 14).

LEGAL MATTERS

Belgium's police and judiciary systems have come under scathing public criticism in recent years following the Dutroux affair (see The 20th Century under History in the Facts about the Cities chapter). A complete revision has been demanded but change is very slow in coming.

Police usually treat tourists with respect and many officers, particularly in Flanders, speak English fluently. Under Belgian law you must carry either a passport or national identity card at all times. Should you be arrested for any reason, you have the right to ask for your consul to be immediately notified.

The EU area in Brussels is regularly targeted for demonstrations by angry farming lobbies or groups incensed at EU-related issues. It's not uncommon for police to seal off entire areas when this happens, though things rarely turn violent.

BUSINESS HOURS

In general, shops are open 8.30 or 9 am to noon or 12.30 pm, and 2 to 6 pm, Monday to Saturday. Some shops in Brussels and Antwerp also open on Sunday; some around Grand Place in Brussels are closed on Monday and some don't close for lunch.

Banks tend to open 9 am to noon or 1 pm, and 2 to 4 or 5 pm on weekdays and Saturday mornings; in the three cities they often don't close for lunch.

There are absolutely no regulations governing trading hours for cafes and pubs – they simply close when the last customer leaves.

PUBLIC HOLIDAYS & SPECIAL EVENTS
Public Holidays

Public holidays in Belgium are:

New Year's Day 1 January
Easter Monday March/April
Labour Day 1 May
Ascension Day 40th day after Easter
Whit Monday 7th Monday after Easter
Festival of the Flemish Community 11 July
(Flanders only)
Belgium National Day 21 July
Assumption 15 August
Festival of the Walloon Community 27
September (Wallonia only)
All Saints' Day 1 November
Armistice Day 11 November
Christmas Day 25 December

Special Events

All three cities have plenty of special events, from jazz marathons and religious processions to local fairs, film festivals and classical music extravaganzas. The tourist offices in each city will be able to give you complete lists. For events related to gays and lesbians, see the Gay & Lesbian Travellers section earlier in the chapter.

In 2002, Bruges will be the Cultural Capital of Europe. At the time of writing, the city was sprucing itself up for this big event.

January
Brussels International Film Festival (☎ 02-227 39 89) This festival has been going for 30 years and runs for 10 days from mid- to late January.
Foire des Antiquaires/Antiekbeurs (☎ 02-513 48 31) Brussels' Palais des Beaux-Arts (Map 4) is the venue for this annual 10-day antique fair (going for almost half a century and usually held in late January or early February), which offers the best from antique dealers in Belgium and neighbouring countries.

February
Bruges Festival A week-long classical music festival in early February.
Comic Strip & Cartoon Film Festival (☎ 02-534 41 25) This 12-day festival is held over two weeks in mid-February and premieres feature-length films and about 100 shorts produced in Belgium and elsewhere.
Carnival Carnival is celebrated throughout Belgium but the most renowned festivities take place in the town of Binche, about one hour's drive south-west of the capital. The highlight is on Shrove Tuesday when the elaborately dressed local men dance in the town's central square.

March
Cinema Novo Film Festival (☎ 050-34 83 54) This 10-day festival is held in mid-March in Bruges and highlights Asian, African and Latin-American films.
Ars Musica (☎ 02-219 26 60) A respected festival of contemporary music which extends from mid-March to early April and attracts a showcase of musicians to various venues in Brussels, including the Palais des Beaux-Arts.

April
Festival van Vlaanderen (☎ 02-548 95 95) Top classical and international music performances are held until October in churches, abbeys, town halls and other historical locations throughout Flanders.
Serres Royales (☎ 02-513 89 40) The magnificent Serres Royales (greenhouses) at the Domaine Royal in Laeken, Brussels, are open to the public for 10 days at the end of April.

May
Heilig-Bloedprocessie The Procession of the Holy Blood is Bruges' most famous annual event. It's held on Ascension Day and celebrates

the drops of Christ's blood that are kept in the town's basilica. On this day, the relic is paraded through town in an elaborate, medieval-style procession. It will be held on 9 May in 2002.

Brussels 20km Run Annual competition held in the streets of the capital on a Sunday in mid-May; it attracts about 20,000 runners.

Brussels Jazz Marathon (☎ 02-456 04 87) The last weekend in May brings jazz bands and enthusiasts to stages all over the city for a series of concerts. A special bus service shuttles passholders from one venue to the next.

Kunsten Festival des Arts (☎ 02-219 07 07) Music, dance, theatre and opera are the varied themes for this Brussels festival held from the middle to the end of May.

Concours Musical International Reine Élisabeth de Belgique (☎ 02-513 00 99) The Queen Elisabeth International Musical Competition is one of Belgium's most prestigious classical music events. It began half a century ago and was inspired by the nation's former queen Elisabeth, who was a violinist. Young talent from around the world is drawn to the month-long competition in three rotating categories – in 2002 it will be violin, in 2003 piano and in 2004 song.

June

Couleur Café (☎ 02-672 49 12) World music, dance, rap and drums come to Brussels for a three-day festival during the last weekend in June.

Ommegang (☎ 02-512 19 61) This medieval-style procession takes place in late June or early July in Brussels. *Ommegang* ('a walk around' in Flemish) dates back to the 14th century, when celebrations were held following the arrival in Brussels of a statue of the Virgin Mary brought by boat from Antwerp. By the 16th century the procession was presided over by royalty and was held to honour Charles V. It is now one of the capital's most famous events. The procession starts at the Place du Grand Sablon and ends in a dance at the illuminated Grand Place. Tickets for the finale cost between €20 and €65 and need to be bought well in advance.

Festival of Wallonia Young Belgian musicians perform classical concerts throughout Brussels and Wallonia until October.

Antwerp Fashion Show One of the city's biggest fashion extravaganzas takes place in the Handelsbeurs in Antwerp over three days towards the end of June. New collections from top Antwerp designers are on the catwalk.

July

Cactusfestival Festival of world music held in

the second weekend of July at the Minnewater in Bruges.

10 Days Off One of the biggest and longest rave parties in Europe held over 10 nights in mid-July in Ghent. A ticket for one night costs €10 or €37 for the whole time.

Foire du Midi A huge, annual, month-long funfair runs from mid-July on Blvd du Midi in Brussels. Expect crowds, a Ferris wheel, roller coasters, *gaufres* (waffles) and much more.

Belgium National Day Celebrations on 21 July include a military procession in the Parc de Bruxelles in Brussels.

Sfinks World Music Festival (☎ 03-455 69 44) A five-day celebration of world music is held in Boechout near Antwerp, at the end of July.

August

Praalstoet van de Gouden Boom The Pageant of the Golden Tree is held every five years in Bruges. It celebrates the marriage of Charles the Bold (Karel de Stoute) to Margaret of York in 1468. The next one will take place from 31 August to 1 September 2002.

Meiboom (☎ 02-217 39 43) The Raising of the Maypole is a folkloric event held annually in Brussels on 9 August. A procession of 'giants' winds down from the Sablon to Grand Place where they plant a maypole.

Tapis des Fleurs Brussels' famous Floral Carpet takes over Grand Place every two years in mid-August. It's a spectacularly colourful three-day event – in 2000, almost 800,000 begonias were used to make a marvellous design representing a lace tablecloth. It is next scheduled for 2002, then 2004.

Jazz Middelheim This biennial, week-long jazz festival in the second week of August is held in Park Den Brandt (Map 11) in Antwerp and is one of the city's biggest shindigs. It will next be staged in 2003.

September

Open Monumentendag/Journées du Patrimoine On selected weekends in September, Belgium opens a handful of protected monuments to the public in what are known as Heritage Days. These events usually fall on the second weekend in September for monuments in the countryside and on the following weekend for those in Brussels.

Ivo Van Damme Memorial (☎ 02-474 72 30) This important athletics meeting attracts a good number of international athletes and is held in early September at the Roi Baudouin stadium at Heysel in Brussels.

Belgian Beer Weekend Brussels' Grand Place comes alive in early September with beer stalls at which visitors can sample about 130 of the nation's many brews.

Les Nuits Botanique (☎ 02-226 12 42) A weekend of rock, world music and pop in the Botanique in Brussels in mid-September.

Antwerp Fashion Week The spotlight hits Antwerp in mid-September every year when the city hosts a week of avant-garde fashion. The event will take on more importance than ever during September 2001 as Antwerp celebrates its Year of Fashion.

December

Marché de Noël (☎ 02-279 40 75) Grand Place in Brussels is the setting for a Christmas craft market held over 10 days during the first fortnight in December and featuring stalls from many EU countries.

Ice Skating Open-air rinks are set up on Grand Place in Brussels, the Grote Markt in Antwerp and the Markt in Bruges for about two weeks from mid-December.

DOING BUSINESS

Brussels makes much of its position as the headquarters of the EU and many international organisations and multinational corporations are based in or around the capital.

If you plan to do business here, start by contacting the trade or commercial office of the Belgian embassy in your country. They can supply the useful publication *Newcomer – An Introduction to Life in Belgium*, which gives information on starting a business. Other guides to track down include Ernst & Young's free *Doing Business in Belgium*, or *Getting Started…Legally: Working in Belgium and Starting a Business* (€12.39) published by the Brussels-based non-profit association, Focus Career Services (see the following list of organisations for contact details).

Once you're in Belgium, the annual *European Public Affairs Directory* may come in useful, depending on your business. It provides contacts for key people in corporations, EU institutions, trade associations and NGOs in Brussels. It's available in selected Brussels bookstores.

The Chambre de Commerce et d'Industrie de Bruxelles (☎ 02-648 50 02, fax 02-646 43 73), Ave Louise 500, B-1050 Brussels, offers assistance to those who

have set up or plan to establish a business. The chamber has about 3000 members and has a business start-up unit.

Ernst & Young (☎ 02-774 91 11), Ave Marcel Thiry 204, B-1200 Brussels, is an international accounting, tax and management-consultancy firm.

Focus Career Services (☎ 02-513 88 03, fax 02-646 96 02), Rue Lesbroussart 23, B-1050 Brussels, offers advice and assistance to newcomers to the EU.

Business Services

Regus provides the complete range of business operations, including fully furnished rental offices and secretarial services. It has several offices in Brussels: the most central is at Ave Louise 65 (Map 6; ☎ 02-535 77 11, fax 02-535 77 00). It also has an office in Antwerp (Map 12; ☎ 03-207 17 77, fax 03-206 17 78) at Koningin Astridplein 7 in the Astrid Park Plaza Hotel. Its Web site is at www.regus.com.

Translate International (☎ 02-373 68 68, fax 02-373 68 63, ⓔ brussels@translate .be), Ave Albert Lancaster 79, B-1180 Brussels, is a reputable service. Expect to pay about €1.25 per line for translations into English.

EGE Stienon (☎ 02-512 32 33, fax 02-514 08 83), Blvd Barthélemy 37, B-1000 Brussels, has interpreters – rates are €370/450 for a half/full day.

Exhibitions & Conferences

Brussels is one of the world's leading conference cities. If you plan a larger event here, contact Brussels Congress (☎ 02-549 50 50, fax 02-549 50 59, ⓔ brussels .congress@euronet.be), which produces *Let's Meet in Brussels*, a free annual publication detailing all the conference venues.

WORK

Nationals from EU countries do not require a work permit to work in Belgium, but they must register with the commune where they intend living and obtain a residence permit from the local town hall as soon as they move to Belgium.

Given Belgium's high unemployment,

chances of finding (legal) work as a non-EU national are slim. Non-EU nationals cannot seek employment without having a work permit issued before they arrive. This is issued by the Ministère de l'Emploi et du Travail (Belgian Ministry of Labour; ☎ 02-233 41 11, fax 02-233 47 38), Rue Belliard 51–3, B-1040 Brussels. The permit will only be issued if your prospective employer can prove that no Belgian or other EU national can do the job.

Due to the country's very high tax rates, Belgium has the fourth highest rate of illegal work in the EU after Greece, Italy and Spain. More than 500,000 people work 'in the black' full-time, representing between 12 and 16% of the nation's economic activity. It's possible to pick up illegal work such as seasonal fruit-picking, for example.

ACCOMMODATION

Brussels, Bruges and Antwerp all offer the whole range of accommodation, from camp sites to hostels, B&Bs, cheap and expensive hotels and long-term options. All become heavily booked in summer, so if you plan to visit from May to September it's wise to make reservations at least several weeks ahead.

The accommodation situation in Brussels is somewhat unusual and great specials can be had – see the boxed text 'Weekend Deals' in the Brussels chapter for details.

Once you're in Belgium, the tourist offices all offer free accommodation-booking services (you pay a deposit that is deducted from your room rate).

Camping facilities in the three cities are nothing to rave about as they're usually remotely located and often framed by noisy motorways. Rates vary widely, but on average you'll be looking at between €6.50 and €12.40 for two adults, a tent and vehicle in a basic camp site.

Youth hostels (*jeugdherberg* in Flemish or *auberge de jeunesse* in French) affiliated with Hostelling International (HI) are present in all three cities, as are similarly-priced private hostels (*jeugdlogies/logements pour jeunes*). The country's two HI organisations are: Vlaamse Jeugdherberg-

centrale (VJH; Map 12; ☎ 03-232 72 18, fax 03-231 81 26, e info@vjh.be), Van Stralenstraat 40, B-2060 Antwerp, which runs hostels in Flanders and Brussels; and Les Auberges de Jeunesse (Map 4; ☎ 02-219 56 76, fax 02-219 14 51, e info@laj.be), Rue de la Sablonnière 28, B-1000 Brussels, which administers Wallonia and Brussels.

Rates at the HI hostels range from €10.65 to €12.64 per night in a dorm, including breakfast. Some of the hostels also have single/double rooms for €20.32/29.74. For details on HI membership, see Useful Cards & Passes in the Documents section earlier in the chapter. There is no age limit for staying at HI hostels. Most charge €3.22 extra for sheets.

B&Bs (*gastenkamers* in Flemish or *chambres d'hôtes* in French) have gained ground enormously in the three cities in the last decade. The tourist offices have lists of B&Bs or you can pick up the *Bed & Breakfast & Rentals* booklet produced by TaxiStop for €4.83 (see the Travel Agencies section earlier in the chapter). B&Bs usually represent excellent value, and charge from about €25 to €50 for a single and from €35 to €65 for doubles. As many B&B rooms are converted attics, some can only be reached up narrow staircases.

Budget hotels charge between about €35 and €50 for a single and from €50 to €70 for doubles. Mid-range hotel prices average €70 to €75 for singles and €62 to €125 for doubles. In Brussels, top-end establishments start at €170/200 for a single/double during the week (but drop considerably at weekends). In Bruges and Antwerp, single/double rooms in luxurious hotels start at €100/125.

For long-term stays, tourist offices have lists of self-contained holiday flats and apartment hotels with rooms containing kitchenettes; we've also listed a few in each of the cities (see the Places to Stay sections). Prices vary depending on whether you're staying at the weekend or midweek, on the number of people and the length of stay. Some of these places will let you stay for a single night, but most won't.

FOOD

Belgian cuisine is highly regarded throughout Europe – some say it's second only to French while in other people's eyes it's equal. Combining Belgian finesse and substantial portions, you'll rarely have reason to complain. All three cities are full of excellent restaurants – both moderate and pricey, relaxed and chic – and it won't take long to discover how seriously the Belgians take the business of eating.

Meat and seafood are abundantly consumed and although there are traditional regional dishes – such as Ghent's famous *waterzooi* (a cream-based fish stew) or *stoemp* (a Flemish variation on mashed potatoes) – you'll find all the most popular dishes have crossed local boundaries. And of course it's not all local fare. Brussels may be small by world city standards but its palate is broad – Italian, Japanese, Irish, Greek, Turkish, North African, Portuguese and Asian cuisines all thrive here.

When eating out, remember it's always much better value to order the suggested menu of the day (*dagmenu* in Flemish or *menu du jour* in French), which usually comprises three or even four courses, rather than selecting individual courses a la carte. Also, the dish of the day *(dagschotel/plat du jour)* often represents good value. The menu term '*min 2 couv*' means a particular dish (most often lobster) is served only to a minimum of two people. Drinks, even bottles of mineral water, are expensive in restaurants.

Breakfast

Many people in Brussels and Flanders sit down to a solid breakfast of sliced cold meats, cheese, bread, butter, jam and coffee, while those in Wallonia tend to content themselves with a coffee and croissant (or bit of baguette), referred to as a continental breakfast by Anglophones. If your survival depends on a hearty start to the day, quiz your accommodation host about his/her style of breakfast as a few hotels still do the meagre 'continental' version.

Snacks

The Belgians swear they invented *frieten/*

frites – chips or fries – and judging by availability, it's a claim few would contest. Their popularity cannot be understated. Every village has at least one *frituur/friture* where frites are served up in a paper cone or dish, smothered with large blobs of thick mayonnaise (or flavoured sauces) until almost unrecognisable and eaten with a small wooden fork in a mostly futile attempt to keep your fingers clean. Expect to pay about €1.50 /1.75 for a small/large portion; sauce is always extra. Standard mayonnaise costs €0.25 while more exotic concoctions such as *Andalouse* (mayonnaise spiked with chilli and spices) cost €0.50.

A *belegd broodje/sandwich garni* is half a baguette filled with an array of garnishings, and is an immensely popular snack food. So too are stuffed *pitas* (pitta breads, also called *gyros*) and Turkish pizza *(pide)*. The latter is a boat-shaped strip of dough about half a metre long that's topped with meat, cheese, eggs or vegetables and baked in a wood-burning oven.

Maatjes are tiny herring fillets eaten raw and traditionally washed down with *jenever/genièvre* (gin). A speciality of pubs in Brussels is a *boterham met platte kaas* – a portion of bread served with a soft white cheese and young radishes and usually accompanied by a fruit-flavoured beer. Top restaurants serve grey or pink North Sea *garnaal/crevettes* (shrimps) and pickled anchovies with aperitifs.

On the sweet side, superb waffles *(wafels/gaufres)* are eaten piping hot from market stalls, as are *oliebollen* (literally 'oily balls'), a Flemish funfair favourite. *Speculoos* (also written as *speculaas*) are thin, crisp, cinnamon-flavoured biscuits devoured all year but especially around 6 December when Sinterklaas/St Nicolas is around. They can be found in supermarkets, bakeries and speciality shops such as Dandoy in Brussels. To round everything off there's chocolate – see the boxed text 'Chocoholics Beware!'.

Starters & Main Dishes

Meat, poultry and hearty vegetable soups figure prominently on menus, but it's mussels *(mosselen/moules)* cooked in white

Chocoholics Beware!

ASA ANDERSSON

Nowhere in the world will test your self-control as much as Belgium. The Belgians have been quietly making some of the world's finest chocolates for well over a century and locals simply regard good chocolate, like good beer, as an everyday part of life.

Filled chocolates, or *pralines* (pronounced 'prah-leens'), are Belgium's forte. They are sold everywhere – from the local bakery and the supermarket deli, to specialist chain stores such as Leonidas and Godiva or, at the top of the range, *confiseries* such as Galler or Wittamer in Brussels and Burie and Del Rey in Antwerp. Prices match quality and reputation – in the better establishments you can be sure that you'll pay for the white gloves they wear to handpick each praline. Count on anywhere between €13 to €38 for a kilo of pralines. If the budget won't stretch that far, pick up a bar of the poor person's equivalent, the elephant-emblazoned Côte d'Or.

When buying pralines, you'll soon discover that the industry has a language all of its own. Terms you may come across are: *caraque*, which is plain or dark chocolate; *ganache*, a blend of chocolate, milk and extra cocoa butter flavoured with coffee, cinnamon or liqueurs; *crème fraîche*, a filling made from fresh whipped cream that's used in the centre of some pralines; *gianduja*, a blend of milk chocolate and hazelnut paste; *praliné*, a mix of chocolate and finely-ground toffee or nuts which can be soft or firm depending on how much chocolate is used; and *praliné nougatine*, ditto but using larger pieces of nuts or toffee to give a slight crunchy sensation.

Ideally, pralines should be served at room temperature, stored at around 15°C and eaten while still in their prime within a fortnight of being made. The best *chocolatiers* (chocolate makers) design their own moulds and hand-make each praline using cocoa butter (not vegetable fat). Rolling of the chocolate 'batter' is what defines its smoothness – grainy chocolate just hasn't been rolled enough! And if you never thought your average bar of chocolate was grainy, you'll think differently after you've been to Belgium.

wine (or a variety of other less traditional sauces) and served with a mountain of frites that's regarded as the national dish. They're cultivated mainly in the Netherlands – the best come from the Dutch town of Yerseke on the Scheldt. The local rule of thumb for mussels is: eat them only during the months with an 'r' in the name and don't touch the ones that haven't opened properly when cooked.

Game, including pheasant and boar, is an autumn speciality from the Ardennes, which is also famed for its hams. Horse, rabbit, hare and guinea fowl are all typical

offerings, as is offal, including kidneys, brains, tripe and liver. In some restaurants you can even suck the marrow out of bones as a starter if you like!

The Belgians cook steak in a way slightly unfamiliar to most English-speaking visitors. *Saignant* (rare) is a euphemism for dripping with blood; *à point* (medium) is what most Anglophones would consider rare, and *bien cuit* is the closest thing you'll get to well done.

Wild mushrooms and sauces made from forest berries often accompany autumn game, and some dishes such as *pintadeau à la bière de framboise* (guinea fowl cooked in raspberry-beer) use the nation's huge range of beers to reveal unique flavours. In spring *asperges de Malines* (asparagus from Mechelen) is a firm favourite; autumn and winter are the seasons for the highly prized *truffel/truffe* (truffle). Originally cultivated for its roots (used in coffee making), chicory (*witloof* in Flemish, *chicon* in French) is now an oft-used vegetable and is eaten cooked or raw.

Surprisingly, Brussels sprouts, thought to have been cultivated in Belgium since the 13th century, rarely make restaurant appearances though they're readily available in supermarkets.

Vegetarians need not fear. Until a decade ago vegetarian restaurants were predominantly hidden behind or above health-food shops and somewhat of an enigma to this heavily meat-based society. These days the restaurant scene is more eclectic, and bistros and cafes also generally have a few vegetarian options (other than unexciting omelettes).

Dining, by the way, doesn't have to take place in a restaurant. Cafes, bistros and brasseries usually all serve food, often at good prices. To assist in translating French and Flemish menus, see the Food sections in the Language chapter.

DRINKS

Beer rules – and deservedly so. The quality is excellent and the variety incomparable (see the special section on Belgium's Glorious Beer for details). Prices match quality, with a 250mL lager costing from €0.85 to €1.23, and a 330mL Trappist beer going for between €1.75 and €3.50, depending on the cafe.

The story doesn't end with beer. Belgian gin is a popular, if potent, drop. Traditionally made from grain spirit, grasses and juniper berries, it is the precursor of modern day gin and has been distilled in Belgium since the Middle Ages when it was considered a medicine, due largely to the healing powers associated with juniper. Like beer, it's hard to ascertain just how many gins are currently made in Belgium – figures range

from 150 to 300. Most jenevers fall into one of two categories: *jonge* (young) or *oude* (old). Oude jenever is considered the best and is typically pale-yellow, has a smooth taste and packs a good punch (35 to 40% alcohol per volume). It's best served in a tall shot-glass cooled in a bed of ice. Expect to pay anywhere from €1.75 to €3.20 for a shot depending on the age and quality. Two specialist gin pubs are De Vagant in Antwerp and 't Dreupelhuisje in Bruges – see the Entertainment section in those cities for details.

Belgium is not known for its wine. However, there is a tiny group of wine-makers in the Hageland region, east of Leuven, based around the village of Rillaar. Their white wines match France's better *vins du pays*.

As for places to drink, Dutch writer Benno Barnard summed it up best: 'Every journey in Belgium, no matter however short, however long, ends up in a cafe.' There's a great variety of drinking establishments: cafes serve alcohol and are open until the early hours of the morning; tearooms don't serve alcohol and close at around 6 or 7 pm – they also serve light meals. A *bruine kroeg* (brown cafe) is a small, old-fashioned pub noted for its decor, while an *eetkaffee* or *eetkroeg* has a more extensive range of food than a normal cafe. Brown cafe, *grand café*, *eetcafé*, *eetkroeg*, *eetkaffee*, *estaminet*, *herberg*, pub, bar, bistro, brasserie – call them what you want – Belgium is chock-full of amazing watering holes. And when the sun comes out the populace emerge for one of the favourite national pastimes – soaking up the sun and a drink at a pavement cafe or, as the Flemish like to put it, *een terrasje doen* (doing a terrace).

SPECTATOR SPORTS
Football

Belgium's football team, the Red Devils, usually qualifies for the two most coveted competitions – the World Cup (held every four years; the next is in 2002) and the European Championship (every four years; next in 2004). Belgium co-hosted the European championships with the Netherlands in 2000. The Red Devils, however, have yet to win a cup, and they are generally well behind France, Italy and the Netherlands in the European pecking order.

Sadly, Belgium is probably best remembered in football terms for the tragedy at Heysel stadium during the European Cup final in Brussels in 1985. Thirty-five supporters of Juventus were killed when Liverpool and Juventus fans clashed. English clubs were banned from European competitions for several years following the disaster and Heysel – the country's premier stadium – was renamed Roi Baudouin.

It's easy enough to get a ticket (€10 to €25) for a local football event – two of the top teams on the national ladder at present are RSC Anderlecht (Brussels) and Club Brugge (Bruges). For details see under Spectator Sports in those cities.

Cycling

Mention cycling in Belgium and it won't be long before the name Eddy Merckx comes up. Merckx was the cycling sensation of the 1960s and '70s and his success has spawned a nation of cycling fans. At weekends it's the norm to see troupes of cyclists of all ages whizzing around country lanes clad in fluorescent lycra gear or pulled up for a drink at their favourite wayside pub. Local racing events get broad coverage on TV and are well supported by the populous.

The cycling season starts in full with the Ronde van Vlaanderen in April. One of the best known events is the Grand Prix Eddy Merckx held in Brussels in May. Top contemporary names include Johan Museeuw, Tom Steels and Andreï Tchmil. Merckx's son, Axel, also pedals in the top ranks.

Tennis

A few Belgian women, including Kim Clijsters and Justine Henin, are making a name for themselves on the international tennis circuit.

BELGIUM'S GLORIOUS BEER

Beer, Glorious Beer! No country in the world boasts a brewing tradition as rich and diverse as Belgium. And nowhere else will you find the quality or quantity of beers that this little nation has to offer. From dark Trappist beers made by monks to golden nectars named after the devil himself…if you like beer, you'll love Belgium, and if you don't like beer yet, you might soon find you do!

A Bit of History

It is St Arnold, the patron saint of brewers, that you have to thank for Belgium's bevy of beers. When plague broke out in the Middle Ages, St Arnold convinced locals to drink beer rather than water. As beer is boiled and water isn't, this so-called 'cure' worked. Beer became an everyday drink – a 'liquid bread' to supplement an otherwise meagre diet.

By the early 19th century, Belgium had over 3000 breweries. However, WWI caused the collapse of half and, by 1946, only 775 breweries remained. These days, 100 breweries compete for the local market, though only a handful have taken on the international arena. This explains why, until the late 1980s, Belgian beer was one of Europe's best-kept secrets.

BELGIAN BEER

1 Trappist	10 Trappist
2 De Dolle Brouwers	11 Hoegaarden
3 Rodenbach	12 Domus; Interbrew
4 De Gouden Boom;	13 Cantillon
De Halve Maan	14 Brasserie à Vapeur;
5 Liefmans	Dubuisson
6 Roman	15 Dupont
7 Duvel	16 Trappist
8 De Koninck	17 Trappist
9 Trappist	18 Trappist

Top: Resist the temptation to sample too many beers on your first night. Photograph by Martin Moos

Beer Types

Walk into a specialist beer cafe in Belgium and you'll be handed a beer menu the size of a book. The country makes between 400 and 800 brews, depending on who you talk to, and beers range from the top-fermented and bottom-fermented to the spontaneously fermented and re-fermented. Few cafes stock every brew but your average pub will have no trouble coming up with 20 different beers and in specialist pubs you'll be looking at several hundred. Resist the over-whelming temptation to sample 10 beers on the first night – Belgians generally stick to one or two types per night, and shine the next day.

Trappist Beers

Belgium's most famous tipples are the Trappist beers, gold or dark in colour, smooth in taste and dangerously strong (from 6% to 11.3% alcohol by volume). Only brews made in one of Belgium's six Trappist monasteries – Westmalle, Westvleteren and Achel in Flanders, and Chimay, Orval and Rochefort in Wallonia – can use the term 'Trappist'. All are re-fermented in the bottle.

The oldest is Westmalle, near Antwerp, which was founded in 1793 and started brewing in 1836. These days it's known for two beers: the deep-brown Double (7%) and the glorious bronze Triple (9%). The latter is one of the nation's favourite beers.

White Beers

White beers – known as *witbier* in Flemish and *bière blanche* in French – are thirst-quenching wheat beers best drunk with a twist of lemon on a summer's afternoon. Pale, cloudy and served in a solid tumbler, the best known and most popular is Hoegaarden, named after a village 40km east of Brussels where this regional beer was revived in the 1960s.

Lambic

The champagne of the beer world – that's the best way to describe *lambic* (*lambiek* in Flemish). Like real champagne, this unique beer takes up to three years to make and comes out sparkling at the end. On the way it spends a night of revelry with wild micro-organisms in a cold attic, and later spontaneously ferments.

Right: The beer can sit in these dusty barrels for up to three years until it reaches perfection.

MARTIN MOOS

Lambic is the traditional beer of Brussels. It comes in several types, the most popular of which is *gueuze* (pronounced 'gerze'), a sour beer made from a mix of different-aged lambics. Then there are fruit lambics such as *kriek* (made with cherries) or *framboise* (with raspberries). Lambics are generally moderate alcohol beers (4% to 6%).

Abbey Beers

There's a plethora of 'abbey' beers on the market in Belgium, such as Grimbergen, Leffe and Maredsous to name but a few, all named after abbeys but no longer made there. Instead, the abbeys sold their labels to the big brewing concerns (such as Interbrew and Moortgat) and these companies now make the 'abbey' beers.

Vlaams Rood

Flemish Red beers are produced in the province of West-Vlaanderen and are best represented by Rodenbach brewery in Roeselare. Rodenbach Grand Cru is a Belgian classic and takes 20 months to mature in huge wooden barrels.

Oud Bruin

Old Brown beers originate from around Oudenaarde and nearby Zottegem in the province of Oost-Vlaanderen and are made by blending young and old beers which undergo a secondary fermentation in the bottle. They're sour with a nutty character – the breweries of Roman at Mater and Liefmans at Oudenaarde are two of the best known.

Saisons

Saisons are 'seasonal' beers made by small breweries such as Brasserie à Vapeur (a steam-powered brewery) in Pipaix, or Dupont in Tourpes, both in the province of Hainaut in Wallonia. Saisons tend to be light-flavoured but hoppy and are best imbibed on a summer's day.

MARTIN MOOS

Left: With around 400 different beers to try, you may be here for some time.

Top 10 Beers

- Duvel
- Westmalle Triple
- Cantillon Gueuze Lambic
- Hoegaarden Witbier
- Timmerman's Kriek Lambic

- De Koninck
- Rodenbach Grand Cru
- Orval
- De Dolle Brouwers Oerbier
- Rochefort #10

Hoogblond

Hoogblond is the name given to golden beers such as Duvel, one of Belgium's most beloved brews. Duvel was invented by the Moortgat brewery at Breendonk immediately after WWI as a victory drink; a passing comment that its taste 'comes from the devil' gave it its name. It comes in a seductive undulating glass and has a creamy, two-inch-thick head that slowly dissolves to reveal a strong, distinct flavour.

Brewery Visits

Not many Belgian breweries open their doors to individual travellers. A few that do include:

Cantillon Brewery – one of the most atmospheric breweries in Belgium. Full of old, dusty, wooden barrels and pungent aromas. See the Musée Bruxellois de la Gueuze in the Brussels chapter for details.

De Halve Maan – in the heart of Bruges. Does tours of its new and old brewing halls. For more details see the Bruges chapter.

De Dolle Brouwers (☎ 051-50 27 81) – a little brewery at Roeselarestraat 12B in Esen, 3km east of Diksmuide. Its name – 'The Crazy Brewers' – says it all. Tours and tastings are held at the weekend.

Facts, Figures & Folklore

- Most beer drunk in Belgium today is made by the Interbrew group based in Leuven, which is the world's third-largest producer.
- Bush, produced by Dubuisson at Pipaix in Hainaut, is the country's strongest beer and at 12% it packs quite a punch.
- As the shape of a glass affects taste and aroma, almost every beer has its own glass. The Kwak glass takes some juggling.
- Pouring techniques differ from one beer to another. Trappist beers should be poured slowly with the glass tilted – aim to have a solid head.

Getting There & Away

AIR

Belgium's national airline is Sabena. Many of the world's airlines fly directly to Brussels' Zaventem airport; however, a greater number fly into other airports in the region, such as Paris, London, Frankfurt or Amsterdam. Depending on where you're coming from, you may want to consider flying into one of these airports. It doesn't cost much to take a train or bus from these places to Belgium. If you're flying from outside Europe, many airlines offer a free return flight within Europe (some airlines even offer two), which is definitely worth considering in your calculations.

Belgium is so small that there are no internal flights between cities.

Departure Tax

Passengers flying from Brussels' Zaventem airport pay a €13.63 departure tax; from Deurne (Antwerp) it's €7.43 and from

Brussels South (Charleroi) it's €4.95. This tax is included in the ticket prices.

The UK & Ireland

There isn't really a low or high season for flights to Brussels or Antwerp: prices depend more on special offers and availability of seats. By taking advantage of special offers (which usually involve booking in advance and being away a minimum number of nights or staying over a Saturday night) you should be able to fly London–Brussels return for between UK£85 and UK£105. British Airways (☎ 0845 773 3377), British Midland (☎ 0870 607 0555), Virgin Express (☎ 020-7744 0004) and Sabena (☎ 0845 601 0933) all fly this route. Their Web sites are at www.britishairways.com, www .iflybmi.com, www.virgin-express.com and www.sabena.com, respectively.

The flight time is one hour and 10 minutes. To compare the difference between flying and travelling there by the Eurostar, see the boxed text 'Plane or Eurostar?' later.

A London–Antwerp flight also takes about one hour, but as there is no competition on this route and few flights, it is not an interesting option. At the time of writing, the only airline servicing the route was the small Flemish company VLM (☎ 020-7476 6677). A one-way/return fare costs UK£110 /170. Its Web site is at www.vlm-airlines .com.

Popular travel agencies include STA Travel (☎ 0870 160 0599), which has an office at 86 Old Brompton Rd, London SW7 3LQ. Visit its Web site at www .statravel.co.uk. usit Campus (☎ 0870 240 1010), 52 Grosvenor Gardens, London SW1W 0AG, has branches throughout the UK. The Web address is www.usitcampus .co.uk.

Other recommended travel agencies include: Trailfinders (☎ 020-7937 1234), 215 Kensington High St, London W8 6BD; Bridge the World (☎ 0870 444 7474), 4 Regent Place, London W1R 5FB; and

Air Travel Glossary

Alliances Many of the world's leading airlines are now intimately involved with each other, sharing everything from reservations systems and check-in to aircraft and frequent-flyer schemes. Opponents say that alliances restrict competition. Whatever the arguments, there is no doubt that big alliances are the way of the future.

Courier Fares Businesses often need to send urgent documents or freight securely and quickly. Courier companies hire people to accompany the package through customs and, in return, offer a discount ticket which is sometimes a bargain. However, you may have to surrender all your baggage allowance and take only carry-on luggage.

Fares Airlines traditionally offer 1st class (coded F), business class (coded J) and economy class (coded Y) tickets. These days there are so many promotional and discounted fares available that few passengers pay full fare.

Lost Tickets If you lose your airline ticket, an airline will usually treat it like a travellers cheque and, after inquiries, issue you with another one. Legally, however, an airline is entitled to treat it like cash and if you lose it then it's gone forever. Take very good care of your tickets.

Onward Tickets An entry requirement for many countries is that you have a ticket out of the country. If you're unsure of your next move, the easiest solution is to buy the cheapest onward ticket to a neighbouring country or a ticket from a reliable airline which can later be refunded if you do not use it.

Open-Jaw Tickets These are return tickets where you fly out to one place but return from another. If available, this can save you backtracking to your arrival point.

Overbooking Since every flight has some passengers who fail to show up, airlines often book more passengers than they have seats. Usually excess passengers make up for the no-shows, but occasionally somebody gets 'bumped' onto the next available flight. Guess who it is most likely to be? The passengers who check in late. If you do get 'bumped', you are normally offered some form of compensation.

Reconfirmation Some airlines require you to reconfirm your flight at least 72 hours prior to departure. Check your travel documents to see if this is the case.

Restrictions Discounted tickets often have various restrictions on them – such as needing to be paid for in advance and incurring a penalty to be altered or cancelled. Others are restrictions on the minimum and maximum period you must be away.

Round-the-World Tickets RTW tickets give you a limited period (usually a year) in which to circumnavigate the globe. You can go anywhere the carrying airlines go, as long as you don't backtrack. The number of stopovers or total number of separate flights is decided before you set off and they usually cost a bit more than a basic return flight.

Ticketless Travel Airlines are gradually waking up to the realisation that paper tickets are unnecessary encumbrances. On simple one-way or return trips, reservations details can be held on computer and the passenger merely shows ID to claim their seat.

Transferred Tickets Airline tickets cannot be transferred from one person to another. Travellers sometimes try to sell the return half of their ticket, but officials can ask you to prove that you are the person named on the ticket. On an international flight, tickets are compared with passports.

Flightbookers (☎ 020-7757 2000), 177–8 Tottenham Court Rd, London W1P 9LF. Their Web sites are at www.trailfinders .com, www.b-t-w.co.uk and www.ebookers .com, respectively.

Also check the Sunday newspapers, the listings magazine *Time Out* or the *Evening Standard* for good-priced tickets.

From Ireland, Aer Lingus (☎ 01-886 8888) has return Dublin–Brussels flights from €160. Check the Web site at www.fly-aerlingus.com. Ryanair (☎ 01-609 7881) offers return flights to Brussels South airport (near Charleroi – for more details see The Airports under Getting Around in the Brussels chapter) for as low as €40. Its Web site is at www.ryanair.ie.

France

There's a network of student travel agencies that can supply discount tickets to travellers of all ages. OTU Voyages (☎ 01 40 29 12 12) has a central Paris office at 39 Ave Georges Bernanos (5e) and many offices around the country. Its Web address is www.otu.fr. Acceuil des Jeunes en France (☎ 01 42 77 87 80), 119 Rue Saint Martin (4e), is another popular discount travel agency.

General travel agencies in Paris that offer some of the best services and deals include Nouvelles Frontières (☎ 08 03 33 33 33), 5 Ave de l'Opéra (1er), with a Web site at www.nouvelles-frontieres.fr, and Voyageurs du Monde (☎ 01 42 86 16 00) at 55 Rue Sainte Anne (2e).

Germany

Cheap tickets in Germany can be purchased at STA Travel (☎ 030-311 0950, fax 313 0948), Goethestrasse 73, 10625 Berlin.

A Frankfurt–Brussels return Apex fare (reserved at least 14 days in advance) will cost about €185. The flight time is one hour.

The Netherlands

Most people travel by train between the Netherlands and destinations within Belgium, and this trend will undoubtedly increase when the Thalys train begins operating on high-speed lines in a couple of years time. That said, there are daily Amsterdam–Brussels flights (45 minutes) – expect to pay about €105 return.

NBBS Reizen is the Netherlands' official student travel agency. You can find them in Amsterdam (☎ 020-624 09 89) at Rokin 66.

The USA

Fares in the high season can cost 40% to 50% higher than those in the low season. High season is roughly from June to mid-September plus the Christmas and New Year period; the shoulder season is from April to May and from mid-September to October; and low is October to March.

Discount travel agents in the USA are known as consolidators (although you won't see a sign on the door saying 'consolidator'). Consolidators can be found through the Yellow Pages or the major daily newspapers. The *New York Times*, *Los Angeles Times*, *Chicago Tribune* and *San*

Plane or Eurostar?

The opening of the Channel Tunnel in 1995 unleashed an all-out fare war among the airlines, the Eurostar and Eurotunnel train services, the bus companies and the ferry operators. Although things have settled down since then, fares between London and Brussels can vary tremendously according to the month, day and time of day you travel, so it's definitely worth shopping around to see what special deals are available. The costs we've indicated are intended as guidelines only.

A London–Brussels flight takes about one hour and 10 minutes and then by train it's another 15 to 25 minutes (depending on which of Brussels' three main train stations you're aiming for) to the city centre. The Eurostar takes two hours and 40 minutes from London's Waterloo station to Brussels' Gare du Midi. In essence, however, there's not much difference in time between a flight and the Eurostar when you take into account getting to/from the airports, check-in times and waiting for luggage.

Francisco Examiner all produce weekly travel sections in which you will find a number of travel agency ads. Ticket Planet (☎ 800 799 8888) is a leading ticket consolidator in the USA and is recommended. Visit its Web site at www.ticketplanet.com.

Council on International Educational Exchange, America's largest student travel organisation, has around 60 offices in the USA and Canada; its head office (☎ 800 226 8624) is in Boston. STA Travel (☎ 800 777 0112) has offices in most major cities. Call the toll-free number (☎ 800 781 4040) for office locations or visit its Web site at www.statravel.com. Another good Web site to try is www.counciltravel.com, where you can reserve plane tickets.

You should be able to fly New York–Brussels return for around US$580 in the low season and US$1020 in the high season. Equivalent fares from the West Coast are US$780 in the low season and US$1200 in the high season.

Canada

Discount air ticket sellers in Canada are also known as consolidators and their air fares tend to be about 10% higher than those sold in the USA. The *Globe & Mail*, *Toronto Star*, *Montreal Gazette* and *Vancouver Sun* carry travel agents' ads and are a good place to look for cheap fares.

Travel CUTS (☎ 800 667 2887) is Canada's national student travel agency and has offices in all major cities. Its Web site is at www.travelcuts.com.

There are return flights to Brussels for about C$1750/3000 from Vancouver in the low/high season and C$780/1080 from Montreal.

Australia & New Zealand

Quite a few travel offices specialise in discount air tickets. Some travel agents, particularly smaller ones, advertise cheap air fares in the travel sections of weekend newspapers, such as the *Age* in Melbourne and the *Sydney Morning Herald*.

In both countries, two well-known agents for cheap fares are STA Travel and Flight Centre. In Australia, STA Travel has offices in all major cities and on many university campuses. Call ☎ 131 776 Australiawide for the location of your nearest branch or visit its Web site at www.statravel.com.au. Flight Centre (☎ 131 600 Australiawide) also has dozens of offices throughout Australia. Its Web site is at www.flightcentre .com.au.

In New Zealand, Flight Centre (☎ 09-309 6171) has a large central office in Auckland at National Bank Towers (on the corner of Queen and Darby Sts) and many branches throughout the country. STA Travel (☎ 09-309 0458) has its main office at 10 High St, Auckland, and has other offices in Hamilton, Palmerston North, Wellington, Christchurch and Dunedin.

There's a big difference between full-price low- and high-season fares but not between discounted fares, so it's worth shopping around in the high season. Book well ahead for the best chance of a good fare deal.

Discounted return air fares to Brussels from Australia on major airlines through reputable agents can be surprisingly cheap. Royal Jordanian Airlines, Lauda Air, Gulf Air and Lufthansa have some good deals. Low-season return fares start at around A$1600 and high-season return fares at around A$1900. One-way flights start from about A$750 in the low season.

From New Zealand, KLM have low-season return fares starting at NZ$2200 and NZ$2600 in the high-season.

Airline Offices

Airline offices (*Luchtvaartmaatschappijen* in Flemish or *Lignes Aériennes* in French) include the following:

Aer Lingus (☎ 02-548 98 48) Rue du Trône 98, B-1050 Brussels
Air Canada (☎ 02-627 40 88) Rue du Trône 98, B-1050 Brussels
Air France (☎ 02-541 42 51) Ave Louise 149, B-1050 Brussels
Air New Zealand (☎ 03-202 13 55) Meir 24, B-2000 Antwerp
Alitalia (☎ 02-551 11 22) Rue Capitaine Crespel 2, B-1050 Brussels
American Airlines (☎ 0800-96156) Rue du Trône 98, B-1050 Brussels

British Airways (☎ 02-548 21 22) Rue du Trône 98, B-1050 Brussels

British Midland (☎ 02-772 94 00) Ave des Pléiades 15, B-1200 Brussels

Cathay Pacific (☎ 02-712 64 48) Ave de Vilvorde 153, B-1930 Zaventem

City Bird (☎ 02-752 52 52) Bldg 117D, Melsbroek Airport, B-1820 Melsbroek

Continental Airlines (☎ 02-643 39 39) Ave Louise 240, B-1050 Brussels

Japan Airlines (☎ 02-745 44 00) Ave Louise 283, BP 6, B-1050 Brussels

KLM (☎ 02-717 20 70) Rue Maurice Charlent 53, 1160 Brussels

Lufthansa Airlines (☎ 02-745 44 88) Brussels National Airport, B-1930 Zaventem

Ryanair (☎ 071-25 12 51) BSCA Building 57, Chemin des Fusillés 1, B-6041 Charleroi

Sabena (☎ 02-723 23 23 for reservations and information, ☎ 0900-00747 for 24-hour flight information) Sabena House, Brussels National Airport, B-1930 Zaventem

United Airlines (☎ 02-713 36 00) Rue du Trône 130, B-1050 Brussels

Virgin Express (☎ 02-752 05 05) Bldg 116, Melsbroek Airport, B-1820 Melsbroek

VLM (☎ 03-285 68 68) Luchthavenlei, B-2100 Deurne

BUS

The three Belgian cities are well connected to the UK, the rest of Europe and Scandinavia by long-distance bus. However, with the increase in availability of low air fares, buses are not necessarily the cheapest public transport to and around Europe. Once again, it pays to shop around.

In Belgium itself, buses are not used to get between cities – this job is left to the efficient train network. However, buses are used to travel between towns and villages in more remote areas.

Eurolines

The easiest way to book tickets is through Eurolines, a consortium of coach operators with offices all over Europe. Its Web site, www.eurolines.com, has links to each national Eurolines Web site.

Eurolines' coaches are fairly comfortable, with reclining seats, on-board toilets and sometimes air-conditioning. They stop frequently for meals, though you'll save a bit by packing your own food.

Discounts depend on the route, but children aged between four and 12 typically get 30% to 40% off, while those aged under 26 and seniors get a 10% to 20% discount on some routes. It's a good idea to book at least several days ahead in summer.

For real coach junkies, the Eurolines Pass gives you unlimited travel between 48 European cities either for 30 days at UK£175/139 (€264/211) for adults/youth and seniors in the low season and UK£245/195 (€370/296) in the high season, or 60 days at UK£219/175 (€327/262) in the low season and UK£283/227 (€430/324) in the high season.

From London's Victoria coach station, Eurolines runs buses to Brussels (8½ hours) and various other cities in Belgium including Antwerp and Bruges. The adult fare to all three cities is UK£32/45 one way/return in the low season, and UK£35/51 in peak season. For seniors or people aged under 26, the one-way/return fare is UK£29/41 in the low season, and UK£33/47 in the high. Should you decide to go only as far as Ostend, the fare is UK£20/35 in the low season and UK£22/39 in the high.

Buses go from London to Dover, from where they cross the Channel using either ferries or Eurotunnel train services. Bookings can be made through Eurolines or any National Express (☎ 0870 580 8080) office.

A central London Eurolines office (bookings ☎ 0870 514 3219, information ☎ 020-7730 8235, fax 7730 8721) is at 52 Grosvenor Gardens, London SW1W 0AU.

In France, the Paris Eurolines office (☎ 08 36 69 52 52, fax 01 49 72 51 61) is at Gare Routière Internationale de Paris, Ave du Général de Gaulle 28, Bagnolet. Check it out at www.eurolines.fr or Minitel 3615 Eurolines. Eurolines' buses depart daily from Paris to Brussels (3¾ hours) and Antwerp (4¾ hours). The one-way/return fare to either is €33/54, or €29.25/49.50 for seniors and those under 26 years.

In Germany, Deutsche Touring/Eurolines buses depart daily from several cities including Aachen, Frankfurt and Cologne to Brussels, Antwerp and Ghent. Frankfurt to Brussels (6¼ hours) costs €28.50/50.50

one way/return. Deutsche Touring/Euro-lines has an office (☎ 069-7903 50, fax 7903 219) at Am Römerhof 17, Frankfurt-am-Main. Its Web site is at www.deutsche-touring.com.

In the Netherlands, Eurolines Nederland (☎ 020-560 87 88, ⓔ info@eurolines.nl) has two offices in Amsterdam – at Rokin 10 and at Amstel Bus Station, Julianaplein 5. Its Web site is at www.eurolines.nl. From Amsterdam, buses run to Antwerp (3¾ hours), Brussels (4¾ hours) and Bruges (4¾ hours). The price is the same for all destinations: adults pay €15.75/24.75 one way/return and seniors and those aged under 26 years are charged €13.50/22.50.

Brussels Eurolines' main office (Map 4; ☎ 02-274 13 50) in Brussels is at Rue du Progrès 80, next to Gare du Nord. Most of its buses depart from here. Tickets can also be bought from offices at Place de Brouck-ère 50 (Map 5; ☎ 02-217 00 25) and Ave Fosny 13 (Map 6; ☎ 02-538 20 49). At peak times, surcharges of €2.47 to €4.95 are added to some fares.

A few popular destinations served by daily Eurolines buses from Brussels include the following (the prices listed are full fares one way/return):

destination	fare	duration (hrs)	frequency (day)
Amsterdam	€15/22.50	4¾	7
Cologne	€18/25.50	4	2
Frankfurt	€25.50/46	6¼	2
London	€43.20/66	8½	3
Paris	€13.70/18.50	3¾	8

Bruges From May to September, one of the Eurolines buses from Brussels to Lon-don picks up passengers at the train station in Bruges. Tickets (€43.20/66 one way/return) can be bought from Reizen Wasteels (Map 10; ☎ 050-33 65 31) at Geldmunt-straat 30a.

Antwerp The Eurolines office (Map 12; ☎ 03-233 86 62) is at Van Stralenstraat 8; buses pick up and set down here. The des-tinations serviced and the fares are the same

as from Brussels – only journey times dif-fer slightly, and never by more than an hour. For details, see the table given for Brussels earlier in this section.

Busabout

This UK-based budget alternative to Euro-lines is aimed at younger travellers, but has no upper age limit. It runs coaches along in-terlocking European circuits which take in 70 European cities. One loop passes through Bruges. Pick-up points are usually conve-nient for hostels and camp sites.

Two passes are available. The Consecu-tive Pass costs UK£169 (or UK£149 for youth and student-card holders) for 15 con-secutive days' travel anywhere on the cir-cuits. The add-on from London to Paris is UK£30 return. There is also a Flexi Pass, which allows 15 individual days' travel within a two-month period, for UK£369 (UK£329). There are also three-week and one/two/three-month passes, as well as various other passes.

You can buy Busabout tickets directly from the company (☎ 020-7950 1661, fax 7950 1662, ⓔ info@busabout.co.uk), 258 Vauxhall Bridge Rd, London, SW1V 1BS, or from suppliers such as usit Campus and STA Travel. For more information visit its Web site at www.busabout.com.

TRAIN
Other Parts of Belgium

Trains are the best way to travel in Bel-gium. Belgium built continental Europe's first railway line (between Brussels and Mechelen) in the 1830s and has since de-veloped an extremely dense rail network. Trains are run by the Belgische Spoorwe-gen/Société National des Chemins de Fer Belges (Belgian Railways), whose logo is a 'B' in an oval. Major train stations have information offices, open until about 7 pm (later in large cities).

There are four levels of service: InterCity (IC) trains (which are the fastest), InterRe-gional (IR), local (L) and peak-hour (P) commuter trains (the latter stop at specific stations only). Depending on the line, there will be an IC and an IR train every half-hour or hour. Trains have 1st- and 2nd-class carriages, and both classes have smoking and nonsmoking sections.

Belgian Railways publish a national timetable *(spoorboekje/indicateur)*, available from major train stations for €3.70. A less-detailed booklet, listing only the most popular IC and IR services, is available free from stations.

For fare and timetable information on all national services call ☎ 02-555 25 55. For international services call ☎ 0900-10366 (€0.45 per minute). Belgian Railways' Web site is at www.b-rail.be and is in Flemish, French, English and German.

Tickets & Rail Passes Second-class train tickets *(gewone biljetten/billets ordinaires)* are 50% cheaper than 1st class. Fares are calculated by distance, with a minimum charge of €1. At weekends, return tickets within Belgium are reduced by 40% for a single passenger or the first in a group and 60% for the rest of the group (to a maximum of six people). For details on discounted excursion tickets, see the boxed text 'B-Excursions'.

Depending on your destination, another option to consider if you're travelling in a small group (three to five people) is a Multi Pass. It costs €34/38/42 for three/four/five people (one person must be over 26 years) and is valid for one journey anywhere in the

B-Excursions

If you intend to do lots of sightseeing, investigate the discounted train excursion tickets known as B-Excursions. These packages include a return 2nd-class ticket plus selected admission fees, brochures and a range of incentives such as a complimentary drink in a local cafe. The price is less than a normal return train ticket plus admission, and almost always represents excellent value. The free booklet *B-Excursions* is available from most railway stations but it's published in French and Flemish only; staff at information offices or ticket windows are usually happy to explain the details.

country. The Rail Pass costs €56/86 in 2nd /1st class, gives 10 one-way trips anywhere and is valid for one year. For those under 26, the equivalent of the Rail Pass is the Go Pass; it costs €38 and is valid for 2nd class only.

A Reductiekaart (Fixed-Price Reduction Card) gives up to 50% off all train tickets for a month and costs €15.86.

Brussels Brussels has three main train stations: Gare du Nord (Map 4; North Station), Gare du Midi (Map 6; South Station), and Gare Centrale (Map 5; Central Station). The latter is a five-minute walk from Grand Place.

Gare du Midi is the main station for international connections: the Eurostar and Thalys fast trains stop here. Most other international trains stop at both Gare du Nord and Gare du Midi (some also stop at Gare Centrale). There are information offices at all three stations. The office at Gare Centrale opens 6.30 am to 9.45 pm daily.

Brussels is well connected with other Belgian cities and towns. Examples of connections include the following (the prices listed are full one-way fares):

destination	fare	duration (mins)	frequency (hour)
Antwerp	€5.08	35	2
Bruges	€9.91	60	2
Ghent	€6.19	40	2
Leuven	€3.59	20	1
Mechelen	€3.09	15	2
Ostend	€12.39	75	1
Ypres	€12.27	105	2
Zaventem airport	€2.35	15	4

Bruges Bruges has just one train station, about 1.5km south of the city centre. The station's information office (Map 9; ☎ 050-38 23 82) opens 7 am to 8.30 pm daily.

To get to Ypres (Ieper in Flemish; €8.42, one to three hours), take the train to Kortrijk where you must wait 35 minutes for the hourly connection. It's well worth buying a B-Excursion ticket (see the boxed text 'B-Excursions') if you're planning a day trip to Ypres. This ticket costs €14.87 and includes a return train fare and admission to three museums. There are regular trains from Bruges to the following destinations:

destination	fare	duration (mins)	frequency (hour)
Antwerp	€10.78	70	1
Brussels	€9.91	60	2
Ghent	€4.58	20	2
Knokke	€2.72	15	1
Ostend	€2.72	15	1
Zeebrugge	€2.10	10	1

Antwerp Antwerp has two main train stations – Centraal and Berchem. Centraal Station is about 1.5km from the old city centre and is where most travellers arrive. Berchem station is some 2km south-east of Centraal Station.

The magnificent Centraal Station (Map 12) is currently undergoing work below ground level to accommodate the Thalys fast train. The work is not expected to be finished until 2005, which means you may find train services into Centraal Station somewhat disrupted. The ticket counters and information offices have been temporarily moved from the main hall to side offices in the main building. National connections from Antwerp include the following trains:

destination	fare	duration (mins)	frequency (hour)
Bruges	€10.78	70	1
Brussels	€5.08	35	2
Ghent	€6.69	45	2
Lier	€1.85	15	1
Mechelen	€2.60	15	2

Centraal Station's train information office (☎ 03-204 20 40) opens 7 am to 10 pm Monday to Saturday, and 7 am to 8 pm on Sunday.

The UK

The Channel Tunnel allows for a land link between Britain and France. The Eurostar passenger train service travels between London–Paris and London–Brussels. The Eurotunnel vehicle service travels between terminals in Folkestone and Calais. This train carries cars, motorcycles and bicycles with their passengers/riders.

In addition to these two services, train-boat-train connections between the UK and Belgium are possible.

Eurostar The highly civilised Eurostar passenger train service takes two hours and 40 minutes to get from London's Waterloo station to Brussels' Gare du Midi, via the Channel Tunnel. Depending on the day of the week and the time of year, there are between 10 and 13 trains per day. Passport and customs checks take place on board, or very cursorily on arrival.

A wide variety of fares is available. The regular 2nd-class fare (known as Standard Flexi) is UK£150/300 one way/return. The equivalent fare in 1st class (meal included) is UK£185/370. These tickets are fully refundable and you can make changes to the date and time of travel.

The other tickets are not as flexible and usually have some sort of conditions attached to them. A 2nd/1st-class Leisure Flexi ticket (return only) costs UK£140/220 and requires that you stay away a Saturday night. The 2nd-class Weekender ticket costs UK£100/200 one way/return and is valid for travel on Saturday, Sunday and public holidays only. In addition, there are often special deals; look out for them on Eurostar's Web site or in your local press.

Youth tickets (UK£45/75 one way/return) are available to those aged under 26; children's fares (from four to 11 years) are UK£29/58 in 2nd class and UK£45/90 in 1st.

You can book tickets from London to Antwerp, Bruges, Ghent and Liège directly through the Eurostar office (you will need to change trains in Brussels). Call Eurostar for details.

Eurostar tickets are sold at Waterloo station and the Eurostar ticket shop at 102–4 Victoria St, London SW1 5JL, as well as at mainline railway stations in the UK. To book by phone, ring Eurostar on ☎ 0870 518 6186 in the UK, ☎ 08 36 35 35 39 in France, or ☎ 0900-10177 (€0.40 per minute) in Belgium. Its Web site is at www.eurostar.com.

Eurotunnel Eurotunnel, the train service

through the Channel Tunnel between Folkestone and Coquelles (5km south-west of Calais) in France, takes cars, motorcycles and bicycles. Trains run 24 hours, year round, with four departures per hour in peak times. During the 35-minute crossing, passengers can sit in their cars or walk around the air-conditioned, soundproofed rail carriage. The entire process, including loading and unloading, takes about an hour.

Fares vary enormously depending on the time of year, the day of the week and time of day. A one-way/return fare for a car (driver and all passengers included) starts at UK£165/215 but prices can increase substantially in peak periods. There are often special promotional fares, such as day trips and mini breaks (return within five days), which are worth investigating.

The fare for a motorcycle (with riders) starts at UK£90 for a same-day return and UK£115 for longer stays. Bicycles can be taken on limited services only.

For information and reservations, contact a travel agent, call the Eurotunnel vehicle service (☎ 0870 535 3535 in the UK, ☎ 03 21 00 61 00 in France, or ☎ 02-717 45 00 in Belgium) or visit Eurotunnel's Web site at www.eurotunnel.com. You can save a small amount of money by booking online.

Train-Boat-Train There are train-boat-train packages in association with Hoverspeed (☎ 0870-240 8070, fax 01304-865 203) running from London's Charing Cross station to various cities in Belgium including Ostend, Bruges, Antwerp and Brussels. The journey to Brussels takes about five hours. The fare tends to fluctuate with season and as it relies on both British and Belgian railways, so contact Hoverspeed for current details. It has a Web site at www .hoverspeed.com.

Continental Europe

As the rail network in this part of Europe is so extensive and fast trains are steadily linking more and more cities, trains are the preferred choice of many travellers getting to Belgium from neighbouring countries. Many of the services are on Thalys trains or

involve a combination of Thalys and ordinary trains.

If you're in Belgium and want to pop across to France, Germany or the Netherlands for a weekend break, you'll find return fares on ordinary trains are discounted by 40% at the weekend. It's worth comparing these with the Thalys weekend deals.

Thalys The Thalys fast trains (a service provided jointly by the Belgian, Dutch, French and German railways) link various cities in Belgium with destinations in the Netherlands, Germany and France. However, there's little difference in journey time between the Thalys and regular trains on the Dutch and German routes as old tracks are still being used through these two countries and in parts of Belgium as well. The tracks are all expected to be upgraded to high-speed lines by about 2005.

There are several types of Thalys tickets available. The most expensive 1st- and 2nd-class fares are the fully flexible, refundable Business tickets. Cheaper fares include the Weekend ticket (valid for travel at the weekend only), the Loisirs (Leisure Return) and the Mini (a nonexchangeable, nonrefundable return); there are limited numbers of these tickets and they need to be booked as early as possible. People aged 12 to 26 get a 50% discount and seniors a 30% discount on one-way fares. For information and reservations see the Thalys Web site at www.thalys.com.

France Thalys fast trains efficiently link Paris with Brussels, Antwerp and Bruges. The trains run almost hourly from Paris Gare du Nord to Brussels (1½ hours) and six or seven times per day to the other two cities.

A regular one-way Paris–Brussels Business fare in 2nd/1st class is €57.75/91.70; a weekend return costs €45.50 in either class. Other examples of 2nd-class Business fares include Antwerp (€61.50, 2¼ hours) and Bruges (€62.75, 2½ hours). For Thalys information and reservations in Paris call ☎ 08 36 35 35 36.

Germany Thalys trains connect Aachen and Cologne with Brussels. Regular Thalys fares are more expensive than ordinary Deutsche Bahn train fares, however, the Thalys discounted return tickets usually work out cheaper than Deutsche Bahn fares.

To Brussels, there are seven Thalys trains per day from Aachen (€21.60 one way, 1¾ hours) and Cologne (€32.25 one way, 2½ hours).

The Netherlands Thalys trains link Amsterdam, The Hague and Rotterdam five times daily with Antwerp and Brussels. From Amsterdam to Antwerp (two hours) you'll be looking at €24.80/29.25 on weekends/weekdays; to Brussels (2¾ hours) it is €29.50/34.75. Alternatively, you can take an ordinary Nederlandse Spoorwegen train to Antwerp (€25, two hours) or Brussels (€30, 2¾ hours).

CAR & MOTORCYCLE

For details on taking a car or motorcycle through the Eurotunnel, see the previous Train section. For information on car ferry services, see the Boat section later in the chapter.

Belgium's motorway system is excellent with, in general, an easy flow of traffic from one side of the country to the other. There are exceptions of course: traffic often comes to a grinding halt on the ring roads around Brussels and Antwerp, and the E40 to the coast is usually crammed on fine weekends in summer. There is also a down side to driving in Belgium – see the boxed text 'Belgian Drivers' for the reasons why.

If you're driving your own car into Belgium, in addition to your passport and driving licence (see Driving Licence under Documents in the Facts for the Visitor chapter) you must carry vehicle registration (proof of ownership) and insurance documents. Motor vehicle insurance with at least third-party cover is compulsory throughout the EU. Your home policy may or may not be extendable to Belgium; it's a good idea to get a Green Card from your home insurer before you leave home. This confirms that you have the correct coverage. All cars should also carry a first aid kit, warning triangle and fire extinguisher.

Road rules are generally easy to understand, although the give way to the right law takes a lot of getting used to (see the 'Belgian Drivers' boxed text for details). Standard international signs are in use and there are good, toll-free motorways. Driving is on the right, and the speed limit is 50km/h in built-up areas, 90km/h outside urban centres and 120km/h on motorways. Seat belts

---

Belgian Drivers

'Aggressive' is the word generally used to describe Belgian drivers, and most foreigners who take to the roads here find it apt. Whether cruising on a sleek highway or bouncing over potholed inner-city streets, drivers have a reputation for being fast, impatient and at times abusive (though rarely incited to road rage). Anyone idling at 120km/h in the fast lane of a motorway will be flashed from behind by speed demons doing 160km/h.

One peculiarity that ensures adrenalin-pumped journeys is the *voorrang van rechts/priorité à droite* (give way to the right) law. Thanks to this rule, cars darting out from side streets sometimes have right of way over vehicles on the main road (but not always – signs with an orange diamond surrounded by white mean the main road has priority). The result: cars with smashed-in passenger-side doors are a common sight.

ASA ANDERSSON

Watch out too at zebra crossings – Belgian drivers generally do not stop for pedestrians, no matter how steely your glare.

are compulsory in the front and rear. The blood-alcohol limit is 0.05%, which means two strong beers and you're over the limit.

More motoring information can be obtained from the Touring Club de Belgique (Map 4; ☎ 02-233 22 11, fax 02-286 33 23), Rue de la Loi 44, B-1040 Brussels. It has a 24-hour Touring Secours breakdown service (☎ 070-34 47 77) which is free for members (nonmembers will be looking at a call-out fee of about €67).

Rental Renting a car for inner-city travel is madness, but having your own wheels certainly makes it easy to nosy around the countryside. If you intend to do so, organise the rental before you leave home – it's usually much cheaper. If that doesn't suit, avoid renting a car from an airport or Gare du Midi in Brussels as tariffs are 15% higher. Details of car hire centres are given in the Getting Around section in each city chapter.

As a guide, the cheapest cars cost about €65 a day, €75 for the weekend or €175 per week. These prices include insurance, VAT and unlimited kilometres. Foreign drivers will need to show their passport or ID card as well as their driving licence, and most car hire companies prefer that you have a credit card. Most companies require drivers to be aged 23 or over and to have been driving for at least one year.

Motorcycles are only available for hire in Brussels; see the Getting Around section in the Brussels chapter for details. Mopeds can be rented in Bruges (see the Bruges Getting Around section).

BICYCLE

Bicycles are popular in flat Flanders where many roads have separate cycle lanes. Bruges and Antwerp have a good network of cycle paths but there are relatively few in Brussels.

Ordinary/mountain bikes can be hired from about 35 train stations around the country for €9.04/16.85 a day (plus a €12.39/37.18 deposit); they must be returned to the same station. For a list of participating stations, pick up the Belgian Railways' *Trein & Fiets/Train & Vélo* brochure from any large train station. It's generally cheaper to hire bikes from private operators who charge about €2.47 per hour or €6.19/8.05 for a half/full day. Most bike rental shops also do repairs.

It costs €3.71 to take a bike on a train and is usually free on ferries crossing the Channel. Bicycles can travel by air. You can sometimes just check it in as baggage (confirm this with the airline in advance). You may have to fold it down and dismantle it as much as possible. Let much (but not all) of the air out of the tyres to prevent them from bursting in the low-pressure baggage hold.

HITCHING

Hitching is never entirely safe in any country in the world, and we don't recommend it. Travellers who decide to hitch should understand that they are taking a small but potentially serious risk. People who do choose to hitch will be safer if they travel in pairs and let someone know where they are planning to go. It's illegal to hitch on motorways in Belgium.

TaxiStop is an agency that matches travellers and drivers headed for the same destination including to places outside Belgium. The fee is reasonable at €0.03 per kilometre. TaxiStop has offices in all three cities – for details see under Travel Agencies in the Facts for the Visitor chapter.

BOAT

Tickets and reservations for ferry services across the Channel between the UK and Belgium are available from ferry operators and travel agencies. Fares and schedules vary widely according to seasonal demand. There's no departure tax when leaving Belgium by sea.

Hoverspeed's (☎ 0870 240 8070) high-speed Seacat catamaran sails from Dover (England) to Ostend in two hours (three to six services a day). The one-way fare for a car plus one adult is between UK£104 and UK£180. Better value are the five-day return fares, which cost from UK£132 to UK£229. Foot passengers are charged UK£28 for both one-way tickets and the five-day return (children UK£15). Hover-speed's Web site is www.hoverspeed.com.

P&O North Sea Ferries (☎ 0870 129 6002) sails overnight from Hull to Zee-brugge (14 hours) and charges between UK£55 and UK£75 one way for a car, or UK£100 to UK£135 return, depending on the season. Adult single/return fares are between UK£33/59 and UK£42/76 depending on the season. Cabins start at UK£68 per person. There are special deals for cars with up to four passengers and discounts for students, those aged under 26 and seniors. Visit its Web site at www.ponsf.com for current details.

Other options to consider are car ferries between Dover and Calais (in France).

For information on train-boat-train packages, see the Train section earlier in the chapter.

ORGANISED TOURS

Many companies in the UK offer package tours to Belgium. Package holidays should not be overlooked – especially for city breaks and short stays – as they often simply comprise accommodation and transport to/from Belgium and can represent excellent value.

Prices depend on the season, the day of the week, the type of accommodation (from one- to five-star hotels to self-catering) and the mode of transport (car, bus, ferry, Eurostar or plane) that you choose.

As an example, two nights in a two-star hotel in Brussels or Antwerp in the low season travelling by train and ferry will cost about UK£120 per person. Add an extra UK£5 for travel by Eurolines coach, UK£50 for the Eurostar train or UK£80 by air.

For more details of tours contact the Belgian Travel Service (☎ 01992-456 323, e belgian@bridge-travel.co.uk), Bridge House, 55–9 High Rd, Broxbourne, Hertfordshire EN10 7DT, or Hoseasons Holidays Abroad (☎ 01502-502 680, e mail @hoseasons.co.uk) at Sunway House, Lowestoft, Suffolk NR32 2LW.

Specialised tours, such as beer or bike trips, can be arranged from the USA. Two companies that organise bike tours in Europe have small sectors taking in Belgium. CBT Bicycle Tours (☎ 800 736 2453, e adventure@cbttours.com), 2506 N Clark St, #150, Chicago, IL 60614, has a 12-day tour from Amsterdam to Brussels (June and July only) for US$2655. Its Web site is at www.cbttours.com. The other company is Euro Bike Tours (☎ 800 321 6060, e info@ eurobike.com), which does a 13-day bike tour (of which only three days are in Belgium) for US$3295. Check its Web site at www.eurobike.com.

Beer tours from the USA are run sporadically – the easiest place to find details is on the Internet. You could try 4Windstours (☎ 509-967 3448, e st4winds@earthlink .net) with a Web site at www.4windstours .com or Global Beer Network (e info@ globalbeer.com) with a Web site at www .globalbeer.com.

From Australia and New Zealand there's little choice in tours to Belgium. Those offered usually include Belgium as part of a Benelux (Belgium/Netherlands/Luxembourg) package. The best place to start looking is the European Travel Office (ETO). Prices are around A$670 per person on a twin-share basis for a three-day tour. ETO has offices in Melbourne (☎ 03-9329 88 44, e etomel@ozonline.com.au), 122 Rosslyn St, West Melbourne, Victoria, 3000 and Auckland (☎ 09-525 30 74, e suntravl @suntravel.co.nz), Suntravel Ltd, 407 Great South Rd, Penrose, New Zealand.

Brussels

- postcode 1000
- pop 977,800
- elevation 57m

Brussels (Brussel in Flemish, Bruxelles in French) is the undisputed crossroads of Western Europe. Situated smack between London, Paris, Amsterdam and Cologne, it is the pulse of the EU and home to people from every country in Europe, plus a whole lot more.

The city's character largely mirrors that of Belgium: confident but modest, and rarely striving to impress. Ask the Brusselaars/Bruxellois what it is that makes their city special and the answers will be varied – great seafood in great restaurants, the smell of hot waffles on a cold winter's day, cafes and pubs that never close, the cosmopolitan but neighbourly feel of the city, forests practically on the doorstep, pheasant and truffles in autumn, comic strips, designer shops…the list goes on.

Visitors, on the other hand, experience other delights – Grand Place, mussels with chips, chocolates and pralines, uncrowded museums, intimate hotels, Art Nouveau and Horta, Tintin, unbelievable beers and more great restaurants and cafes.

Brussels has all of the above, and a lot more. Among its most intriguing and invigorating qualities are its contrasts and contradictions. The architecture ranges from monumental edifices such as the Palais de Justice to the discreet facades of Art Nouveau houses, before making a quantum leap to the gleaming modernity of the EU's glass city. Bureaucrats and red tape operate alongside the laid-back locals who value the city's relaxed pace and casual atmosphere. Brussels is home to the EU's key decision-making bodies and also the North Atlantic Treaty Organisation (NATO); at the same time the city uses a symbol of a little boy urinating to sell itself around the world.

Such contrasts are characteristic of Surrealist art, which embodied the spirit of the capital in the 1920s and was captured by leading local exponents René Magritte and Paul Delvaux. Their works are displayed in the Musées Royaux des Beaux-Arts, the city's most prestigious museum, which also showcases masterpieces from a very different world – that of the Flemish Primitives, Breugel and Rubens.

Brussels sits in Flanders, north of Belgium's Linguistic Divide (see the boxed text 'The Linguistic Divide' in the Facts about the Cities chapter for details). It is composed of 19 *communes* (municipalities), collectively known as the Brussels Region (Brussels Gewest in Flemish, Région de Bruxelles in French). This region is the only area in Belgium to be officially bilingual and the communes often (but not always) have two names – the original Flemish plus a French version; thus you'll see signs for the commune of Elsene (as it's known in Flemish) and Ixelles (as it's called in French). This at times confusing system is paralleled in many aspects of Belgian life and is one of the most obvious signs of the underlying tensions between the Flemish and Walloon communities. As the majority of people in Brussels speak French, we've used French place/street names throughout the Brussels chapter and hope that doing so hasn't irritated or upset too many Flemish. To compare neighbourhood names, see the list of alternative place names in the Appendix.

At the end of the day, Brussels is what you make it. It can be hip, it can be dull – it's a city of contrasts.

Getting Around

ORIENTATION

Most of the Brussels region is surrounded by a motorway – the Ring – which provides easy access to much of the central district. Another ring – the Petit (small) Ring – encases the old city centre in a pentagon of boulevards that allows rapid transit.

Central Brussels is divided into two main areas – the Lower and Upper Towns. The

Lower Town (Map 5) comprises the medieval centre and is based around the imposing Grand Place, a former market square. This area is easy to get around on foot, its cobbled streets leading to popular quarters such as Ilôt Sacré, Ste Catherine, St Géry and, to the south, the Marolles, an old working-class neighbourhood where some locals still speak Bruxellois, the city's old dialect based on a mixture of Flemish and French.

The Upper Town has a vastly different atmosphere. It rises to the east and south-east of Grand Place and was the traditional base of Belgium's French-speaking elite. Thus you'll find wide boulevards flanking monumental buildings such as the Palais Royal and the Palais de Justice, as well as the Belgian parliament and government headquarters, some major museums and chic shopping precincts based around the Sablon and Ave Louise areas.

Although there's plenty to see within the Petit Ring, Brussels extends much farther. The modern EU quarter (Map 7) – look for signposts to Europese Instellingen/Institutions Européennes – lies to the east and borders the trendy Ixelles district, which straddles Ave Louise. Ixelles and its neighbour, St Gilles, are known for their many Art Nouveau buildings. St Gilles also has a down-at-heel quarter based around the Gare du Midi area. South of Ixelles, the affluent commune of Uccle flanks the Bois de la Cambre, a popular park that eventually joins the Forêt de Soignes.

North of the old city centre is a business district built around Blvd Émile Jacqmain and resembling a miniature Manhattan. Nearby are two immigrant neighbourhoods, St Josse and Schaerbeek. The Canal de Willebroek separates these communes from Laeken and the Domaine Royal, the main residence of Belgium's royal family. Just north-west of here is Heysel, site of the infamous soccer stadium disaster of 1985 and home to the Atomium, a space-age leftover from the 1958 World Fair, and Bruparck, a multifaceted entertainment complex.

Last, north-west of the centre are the little-visited communes of Koekelberg and

What Street is This?

First-time visitors to Brussels are often flabbergasted by its peculiarly long street names. Blue-and-white street-corner plaques proclaim titles like 'Petite Rue de la Violette Korte Violetstraat' or 'Place de la Vieille Halle aux Blés Oud Korenhuis'. And these aren't isolated cases. It's tricky recalling what street a great cafe is on when it's almost impossible to get your tongue around the name.

They become more manageable when you remember that it's two names in one – the French followed by the Flemish. Thus, Little Violet Street is actually Petite Rue de la Violette in French and Korte Violetstraat in Flemish. Note also that, in French, *rue* (street) comes at the start of the name while in Flemish *straat* is tacked onto the end.

Jette; the latter is home to the new Musée Magritte. To the south-west is Anderlecht, best known for its soccer team but also boasting some interesting museums.

Brussels has three main train stations – Gare du Nord, Gare Centrale and Gare du Midi. For details see the Train section in the Getting There & Away chapter.

THE AIRPORTS

Belgium's main international airport is Brussels National airport, commonly known as Zaventem airport (Map 3). The only other international airports near the capital are Brussels South, 55km south of the Brussels (near the city of Charleroi) and used mainly by Ryanair for flights to/from Ireland, and Deurne (see the Antwerp chapter for details).

Zaventem airport is 14km north-east of Brussels. The airport terminal has a decent array of bars, restaurants, duty-free shops and other facilities. There are two main parts (or concourses) to the terminal: C (for flights to/from all Schengen countries) and B (for all other flights).

The terminal building is five storeys high and is relatively compact. The building's top level (4), known as the Promenade, includes shops and a cafeteria with a view of the runways. Level 3 is the departures hall, where you'll find an information desk and free airport maps. The arrivals hall is on level 2. Facilities here include car rental agencies and tourist information offices (see the Tourist Offices section in the Facts for the Visitor chapter). The bus terminus and luggage storage lockers are on the ground floor. The train station is on the lowest level (-1).

For all airport and flight information ring ☎ 02-753 39 13.

TO/FROM THE AIRPORTS

A shuttle train – the Airport City Express – runs roughly every 15 minutes between Zaventem airport and Brussels' three main train stations. The trip takes 15 minutes to Gare du Nord, 20 minutes to Gare Centrale and 25 minutes to Gare du Midi; a one-way ticket in 2nd/1st class costs €2.35/3.59. From the airport to the city, the first train departs at 5.32 am; the last leaves at 12.20 am. From Gare Centrale, the first train to the airport departs at 4.48 am and the last is at 11.16 pm.

On weekdays, bus BZ runs between the airport's bus terminal and Gare du Nord (€2.23 one-way, 35 minutes). During weekdays, this bus departs from the airport half-hourly from 6.20 to 8.25 am and hourly from 9 am to 11 pm. From Gare du Nord it departs half-hourly from 5.45 to 8.15 am and then hourly until 10.20 pm. On Saturday, it runs every two hours – the first departure from the airport is 7.05 am and the last is 9.05 pm.

Sabena operates a bus between Zaventem airport and Antwerp (€6.19 one-way, 40 minutes; pick up and drop off at De Keyserlei 45, Antwerp; Map 12). It runs hourly from 5.30 am to 10 or 11 pm, and leaves from the Zaventem bus terminal.

The taxi fare between the airport and central Brussels is €25 to €30; taxis wait outside the arrivals hall. Official taxis have a yellow and blue 'Taxi' sign and some also have an orange and white windscreen sticker indicating a 25% reduction on the return journey (valid for two months).

To Brussels South airport (used mainly by Ryanair for flights to/from Ireland),

there's a daily Ryanair bus (timed to coincide with flight schedules) that departs from The Wild Geese, an Irish pub at Ave Livingstone 2 (Map 7) in Brussels' EU area. The fare is €6.19 one way.

PUBLIC TRANSPORT

Brussels' modern and efficient public transport system is operated by the Société des Transports Intercommunaux de Bruxelles (STIB in French, MIVB in Flemish). The metro, trams, premetro (trams that go underground for part of their journey) and buses make up the network.

There are STIB ticket kiosks dotted all around the city. The most central is outside the Bourse (Map 5) on Blvd Anspach; it opens 6.20 am to 5 pm weekdays. Others are located in the following metro stations: Porte de Namur (Map 6), Rogier (Map 4) and Gare du Midi (Map 6). Free transport maps are available from the ticket kiosks and the tourist office.

Brussels' public transport generally runs from about 5.30 am to 11 pm or midnight. For more information, drop into the STIB/MIVB information office (Map 5; ☎ 02-515 20 00) at 31 Rue l'Évêque.

Tickets & Passes

Tickets are valid for one hour and are sold at metro stations, STIB kiosks, some newsagents and on buses and trams. The pricing system is simple – a single-journey ticket costs €1.24, five/10-journey tickets cost €5.95/8.86 and a one-day pass for unlimited travel costs €3.47. Tickets must be validated at the start of your journey in machines located at the entrance to metro platforms or inside buses and trams. Travelling without a validated ticket (random checks are made) can incur a fine of €55.

The Tourist Information Brussels (TIB) office on Grand Place sells one-day passes as well as a Tourist Passport, which comprises two one-day passes and discounts to various sights.

Metro

Brussels' metro system (Map 2) opened in 1965. Metro stations are marked by rectan-

Art in the Metro

You many think that when you've seen one metro station you've seen them all, but that's not so in Brussels. Nearly 60 works of art adorn the city's metro and premetro stations. The STIB brochure *L'Art dans le Métro* lists what you can see; highlights include:

Bourse metro station (Map 5): Paul Delvaux's *Nos Vieux Trams Bruxellois* depicts old trams in the capital.

Porte de Hal metro station (Map 6): comic-strip artist François Schuiten's wall compositions entitled *Le Passage Inconnu* (The Unknown Passage) merge old trams and futuristic vehicles in scenes mirrored in his best cartoons.

Horta premetro station (Map 6): relics from Horta's Maison du Peuple have been integrated into the station's foyer.

Stockel metro station (Map 3): the walls are adorned with life-sized paintings of Tintin and pals.

gular signs with a white 'M' on a blue background. There are three metro lines: Line 1A goes from Roi Baudouin station to Herrmann-Debroux; Line 1B runs from Bizet to Stockel; and Line 2 is a loop that joins Simonis with Clémenceau, basically following the Petit Ring. There's a train roughly every 10 or 15 minutes.

Tram, Premetro & Bus

Tram and bus stops have red-and-white signs. Unfortunately there's no central transport hub for buses or trams, so you'll need to pick up the STIB's free transport map. A few of the most common central bus stops include the STIB information office on Rue l'Évêque (Map 5), outside Falstaff cafe on Rue Henri Maus (Map 5), next to the GB supermarket on Rue des Halles (Map 5) and next to Gare Centrale (Map 5).

Premetro trams (Map 2) run mainly between Gare du Nord (Map 4) and Gare du Midi (Map 6), travelling underneath the ruler-straight boulevard known consecu-

tively as Adolphe Max/Anspach/Maurice Lemonnier. They also dive below ground in a few other places around town.

Train

Trains are of minimal use for getting around in Brussels. For visitors, their main role is to get between the city centre and Zaventem airport (see To/From the Airports earlier in the chapter). For information on train services to other cities in Belgium and destinations farther afield, see under Train in the Getting There & Away chapter.

CAR & MOTORCYCLE

Driving in Brussels has its thrills – see the boxed text 'Belgian Drivers' in the Getting There & Away chapter for details of what to expect. Additionally, there are potholes, traffic jams and tunnels where drivers love to speed. The slightest hiccup on either ring road brings traffic to a halt, and don't consider leaving by car on Friday afternoon unless you love congestion. For information on road rules, see under Car & Motorcycle in the Getting There & Away chapter.

Parking poses the usual problems. Signs saying *betalend parkeren/stationnement payant* mean that you must pay for street parking. Green ticket-machines issue one /two-hour tickets for €1/2.50 (two hours is the maximum).

Multistorey and underground car parks, dotted around the centre, are generally closed between 1 and 6 am. Two central car parks are Inno Parking (Map 5; €1.86 /9.05/12.77 for one/five/24 hours), accessed from Rue du Damier, and Parking 58 (Map 5; €1.73/12.39 for one/24 hours) on Rue de l'Évêque. There's a great view of the city from the 10th floor of Parking 58.

Car Rental

The major car rental companies have offices at Gare du Midi, Zaventem airport and offices around town. Take note, rentals from Zaventem and Gare du Midi cost 15% more due to extra taxes.

Rental companies in Brussels include:

Avis (Map 6; ☎ 02-537 12 80) Rue Américaine 145

Budget (Map 6; ☎ 02-646 51 30) Ave Louise 327b
Hertz (Map 5; ☎ 02-513 28 86) Blvd Maurice Lemonnier 8
National/Alamo (Map 3; ☎ 02-753 20 60) Zaventem airport

Motorcycle Rental
Baele & Schmitz (Map 3; ☎ 02-762 60 27) at Chaussée de Louvain hires 50cc scooters for €14.87/124 per day/week, and Yamaha motorcycles (600cc to 1100cc), which cost €69.41 per day or €347 to €594 per week. A hefty deposit of €991/1859 is required for scooters/motorcycles.

TAXI
Taxis are metered and expensive, and the cabbies have a reputation for pugnacious driving. Taxes and tips are officially included in the meter price, so ignore demands for extra service charges.

The basic rate is €2.35, plus €0.99 per kilometre within the Brussels region, or €1.98 per kilometre outside. Between 10 pm and 6 am an additional €4.21 is charged. The waiting rate is €19.83 per hour. Generally, you'll find taxis near all three central train stations as well as outside the Hôtel Amigo (Map 5) near Grand Place and at Place Stéphanie (Map 6) on Ave Louise. Alternatively, call Taxis Bleus (☎ 02-268 00 00) or Taxis Verts (☎ 02-349 49 49).

BICYCLE
Cycling in central Brussels is not for the faint-hearted – intolerant drivers, slippery cobblestones and tram tracks are all possible hazards. That said, there are some bike lanes (usually painted red and marked with white lines) and paths separated from the traffic.

Dedicated cyclists should head to Uccle where La Selle à Deux Roues (Map 3; ☎ 02-375 32 72) at Rue Édith Cavell 216 rents out bikes for €9.04 per 24 hours. It's closed Sunday and Monday. Bus No 60 stops nearby. From here it's an easy cycle to the Bois de la Cambre and Forêt de Soignes.

ORGANISED TOURS
Bus, walking and theme tours of the city are all available in English as well as in German, Japanese, Flemish and French. Though many visitors shun bus tours, they are a good way to get an overview of the city in a short time (particularly as many of the sights are scattered over a wide distance). Afterwards you can concentrate on the sights within the centre and/or leisurely revisit outlying attractions. Most of the following tours can be booked at the TIB.

The main bus operator is De Boeck (Map 5; ☎ 02-513 77 44), Rue de la Colline 8, which has a 2¾-hour tour of all the major sights costing €19.83 (seniors and students €17.84, children €9.91). It also runs the cheaper Visit Brussels Line, double-decker buses that stop at 12 places including the Atomium, Place Royale and Rond Point Schuman. You can hop on and off as often as you like. These blue-and-yellow buses depart from Gare Centrale every half-hour between 10 am and 3 pm. Tickets (€12.15) can be bought on the bus (seniors and students €11.16, children €7.44).

Another new bus option is the double-decker, open-roof City Sightseeing Bus operated by Open Tours (☎ 02-466 16 25). Its 1½-hour tour costs €11.15 (children free) and buses depart daily from Gare Centrale.

For something a bit more intimate there's a mini-bus tour (maximum eight people) run by The Human Profile (☎ 02-715 91 20). It winds in and out of narrow cobbled streets in the old centre (something the big buses can't do) and costs €24.78 for three hours. It departs daily at 10 am and 2 pm from Grand Place 10 (Map 5).

Chatterbus (☎ 02-673 18 35), based at Rue des Thuyas 12, runs a 2½-hour walking tour of the old centre in summer (15 June to mid-September), departing daily at 10 am from Galeries St Hubert (Map 5). The cost is €7.43. Chatterbus also organises theme tours (such as a cafe and pub crawls) using public transport.

In summer, horse-drawn carriages do circuits of the Lower Town starting from Rue Charles Buls, near Grand Place. A 20-minute ride costs €14.87.

Atelier de Recherche et d'Action Urbaine (ARAU; Map 5; ☎ 02-219 33 45), Blvd Adolphe Max 55, is a heritage conservation group set up in 1969. It runs a variety of theme tours to Art Nouveau buildings, Art Deco houses, the EU quarter, the Grand Place area and the Marolles. They're highly recommended, especially if you're keen to get into some of the private Art Nouveau showpieces. There are usually only one or two tours per theme per month, so you either have to plan your visit or take pot luck that you'll be there for a particular tour. The cost is €14.87 (under 26 years €12.39) for bus tours and €7.43 for walking tours. The Art Nouveau bus tours (three hours) are held on the second and forth Sunday of the month (May to July, September and October only) at 9.45 am. Most tours depart from Place Brouckère, and some tours are conducted in English. Reservations are necessary – you can book and pay at the TIB, which also has full details of ARAU's seasonal program.

Things to See & Do

Highlights

- Soak up the ambience of Grand Place on a summer's evening

- Seek out old masters and Surrealists at the Musées Royaux des Beaux-Arts

- Revel in the world of Art Nouveau at the Musée Horta

- Combine comics with Art Nouveau at the Centre Belge de la Bande Dessinée

- Delve into Art Deco at the engaging Musée David et Alice Van Buuren

- Taste a true Brussels brew at the Musée Bruxellois de la Gueuze

- Sample the city's many fabulous restaurants and cafes

GRAND PLACE (MAP 5)

Brussels' magnificent central square, Grand Place, tops every newcomer's itinerary. It boasts the country's finest baroque guildhalls, the beautiful Hôtel de Ville (town hall),

popular pavement cafes and intimate restaurants – a combination that lures tourists in droves. Hidden at the very core of the old town, it's only revealed as you enter from one of the narrow side alleys – a discreet positioning that simply adds to its charm.

The square dates from the 12th century and was once marshland. By the mid-14th century, Brussels was booming through the cloth trade and the patronage of the dukes of Burgundy. A prosperous market covered not only Grand Place but also the neighbouring streets, as is evident from names such as Rue au Beurre (butter street), Rue des Bouchers (butchers' street) and Rue du Marché aux Poulets (chicken-market street). The city's increasingly wealthy merchant guilds established headquarters – guildhalls – on the square. The construction of the Hôtel de Ville sealed Grand Place's role as the hub of commercial, political and civic life in Brussels. Medieval tournaments and public executions took place here before exuberant crowds.

In 1695 much of central Brussels, including Grand Place, was bombarded for 36 hours under the orders of Louis XIV of France. Most of the guildhalls, as well as thousands of houses and 16 churches, were destroyed in the attack, which was designed to distract the allied forces of England and the Spanish Netherlands, with whom the French king was at war. Except for Hôtel de Ville, nearly all the buildings that you see on Grand Place today are 17th-century replacements.

Hôtel de Ville

The splendid Gothic Hôtel de Ville was the only building on Grand Place to escape the 1695 French bombardment – ironic considering that it was the primary target. It's a superb structure, with a creamy facade covered with stone reliefs and an intricate 100m-high tower topped by a gilded statue of St Michel, the city's patron saint. The building is not symmetrical – the left-hand side was begun in 1402 but the right wing wasn't added until 1444 and is, due to space constraints, shorter. Guided tours (€2.47) in English are run at 3.15 pm on Tuesday and

BRUSSELS

ALBERT COLE

The magnificent Hôtel de Ville on Grand Place

Wednesday (with an extra tour at 12.15 pm on Sunday from 1 April to 30 September).

Guildhalls

The splendour of Grand Place is due largely to its antique frame of guildhalls. Each merchant guild erected its own building, which is named (there were no street numbers back then) and adorned with gilded statues and elaborate symbols related to its trade. When the guildhalls were obliterated in the 1695 bombardment, the guilds rallied and rebuilt their headquarters in under five years, using stone (rather than partial timber as before) for the facades and adding fanciful baroque touches to the gables.

Some of the highlights include:

Maison du Roi (King's House) Opposite the Hôtel de Ville, this dark, brooding building is somewhat inappropriately named as it was never home to royalty. These days it houses the Musée de la Ville de Bruxelles.

No 1: Maison des Boulangers (Bakers' House) Le Roy d'Espagne, one of the most popular cafes on the square, occupies this building, which belonged to the bakers' guild. The gilded bronze bust above the door represents their patron, St Aubert.

No 2: La Brouette (The Wheelbarrow) Faint gold wheelbarrows can still be seen above the door of this house, which was home to the grease-makers. The statue of St Gilles was added in 1912.

No 4: Le Sac (The Bag) This building was the headquarters of the cabinet-makers (and now houses Thomas Cook).

No 5: La Louve (The She-Wolf) The archers' guild topped their building with a golden phoenix rising from the ashes to signify the rebirth of Grand Place after the bombardment. A statue of the She-Wolf can be seen above the doorway.

No 6: Le Cornet (The Horn) The boatmen's guild is easily identified by its incredibly ornate, stern-shaped gable.

No 7: Le Renard (The Fox) This house served the haberdashers.

No 8: L'Étoile (The Star) Across Rue Charles Buls from the Hôtel de Ville, this is the smallest building on the square. Here Everard 't Serclaes, the city's hero and modern-day good-luck charm, died.

No 9: Le Cygne (The Swan) Adorned with a huge swan and built in classical style, this house originally served the butchers' guild. Nowadays it's home to the finest restaurant on the square, La Maison du Cygne.

No 10: L'Arbre d'Or (The Golden Tree) Hops plants climbing up columns hint at this building's former and current role as the brewers' headquarters and Musée de la Brasserie.

Nos 26 & 27: Le Pigeon This guildhall belonged to the city's artists. Later, Victor Hugo lived here during his exile from France in 1852.

Musée de la Ville de Bruxelles

The Brussels City Museum (☎ 02-279 43 58) is in the Maison du Roi on Grand Place. The museum occupies three floors and provides a historical overview of the city through old maps, architectural relics, paintings, three-dimensional models, tapestries and, displayed on the ground floor, Pieter Breugel the Elder's *Cortège de Noces* (Wedding Procession) of 1567.

One room on the 3rd floor is devoted to the worldly wardrobe of Manneken Pis, Belgium's national symbol (for more details see that entry later in the chapter). Only one-sixth of his 675 garments is ever on display; the rest are locked away in the cupboards below.

The museum opens 10 am to 12.30 pm and 1.30 to 5 pm Monday to Thursday (until 4 pm between 1 October and 31 March), and 10 am to 1 pm at the weekend. Admission costs €2.50 (students and seniors €2).

Musée du Cacao et du Chocolat

The Museum of Cocoa and Chocolate (☎ 02-514 20 48) at Grand Place 13 is devoted to an enticing theme but has little of substance to support it. The admission cost of €5 (students €3.75) entitles you to one chocolate-dipped biscuit, a wander through some unimpressive exhibits and a peek at a praline-making demonstration. For this sort of money you might be better off crossing the square to Godiva or Galler and indulging in a box of the real thing. The museum opens 10 am to 5 pm Tuesday to Sunday.

Musée de la Brasserie

The Brewery Museum (☎ 02-511 49 87), Grand Place 10, occupies the basement of the brewers' guildhall, L'Arbre d'Or. In two words: don't bother. If you want to see a real brewery, head to the Musée Bruxellois de la Gueuze in Anderlecht.

SOUTH OF GRAND PLACE (MAP 5)
Rue Charles Buls

Rue Charles Buls leads off the south-western side of Grand Place. It paves the way to Manneken Pis and, not surprisingly, is lined with lace and trinket shops. At the start of the street, in a small arcaded gallery, you'll find an 1899 gilded **Art Nouveau plaque** dedicated to the city from its appreciative artists. Next to it is a reclining **statue of Everard 't Serclaes**, a 14th-century hero who defended the city – rub his gleaming torso for good luck.

Musée du Costume et de la Dentelle

A stone's throw from Grand Place and well worth an hour or so is the Costume and Lace Museum (☎ 02-512 77 09), Rue de la Violette 6. Superb displays of antique and modern lace are displayed on three floors and include the sombre black attire once worn by women *en promenade* (out walking) and the more colourful lace gowns for women *en visite* (visiting). Note also the antique underwear, including an old *buste-houder* (bra). Unfortunately, explanations are in Flemish and French only.

The museum opens 10 am to 12.30 pm and 1.30 to 7 pm daily except Wednesday (until 4 pm from 1 October to 31 March). Admission costs €2.

Manneken Pis

Despite being a national symbol and known throughout the world, this fountain with a little boy cheerfully taking a leak never fails to disappoint visitors due to its size (it's tiny). It's on the corner of Rue de l'Étuve and Rue du Chêne, three blocks from Grand Place.

The present-day bronze Manneken Pis was sculpted by Jerôme Duquesnoy in 1619, but a stone version – named Little Julian – stood here from the mid-14th century. The statue's origins are lost in legend: some say he's modelled on a boy who extinguished a fire, others say he was the son of a nobleman. Whatever, the people of Brussels have adopted him as the symbol of their indomitable and irreverent spirit, and on occasion dress him up in one of his 675 costumes. Kitsch? Well, there's more – his little 'sister', Jeanneke Pis, squats in an alley a few blocks away.

Fondation Jacques Brel

The Jacques Brel Foundation (☎ 02-511 10 20), Place de la Vieille Halle aux Blés 11, is an archive centre-cum-museum dedicated to the Belgian singer whose passionate but often bitter, anti-bourgeois songs earned him a huge following at home and in France. For more, see the boxed text 'Jacques Brel' in the Facts about the Cities chapter.

The centre features a permanent exhibition entitled *Avec Brel – un soir de tournée*, which intimately recreates an evening on the road with Brel in 1958 (French explanations only). It opens 11 am to 6 pm Tuesday to Saturday and admission costs €5 (students €3.70).

BRUSSELS

NORTH OF GRAND PLACE
Bourse (Map 5)
A block from Grand Place is the Belgian Stock Exchange on busy Place de la Bourse. It occupies a grandiose neoclassical edifice from 1873 that has recently been cleaned and is in better shape than it has been for years. The facade is festooned with friezes and sculptures of exotic fruits, reclining nudes, lunging horses and a multitude of allegorical figures.

Next to the Bourse, on Rue de la Bourse, is a small archaeological museum, **Bruxelaa 1238**, where you can see the excavation of a 13th-century chapel. An English-language tour of Bruxelaa 1238 is conducted on Wednesday at 10.15 am (reservations are necessary; ask at the TIB).

Église St Nicolas (Map 5)
Next to the Bourse and easily overlooked is the Church of St Nicolas, Rue au Beurre 1. This pint-sized edifice is encrusted with shops and is as old as Brussels itself. Heavily restored through the centuries, the dark and sombre interior is noted for the unusual angle at which its three aisles were built. The church opens 7.45 am to 6.45 pm weekdays and 9 am to 6 pm at the weekend.

Galeries St Hubert (Map 5)
Just one block from Grand Place, the glass-vaulted Galeries St Hubert is *the* place to seek refuge on a rainy day. Built in 1846 as Europe's first shopping arcade, it comprises three connecting sections: Galerie du Roi, Galerie de la Reine and the smaller Galerie des Princes at the side. Recent renovation has returned it to its former glory (despite the imitation marble wall panels). The Galeries contain an eclectic mix of fashion, chocolate, book and music shops as well as restaurants, cafes and a cinema.

Rue des Bouchers (Map 5)
Leading off from Galeries St Hubert in a lively little quarter known as **Ilôt Sacré** is the famous Rue des Bouchers. Whether you decide to eat at one of the many seafood restaurants here or not, this pedestrianised cobbled street is a spectacle not to be missed. Both sides of the street are packed with tables where you can dine throughout the year (overhead heaters supposedly keep frostbite at bay in winter) and hard-sell waiters entice would-be diners with displays of marine delicacies and the odd novelty (singing fish are the latest attention-grabbing devices being used). Many of the restaurants are not recommended but there are exceptions, including Chez Léon and Aux Armes de Bruxelles (see the Places to Eat section later in the chapter).

Jeanneke Pis (Map 5)
Manneken Pis' female counterpart is Jeanneke Pis, at Impasse de la Fidélité off Rue des Bouchers. This little girl, gleefully squatting as she wees, was erected in 1985 by Denis Adrien Debouvrie 'in honour of loyalty'. Loyalty to what we're not sure, but certainly there's no bond between her and the tourist office, whose official guidebook doesn't even acknowledge her existence.

Cathédrale des Sts Michel & Gudule (Map 4)
This splendid twin-towered cathedral at Parvis Ste Gudule is named after Brussels' male and female patron saints. After years of renovation, it now sits gleaming on the hillside to the north of Gare Centrale. The rather out-of-the-way location means it is often overlooked – lost between the lower and upper towns and not on any of the paths most visitors tread.

Begun in 1226, the cathedral took some 300 years to build and consequently reveals a blend of styles – from Romanesque through all the stages of Gothic and right up to Renaissance. The interior is light and airy but almost bereft of decoration due to plundering, first by Protestants in the 17th century and later by the French army. Beautiful stained-glass windows flood the nave with light and the enormous wooden pulpit, depicting Adam and Eve being driven out of Eden by fearsome skeletons, is worth inspecting. In the crypt are the remains of an 11th-century Romanesque chapel.

The cathedral opens 8 am to 6 pm daily, admission to the crypt costs €0.99.

BRUSSELS

Centre Belge de la Bande Dessinée & Grand Magasin Waucquez (Map 4)

The Belgian Centre for Comic Strip Art (☎ 02-219 19 80) at Rue des Sables 20, about 800m from Grand Place, should not be missed. The centre is a tour through the country's rich, vibrant comic-strip culture, tracing the history from its earliest beginnings to contemporary favourites. It has a bookshop, a library, a lovely *brasserie* (cafe) and several floors of exhibits, all housed in one remarkable building, the **Grand Magasin Waucquez**.

This former department store was created by Victor Horta in 1906 for the Waucquez family textile business. The use of skylights and windows to provide light are pure Art Nouveau, though the building is not as decorative or supple as some of Horta's other creations. Despite standing empty for 16 years, it was spared from the demolition madness that stripped Brussels of other Art Nouveau showpieces and is now worthy of a visit in itself.

An English-language booklet (free but to be returned) leads you through the various storeys and displays. Fans of Hergé will find a much photographed replica of Tintin's red and white rocket, plus plenty of examples of his work. The top level traces the evolution of Belgian comics from the 1960s to the present day. For more on Belgian comics, see the following boxed texts: 'The Art of Belgian Comics' in the Facts about the Cities chapter; 'Tintin & Hergé' below and 'Murals of Brussels', later in the chapter, for a comic-strip walking tour.

The centre opens 10 am to 6 pm Tuesday to Sunday; admission costs €6.20 (children €2.50).

Rue Neuve Area (Map 5)

Rue Neuve is the city's pedestrianised shopping heart. It's generally teeming with people and is best avoided on Saturday afternoon.

One of the few sights in this area is **Église Notre Dame du Finistère**, an 18th-century church that sits in vivid contrast to the modern mania around it. Nearby is the sombre **Place des Martyrs**, with its monument to the 467 who died in the 1830 revolution. Rejoin Rue du Neuve to meander through **Passage du Nord**, an elegant 19th-century shopping arcade. Rue Neuve terminates at Place de la Monnaie, a rather ugly square that's home

Tintin & Hergé

He's small, quiffed, almost asexual and sanctimonious, his dog is a pragmatic smart aleck with a penchant for booze and his mate is a drunkard. Since their birth in 1929, Tintin and pals have become a Belgian comic-strip phenomenon, loved (and occasionally loathed) around the world.

Meanwhile, back in Brussels, their creator, Hergé (1907–83), is not having it so easy. In recent years he has come under flack for the racial stereotypes portrayed in some early books (such as *Tintin au Congo*, in which the Africans are portrayed as timid and subservient) and for his alleged collaboration during WWII (unlike others, Hergé continued working for *Le Soir Volé*, a newspaper that printed German propaganda). His advocates point out that when Hergé wrote his first three books – *Tintin au pays des Soviets*, *Tintin au Congo* and *Tintin en Amérique* – the time was 1929 to 1932, colonialism was not a dirty word and Tintin was simply a journalist reflecting that era.

Has all this controversy tarnished the books' sales or reputation? Great snakes, no! More than 200 million books covering the young reporter's global adventures and mishaps have been sold in 58 languages (Tintin and Snowy are known in French as 'Tintin et Milou' and in Flemish they're 'Kuifje en Bobbie'). As for Hergé, he's remembered as one of Belgium's best. To see some of his art, head to the Centre Belge de la Bande Dessinée.

to Brussels' opera house, the **Théâtre Royal de la Monnaie** (for more details see the boxed text 'A Revolutionary Performance' in the Facts about the Cities chapter).

STE CATHERINE AREA (MAP 5)

The appealing Ste Catherine quarter lies across the busy Blvd Anspach to the north-west of Grand Place. An excellent **view** of the area, and much of Brussels for that matter, can be had from Parking 58, a public car park on Rue de l'Évêque. Take the elevator to the (open-air) 10th storey.

The Ste Catherine area is noted for its many seafood restaurants, which are based around the **Marché aux Poissons**, or Vismet. As its name suggests, it was the city's fish market in earlier times.

Église Ste Catherine

This 19th-century church at Place Ste Catherine is the nominal heart of the area. It is built on the site of a 12th-century chapel that once adjoined the city ramparts. The outside is an unimpressive hotchpotch of styles; it's cool and austere inside. Take a look at the small 15th-century black statue of the Virgin and Child near the glass partition; Protestants hurled it into the Senne in 1744, but locals found it floating on a chunk of turf and fished it out. The church opens 8.30 am to 5 or 6 pm daily (closed Sunday afternoon).

Maison La Bellone

One block from Place Ste Catherine is the Maison La Bellone, Rue de Flandre 46, a stunning 18th-century building with a glass-vaulted courtyard that is used for occasional concerts. It's at the end of an arcade and is easy to miss – look for the sign. It opens 10 am to 6 pm Tuesday to Friday (closed in July). Admission is free.

Église St Jean Baptiste au Béguinage

From Maison La Bellone, cross over Marché aux Poissons and you'll soon arrive at Église St Jean Baptiste au Béguinage at Place du Béguinage. The imposing facade of this church is deemed by many to be the most

beautiful in Belgium. The church dates back to the 17th century and was designed by Luc Fayd'Herbe, a student of Rubens, which explains its strong Italian-Flemish baroque style. In November 2000, a fire swept through the church gutting the interior but luckily sparing the facade. It's expected to be closed for several years; in the meantime you can still view the outside.

Tour Noire

This historic tower, on the southern side of Place Ste Catherine, formed part of the city's original wall. These days it is dwarfed by the Novotel hotel which was built around it in the late 1990s.

ST GÉRY AREA (MAP 5)

The St Géry area, south of the Ste Catherine quarter, is one of Brussels' little secrets. It was in this quarter that Brussels came into being – St Géry, the bishop of Cambrai and Arras, built a chapel here in 695 and from that the city grew. For years, visitors have hesitated to cross Blvd Anspach and explore this area – it's well worth doing so.

The area's hub is Place St Géry, an engaging little square that is surrounded by popular cafes and dominated by the **Halles St Géry** (☎ 02-289 26 66), a former meat market. Renovated a decade ago, the Halles hosts a permanent exhibition on the architectural patrimony of the Grand Place area and an ecology shop. It has a cafe that's open day and night.

From a public courtyard off Place St Géry (go through the black steel gates next to the bistro La Lion St Géry), there's a lovely view of **Église Notre Dame des Riches Claires**, an intriguing asymmetrical church. Nearby is the **Nero** mural, one of many comic-strip murals in this area (see the boxed text 'Murals of Brussels' later for details).

Head up Rue du Pont de la Carpe to Rue des Chartreux, a charming street renovated in 1999 and now boasting innovative tree-shaped street lamps. **Le Greenwich** at No 7 is a great cafe to pause for a drink, or proceed to No 42 where (weekdays only) you can push open the black door to reveal part of a 12th-century sandstone **tower**, one of 50 such defensive towers that once stretched for 4km around the old city centre.

Directly opposite is **Album** (Map 5; ☎ 02-511 90 55), Rue des Chartreux 25, a little museum that changes its focus every year or so to keep pace with the times and stimulate debate. Its newest theme, advertising, is a look at Belgian culture and social issues. Housed in a former watchmaker's shop, it opened in 1997 and is run by an enthusiastic young couple. The interactive exhibits are fresh, engaging and multilingual (French, Flemish and English). The pricing policy is simple – the longer you stay the more you pay (ranging from €1.25 for 15 minutes to €5 for 1½ hours). Album opens from 1 to 6 pm daily except Wednesday.

First there was Manneken Pis, then Jeanneke Pis now Zinneke Pis or, more correctly, **Zinneke**, a statue of a mongrel dog with its leg cocked on the corner of Rue des Chartreux and Rue du Vieux Marché aux Grains. Designed by Flemish sculptor Tom Frantzen, Zinneke embodies Brussels' cosmopolitan nature and is another example of the city's irreverent spirit.

One of the city's Art Nouveau gems is concealed nearby. Continue along Rue du Vieux Marché aux Grains to the Leda 41 shop and go through the neighbouring black doors to a small courtyard (this is private property but the owners do not mind if visitors peek inside; take note that the doors are open 7 am to 5 pm on weekdays; on Saturday you must ask at the Leda 41 shop and on Sunday there's no access). From the courtyard you can see two superb old **stained-glass windows**. One features a young lady in a flowing white gown standing before a pond with a swan in it, the other an exotic Chinese woman.

Rue Antoine Dansaert is the border between the Ste Catherine and St Géry areas. It was once a quiet street where farmers from Flanders came to buy hardware; it's now home to a cluster of avant-garde **fashion shops** (see the Shopping section later in the chapter).

A vestige of Belgium's colonial heyday is found at Rue Antoine Dansaert 75–9. The upper facade of this **Art Deco building** is adorned with ceramics featuring bananas and orange trees. Designed by Eugène Dhuicque, the building was the headquarters of a company that imported exotic fruit from Africa.

MAROLLES (MAP 6)

The Marolles district lies between Grand Place and Gare du Midi. Despite slow gentrification, the area is still full of working-class kudos. The quarter's best-known attraction is the **Place du Jeu de Balle flea-market** (see under Markets in the Shopping section later).

The **Église Notre Dame de la Chapelle**, Rue des Ursulines 4, rises between the Marolles and the Sablon. Built in Romanesque Gothic style, it is Brussels' oldest church, founded in 1134. Inside, there's a chapel devoted to Pieter Breugel the Elder, who lived nearby. The church opens 9 am to 5 pm weekdays and 11.30 am to 4 pm at the weekend between June and September.

The nearby **Musée Breugel**, Rue Haute 132, occupies the house where Pieter Breugel the Elder lived and died (for details see the boxed text 'The Breugel Family' later). The museum is only open by reservation – ask at the TIB.

PLACE ROYALE AREA (MAP 4)

The busy Place Royale is the heart of the Upper Town, sitting on high ground immediately above Gare Centrale. The Upper Town is more spacious than its lower counterpart and distances here are greater. The easiest way to arrive here from Gare Centrale is via the **Mont des Arts**, an open-air stairway. At the centre of Place Royale stands a **statue of Godefroid de Bouillon**, an 11th-century crusader considered one of Belgium's ancient heroes.

Musée des Instruments de Musique & Old England Building

This museum (☎ 02-545 01 30) stands proudly at Montagne de la Cour 2, at the top of Mont des Arts. It boasts one of the world's biggest collections of musical instruments and, what's more, it is newly relocated in the fabulous Old England

Murals of Brussels

Brussels' Comic Strip Route is a series of giant comic-strip murals and colourful statues that enliven facades in back alleys and main thoroughfares throughout the old city centre. The route was set up in the 1990s to bring some of the wealth of comic artistic talent into the daily life of the city.

Moseying past the murals, or at least some of them, is an excellent way to explore less-visited neighbourhoods and discover the city's nooks and crannies…and there are lots of them. You'll be looking at a good three-hour walk to trace the entire 6km circuit, which is detailed in the publication *Comic Strip Walk* available from the TIB (€1.25). The following is an abbreviated version that can be done in roughly an hour, taking in a cross-section of comic styles and talent. It's marked on the Comic Strip Route map.

Start at Place St Géry where you'll find **Nero** (1) by Marc Sleen, an immensely popular series that started in 1947. Nero is the character at the top of the tree, and the series revolves around his day-to-day adventures.

Take Rue du Point de la Carpe north to Rue des Chartreux where, halfway along, rises **L'Archange** (2) by Yslaire (his real name is Bernard Hislaire). This narrow, sepia-toned panel with its whimsical angel overlooking graffiti contrasts the light and heavy sides of life.

Continue along this street to Rue des Fabriques where at No 21, just after the intersection with Rue du Rempart des Moines, appears the nautical **Cori Le Moussaillon** (3) by Bob De Moor (turn around or you'll miss it). Directly ahead and demanding attention is **The Dreams of Nic** (4) by Hermann. This huge mural occupies an entire wall and evokes childhood fantasy with flying elephants and turtles.

Turn left into Rue de la Senne then left into the second street, Rue 't Kint. One block on, at the corner of Rue de la Buanderie, a bank robbery is going on overseen by the most stupid dog in the West, Ran Tan Plan, and cartoon hero, **Lucky Luke** (5). Morris' Western parody first came out in 1946 and, even these days, Lucky Luke still shoots quicker than his shadow.

Retrace your steps to Rue de la Senne, turn left and continue to Rue du Petit Rempart for one of the best murals in the series, **La Marque Jaune** (6). Here, Edgar P Jacobs' heroes, Blake and Mortimer, are in London solving the case of the stolen royal crown. In the afternoon, this bright mural is in full sun and brings life to a somewhat down-at-heel neighbourhood.

Take Rue d'Anderlecht and then turn right into Rue de la Verdure. Follow it for three blocks until you're greeted by **Isabelle** (7; by Willy Maltaite aka Will), a little red-headed girl pictured with the beguiling Calendula, a witch, and Ursula, the fearless aunt.

At Blvd Maurice Lemonnier, turn left and, should you wish, get sidetracked in **Pêle Mêle** (8), a second-hand bookshop at Blvd Maurice Lemonnier 55, which has a decent section on comics.

Cross over Blvd Maurice Lemonnier and continue north up it through Place Fontainas and turn

---

building, a former department store and Art Nouveau showpiece. Built in 1899 by Paul Saintenoy for an English company, the building's predominantly black facade is a swirl of wrought iron and arched windows. Though empty for many years, it miraculously escaped demolition and, in June 2000, metamorphosed into this wonderful museum.

The museum has some 7000 instruments but only about a quarter are on display. The collection covers instruments from around the world but Europe is the strong point. State-of-the-art technology means you get to hear many of the instruments through personal headsets as you wander around.

It opens 9.30 am to 5 pm Tuesday, Wednesday and Friday, until 8 pm on Thursday, and 10 am to 5 pm at the weekend. Admission costs €3.71 (children €1.23,

Murals of Brussels

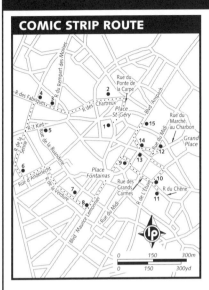

COMIC STRIP ROUTE

right into pedestrianised Rue du Bon Secours and **Ric Hochet** (9) by Tibet. You can tell by the clothes that this comic series, about the adventures of a dashing journalist-cum-sportsman, dates to the mid-1950s.

Turn right then immediately left into Rue des Grands Carmes, which leads past **Manneken Pis** (10) and to the colourful **Olivier Rameau** (11), half way up Rue du Chêne. This strip, by Dany, shows Alice being invited into Rameau's world of marvels; interestingly, a nearby shop sells fireworks.

Backtrack and turn right into Rue de l'Étuve, take the first left into Rue du Lombard then the first right to bring you to the junction of Rue du Midi and Rue du Marché au Charbon. Looming in a dark corner at Rue du Marché au Charbon 60 is **Le Passage** (12) by François Schuiten, arguably Belgium's best-known contemporary comic artist. This narrow strip is a scene from *Brüsel*, part of his famous *Les Cités Obscures* series from 1982. It invites you to wander into a city of the future, or past, when Brussels had many hidden quarters and dead-end alleys.

Head back towards Blvd Anspach and you'll soon see the suave **Victor Sackville** (13). Francis Carin started this ongoing series in 1985; it's about an English spy who travels through Europe during WWI.

At this point, turn around to see **Broussaille** (14) by Frank Pé. This mural was painted in 1991 and was the city's first; it depicts a young couple arm-in-arm discovering Brussels. Interestingly, this strip is located in Brussels' gay nightlife hub and, in the original version, it was difficult to tell whether the couple was gay or not. Gay establishments used the mural to promote their quarter until 1999 when the mural was repainted and the figure with the black hair was given a more feminine hairstyle, earrings and (slightly) bigger breasts!

Follow Plattesteen to Blvd Anspach, turn right and two blocks along at No 100 you'll find **Brüsel** (15), one of two shops in the city devoted entirely to comics. Happy browsing!

The Marolles neighbourhood also has quite a few murals – you'll find these marked on Map 6.

---

seniors and students €2.47). It's free on the first Wednesday of the month after 1 pm.

Musées Royaux des Beaux-Arts

The Royal Museums of Fine Arts (☎ 02-508 32 11) is actually a single museum divided into two sections – the Musée d'Art Ancien and the adjoining Musée d'Art Moderne. It has two entrances – at Place Royale 1 and Rue de la Régence 3. If you wish to work your way chronologically through the paintings, it's best to enter through the latter.

The museum houses Belgium's premier collections of ancient and modern art and is particularly well endowed with works by Pieter Breugel the Elder, Rubens and the Belgian Surrealists. You can visit its Web site at www.fine-arts-museum.be.

Both sections are large and you'll need a good day here if you want to do them justice.

The Breugel Family

The Breugels dominated Flemish art in the latter half of the tumultuous 16th century and early into the next. The family comprised Pieter Breugel the Elder (around 1525–69) and his two sons, Pieter the Younger and Jan. There's some confusion in art circles over the spelling of their names – Breugel the Elder is believed to have dropped the 'h' from his name, but both sons retained it. Other variations are Bruegel/Brueghel.

No matter how you spell it, Breugel the Elder was undeniably the family's master. His work ranged from powerful drawings of the Alps, produced during a two-year visit to Italy early in his career, to macabre, satirical allegories likened to the work of Hieronymus Bosch who was active in the art world half a century earlier. But it's for his quirky scenes of contemporary peasant life, woven around portentous religious events and myths, that Breugel the Elder is best remembered.

After marrying the daughter of Pieter Coecke van Aelst, an Antwerp artist to whom he'd been apprenticed, Breugel moved to Brussels and lived on the edge of the Marolles district (the house is now the Musée Breugel), where he painted some of his best works.

His first son, Pieter the Younger, largely copied his father's style but later earned the nickname 'Hell Breughel' for his preoccupation with scenes of damnation. Jan Breughel spent most of his artistic life in Antwerp and was a colleague of Rubens. His sensitive paintings of landscapes and flowers led to his sobriquet of 'Velvet'.

The best place to see works by Breugel the Elder is Vienna's Kunsthistorisches Museum. In Belgium you'll have to be content with the excellent collection of family works in Brussels' Musées Royaux des Beaux-Arts as well as the smaller collection at the Museum Mayer Van den Bergh in Antwerp.

A free colour-coded map of the museum is provided by the cashiers. If you plan your visit for a Wednesday, you may be able to use the lunchtime concert (€4.95) held in the Musée d'Art Ancien at 12.40 pm as a break between the two sections.

From the main hall you walk up to the **Musée d'Art Ancien**. Paintings from the 15th and 16th centuries (blue route) start with the Flemish Primitives and include works by Rogier Van der Weyden, Dirk Bouts, Hans Memling and, in Room 21, Gerard David, who is considered to be the last artist of this period. Room 22 moves onto Quinten Matsijs, whose works demonstrate a turning point in Flemish art as traditional realistic scenes were gradually dropped in favour of the more flamboyant Renaissance style imported from Italy.

Room 31 is devoted to paintings by the Breugel family, in particular Pieter Breugel the Elder. The mysterious *Fall of Icarus* is one of his most famous works, although *De Volkstelling* (The Census at Bethlehem, painted in 1566) is more typical of his distinctive peasant scenes. *The Fall of the Rebel Angels* (1562) is characteristic of his gruesome religious allegories.

Up on the next level are works from the 17th and 18th centuries (brown route). Magnificent paintings by Rubens are the prime attractions here. Room 52 is devoted to portraits and small, engaging sketches (such as *Studies of a Negro's Head*), while Room 62 holds gigantic masterpieces, including the acclaimed *Adoration of the Magi* and the moving *Ascent to Calvary*. Jordaens, one of Rubens' contemporaries, is well represented in Room 57.

Descend to the main hall and take the escalators down to level -2 and the entrance to the **Musée d'Art Moderne**. This gallery has two parts – the somewhat dull 19th-century section (yellow route; often closed at the weekend), which begins at level -2 and rises for five storeys, and 20th-century art (the green route), which occupies a subterranean gallery that meanders for another six levels below ground.

A few 19th-century highlights to watch

out for are sculptures by Constantin Meunier and Ensor's macabre fighting skeletons.

However, it's the 20th century that draws most of the attention, particularly the work of Belgian Surrealists René Magritte (on level -6) and Paul Delvaux (level -5). Other national artists include Léon Spilliaert and Rik Wouters, both of whom belonged to the Fauve group of painters. Works by artists from the Jeune Peinture Belge group – such as Gaston Bertrand, Anne Bonnet and Louis Van Lint – can also be seen on level -6. The international scene is much less extensive but look out for Francis Bacon's delightful *Le Pape aux Hiboux* (Pope with Owls) near the start.

The museums' opening hours vary from section to section – some sections close for lunch at noon, others at 1 pm. Basically the opening hours are 10 am to noon or 1 pm and 1 or 2 to 5 pm daily (except Monday). Admission costs €4.95 (students €3.47), but is free after 1 pm on the first Wednesday of the month. To get there use Parc metro station or take tram No 92, 93 or 94.

Église St Jacques sur Coudenberg

This graceful neoclassical church on Place Royale was built in 1775. It resembles a Roman temple, which explains why the French turned it into a Temple of Reason and later a Temple of Law during their reign. In 1802 it reverted to being a Catholic church. The interior is impressively light and airy. The church opens 10 am to 5 pm Tuesday to Saturday.

NORTH OF PLACE ROYALE (MAP 4)

Palais Royal

The Royal Palace at Place des Palais overlooks the southern end of the Parc de Bruxelles. The 19th-century palace is a long, low, cream-toned building that commands little attention these days as it no longer houses the royal family (since the death of Queen Astrid, wife of Léopold III, Belgium's monarchs have lived at Laeken, though the Palais Royal is still their official residence).

It stands on the site of the former palace of the dukes of Brabant, which was razed in 1731. Two mansions were subsequently built and these were converted into a residence by William I, ruler of Belgium and the Netherlands, in the early 19th century. In 1862 King Léopold II, the monarch responsible for many of Brussels' gargantuan monuments, extended it.

The palace opens for visits 10.30 am to 4.30 pm Tuesday to Sunday, from the end of July to early September. Admission is free.

Musée de la Dynastie

Next to the Palais Royal is the Dynasty Museum (☎ 02-502 25 41). The plush apartment rooms house a dreary dynastic history of Belgium since independence, as well as a captivating memorial to King Baudouin. An English-language audio guide (lasting 1½ hours) is available. The museum opens from 10 am to 6 pm daily (except Monday); admission costs €6.20 (students €5).

Parc de Bruxelles

Brussels' largest central patch of greenery is the Parc de Bruxelles (metro Parc), an old, formal park flanked by the Palais Royal and the Palais de la Nation (Belgium's parliament). The park was the site of a poultry yard in the 11th century and was formerly laid out under the dukes of Brabant. It's dotted with classical statues and is framed by trees whose branches have been mercilessly trellised. For more information on parks in and around Brussels, pick up the *Discovering Brussels Through its Green Areas* booklet from the tourist office.

Musée du Cinéma

The Cinema Museum (☎ 02-507 83 70), inside the Palais des Beaux-Arts at Rue Baron Horta 9, has a small permanent exhibition dedicated to the evolution of movie-making. However, the museum's main focus is screening classic and silent movies (for details see under Cinemas in the Entertainment section later in the chapter). It opens 5.30 to 10.30 pm; admission is included in the price of a movie ticket.

Musée Charlier

The Charlier Museum (☎ 02-218 53 82, metro Madou) at Ave des Arts 16 is a splendid collection of decorative and applied arts. It's named after Guillaume Charlier, a 19th-century Brussels sculptor who lived in this town house for a time, and is packed with antique furniture, Flemish tapestries and works of art. The museum opens 10 am to 5 pm on Monday and 1.30 to 5 pm Tuesday to Friday. Admission costs €2.47.

Colonne du Congrès

The Congress Column on Place du Congrès was erected in 1850 to commemorate the National Congress of 1831, which proclaimed the Belgian constitution. It was designed by Joseph Poelaert, soars 25m high and is crowned by a statue of Léopold I. At its base burns the eternal flame, a homage to the Belgians who died during WWI and WWII. Though at a good elevation, the view from this square is quite drab.

To get to the column head for Botanique or Madou metro station, or take bus No 29 or 63.

SOUTH OF PLACE ROYALE (MAP 6)
Église Notre Dame du Sablon

Flamboyant Gothic is the style of this large but somewhat gloomy church at Rue de la Régence 3 bis, just down the road from the Musées Royaux des Beaux-Arts. It began as a chapel, built by the archers' guild in the 13th century, but was enlarged in the 15th century when pilgrims descended in droves following the arrival here of a small statue of the Madonna reputed to have healing powers. The statue has long since gone and the inside is now best noted for its 11 impressive stained-glass windows and the chapel of the local Tour et Tassis family, who founded Belgium's postal service. The church opens 9 am to 6 pm weekdays (from 10 am at the weekend).

Place du Petit Sablon

About 200m uphill from Place du Grand Sablon, this charming little garden is framed by 48 bronze statuettes depicting the medieval guilds. At its heart is a monument to counts Egmont and Hoorn, who were beheaded on Grand Place in 1568 for defying Spanish rule.

Palais de Justice

This colossal law court (☎ 02-508 65 78, metro Louise) on Place Poelaert was one of Léopold II's most stupendous projects. Larger than St Peter's in Rome, it was purposely sited on a hill above the working-class Marolles area as a symbol of law and order. Its design, based on ancient Egyptian temple architecture, is equally intimidating. It was created by the architect Joseph Poelaert, who died during its construction in 1879; legend has it he was struck by illness brought on by witchcraft attributed to the many residents who were evicted to make way for the building.

It's possible to go inside from 9 am to 3 pm on weekdays; admission is free. From the nearby viewing platform there's a good view over northern Brussels.

EU AREA (MAP 7)

The EU area is bordered by the Petit Ring to the west and Parc du Cinquantenaire to the east. Totally abandoned at the weekend, it comes to life on weekdays when it takes on a very business-as-usual air. Although it's not a district for idle wandering, the area does offer some interesting sights, including Art Nouveau houses, museums and the European Parliament building (see the boxed text 'The EU in Brussels' later).

Art Nouveau Architecture

Dotted around the EU area are superb Art Nouveau buildings including:

Maison St-Cyr (Square Ambiorix 11, metro Schuman) The narrow facade of this building (now privately-owned flats) is an extravagance of knotted and twisted ironwork. It was built in 1903 for the painter Léonard St-Cyr by Gustave Strauven (1878–1919), who worked as an apprentice to Horta and also built Art Nouveau houses in Schaerbeek.

Hôtel Van Eetvelde (Ave Palmerston 2–4, metro Schuman) While the outside of this building is unusual, the interior is a Horta masterpiece

(1895–1901). It was commissioned by Baron Van Eetvelde, Minister for the Congo at that time and the country's highest paid civil servant. Exotic timbers stud the interior, which has a central glass dome infused with African-inspired plant motifs. It's now owned by a gas company, and admission is limited to ARAU tours (see the Organised Tours section earlier in the chapter).

Maison Cauchie (☎ 02-673 15 06, Rue des Francs 5, metro Mérode) Built in 1905, this stunning house was the home of architect and painter Paul Cauchie (1875–1952) and its sgraffito facade, adorned with graceful female figures, is one of the most beautiful in Brussels. A petition saved the house from demolition in 1971 and since 1975 it has been a protected monument. Bought and restored by Guy Dessicy, founder of the Centre Belge de la Bande Dessinée, it's worth trying to time a visit to the first Saturday or Sunday of the month, when the house opens to visitors (from 11 am to 6 pm; admission costs €3.70). If that's not possible, the facade alone warrants a visit.

Musée des Sciences Naturelles de Belgique

The excellent Museum of Natural Sciences (☎ 02-627 42 38), Rue Vautier 29, is a large complex on a hillock overlooking Parc Léopold. The superb collection spans several floors; however, the star attractions are the fossilised skeletons of 29 iguanodons – two-legged, 10m-high dinosaurs that lived 135 million years ago – found in a coal mine in Bernissart, a village near Mons, in 1878.

The museum opens 9.30 am to 4.45 pm Tuesday to Saturday and 9.30 am to 6 pm on Sunday. Admission costs €3.72 (students €2.47); it's free after 1 pm on the first Wednesday of the month. To get there take bus No 34 or 80.

Musée Antoine Wiertz

This museum (☎ 02-648 17 18), Rue Vautier 62, is just down the road from the Natural Science Museum and a stone's throw from the European Parliament. If you're into the shocking or nasty, it may appeal. Antoine Wiertz was a 19th-century Brussels artist bent on painting giant religious canvases depicting hell and other frenzied subjects. The building was Wiertz's home and studio.

The museum opens 10 am to noon and 1 to 5 pm Tuesday to Friday and alternate weekends. Admission is free. To get there take bus No 34 or 38.

Parc du Cinquantenaire

Cinquantenaire (metro Mérode) is a large park built by Léopold II. It borders the EU quarter at the end of Rue de la Loi and Rue Belliard and has one of the city's many road tunnels running beneath it. It's best known for its cluster of museums – art, history, military and motor vehicles – and the massive Arcade du Cinquantenaire, which rises majestically from its eastern end.

Arcade du Cinquantenaire This triumphal arch and the two monumental buildings it connects were built by Léopold II to host an exhibition in 1880 celebrating the 50th anniversary of Belgian independence (although the arch wasn't finished until 1904). The vast complex reflects the rich and expansive mood that permeated Belgium at that time. In summer, the area is put to good use with a popular drive-in cinema (see Cinemas under Entertainment later in the chapter for more details).

Musées Royaux d'Art et d'Histoire The Royal Art and History Museums (☎ 02-741 72 11) in the southern wing of the Cinquantenaire buildings are chock-a-block with antiquities from all over the world. Unfortunately, all labelling is in French and Flemish only, but an English-language booklet is available for €4.46.

The museums open 9.30 am to 5 pm Tuesday to Sunday. Admission costs €3.70 (students €2.50); it's free after 1 pm on the first Wednesday of the month.

Musée Royale de l'Armée et d'Histoire Militaire The Royal Museum of Army and Military History (☎ 02-737 78 11) occupies the vast northern wing of the Cinquantenaire complex. This huge museum was opened nearly a century ago and boasts a staggering collection of all things military dating back to Belgian independence. Most spectacular are the galleries of

The EU in Brussels

The capital of Europe...that's Brussels' big boast and it's all thanks to its position as the headquarters of the European Union (EU). The EU is an economic and political union that was formally established by the Maastricht Treaty in 1993. At present it is made up of 15 countries stretching from the Arctic Circle to the Mediterranean Sea. About 370 million people, or 8% of the world's population, live within the EU. A dozen other nations – mainly Eastern European countries such the Czech Republic, Latvia and Romania – are currently negotiating to join the EU. The first of these countries could do so by 2003–4.

As the capital of this international union, Brussels has, of course, fared well. Multinationals, foreign companies and international agencies have been lured to base themselves here and parts of the city are now full of Eurocrats, bureaucrats, corporate lawyers, lobbyists, interpreters and journalists, all bent on working, manipulating, watching or reporting the political goings on. All this, of course, has a knock-on effect of creating local jobs, particularly in the hotel and hospitality industries.

On the flip side, there are also plenty of Eurosceptics who lament the EU's excesses (the European Parliament building cost US$1.6 billion but its debating chamber is used for just a few weeks each year), and complain about the high salaries paid to EU civil servants and the size of the bureaucracy that runs the show. EU institutions employ about 27,000 people, of which 18,000 work in Brussels for the European Commission, the EU's executive arm. The average Belgian, too, feels far removed from all the EU hype and there are those who resent the fact that the Quartier Léopold, a residential suburb with distinctive townhouses, has been largely demolished to make way for this real-life Gotham City.

The EU area (Map 7) lies to the east of the city centre. The two main thoroughfares – Rue de la Loi and Rue Belliard – are lined with ugly EU and government offices and are always bellowing with traffic. Parts of the district are derelict construction sites while other areas are being claimed for further EU expansion.

As a visitor, there's little to see and the area is not visually appealing. The most famous building is the four-winged **Berlaymont** at Rond-Point Schuman (metro Schuman). Built in 1967, it was the European Commission's bustling headquarters until 1991 when it was evacuated after asbestos started leaking from the building. Work to remove the 1400 tonnes of hazardous material has been going on for years, and for a long time the building was a ghost of its former self, all draped in white like a Christo piece of art. The commission staff now work in various buildings around the city but

---

tanks, planes and armoured cars. For something different, take the elevator to the top floor, where an outside balcony affords good city views.

The museum opens 9 am to noon and 1 to 4.45 pm Tuesday to Sunday; admission is free.

Autoworld As its name suggests, Autoworld (☎ 02-736 41 65) has a huge collection of vintage cars, both local and international. With over 400 vehicles on display, it's one of the biggest such ensembles in Europe.

Autoworld opens 10 am to 5 or 6 pm

daily and admission costs €4.95 (students €3.70).

IXELLES & ST GILLES
Musée Horta (Map 6)

This museum (☎ 02-543 04 90), Rue Américaine 25 in St Gilles, occupies the two adjoining Art Nouveau houses that Victor Horta designed and built between 1898 and 1901 and is where he lived until 1919 (for more on Horta see the Art Nouveau in Brussels special section).

From the outside, the most noticeable thing is usually the queue of people waiting to get in. In typical Horta style it is the in-

The EU in Brussels

should move back in once the Berlaymont is habitable (expected to be at the end of 2002).

Opposite the Berlaymont is the headquarters of the **Council of the European Union** (also known as the Council of Ministers), a pink granite building at Rue de la Loi 175. The council is the EU's main decision-making body and must approve all EU laws. It moved into this building in 1995 and has already outgrown its new premises.

The distinctive domed **European Parliament** building, Rue Wiertz 43, sits next to Parc Léopold to the south-west of Rond-Point Schuman. Opened in 1998 by King Albert II, it's all steel and blue glass and is nicknamed 'Caprice des Dieux' (Whim of the Gods) as it's shaped like a French cheese of that name. The European Parliament is the legislative branch of the EU and elections for the 626 members are held every five years (the next will be in 2005). It is the only EU institution that meets and debates in public.

It's possible to sit in on a parliamentary session in the visitor's gallery of the parliament's huge debating chamber, known as the hemicycle, or to simply tour the hemicycle when parliament is not meeting. Free tours, using multilingual headphones, are held at 10 am and 3 pm Monday to Thursday, 10 am Friday, and 10 and 11.30 am and 2.30 pm Saturday. Tours start at the visitors centre (Map 7; ☎ 02-284 34 57), which is attached to the Paul-Henri Spaak section of the parliament building. Incidentally, this section is named after Belgium's most famous statesman, Paul-Henri Spaak (1899–1972) who is remembered as 'Mr Europe' for his tireless efforts in creating a united Europe.

The easiest way to get to the European Parliament from central Brussels is with bus No 38 (direction Homborch; it departs every 15 minutes from next to Gare Centrale) to the stop De Meeus on Rue du Luxembourg. From this street you get a good view of the parliament building's blue dome and the contrast between the new (it) and the old (Gare du Luxembourg – this ornamental building is the oldest standing train station in Belgium and is currently threatened due to plans to expand the parliamentary complex). Pass through Gare du Luxembourg and cross the concrete mess behind it to arrive at the Info Point. The Paul-Henri Spaak entrance is now directly in front of you (at the end of the covered passageway) and the visitors centre is down to your left.

Everywhere in Brussels – in shops, on car licence plates, on buildings, T-shirts and umbrellas – you'll see a dark blue flag featuring a circle of 12 five-pointed gold stars. It's the EU flag. It was originally designed for the Council of Europe (an intergovernmental organisation that is not part of the EU) in the early 1950s and was adopted by the European Commission in 1985.

---

side that tells the story. There are airy rooms radiating from an iron-laced staircase, mirrored cabinets, glorious timber panelling, intimate stained-glass inlays and even curled door-handles. A new basement section holds a model of Horta's famous Maison de Peuple (now demolished; the wrought iron staircase leading to the basement was saved from that building).

Unfortunately, all this splendour dims somewhat when it's too crowded: time your visit for a weekday. It opens 2 to 5.30 pm Tuesday to Sunday; admission costs €3.70/5 on weekdays/weekends. To get there take tram No 91 or 92 from Place Louise.

Other Art Nouveau Architecture (Map 6)

Ixelles and St Gilles hold the city's greatest concentration of Art Nouveau buildings and it was here that Horta and Hankar, one of Horta's contemporaries, first introduced the style. Some highlights include:

Hôtel Solvay (Ave Louise 224) Horta designed this in 1894 at the age of 33 and it is considered his best work. It was commissioned by the Solvay family, prominent industrialists (see under Science in the Facts about the Cities chapter) who gave him free rein in matters of design and budget. The outside is studded with Art Nouveau elements – note the caramel-toned

Art Nouveau Walking Tour

The following walking tour takes in Art Nouveau buildings in two districts – the EU area (Map 7) and the adjoining neighbourhoods of Ixelles and St Gilles (Map 6). It covers the most famous works as well as beautiful and interesting buildings by lesser known architects. For more details on each building refer to the main entry in the text.

The whole tour can be done in about four hours (not including a stop for lunch or time spent inside the few buildings that are open to the public). If you start in the morning (around 9.30 am), the sun should be shining on some of the most beautiful facades as you reach them, you'll be in time for lunch in one of the restaurants, cafes or sandwich bars around Rue du Bailli in Ixelles, and you will find the Musée Horta and Hôtel Hannon open by the time you arrive (note, both are closed on Monday and Hôtel Hannon is also closed at the weekend). Public transport has been incorporated into the tour when necessary (a one-day pass will stand you well).

For a shorter version of the tour (roughly one hour), pick it up at Hôtel Solvay (tram Nos 93 or 94 from Place Louise to tram stop Lebroussart) but note that by starting here you'll miss some of the most beautiful facades.

From Gare Centrale, take bus #63 (direction Maes) to the stop Ambiorix on Square Ambiorix in the EU area (Map 7). Cross the square to the **Maison St-Cyr** at Square Ambiorix 11. Head west along the road, noting the ceramic tiles of Villa Germaine at Ave Palmerston 24, until you reach Horta's **Hôtel Van Eetvelde** at Ave Palmerston 4.

Return to Square Ambiorix and cross it to Ave Michel-Ange where you'll pass a lovely **stained-glass window** depicting an egret adorning the doorway at No 64. Continue to the circular mosque at the north-western corner of Parc du Cinquaintenaire. Cross round to the left of the mosque where there's a gate into the park. Walk through the park and under the Arcade du Cinquintenaire. Cut through the gardens on your right, exiting at Rue des Francs where the grey-and-gold facade of Paul Cauchie's **Maison Cauchie** is immediately visible on the other side of Ave des Gaulois. This is the end of the EU section of the tour.

From Maison Cauchie, head east along Ave des Gaulois to Merode metro station and take the metro (either line 1A direction Roi Baudouin or line 1B direction Bizet) to the stop Parc. Exit the metro station and cross diagonally to the tram stop on Rue Royale. Take tram No 93 (direction Marie-José) or No 94 (direction Wiener) for nine stops to the stop Vleurgat.

Cross Ave Louise and continue south to Rick's, a bar/restaurant whose outback courtyard affords a good view of the curved windows of Horta's **Hotel Hallet**, Ave Louise 346. Ask the publican if you can take a peek – they generally don't mind. At the time of writing, Hôtel Hallet (built 1902)

wrought-iron, the swirling street number and curvaceous doorbell – and is worth a look. As for seeing the inside, you'll have to part with €450 (that's the price for a one-hour visit for a maximum of 20 people) to gain entrance. Ask at the TIB if you're interested.

Hôtel Tassel (Rue Paul Émile Janson 6) The Hôtel Tassel (1893) is another of those gems that only a few ever see. It's the office of an architect firm and even ARAU rarely gets permission to take visitors inside the building that got the Art Nouveau ball rolling. The facade is quite conservative but inside Horta let loose with his whiplash effect, or 'Horta line', that embraces the floors, walls and ceilings.

Maison Hankar (Rue Defacqz 71) Together with the nearby Hôtel Tassel, this was one of the first Art Nouveau houses in Brussels, built by Paul Hankar for himself in 1893. He employed red brick – a colour not often seen in buildings of this style – and sgraffito was used at the top in the three little panels entitled *jour* (day), *soir* (evening) and *nuit* (night).

Hôtel Hannon (☎ 02-538 42 20, Ave de la Jonction 1) This lovely building, with its stained glass and external stone frieze, was designed in 1902 by Jules Brunfaut. It's now a photography gallery, Espace Photographique Contretype, and is one of the few Art Nouveau buildings that is readily accessible to the public.

Art Nouveau Walking Tour

was in the throes of much-needed restoration, but it's worth a look anyway.

Make your way north now to two groups of houses designed by Antoine Blérot. The first two, at **Rue Vilain XIV 9 and 11**, are noted for their sgraffito and are signed and dated (1902) by Blérot. The other pair, with excessive wrought-iron railings, is round the corner at **Ave du Général de Gaulle 38 and 39**, overlooking the Étangs d'Ixelles (Ixelles Ponds). Blérot's own home stood between these two groups until it was destroyed in the 1960s. A prolific builder with great imagination, Blérot designed 40 houses all up, each externally different from the next.

Continue to **Rue du Lac 6**, one of 11 houses in this area designed by Ernest De Lune. It has a fantastically tall stained-glass window and a lovely 2nd-floor balcony. Rejoin Ave Louise and follow it northwards to Horta's **Hôtel Solvay** at Ave Louise 224.

Cross Ave Louise to arrive at **Hôtel Tassel**, Rue Paul Émile Janson 6. Now weave your way past two houses by Paul Hankar. The first, the large **Maison Camberlaini** at Rue Defacqz 48, is rather dilapidated. The second, **Maison Hankar**, is at Rue Defacqz 71. Backtrack to the junction with Rue Faider and turn right into it for Albert Roosenboom's creation at **Rue Faider 83**, which has simple Art Nouveau tones, including a beautiful, gilded sgraffito design at the top. Roosenboom also signed this house.

Continue south along this road to Rue du Bailli, a good area for a pit stop. Follow Rue du Bailli westwards to Église des Augustins (the baroque facade of this church dates to 1620 and originally stood on Place de Brouckère in central Brussels) and go round to **Rue Africaine 92**, designed by De Lestrée in 1903. It has creamy tones and harmonious lines plus a big circular window, a favoured feature of many Art Nouveau houses. From here it's a short walk to the **Musée Horta** at Rue Américaine 25.

The tour's last two houses are two (big) blocks south down Chaussée de Charleroi. Jules Brunfaut's **Hôtel Hannon** is at Ave de la Jonction 1. Close by is the **Clinique Van Neck** at Rue Wafelaerts 53, the last Art Nouveau house to be built in Brussels. It was designed by Antoine Pompe in 1910 (his name and the date can just be made out to the left of the door) as a clinic for Doctor Van Neck. It's all very straight and the wrought-iron has few embellishments, making it a good example of the transition which was taking place from Art Nouveau to Art Deco.

From here, walk back to the tram stop Ma Campagne at the intersection of Chaussée de Charleroi and Chaussée de Waterloo to take tram No 92 (direction Ste Marie) back to town. Alternatively, stay on this tram until it reaches **De Ultieme Hallucinatie** (Map 4; tram stop Gillon), Rue Royale 316, and finish the tour with a drink in one of Brussels' most famous Art Nouveau cafes.

It opens 1 to 6 pm Tuesday to Sunday; admission costs €2.50; tram No 92 stops nearby.

Porte de Hal (Map 6)

The mighty Porte de Hal on Blvd du Midi marks the southernmost point of the Petit Ring. This sturdy tower is the sole remaining medieval gate (extensively renovated in the 18th century) of the seven that made up the city's second perimeter wall. When the other gates were demolished at the end of the 18th century, Porte de Hal was spared as it was being used as a prison.

Musée Constantin Meunier (Map 3)

This intimate museum (☎ 02-508 32 11), Rue de l'Abbaye 59, is in the southern part of Ixelles. Constantin Meunier (1831–1905) was a Brussels-born artist who is best known for his bronze sculptures. The museum occupies the town house where he lived and worked for the last few years of his life. Meunier was a social realist and his art was fed by his concern for the plight of the working classes. Heavy and dark, his work typically depicted the harsh conditions under which coal miners or dock workers toiled, and his larger-than-life bronzes are emotive and heroic. The museum opens 10 am to noon and 1 to 5 pm Tuesday to Friday, and alternate weekends. Admission is free. To get there take tram No 93 or 94.

Musée Communal d'Ixelles (Map 6)

The Ixelles Museum (☎ 02-511 90 84) at Rue Van Volsem 71 has a small but engaging collection of modern Belgian and French art. It covers most of the 19th- and 20th-century movements and features works by Magritte and Delvaux. The museum opens from 1 to 6.30 pm Tuesday to Friday and 10 am to 5 pm at the weekend; admission is free. Take tram No 81 or 82 to get there.

Bois de la Cambre (Map 3)

This forest separates Ixelles and Uccle and is named after the Abbaye de la Cambre, a former 12th-century convent. The park was established in 1862 and joins the much larger Forêt de Soignes (see the Excursions section later in the chapter). Tram Nos 93 and 94 from Place Louise stop close by.

UCCLE
Musée David et Alice Van Buuren (Map 3)

This exquisite little museum (☎ 02-343 48 51) at Ave L Errera 41 is located in the former house of Dutch banker David Van Buuren, a wealthy collector and patron of the arts who built this Art Deco showpiece in 1928. Five rooms are open to the public and are crammed with ancient paintings, sublime furnishings, stained glass and carpets (the meticulous staff ensure plastic shoe-coverings are donned before entering).

The museum opens 1 to 6 pm on Sunday and 2 to 6 pm on Monday. Admission costs a hefty €7.43 (students €4.95). To get there take tram No 23 or 90.

ST JOSSE & SCHAERBEEK
Le Botanique (Map 4)

Le Botanique (☎ 02-218 79 35, metro Botanique), at Rue Royale 236 on the edge of St Josse, is the cultural centre of Brus-

sels' French-speaking community (and hence is also known as the Centre Culturel de la Communauté Française). The impressive neoclassical glass building dates back to 1826 and originally housed the city's botanical garden. These days it supports a solid program of cultural events, including theatre, exhibitions and concerts.

Halles de Schaerbeek (Map 4)

This former food market, Rue Royale Ste Marie 22a, is just past Église Ste Marie in the southern part of Schaerbeek. Built in 1901, it is one of the city's few examples of industrial architecture and has recently been restored as a venue for the performing arts. Tram Nos 92 and 93 go there.

LAEKEN (MAP 8)
Domaine Royal & Parc de Laeken

The Domaine Royal, or royal estate, is the home of Belgium's ruling family. It spreads out to the east of Ave du Parc Royal and the main building, the Château Royal de Laeken, is occupied by Prince Philippe and Princess Mathilde. On the opposite side of the road is Parc de Laeken, a partly private, partly public park that stretches to the Atomium. In this park is the Villa Belvédère, home of King Albert II and Queen Paola, while the former queen, Fabiola (the widow of King Baudouin), inhabits nearby Château Stuyvenbergh. All the chateaux are out of bounds to tourists, but the nearby Serres Royales, the Pavillon Chinois and the Tour Japonaise can all be visited, as can the park's focal point, a statue of Léopold I erected in 1880.

Serres Royales These enormous royal greenhouses at Ave du Parc Royal 61 were built by Alphonse Balat (Horta's teacher) during the reign of Léopold II. Fuchsias and all sorts of tropical species thrive inside and people come from all over Belgium to see them during the 10 days each year (between the end of April and early May) that the greenhouses are open to the public. Expect formidable queues.

[continued on page 113]

ART NOUVEAU IN BRUSSELS

Art Nouveau was a brilliant, albeit brief, decorative art and architectural movement that shattered historicism in art and ushered in a new style throughout parts of Europe at the end of the 19th century. It swept through several European cities, among them Paris, Barcelona, Vienna, Glasgow and Brussels, and went under several names, including 'Liberty Style', 'Jugendstil' and, in Belgium, 'Art Nouveau'.

The movement's most visible form was architecture, and everything from department stores and schools to shops and private homes came under its influence. However, it was more versatile than just architecture and almost nothing in the realm of decorative arts escaped its touch. Banisters and beds, cupboards and cutlery, door handles and jewellery were all moulded along Art Nouveau lines. In Brussels, the movement's leading exponent was Victor Horta, but other architects also played key roles, including Paul Hankar and Henry Van de Velde and, to a lesser degree, Antoine Blérot, Ernest De Lune, Gustave Strauven, Paul Saintenoy and Paul Cauchie.

Art Nouveau is characterised by its use of sinuous lines – organic tendrils, feminine curves and floral motifs were all radically used to break free of the restrictive classical styles. Architects and designers seized on the shapes of nature and favoured the use of steel (the 19th century's most recent invention), glass and exotic timbers. Intricate wrought-iron balconies, round windows, frescos and sgraffito (an incised mural or ceramic decoration) were employed in combination to give buildings a hallucinogenic look. One Art Nouveau cafe in Brussels is now even named De Ultieme Hallucinatie (The Ultimate Hallucination).

But it wasn't only about facades. Horta preferred buildings that were relatively plain from the outside but overwhelmingly ornate

Title page: Detail of the stunning sgraffito facade of Maison Cauchie (photograph by Leanne Logan)

Left: The intricate detail used by Horta on the Hôtel Solvay is considered to be his finest work.

within. His Hôtel Solvay and Hôtel Van Eetvelde (*hôtel* here referring to a townhouse) are Brussels' best examples.

Art Nouveau architecture made its first appearance in Brussels in 1893. In this year Horta designed the Hôtel Tassel in Ixelles for Émile Tassel, a prosperous industrialist. At the same time, Paul Hankar built a unique house for his own use a few blocks away. In 1895, Henri Van de Velde built his home, the Villa Bloemenwerf, in Uccle.

From here the movement flourished, fed by a ballooning population. Between 1870 and 1910, Brussels' inhabitants rose from 250,000 to 800,000 and, due to the wealth pouring in from industry and the Congo, a middle class emerged. This bourgeoisie wanted new homes and, while conventional types chose villas in outlying suburbs or large terraced townhouses, independent thinkers opted for Art Nouveau, a style that was able to express their individuality. Indeed, it was the wealth of a relatively small number of generous, progressive-thinking patrons that supported the movement.

So too did the current political climate. At the time the nation was dominated by the Catholic conservatives and, by the mid-1880s, political discontent was high. Only a tiny fraction of the population was eligible to vote and, following workers riots in many cities, the Belgian Socialist Party led a successful campaign to gain universal male suffrage, introduced in 1893. Unusual for its time, the Socialist Party encouraged the artistic avant-garde and, with building having become an ideological means of expression, many Socialists and Liberals chose Art Nouveau.

As quickly as it flowered, Art Nouveau fell out of fashion. Brussels' last building, a doctor's clinic designed by Antoine Pompe, was completed in 1910. Gone was the sensuous form that typified the style. In its place evolved the modern, clean-cut style of Art Deco.

Although Art Nouveau has at times been dismissed as bourgeois decorative excess, the movement also had a social vein. Horta, like many of his contemporaries, was committed to creating works for the people rather

Right: Every type of household object was subject to Art Nouveau design, as this curvaceous chair by Victor Horta testifies.

LEANNE LOGAN

than the bourgeoisie, though in most cases it was the latter who paid for their bread and butter.

The most famous public building of this era was the Maison du Peuple, commissioned by the Socialist Party and built by Horta from 1896–9 on Place Vandervelde, just below the Sablon. It was the party's headquarters and housed offices and a large meeting/entertainment hall. A daring glass-vaulted building, it featured all of Horta's trademarks, particularly his love of creating transparent places in which light was free to play. Sadly, the building was eventually abandoned and in 1965, amid an international outcry, it was torn down.

The Maison de Peuple was not the only Art Nouveau building to fall under the demolition ball. Until recently, the works of Horta and his contemporaries were disregarded in the capital. The private home of

LEANNE LOGAN

Left: The elegant Old England building has been given a new role housing the Musée des Instruments de Musique

EDWARD SNIDERS

Antoine Blérot, one of the city's most prolific Art Nouveau architects, was destroyed in 1964 and other buildings either disappeared or were threatened with destruction throughout the 1970s. Since then, the city has been severely criticised for failing to protect its architectural heritage.

Thankfully, where Art Nouveau buildings are concerned at any rate, those days have passed and most buildings of this genre in Brussels are now protected monuments. Two of the city's finest *fin-de-siècle* department stores, the Old England building and the Grand Magasin Waucquez, both in the heart of Brussels, have been superbly restored and now house acclaimed museums.

While the old city centre boasts some fine Art Nouveau examples, to really explore it's necessary to go farther afield, primarily to the neighbourhoods of Ixelles, St Gilles, the EU area and Schaerbeek.

Brussels' Department Stores

Art Nouveau's flowering helped the rise of a new type of commercial space – the department store. Although such shops predate Art Nouveau (Le Bon Marché, built in Paris in 1869, is generally considered to be the first), this new, versatile movement was well suited to provide equally versatile spaces for a burgeoning breed of shoppers. By using steel and glass, the architects were able to design exotic buildings with large windows that offered passers-by a view of the many enticing products inside. Once within, shoppers had a light and airy environment in which to browse and buy and, before long, 'window shopping' and shopping itself became a new leisure activity for the middle classes. Department stores often featured restrooms and many also had cafes.

Brussels' architects Victor Horta, Paul Saintenoy and Paul Hankar were all commissioned to design shops in the Art Nouveau style. The largest department store of the time was À l'Innovation, built on the city's main shopping thoroughfare, Rue Neuve, from 1900–3, and designed by Horta. The drab buildings that flanked it simply heightened, by their contrast, its attention-demanding facade. Unfortunately, À l'Innovation was destroyed by fire in 1967.

Two Art Nouveau department stores which do remain and which can still be visited today are the Grand Magasin Waucquez (now the Centre Belge de la Bande Dessinée) and the Old England building (now the Musée des Instruments de Musique). Details of both can be found in the Things to See & Do section of the Brussels chapter.

Top: Discrete Art Nouveau facades hide round every corner in Brussels, particulary in Ixelles and St Gilles.

Ixelles and adjoining St Gilles are known as the 'cradle of Art Nouveau', while the EU area has some of the city's most stunning facades. Schaerbeek also has some nice examples, but most of the houses are rundown and few visitors end up there.

Many Art Nouveau buildings are privately owned and are therefore closed to the general public. The only way to get inside some – such as Horta's famous Hôtel Van Eetvelde – is on a highly recommended guided tour conducted by the Atelier de Recherche et d'Action Urbaine, or ARAU (for details see under Organised Tours in the Getting Around section of the Brussels chapter). ARAU tours are, however, infrequent and you've got to be lucky to be in Brussels on the day one is running. Fortunately, many Art Nouveau buildings are enticing for their facades alone and can be enjoyed simply by wandering past. In the Brussels chapter you'll find a comprehensive walking tour that includes famous and little-known buildings in the EU area, Ixelles and St Gilles.

Horta and contemporaries

Victor Horta (1861–1947) pioneered a new concept of total design whereby everything – from the building itself to the furniture, wallpaper and door hinges – were designed in harmony with each other. Also central to his concept was the individuality of the house – the design must meet the needs and way of life of the client. Horta proudly exposed rather than concealed steel, and his work was known for its swirling ironwork, elaborate masonry and revolutionary use of natural light.

Top: The sinuous lines of Hôtel Solvay

Left: The use of elaborate stained glass, seen here at Blerot's La Porteuse d'Eau, is pure Art Nouveau.

Born in Ghent, Horta studied at the École des Beaux Arts in Brussels under Léopold II's architect, Alphonse Balat, who was responsible for designing the enormous royal greenhouses in Laeken and whose work was to influence Horta's love of steel and glass. But Balat was a traditionalist and the young Horta needed to look farther afield for more radical inspiration. He found it in the designs of William Morris, a leading member of the English Arts & Crafts movement that flourished just before Art Nouveau but busied itself with decorative arts rather than architecture.

Horta grasped this new style and worked it into architecture, shocking the architectural world with his Hôtel Tassel built in Ixelles in 1893. Balat is reported to have wept upon seeing it while French architect Hector Guimard quickly adapted Horta's revolutionary coiled line to make, among other things, the famous entrances to Paris' metro stations.

From here Horta entered his most productive period, designing over 40 buildings from private residences to department stores and public buildings during the next 12 years. The Hôtel Solvay and Hôtel Van Eetvelde are considered to be his masterpieces. After the Maison du Peuple he turned his talent to his own house at Rue Américaine (now the Musée Horta), then À l'Innovation department store (see the boxed text 'Brussels' Department Stores' earlier) followed by his final Art Nouveau building, the Grand Magasin Waucquez (now the Centre Belge de la Bande Dessinée). Horta's exile in England and the USA during WWI marked a transition in style – Art Nouveau's flowing form was replaced with the severe lines of Art Deco – and his bold Palais des Beaux-Arts (1922–8) – a multipurpose entertainment centre that is still used in Brussels today – is evidence of the change.

Another of the movement's leading figures was Paul Hankar (1859–1901). Hankar studied sculpture at the École des Beaux Arts in Brussels but in 1888 went into interior design. He too was strongly influenced by the English Arts & Crafts movement, and the interiors of some of the restaurants, galleries and many shops that he created had

Top: Horta designed his own home at Rue Américaine where he lived until 1919. It is now the Musée Horta.

elements similar to those of famous Glasgow designer Charles Rennie Mackintosh. The only surviving Hankar shop-front (Map 4; formerly a shirt-maker and now a florist) is at Rue Royale 13. Hankar died in January 1901 after a long illness that had slowed his activities for several years but his work influenced a generation of architects including Paul Hamesse and Antoine Pompe.

Henri Van de Velde (1863–1957) trained in Antwerp and Paris and was a painter before he turned his hand to architecture and decorative arts. Unlike Horta, he designed few houses – the best known is his own home, Villa Bloemenwerf, Vanderaeylaan 102 in Uccle; however, it's unexceptional from the outside and the public can't access it. Van de Velde concentrated on creating furniture, ceramics and jewellery and he also designed the Netherlands' famous Kröller-Müller museum. In 1901 he became artistic director of the Staatliches Bauhaus school of design in Weimar, a predecessor to Germany's Bauhaus school of functionalist architecture.

For details on specific Art Nouveau buildings in Brussels, see the Things to See & Do section of the Brussels chapter.

LEANNE LOGAN

Left: The predominant black facade of the Old England building is a swirl of wrought iron and arched windows.

[continued from page 104]

Check with TIB for exact dates and prices. To get there head for the Bockstael metro station, and then take tram No 53.

Pavillon Chinois & Tour Japonaise The Chinese pavilion and Japanese tower on Ave Van Praet stand almost opposite each other on the edge of the Domaine Royal. Both are leftovers from the reign of Léopold II – he had them built after seeing similar constructions at the World Fair in Paris in 1890. The former houses an extensive collection of Chinese porcelain; the latter is used for temporary exhibitions. Both are open 10 am to 4.45 pm Tuesday to Sunday and a ticket to both costs €2.97 (free on the first Wednesday of the month from 1 to 4.45 pm). Tram Nos 23 and 52 go there.

Atomium

The Atomium (☎ 02-474 89 77) on Blvd du Centenaire is a space-age leftover from the 1958 World Fair. The structure was designed by engineer André Waterkeyn and is a model of an iron molecule – enlarged 165 billion times. Originally it was to be demolished after 1958 but it became a symbol of postwar progress and is now a city icon. A high-speed elevator whizzes visitors to the top ball, where there's a restaurant and viewing platform. To descend there's a series of escalators. Talk of restoring the Atomium has been going on for years and in 2000 the Belgian government pledged €990,000 for repairs. The total bill, however, is expected to be about €25 million, so it's still unknown if or when work will be carried out.

The Atomium opens 9 am to 8 pm daily (10 am to 6 pm from 1 September to 31 March); admission costs €4.95 (students €3.71). To get there head for Heysel metro station or take tram No 81.

Parc des Expositions

Also known as the Palais de Centenaire, this huge trade fair area at Place de Belgique was built in 1935 to commemorate a century of independence and is still regularly used for conferences and conventions.

Bruparck

This modern leisure complex (☎ 02-474 83 77, metro Heysel), Blvd du Centenaire 20, incorporates the giant Kinepolis cinema (see the Entertainment section later), the Océade water fun-park, Mini Europe (highlights from around the continent in miniature) and the Village (a leisure centre). Admission to the Bruparck area is free, but there are admission costs for each of the attractions.

KOEKELBERG & JETTE
Basilique Nationale de Sacré-Cœur (Map 3)

This mighty basilica at Parvis de la Basilique 1 sits at the end of the ruler-straight Blvd Léopold II in Koekelberg. It's the world's fifth largest church and also arguably the city's most ghastly religious edifice, a discordant mix of neo-Gothic and Art Deco. It was started in 1905 but the plans were modified in the 1920s due to financial constraints and the building was not actually finished until many decades later.

It opens 8 am to 5 or 6 pm and admission is free (there's a €2.47 charge if you want to climb the dome for a city view). To get there head for Simonis metro station and then take bus No 87.

Musée Magritte (Map 3)

The Musée Magritte (☎ 02-428 26 26) at Rue Esseghem 135 in Jette occupies the house where René Magritte, Belgium's most famous Surrealist artist, and his wife Georgette lived from 1930–54. It's an anonymous, suburban, yellow-brick house which comes as a surprise given Magritte's paintings.

The museum opened in 1999 and is, by its very nature, small. Only 20 visitors at a time can fit in; others have to wait on the street. It was the private initiative of a friend of the widow Magritte and, with little support from the Belgian state, the curators have painstakingly assembled hundreds of original items – from Magritte's passport to paintings, photos, furniture and a pipe. Not everything's original but there's more than enough for visitors to get an inkling into Magritte's private world. For more on Magritte, see the boxed text 'René Magritte' in the Facts about the Cities chapter. The museum opens 10 am to 6 pm Wednesday to Sunday; admission costs €6 (those under 23 years €5). From central Brussels, take the metro to Belgica and then tram No 18 for three stops.

ANDERLECHT
Musée Bruxellois de la Gueuze (Map 4)
Anyone with even a vague interest in Belgian beer must not miss the excellent Brussels Gueuze Museum (☎ 02-521 49 28) at Rue Gheude 56, about a 10 to 15-minute walk from Gare du Midi. It's not so much a museum as a self-guided tour through the family-run Cantillon brewery, where the owners still proudly use traditional methods to make their fine *lambic* beers (see the Belgium's Glorious Beer special section for details). After a brief introduction, you make your own way around the ancient, and at times dusty, complex before returning to sample one of the brews. The museum opens 8.30 am to 5 pm weekdays and 10 am to 5 pm on Saturday. Admission costs €2.47. To get there head for Lemonnier premetro station or Gare du Midi metro station.

Musée du Béguinage (Map 3)
The Beguine Convent Museum (☎ 02-521 13 83) at Rue du Chapelain 8 is a minute's walk from Maison d'Erasme (see the following entry). The pint-sized *begijnhof* (see the boxed text 'Begijnen & Begijnhoven') was founded in 1252 and the two brick buildings were home to eight women.

Admission costs €1.23 and includes entry to Maison d'Erasme; it opens 10 am to noon and 2 to 5 pm daily except Tuesday and Friday.

Maison d'Erasme (Map 3)
The Erasmus House (☎ 02-521 13 83, metro St Guidon) at Rue du Chapitre 31 was where the great philosopher stayed for several months (see the boxed text 'Erasmus – Renaissance Man' in the Facts about the Cities chapter for more details about his life). The five rooms are crammed with artefacts, including a fragment of Erasmus' coffin, portraits by famous artists and old editions of his writings.

It opens 10 am to noon and 2 to 5 pm daily except Tuesday and Friday. Admission costs €1.23 and includes admission to the nearby Musée du Béguinage (see the previous entry).

Begijnen & Begijnhoven

The *begijnen* (Beguines) were a Catholic order of unmarried or widowed women that was founded in the 12th century in the Low Countries. The order was established largely due to the gender imbalance caused by the Crusades to the Holy Land – large numbers of men embarked on the Crusades but many never returned.

With little prospect of marriage, many single women joined forces for mutual support and set up religious communities, known as a *begijnhof* (*béguinage* in French). These communities (*begijnhoven* in plural) adhered to vows of obedience and chastity but not, unlike nuns, poverty. The women were often from wealthy families and devoted their time to caring for the elderly and sick, and work such as making lace and textiles from which they earned their living. Also, benefactors would pay the Beguines to pray for them, and so their communities were able to be independent.

Most begijnhoven are clusters of small houses surrounded by a protective wall and built around a central garden and church. Many Flemish cities still have a begijnhof – one of the best preserved and most beautiful can be found in Bruges. Most of the begijnhoven are still inhabited, though rarely by Beguines. At the beginning of the 20th century there were about 1500 Beguines in Belgium but the order has now virtually died out. In 1998, the unique heritage of these communities was recognised and 13 of the country's 20 begijnhoven were added to UNESCO's World Heritage List.

WHAT'S FREE

A handful of the city's museums offer free admission after 1 pm on the first Wednesday of the month, including the Musées Royaux des Beaux-Arts, the Musée des Instruments de Musique, the Musée des Sciences Naturelles de Belgique, the Musées Royaux d'Art et d'Histoire, and the Pavillon Chinois and Tour Japonaise. Others, such as the Musée Constantin Meunier, the Musée Communal d'Ixelles, the Musée Antoine Wiertz and the Musée Royal de l'Armée et d'Histoire Militaire, are free every day.

All of the city's churches are free. In summer there are classical concerts on Sunday in the Bois de la Cambre.

ACTIVITIES
Fitness Centres

Brussels' fitness scene is considered by many to be quite austere. Top-end hotels generally have some sort of gym and a sauna and, very occasionally, an indoor swimming pool. For aerobics classes try a private fitness club.

A small but well-run central gym is John Harris Fitness (Map 5; ☎ 02-219 82 54) in the Radisson SAS hotel at Rue du Fossé aux Loups 47. A one-day pass costs €24.54, or there's a 10-session pass (valid for six months) for €171.

Much cheaper is Fitness La Salle (Map 4; ☎ 02-513 26 16), Rue Rogier Van der Weyden 3, on the 1st floor of the Palais du Midi. One session at this basic gym costs €5, a 10-session card costs €50 and there are one/three-monthly passes for €40/90.

Belle Fitness (Map 5; ☎ 02-513 98 08), Rue des Chartreux 17, is a female-only gym; monthly membership costs €25.

Jogging

Popular running paths meander through the Bois de la Cambre and Parc de Woluwé (Map 3) and around the *étangs* (ponds) at Ixelles (Map 6) and Mellaerts (Map 3). For something more central try Parc de Bruxelles (Map 4) or Parc du Cinquantenaire (Map 7).

Swimming

Belgium isn't much of a swimming nation but those interested in unusual pools might want a dip at Piscine Victor Boin (Map 6; ☎ 02-539 06 15), Rue de la Perche 38, in St Gilles. It is a covered, Art Deco pool with a *bain turc* (Turkish bath), reserved for women on Tuesday and Friday, at the rear; it is reserved for men on the other days of the week, but closed on Sunday. A single pool ticket costs €1.73. It opens 8 am to 7 pm weekdays (from 2 pm on Wednesday) and 9 am to 9 pm on Saturday. Premetro No 55 or tram No 81 or 18 will drop you nearby.

Billiards

Cercle Royal de Billard (Map 4; ☎ 02-511 10 08), on the 3rd floor of the Palais du Midi at Rue Rogier Van der Weyden 3, is a sedate billiard hall. Tables cost €2.50 for one hour.

Ice Skating

For the last couple of years Grand Place has been the setting for one of Europe's most picturesque *patinage à glace* (ice-skating) rinks. It operates for the last two weeks of December; the TIB will have exact dates. Expect to pay €4.95 for one hour including skate hire (children €2.47).

The Patinoire at Forest National (Map 3; ☎ 02-345 16 11), Ave du Globe 36, has an indoor rink. Admission costs €5/2.50 and skate hire is €2.47. Bus No 48 stops nearby or take tram No 18.

Squash & Tennis

Flanders Gate Squash Club (Map 4; ☎ 02-512 98 23), Blvd Barthélémy 17, has six courts. Members/non-members pay €5/7.50 per half-hour or €40/62.50 for a 10-session card.

Centre Sportif de la Woluwé-St-Pierre (Map 3; ☎ 02-773 18 20) at Ave Salomé 2 in Woluwé-St-Pierre is a huge sporting complex with squash and tennis courts. Rates range from €5 to €6.50 per half-hour for squash and €6.75 to €17 for tennis (depending on the time of day). From Montgomery metro station take tram No 39 to Ave Orban.

Chess

For a spot of chess head to Le Greenwich (Map 5), an old-world cafe in the heart of town or, for something less smoky, De Ul-tieme Hallucinatie (Map 4; for more details see under Pubs & Bars in the Entertainment section later).

Skiing & Snowboarding
Yeti Ski (Map 3; ☎ 02-520 77 57), at Drève Olympique 11, near the Royal Amicale Golf Club in Anderlecht, boasts an artificial slope for practising skiing/snowboarding techniques (€7.50 per hour plus ski/snow-board hire at €2.50/5). Take bus No 47 to the Pede Sport stop.

Golf
There are several courses in and around Brussels. The Royal Amicale Golf Club (Map 3; ☎ 02-521 16 87) at Rue Scholle 1 in Anderlecht has 18 holes. Green fees are €30/45 per week/weekend.

COURSES
Language
Foreign schools, cultural centres and private language schools all offer language courses. If you're living in Brussels, the cheapest courses are those run by each of the com-munes; look in the White Pages under *Ad-ministration Communale/Gemeentebesturen.*

Private language schools offer intensive tuition and greater flexibility, but are more expensive. Prices vary greatly: from about €175 for a short course to €500 for a longer period.

A few places to investigate include:

Alliance Française (Map 3; ☎ 02-732 15 92) Ave de l'Émeraude 59. This centre is dedicated to teaching the French language and culture.
Eurospeak (Map 6; ☎ 02-511 89 12) Rue de Stassart 49. Flemish and French courses (maxi-mum of six people) are offered. The 27-hour course costs €295.
Nederlands Taalinstituut (Map 4; ☎ 02-219 03 27) Rue de l'Association 56. This place offers private and group courses in many European languages.

Beer
Beer Mania *(Map 6; ☎ 02-512 17 88,* **e** *beermania@skynet.be)*, on Chaussée de Wavre 174, is a shop specialising in beer.

The guy who runs it also holds beer appre-ciation sessions (minimum 10 people, €4.95 per person). You need to reserve in advance – for more details see Beer in the Shopping section later in the chapter.

Places to Stay

The area round Grand Place is rich in hotels, but other neighbourhoods not to overlook include the lovely Ste Catherine quarter and the Ave Louise district. The rates below include the 10% city tax, 6% VAT and 16% service. Breakfast is included in the price, unless otherwise stated.

PLACES TO STAY – BUDGET
Camping
Beersel (☎ 02-331 05 61, fax 02-378 19 77, Steenweg op Ukkel 75) is a small ground about 10km south of central Brussels in Beersel. It charges €2.47/1.98 for adults /children and €1.98/1.23 for a tent/car plus a €0.99 per person per day tourist tax. It

---

Weekend Deals

Brussels' accommodation scene has under-gone rapid transformation over the past decade or so and there's now a plethora of hotels, particularly ultra-expensive options aimed at EU visitors and business travellers. The result of this boom is a price war among hotels and some good deals for tourists. At the weekend, when all the Eurocrats and businesspeople have evacuated and the EU quarter is dead, many hotels around the city drop their rates dramatically. For example, the sumptuous Hôtel Metropole reduces its rate by 30% and the Hôtel Amigo and Conrad International by 50%. Breakfast at top-end hotels is usually included in the price at the weekend also.

Note that some establishments also drop their rates during the summer holiday months (roughly the last week of July and all of Au-gust). You'll find details of normal and week-end rates in the hotel listings in this chapter.

opens year round. Tram No 55 (direction Uccle) stops 3km away, from where you take bus UB (direction Halle) to Beersel.

Hostels

Brussels' most central hostel is the popular **Sleep Well** *(Map 4; ☎ 02-218 50 50, fax 02-218 13 13, e info@sleepwell.be, Rue du Damier 23)*. It's a big, bright, modern place with single/double rooms for €20.19/35.95. Triples/quads cost €15.98/16.23 per person and six/eight-bed rooms cost €13.88/12.14 per person. All bathroom facilities are communal. It's closed from 10 am to 4 pm.

There are three HI-affiliated hostels and all have single/double rooms for €20.32/29.75 as well as dorms, which range in size from four beds (€12.64 per person) up to 14 beds (€10.65). None of the HI hostels has kitchens for travellers to use.

The most central HI hostel is **Bruegel** *(Map 4; ☎ 02-511 04 36, fax 02-512 07 11, e jeugdherberg.bruegel@ping.be, Rue du St Esprit 2)*. It's popular with young groups, closes from 10 am to 1 pm and has a 1 am curfew. All the dorms here are quite large (12 beds).

About 1.25km west of Grand Place is the second HI hostel, **Génération Europe** *(Map 4; ☎ 02-410 38 58, fax 02-410 39 05, e brussels.europe@laj.be, Rue de l'Éléphant 4)*. It has a large garden and secure private parking. The rooms are modern and have private toilet and shower. It's closed between 11 am and 3 pm. The closest metro station, Comte de Flandre, is a five-minute walk from the hostel.

The third HI hostel is **Jacques Brel** *(Map 4; ☎ 02-218 01 87, fax 02-217 20 05, e brussels.brel@laj.be, Rue de la Sablonnière 30)*. It is near the Madou metro station and 1km uphill from Gare Centrale (or take bus No 66). It has recently been renovated and has singles/doubles with private bathroom facilities as well as a range of dorms (from three to 14 beds). Street parking is possible.

A few blocks farther north is the **Centre Vincent Van Gogh** *(Map 4; ☎ 02-217 01 58, fax 02-219 79 95, e chab@ping.be, Rue Traversière 8)*. It's relaxed and hip. Singles

/doubles cost €17.35/28.78, four/six-bed dorms cost €11.90/10.16 per person and beds in a dorm (eight to 10 beds) are €8.43. ISIC cardholders get a 10% discount. Facilities include a courtyard, bar, laundry and a small kitchen for guests to use. It's 1.2km uphill from Gare Centrale, or take the metro to Botanique or bus No 65.

B&Bs

For B&B accommodation in Brussels contact **Bed & Brussels** *(Map 6; ☎ 02-646 07 37, fax 02-644 01 14, e info@bnb-brussels.be)*, Rue Kindermans 9, or visit www.bnb-brussels.be. The cheapest B&B rooms have communal bathroom facilities and cost from €27/42 for a single/double. Rooms in the mid-range have private bathrooms and go for around €35/49. The most expensive are in apartments or villas and cost from €49.33/66.68. Children aged under three are free; for under-12s the price is €14.87.

Most B&Bs require a minimum stay of two nights, though a few accept overnighters. One such place is **B&B Guilmin** *(Map 6; ☎ 02-512 92 90, fax 02-502 41 01, e ph.guilmin@belgacom.net, Rue de Londres 19)*. Don't be bothered by the revolting facade – this is a delightful place to stay. The four rooms are large, charming and all have different decor. Trône metro station is 600m away. The price is €57/77 for one/two people (an extra €12.50 is levied per room for stays of one night).

Hotels

Central Brussels' cheapest hotel is **Pacific Sleeping Hôtel** *(Map 5; ☎ 02-511 84 59, Rue Antoine Dansaert 57)*. This old-fashioned place started at the turn of last century and it still has the atmosphere of a village thrift shop. Unfortunately, it's expected to close in 2004 when the lease expires. In the meantime, single/double rooms cost €27.25/44.60 with communal bathrooms (showers cost an extra €2.50). Doubles with a dinky private shower cost €57.

The friendly and unpretentious **Hôtel La Vieille Lanterne** *(Map 5; ☎ 02-512 74 94, fax 02-512 13 97, Rue des Grandes Carmes*

29), above a lace shop opposite Manneken Pis, has just six comfortable rooms for €62/73.10, all with private bathrooms.

In the Ste Catherine area, the only budget place to stay is **Résidence Les Écrins** *(Map 5; ☎ 02-219 36 57, fax 02-223 57 40,* **e** *les.ecrins@skynet.be, Rue du Rouleau 15)*. It's a small hotel with 11 simple, bright, modern rooms (all with TV and telephone) for €39.66/47.10 (communal bathroom) or €61.20/74.40 (private facilities).

For a taste of true Marolles atmosphere head to **Hôtel Galia** *(Map 6; ☎ 02-502 42 43, fax 02-502 76 19,* **e** *hotel.galia@ skynet.be, Place du Jeu de Balle 15–16)*. Overlooking the city's famous bric-a-brac market, this place has clean, decent-sized rooms, each with a tiny shower and toilet closet. Prices start at €49.57/54.53.

Hôtel à la Grande Cloche *(Map 4; ☎ 02-512 61 40, fax 02-512 65 91,* **e** *info @hotelgrandecloche.com, Place Rouppe 10–12)* is a relatively large, welcoming and well-kept establishment on the edge of the Marolles, and one of the best in this category. Doubles cost €43.38/58.25 without /with a small, partitioned shower, or €70.64 with an ordinary bathroom. Parking is possible on the square in front.

The friendly, family-run **Hôtel Sabina** *(Map 4; ☎ 02-218 26 37, fax 02-219 32 39, Rue du Nord 78)* near Place Madou is very good value. It has something of an old-world atmosphere and is popular with weekend travellers and weekday Eurocrats. The light, airy rooms cost €54.53/66.93, all with private bathrooms. Street parking is possible.

Just off Ave Louise and excellent value is the homely **Hôtel Rembrandt** *(Map 6; ☎ 02-512 71 39, fax 02-511 71 36, Rue de la Concorde 42)*. This pale-pink corner hotel boasts immaculate rooms (although they're a tad small) with classical furnishings and old paintings. Rooms with a shower go for €34.70/57, and those with a private toilet as well cost €57/73.32.

PLACES TO STAY – MID-RANGE
Grand Place Area
Hôtel St Michel *(Map 5; ☎ 02-511 09 56, fax 02-511 46 00, Grand Place 11)* is Grand

Place's *only* hotel. It's overpriced for what you get but the staff are welcoming and what more can we say about the location? The hotel has no dining room, so breakfast is served either in your room or in a cafe on the square. Single/double rooms at the front with views of the square cost €109/130; those at the back cost €81.80/97.91.

Half an alley from Grand Place is tiny **Hôtel Sema** *(Map 5; ☎ 02-514 07 60, fax 02-548 90 39, Rue des Harengs 6–8)*. The 10 rooms are a bit dark during the day (it's sandwiched between taller buildings); however, they're spacious, stylishly furnished and all have neat bathrooms. The location is excellent. The price is €111/123, or €86.76 for either a single or double at the weekend.

Hôtel Arlequin *(Map 5; ☎ 02-514 16 15, fax 02-514 22 02,* **e** *arlequin@skynet.be, Rue de la Fourche 17)* is also superbly located, a feature you'll appreciate when dining in the 7th-floor (buffet) breakfast room. The rooms themselves are somewhat ordinary and quite small, but are decently priced at €76.84/114 (reduced to €59.49 /76.84 at the weekend).

Hôtel Mozart *(Map 5; ☎ 02-502 66 61, fax 02-502 77 58,* **e** *hotel.mozart@skynet .be, Rue du Marché aux Fromages 23)* is a romantic and well-located little gem. It has seductive, salmon-toned rooms with beamed ceilings, period paintings and a mix of antique and modern furnishings. It's on a noisy nightlife street and there's a club opposite so request a room at the back. Rates start at €70/87.50, or €112 for a triple.

Friendly **Hôtel La Légende** *(Map 5; ☎ 02-512 82 90, fax 02-512 34 93,* **e** *hotel_la legende@hotmail.com, Rue du Lombard 35)* has small, old rooms for €70.64/79.32 or nice newer rooms from €89.24/97.91. At the weekend, prices drop by about €5. There's a cosy mezzanine breakfast room.

Ste Catherine
One of the most charming hotels in this price bracket is **Hôtel Noga** *(Map 5; ☎ 02-218 67 63, fax 02-218 16 03,* **e** *info@ noga_hotel.com, Rue du Béguinage 38)*. A mix of the modern and old, it's a feast for the eyes with rich colour schemes and

spacious rooms, all with individual decor. Prices for singles/doubles/triples start at €73.12/86.76/109; rooms are discounted at the weekend and in summer.

Hôtel Welcome (Map 5; ☎ 02-219 95 46, fax 02-217 18 87, e reservation@hotel welcome.com, quai au Bois à Brûler 23) is Brussels' smallest hotel. The six rooms are decked out in rich, rustic tones and prices go from €54.53/64.45. The breakfast room (originally a stable) features a delightful wall mosaic. Breakfast costs €7.43 extra.

At the opposite end of the spectrum and at the top-end of this price bracket is the 217-room *Novotel Tour Noire (Map 5; ☎ 02-505 50 50, fax 02-505 50 00, e H2122@accor .hotels.com, Rue de la Vierge Noire 32)*. This big hotel has been carefully draped around the Tour Noire, a historic tower. Rooms cost €147/152 (breakfast costs an extra €13.63). During weekends these same rooms cost €116 (breakfast included).

Gare du Nord Area
This area rates poorly with tourists but those into modern Belgian art should consider the *Art Hotel Siru (Map 4; ☎ 02-203 35 80, fax 02-203 33 03, e art.hotel.siru@ skynet.be, Place Rogier 1)*. This Art Deco hotel boasts works by 130 contemporary Belgian artists. Some rooms feature mundane art pieces, others are surreal and there are a few bordering on nightmarish. Many of the rooms are small and weekday prices are inflated at €136/153. Weekend deals (€96.67) are more reasonable.

Gare du Midi Area
There's little to recommend hotels in this quarter but the *Hôtel Ustel (Map 6; ☎ 02-520 60 53, fax 02-520 33 28, e hotel.ustel@ ping.be, Square de l'Aviation 6–8)* is worth mentioning. The 94 rooms are hidden behind a 19th-century façade and the hotel's restaurant, La Grande Écluse, is an industrial delight (see Places to Eat later). It costs €96.67 /118, or €74.36/86.76 at the weekend.

Ave Louise
The *Hôtel De Boeck's (Map 6; ☎ 02-537 40 33, fax 02-534 40 37, e hotel.deboecks*

@euronet.be, Rue Veydt 40) is a decidedly old-fashioned and somewhat spartan hotel located on a quiet backstreet in this ritzy area. If your needs are modest, it will suffice. Single/double rooms start at €69.41/ 89.24. It's 800m from Place Louise, or you can take tram No 93 or 94 and walk two blocks.

EU Area
The small, old-fashioned *Hôtel Marie José (Map 4; ☎ 02-512 08 43, fax 02-512 46 04, e chezcallens@village.uunet.be, Rue du Commerce 73)* is in the heart of the government and administrative district on the edge of the EU quarter. Good-sized rooms and friendly service make it popular with businesspeople. Prices range from €69.41 to €87.76 for singles and €81.80 to €99.15 for doubles. At the weekend rates drop to €64.45/71.88.

PLACES TO STAY – TOP END
Grand Place Area
Hôtel Métropole (Map 5; ☎ 02-217 23 00, reservations ☎ 02-214 24 24, fax 02-218 02 20, e info@metropolehotel.be, Place de Brouckère 31) is the city's sumptuous, late-19th-century showpiece. An opulent French Renaissance-style foyer with marble walls and coffered ceiling leads to an imperial reception hall backed by beautifully etched stained-glass windows.

The hotel was built in 1885 and is still owned by the Wielemans, a Bruxellois family. Single rooms range from €262 to €362 and doubles cost from €312 to €412. Email reservations attract a 30% discount (during the week only). At the weekend, rates drop to between €111 and €210. Unlike the lavish entrance, the elegant rooms tend to be quite soberly furnished. A buffet breakfast is included.

Tucked away in a corner one block from Grand Place is *Hôtel Amigo (Map 5; ☎ 02-547 47 47, fax 02-513 52 77, e hotelamigo@ hotelamigo.com, Rue de l'Amigo 1–3)*. This 18th-century-style hotel was built in the 1950s on the site of a former prison and is full of antique furniture and tapestries. Singles/doubles start at €322/347 but drop to

€148/173 at the weekend. Suites range from €743 to €2100. A continental breakfast served in the room is included, or there's a buffet version for €22.

The city's most charming address is **Hôtel Le Dixseptième** (Map 5; ☎ 02-502 57 44, fax 02-502 64 24, *e* ledixseptieme@ net7.be, Rue de la Madeleine 25). The discreet facade hides 24 rooms that are sumptuously decorated, and they are all unique. There are two sections: modern spacious studios at the rear, featuring innovative furnishings and kitchenettes; and suites in Louis XVI style with large salons, beamed ceilings and fireplaces. Room rates range from €171 to €319 for singles and €196 to €345 for doubles; at the weekend rates start at €124/149. A buffet breakfast is included.

The **Radisson SAS** (Map 5; ☎ 02-219 28 28, fax 02-219 62 62, *e* dirk.ghysels @radissonsas.com, Rue du Fossé aux Loups 47) is a big American/Scandinavian hotel. It caters predominantly for businesspeople and rates highly for efficient service and facilities. Seven stories high and built around a glass-covered atrium, it's polished but somewhat cool in tone. Rooms start at €322, or €171 at the weekend. The buffet breakfast costs €24.54 extra.

Ave Louise & Ixelles

Brussels' finest hotel is arguably the **Conrad International** (Map 6; ☎ 02-542 48 00, fax 02-542 42 00, *e* bruhc_rm@hilton.com, Ave Louise 71). This palatial, classical-style hotel has creamy tones and wrought iron, and is a harmonious blend of opulence and efficiency. Prices start at €409/433. At the weekend you can have a room for €159/209 (buffet breakfast included).

The friendly **Hôtel Manos Stéphanie** (Map 6; ☎ 02-539 02 50, fax 02-537 57 29, *e* manos@manoshotel.com, Chaussée de Charleroi 28) is an intimate hotel on a busy boulevard just off Ave Louise. The plush Louis XVI interior sports rooms for €179 /204, discounted to €90/100 at the weekend. Breakfast is included in the price and is taken in a saccharine-sweet breakfast room.

EU Area

The elegant **Hôtel Stanhope** (Map 6; ☎ 02-506 91 11, fax 02-512 17 08, *e* summit hotels@stanhope.be, Rue du Commerce 9) is close to the Trône metro station. The 50 rooms occupy three townhouses and are lavishly furnished with late-19th-century, English-style decor. It's popular with wealthy Americans and businesspeople. Rooms cost €245/370 (buffet breakfast costs €21 extra), dropping to €149/171 at the weekend (including breakfast).

Zaventem Airport

The **Sheraton Brussels Airport** (Map 3; ☎ 02-710 87 77, fax 02-725 11 55, *e* uvg .gateways@skynet.be) is opposite the airport departures hall. Sound-proof rooms start at €371 and are reduced to €122/146 for a single/double on Friday and Saturday night.

LONG-TERM RENTALS

The TIB has lists of hotels and serviced apartments with fully equipped rooms.

Hôtel Albert (Map 4; ☎ 02-217 93 91, fax 02-219 20 17, *e* info@hotelalbert.be, Rue Royale Ste Marie 27–9) is opposite the Halles de Schaerbeek. It has hotel rooms but also 'mini-flats' with kitchenettes costing €61.97/79.32 for singles/doubles. Tram Nos 93 and 94 from Rue Royale stop nearby.

Citadines Apart'Hotel (Map 5; ☎ 02-221 14 11, fax 02-221 15 99, *e* resa@citadines .com, Quai au Bois à Brûler 51), in the Ste Catherine area, is part of a French hotel chain targeting businesspeople. It has 125 studios and 44 apartments. Studios (for one or two people) cost €91.72/577 per day /week and apartments (up to four people) cost €133/840. Rates are reduced for stays of more than one month.

Hotel Euroflat (Map 7; ☎ 02-230 00 10, fax 02-230 36 83, *e* reservation@hoteleuro flat.be, Blvd Charlemagne 500) is a sterile hotel opposite the Berlaymont. It's handy for EU business and has single/double rooms with kitchenettes for €142/166 per night, or €772/911 per week.

Résidence Parnasse (Map 6; ☎ 02-505

Brussels' sleek and efficient tram system – if only European politics ran as smoothly…

EDWARD SNIJDERS

Grand Place's flower market in full blossom

MARTIN MOOS

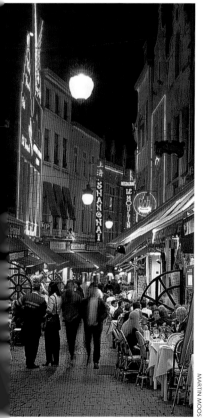

MARTIN MOOS

...y Rue des Bouchers for a real taste of Brussels.

View the capital from the top of the Atomium.

MARTIN MOOS

DOUG McKINLAY

Eating out in Brussels is also a feast for the eyes.

DOUG McKINLAY

Don't miss that Belgian bivalve classic, *moules*.

EDWARD SNIJDERS

Crowds historically gathered at Grand Place for executions – today's entertainment is a bit more civilised

98 00, fax 02-505 99 00, **e** *rainbow@ residenceparnasse.com, Rue d'Idalie 8)* has a great location overlooking the European Parliament and chic, fully equipped apartments. The minimum rental is one month, and rates start at €1795 per month.

Places to Eat

Dining out is one of the true pleasures of Brussels. The city is overly endowed with quality restaurants and although many visitors on a first-time trip stick to the restaurants lining Rue des Bouchers and the other cobbled streets around Grand Place, it's well worth being adventurous and heading farther afield. The city's cosmopolitan nature means there is no shortage of Italian, Japanese, Spanish, Turkish, Greek, American and Irish cuisine, and African cuisine is also starting to make its mark.

PLACES TO EAT – BUDGET
Grand Place Area
One of the most popular tourist eateries in the heart of the city is *Chez Léon (Map 5;* ☎ *02-513 04 26, Rue des Bouchers 18).* This rambling place occupies several gabled houses on Brussels' famous dining street and offers fast service, big helpings of mussels and chips, and free meals for the kids (an obvious winner with families).

For no-nonsense Italian cuisine try *Rugantino (Map 5;* ☎ *02-511 21 95, Blvd Anspach 184).* This restaurant is a little morsel of Italy with a simple menu, good prices, great food and loud voices emanating from the kitchen. Mains range from €6.94 to €11.65. It's closed on Sunday.

African restaurants are at last springing up around Brussels. The closest to Grand Place is *Waka Moon (Map 5;* ☎ *02-502 10 32, Rue des Éperonniers 60).* This tiny restaurant has a strong following amongst the city's Congolese community, and does a very good *maafé* (lamb in peanut sauce) for €9.66.

Casual, velveteen, muted...that's the atmosphere at *Centre Hémisphère (Map 5;* ☎ *02-513 93 70, Rue de l'Écuyer 65).* This

luscious cafe/bistro is adorned with ruby cushions, soft sofas and lovely lanterns, giving it a silky, Oriental ambience. Staples include *plats du jour* (dishes of the day) from €7.43 to €9.91 and *pitas* (pitta bread sandwiches) for around €4.20. It's closed on Sunday.

Inno department store's *Lunch Garden (Map 5;* ☎ *02-212 85 89, Rue Neuve 111)* is a self-service cafeteria with cheap meals. It opens 9.30 am to 5 pm Monday to Saturday.

If you're just after *frites* (chips or French fries) or a pita, take your pick of the swarm of places along Rue du Marché aux Fromages (Map 5). Most are open from lunchtime until 6 am and serve basic pitas from €2.97, a *brochette* (kebab) for €7.43 and vegetarian pitas. You can dine in or take away.

Sandwich bars are dotted around town. One of the most ubiquitous is *Panos (Map 5;* ☎ *02-513 14 43, Rue du Marché aux Herbes 85)* where you can buy a *belegd broodje/sandwich garni* (half a filled baguette) for around €2.

Crock'In (Map 5; ☎ *02-223 29 61, Blvd Anspach 64)* is another sandwich bar but it also has a small dine-in area. It opens 7 am until 6.30 pm daily.

Belgium's home-grown hamburger chain is *Quick.* It has branches around the city including one at Rue du Marché aux Herbes 103 (Map 5; ☎ 02-511 47 63).

Self-caterers will find a *GB* supermarket *(Map 4;* ☎ *02-226 66 11)* in the basement of the City 2 shopping centre on Rue Neuve. More central options include the *GB (Map 5;* ☎ *02-549 04 11)* on the corner of Rue des Halles and Rue du Marché aux Poulets (the food section is in the basement) and the small, very crowded *AD Delhaize (Map 5;* ☎ *02-512 80 87, Blvd Anspach 63).* They're all open from 9 am to about 8 pm Monday to Saturday (the AD Delhaize also opens 9 am to 6 pm on Sunday).

St Géry
Spend any time in Belgium and you'll soon come across *Le Pain Quotidien/ Het Dagelijks Brood (Map 5;* ☎ *02-502 23 61, Rue Antoine Dansaert 16).* This national chain of bakeries-cum-tearooms offers

wholesome bread, savoury pies and filled sandwiches (€3.96 to €5.57) and they're excellent places for breakfast (€2.72 to €5.20), lunch or a snack. The decor at each place is similar – fashionable country-style with diners eating together at one big wooden table in a smoke-free environment. The chain has branches around Belgium, and they're generally open 7 am to 5 or 6 pm daily.

Fin de Siècle (Map 5; ☎ 02-513 51 23, Rue des Chartreux 9) is a cavernous bistro known for its convivial atmosphere; it's popular with the 20- to 40-something crowd. The blackboard menu sports a few vegetarian options and meals are mostly in the €8.90 to €13 bracket. It's closed on Monday.

Rue des Chartreux has two innovative tearooms. *AM Sweet (Map 5; ☎ 02-513 51 31, Rue des Chartreux 4)* doubles as a sweet shop and you can order a chocolate Zinneke (modelled after the statue of the dog that's located just up the street) to accompany your cuppa. It opens 9 am to 6.30 pm Monday to Saturday. The other is *Arteaspoon (Map 5; ☎ 02-513 51 17, Rue des Chartreux 32)*, which is also a contemporary art space for alternate young artists.

For a sober but stylish Mediterranean restaurant-cum-bar there's *Mamesse (Map 5; ☎ 02-512 34 30, Rue St Christophe 20)*. It's all red tiles and ochre tones. Mains cost from €7.35 to €11.15; it opens for dinner only (closed Sunday).

Nearby is *Den Teepot (Map 4; ☎ 02-511 94 02, Rue des Chartreux 66)*, an old-guard vegetarian restaurant. It's above a health-food shop, caters largely for local workers and opens for lunch only (Monday to Saturday).

Marolles

After rummaging through the flea market, a good place to put your feet up is *Brasserie La Clef d'Or (Map 6; ☎ 02-511 97 62, Place du Jeu de Balle 1)*. It has been serving *soupe de la maison* (soup of the house; €1.61) and a good *croque monsieur* (grilled ham and cheese sandwich; €2.60) to market vendors and visitors for years. It's an unpretentious establishment open 5 am to 5 pm daily (except Monday).

Eetcafé Het Warm Water (Map 6; ☎ 02-513 91 59, Rue des Renards 19) is one of several eateries on this pleasant pedestrianised street. It's a comfy, Dutch kitchen-style place with mustard decor and wooden tables. It does breakfast as well as snacks (vegetable pies for €3.22 or soup for €1.61) and it opens 8 am to 5 pm daily (except Wednesday).

For something a bit more contemporary head to *Ici Même (Map 6; ☎ 02-502 54 24, Rue Haute 204)*. The violent orange facade of this place is enough to turn anyone off, but the mix-and-match menu, including many aromatic dishes from the south of France, is great (for vegetarians too). Expect to pay about €7.50/11.25 at lunch/dinner.

Gare du Midi Area

For moussaka and retsina, try one of the unpretentious little Greek restaurants on Rue d'Argonne. *Le Cheval de Troie (Map 6; ☎ 02-538 30 95, Rue d'Argonne 32)* serves a good plat du jour for €5.45. It's closed on Wednesday.

For picnic supplies, there's a handy *GB Express (Map 6; ☎ 02-526 93 30)* supermarket inside Gare du Midi, open daily from 8 am to 9 pm.

Sablon

This area is not known for cheap eats but *Le Perroquet (Map 6; ☎ 02-512 99 22, Rue Watteeu 31)* is an exception. This smooth Art Nouveau cafe is where young Anglophone expats love to gossip and smoke. There are reasonably priced drinks, an excellent range of salads (€4.46 to €9.17) and exotic stuffed pitas (€4.46 to €7.18), including vegetarian options.

Le Pain Quotidien (Map 6; ☎ 02-513 51 54, Rue des Sablons 11) is another branch of this successful chain (see under Grand Place Area earlier in this section).

La Pirogue (Map 6; ☎ 02-511 35 25, Impasse St Jacques 12) is a neat Senegalese bistro on a quiet pedestrian street just off Place du Grand Sablon. Homemade ginger beer is the house speciality, and it goes down well with mains (€7.43 to €10.78) such as *bine bine* (shrimps combined with mango and pineapple).

St Josse

For good, cheap Turkish fare head to one of the many *pide* (Turkish pizza) joints in St Josse. The city's oldest and arguably best is *Metin (Map 4; ☎ 02-217 68 63, Chaussée de Haecht 94)*. It started in 1978, about 15 years after the first Turkish immigrants moved into this neighbourhood, and continues to draw plenty of local diners (closed Tuesday). Pide prices range from €3.47 to €5.57, depending on toppings. Bus No 65 from Gare Centrale stops close by.

Porte de Namur

One of the best-known eateries in this area is *L'Ultime Atome (Map 6; ☎ 02-511 13 67, Rue St Boniface 14)*. This corner brasserie/bar is positively alive with conversation and music and attracts a vibrant, eclectic crowd. The kitchen opens non-stop from noon until midnight and there's a wide range of eats that includes vegetarian fare (main courses range from €7.43 to €15.36).

Just around the corner is *Yamato (Map 6; ☎ 02-502 28 93, Rue Francart 11)*, a teeny Japanese eatery where a dozen people line the main bar while others wait in the sidelines. It's closed Sunday and Monday, and is full almost every other day.

Filling up is what *La Canardière (Map 6; ☎ 02-512 26 20, Rue de Stassart 17)* and the next-door *Spaghetteria (Map 6; ☎ 02-514 03 21, Rue de Stassart 19)* are all about. These two tiny restaurants pump out huge bowls of pasta to students and late-night diners. You can eat as much spaghetti as you want for about €5.45, but extra sauce costs €0.74. They're open for lunch and dinner (evenings only at the weekend).

Ave Louise & Ixelles

A cheap place for lunch in this otherwise pricey area is *Lunch Garden (Map 6; ☎ 02-512 96 18, Ave Louise 12)*, a self-service cafeteria in the Inno department store. It's on the 2nd floor and opens from 10 am to 4.30 pm Monday to Saturday. A fast food

option is *Hector Chicken (Map 6; ☎ 02-511 52 22, Ave de la Toison d'Or)*.

Head deeper into Ixelles and you'll find the modern *L'Amour Fou (Map 6; ☎ 02-351 43 94, Chaussée d'Ixelles 185)*. This long cafe/bar draws a young casual crowd for drinks or a meal. The menu features bistro-style food such as salads (€7.44), pasta (€8.06), *stoemp* (Flemish-style mashed potatoes served with bacon and sausages; €7.93) and steaks (€10.16); the kitchen opens 9 am to midnight daily. Take bus No 54 or 71.

Funky little *Touch & Go (Map 6; ☎ 02-640 55 89, Rue de Livourne 131)* is part of a small chain pushing stuffed pitas. Prices range from €3.09 to €4.70; vegetarians are catered for. It opens daily for lunch and dinner (until 1 am at the weekend). Tram Nos 93 and 94 stop nearby.

Plenty of eateries compete at the intersection of Chaussée de Boondael and Ave de l'Université near the Université Libre de Bruxelles. One that's cheap and always moving is *La Petite Planète (Map 3; ☎ 02-640 45 11, Chaussée de Boondael 467)*, a modern pita bistro that's open 24 hours daily.

Self-caterers can head to the *Nopri* supermarket *(Map 6; ☎ 02-648 38 78, Rue du Bailli 63)*, open 9 am to 7 pm Monday to Saturday.

EU Area

For the best frites in the city you'll have to head to *Maison Antoine (Map 7; Place Jourdan)*. This *friture* (chip shop) has been operating for half a century on this old-fashioned square near the EU quarter, and at lunch time you'll need to queue. It opens 11.30 am until 1 or 2 am daily. Bus No 34 from the stop next to the Bourse will eventually get you there.

The *Sushi Factory (Map 7; ☎ 02-230 74 32, Blvd Charlemagne 44)*, close to the Berlaymont, is good for a quick Japanese snack.

PLACES TO EAT – MID-RANGE
Grand Place Area

The hordes of restaurants lining Rue des Bouchers are largely overpriced; of these places, *Aux Armes de Bruxelles (Map 5;*

☎ *02-511 55 98, Rue des Bouchers 13)* stands out as the exception. A battalion of elderly, starched waiters marches around this large, traditional establishment serving ample portions of Belgian classics such as *moules-frites* (mussels and chips) and *waterzooi* (a cream-based fish stew). Prices range from €13.26 to €22.19, or there are good-value three-course *menus* starting at €27.27. The kitchen opens from noon to 11 pm.

Slightly cheaper but also very good is ***Taverne du Passage*** *(Map 5; ☎ 02-512 37 32, Galerie de la Reine 30)* in the Galeries St Hubert. It has been around since 1928 and stepping through the draped doorway here is like being zapped back a century or two. Friendly service and hearty servings of Belgian cuisine make it a winner. Mains range from €13.88 to €20.

Brasserie de la Roue d'Or *(Map 5; ☎ 02-514 25 54, Rue des Chapeliers 26)* pays homage to the city's Surrealist artists and has well and truly hooked many locals. The food is traditional and excellent, and the kitchen opens daily until midnight. Expect prices between €12.39 to €19.83.

Al Barmaki *(Map 5; ☎ 02-513 08 34, Rue des Éperonniers 67)* is a spacious Lebanese restaurant with an unfussy approach to food. The atmosphere is casual, the decor simple and uncluttered and vegetarians are well looked after. It's closed on Sunday.

Planète Chocolat *(Map 5; ☎ 02-511 07 55, Rue du Lombard 24)* is a shop-cum-cafe specialising in pralines, cakes and hot chocolate drinks. On Sunday afternoon they stage an immensely popular *thé-dansant* (tea dance), where you can get up and jive to everything from contemporary to classical music. It opens 10 am to 6.30 pm Tuesday to Saturday and 2 to 9 pm on Sunday.

St Géry

It's rare to see ***Bonsoir Clara*** *(Map 5; ☎ 02-502 09 90, Rue Antoine Dansaert 18)* anything but full. This twin-salon restaurant with its intimate, quirky design serves generous portions of modern European food with full-bodied flavour. At lunchtime, a meal and coffee costs €12; at dinner main courses range from about €11 to €18.50.

Next door is ***Kasbash*** *(Map 5; ☎ 02-502 40 26, Rue Antoine Dansaert 20)*, a dark and intimate Moroccan restaurant where you dine by the light of 1001 lanterns (at least that's how it seems). Typical fare includes couscous (€10 to €13.65), lamb *brochettes* (€13.65) and *tajines* (spicy meat-based stews; around €13).

Just up the street is the well-established Vietnamese ***La Papaye Verte*** *(Map 5; ☎ 02-502 70 82, Rue Antoine Dansaert 53)*. It's good for an easygoing meal, prices are reasonable (€7.43 to €12.39 for mains) and vegetarians should find something to their liking here.

For traditional food, including a range of dishes cooked in local Cantillon brews, head to ***In 't Spinnekopke*** *(Map 4; ☎ 02-511 86 95, Place du Jardin aux Fleurs 1)*. This cosy *estaminet* (tavern) dates back to the 18th century and is quintessentially Belgian – checked tablecloths, penguin-style waiters and a long list of classic dishes written in both French and Brussels dialect. Reservations are necessary. It's closed at lunchtime on Saturday and all day Sunday. Mains are in the €11.15 to €19.21 bracket.

Ste Catherine

Seafood is the staple on Quai aux Briques and one of the oldest establishments is ***Jacques*** *(Map 5; ☎ 02-513 27 62, Quai aux Briques 44)*. This friendly, down-to-earth restaurant has been around for over 60 years and these days attracts an older, largely local crowd. Excellent fish meals cost from €11.40 to €20.82 and mussels cost €14.87. For lobster you must ring a day in advance.

A new kid on the block and conducive to a romantic night out is ***Le Vistro*** *(Map 5; ☎ 02-512 41 81, Quai aux Briques 16)*. This little seafood restaurant is sandwiched in amongst the big guns and offers a very good three-course seafood *menu* for €27.14. It's closed lunchtime Saturday and all day Sunday.

Marolles

L'Étoile d'Or *(Map 4; ☎ 02-502 60 48, Rue des Foulons 30)* is better known to residents of this old quarter as 'De Rotte Planchei' (The Rotten Wooden Floor). This engaging restaurant started in 1900 as a cafe but was restored in the 1990s. It features the original stove, fresh flowers and excellent Belgian food, some of which is cooked with the local Cantillon brews. Main courses hover around the €11.15 to €15.61 range. Reservations on Friday and Saturday nights are essential.

The appropriately named **Bazaar** *(Map 6; ☎ 02-511 26 00, Rue des Capucins 63)* is a large baroque restaurant (complete with downstairs bar and nightclub) specialising in world cuisine (main courses are in the €11.40 to €16.36 category). The decor of this place was inspired by a dream and it has struck a chord with locals – reservations are necessary at the weekend (closed Monday). It has no signpost – look for the green facade and fake stained-glass wall.

For something a bit beefier try **Au Stekerlapatte** *(Map 6; ☎ 02-512 86 81, Rue des Prêtres 4)*. The grungy facade hides a cavernous bistro where the approach is casual, the menu extensive and the portions large. Meat, fish and fowl – cooked in traditional Belgian ways – are the main-course staples (€12.89 to €17.35). For starters, try local offerings such as *Bloempanch à la Bruxelloise* (fried black pudding with a caramelised apple topping). It's closed on Monday.

Gare du Midi Area

An excellent choice in this somewhat desolate area is **La Grande Écluse** *(Map 6; ☎ 02-522 30 25, Ave Poincaré 77)*, attached to Hôtel Ustel. This restaurant occupies a converted 19th-century lock that, until 1930, controlled the flow of the now underground River Senne. The polished infrastructure makes a fascinating setting and the restaurant itself runs like a well-oiled machine. Main courses average about €13.80.

Sablon

Pedestrianised Rue de Rollebeek is the main hunting ground for diners in the Sablon. Of the restaurants lining this street, **Tout & n'Importe Quoi** *(literally 'everything and whatever'; Map 4; ☎ 02-513 27 33, Rue de Rollebeek 21)* stands out for its

minimalist, modern decor and well-priced French/Belgian cuisine (mains cost from €12.14 to €16.11).

Porte de Namur

For delicious meat and vegetarian dishes, using only organic produce, there's **Table d'Hôte Bio** *(Map 6; ☎ 02-513 60 35, Rue Ernest Solvay 20)*. This tiny restaurant has just six tables and warm, rustic tones. Mains cost between €14.50 and €22. It's closed on Sunday.

Ave Louise, Ixelles & St Gilles

Pedestrianised Rue Jourdan and Rue Jean Stas are lined with little cafes, trendy brasseries and pricey restaurants where the sophisticated set stops for a bite between boutiques.

Firmly ingrained on the ladies' lunch circuit is **La Crêmerie de la Vache** *(Map 6; ☎ 02-538 28 18, Rue Jean Stas 6)*. This bakery-cum-tearoom does open sandwiches, quiches, ice creams and kill-for cakes; it opens 8 am to 7 pm daily.

Il Rinascimento *(Map 6; ☎ 02-534 75 20, Rue Jourdan 14)* is a good Italian restaurant; the pizzas are baked in a wood oven and the staff are winners. Count on about €8.06 to €11.53 for a main meal.

Big, brash and always busy – that's **Rick's** *(Map 6; ☎ 02-647 75 30, Ave Louise 344)*. This American bar and restaurant is much loved by US businessmen. While the menu holds few surprises – spare ribs (€17.22), imported T-bone steaks (€27.14), burgers and beans – the food is very good and the weekend brunch (€14.74) is something of an institution. It opens daily from lunchtime to midnight.

Arguably the best *glacier* (ice-cream seller) in this part of the city is **Le Framboisier** *(Map 6; ☎ 02-647 51 44, Rue du Bailli 35)*. Traditional-style ice cream with imaginative flavours (such as fresh flowers) and sorbets made from Cantillon beers are the specialities of this shop/cafe. In summer you can beat a cool retreat to the garden out back. It opens noon to 11 pm (it's closed on Monday).

Notos *(Map 6; ☎ 02-513 29 59, Rue de*

Livourne 154) is a sleek little Greek restaurant newly relocated to this neighbourhood. There's no plate-smashing or faded posters of sun-soaked isles here; instead the refined ambience is backed up by superb Greek food with an imaginative twist. Main courses are in the €11.89 to €16.60 range. It's closed Sunday and Monday.

La Tsampa (Map 6; ☎ 02-647 03 67, Rue de Livourne 109) is a vegetarian restaurant attached to a health-food shop. It closes early (9.30 pm) but the atmosphere is agreeable, the food good (€8.67 for the dish of the day), and there's a small garden out back. It's closed on Sunday; tram No 93 stops near by on Ave Louise.

Fashionable restaurants and brasseries are all the rage on Rue du Page near the Musée Horta. One that's recommended is *Le Fils de Jules (Map 6; ☎ 02-534 00 57, Rue du Page 35)*, a yuppie outpost that does superb Basque and Landaise (from Landes in south-western France) cuisine. Main meals hover around the €17.35 mark (it's closed for lunch at the weekend). The interior is dark and inviting.

L'Amadeus (Map 6; ☎ 02-538 34 27, Rue Veydt 13) is an exotic establishment ideal for either a romantic tryst or a casual night out. It has two sections – a street-front wine and oyster bar and an intimate restaurant at the rear. It's a clever combination and attracts a loyal clientele. Mains cost between €13.51 and €21.94. It opens daily (except at lunchtime on Monday) and can be reached by tram No 91.

Trave Negra (Map 6; ☎ 02-539 28 87, Rue Théodore Verhaegen 9) in St Gilles is one of the city's best Portuguese restaurants. Belgium is home to about 45,000 Portuguese and two-thirds of the community live in the capital, mainly around St Gilles. This little restaurant offers excellent *salmão grelhado* (grilled salmon; €13.88) as well as a range of tasty national specialities. It's closed on Monday.

Down near the Université Libre de Bruxelles is *Le Doux Wazoo (Map 3; ☎ 02-649 58 52, Rue du Relais 21)*. It's well known for an outstanding wine list and delicious French/Belgian cuisine (mains cost from

€13 to €17.97) together with unfailingly friendly service. Tourists are a rare sight in this area but if you feel like exploring, bus No 95 from the Bourse will land you close by.

EU Area
Rue Archimède is lined with restaurants with English-language menus and pubs where Anglophones gather to drink and eat.

Rosticeria Fiorentina (Map 7; ☎ 02-734 92 36, Rue Archimède 43) has changed little over the years despite its perennial rave reviews. Hearty Italian cuisine (from €9.91 to €12.39) is served on paper tablecloths in unpretentious old-world surroundings.

At the other end of the spectrum is *Sotto Ripa (Map 6; ☎ 02-230 01 18, Rue du Luxembourg 60)*, an innovative and upmarket Italian/Mediterranean joint with mains starting at €14.87.

PLACES TO EAT – TOP END
Grand Place Area
The *Café Métropole (Map 5; ☎ 02-219 23 84, Place de Brouckère 31)* is part of the Hôtel Métropole. The cafe oozes splendour, with Art Deco chandeliers, plush leather upholstery and crisply attired waiters. It's a grand place to indulge in a coffee and cake.

The best you'll get on Grand Place is *La Maison du Cygne (Map 5; ☎ 02-511 82 44, Rue Charles Buls 2)*. This sophisticated restaurant occupies an elaborate guildhall and offers a few tables with much-cherished views over the square. The French/Belgian cuisine changes with the season. The lunchtime set *menu* (€35.94) is favoured by local businesspeople; at dinner (when the *menu* costs €61.97) it's the domain of the international well heeled. It is closed Saturday lunchtime and all day Sunday.

Marolles
Ask any Bruxellois to name the city's finest restaurant and the answer is always *Comme Chez Soi (Map 4; ☎ 02-512 29 21, Place Rouppe 23)*. Chef Pierre Wynants' innovative cuisine is dotted with seasonal stars like *truffes fraîches* (fresh truffles) and backed up with the likes of *faisan* (pheasant), fillets of

sole, caviar and sautéed pigeon. A good bite out of your weekly wage can be sunk here on a main course alone (€24.78 to €99) while four-course *menus* start at €53.29. Reservations are necessary. It opens for lunch and dinner and closes Sunday and Monday and all of July.

Sablon
Watching the Sablon's parade of fur coats, felt hats and overfed poodles is best undertaken at *Wittamer (Map 6; ☎ 02-512 37 42, Place du Grand Sablon 12–13)*. This exclusive patisserie has a 1st-floor tearoom where you can sip coffee and eat luscious gateaux (€8.92), and observe the bourgeois. It opens 10 am to 4 pm daily (except Monday).

Ave Louise & Ixelles
The gleaming brass interior of *La Quincaillerie (Map 6; ☎ 02-538 25 53, Rue du Page 45)* gives a clue to this sleek restaurant's former life as a hardware shop. Book a table for two on the 1st-floor gangway to best appreciate the setting. What's on depends on the vagaries of the season but seafood is the speciality and the oyster bar here is famous. Expect to pay about €25 for a typical main course. It's closed for lunch at the weekend.

L'Atelier de la Truffe Noire (Map 6; ☎ 02-640 54 55, Ave Louise 300) is a *très chic* brasserie attached to an expensive *traiteur* (delicatessen/grocery). Minimalist decor, warm tones and the inflated prices of the food (mains around €19.80) attract an urbane clientele. It opens 8.30 am to 6.30 pm daily (until 3 pm on Monday).

Entertainment

The English-language magazine *Bulletin* (see Newspapers & Magazines in the Facts for the Visitor chapter) has a What's On guide with good coverage of contemporary and classical live music, theatre, dance, opera, cinema and visual arts exhibitions.

Tickets for classical and contemporary events can be booked and bought through box offices or at FNAC (Map 4; ☎ 02-209 22 39), Rue Neuve, in the City 2 shopping centre. It opens 10 am to 7 pm Monday to Saturday. Call Centre (☎ 0800 212 21 in Belgium or ☎ 02-501 29 47 from abroad) takes bookings for opera and classical music events.

Another ticket agency for contemporary live gigs is Caroline Music (Map 5; ☎ 02-217 07 31), Passage St Honoré 20. This record shop also stocks fliers for smaller bands and has a whiteboard listing big events. Pick up the free, monthly *Mofo*, *Rif Raf* or *The Ticket* gig guides.

PUBS & BARS
Brown Cafes
A minute's walk from Grand Place – at the end of easily missed alleys – are four old taverns. The best known is *Toone* (Map 5) at the Théâtre Royal de Toone (see under Theatre later in this section), with a fireplace, wooden benches and ancient puppets dangling from the ceiling. There's also a nonsmoking section. You enter from either Petite Rue des Bouchers 21 or Impasse Schuddeveld 6.

Another is *Au Bon Vieux Temps (Map 5; ☎ 02-217 26 26, Rue du Marché aux Herbes 12)*, which is the cheapest of the lot. Next door, *À l'Imaige de Nostre Dame (Map 5; ☎ 02-219 42 49, Impasse des Cadeaux 6)* is reminiscent of an old Flemish kitchen and its ambience is warm and welcoming.

The last of the four is *À la Bécasse (Map*

Brussels' Top 10 Bars

- À la Mort Subite
- Le Cirio
- Le Greenwich
- Toone
- Bizon
- Roi des Belges
- Het Biercircus
- La Fleur en Papier Doré
- L'Ultime Atome
- De Ultieme Hallucinatie

BRUSSELS

5; ☎ 02-511 00 06, Rue de Tabora 11). It has just one hall with long rows of tables, good-hearted revelry and lambic and kriek beers served in earthenware pots. In all it's reminiscent of a scene from the days of Breugel.

Le Greenwich (Map 5; ☎ 02-511 41 67, Rue des Chartreux 7) is an eccentric cafe with wood panelling and mirrored walls. It has been attracting chess-players for decades – grandmasters such as Gary Kasparov and Anatoly Karpov have entered its hall and even Magritte used to get thrashed here. The atmosphere is always thick with smoke and concentration, the lack of music makes it a pleasant spot to read a newspaper, and the beers are cheap.

Another favourite of Magritte and his Surrealist pals was *La Fleur en Papier Doré (Map 4; ☎ 02-511 16 59, Rue des Alexiens 53).* The nicotine-stained walls of this dark cafe are covered with their writings and scribbles. These days it draws a cross-section of customers, from intellectuals to Eurocrats, young and old, dull or animated.

El Metteko (Map 5; ☎ 02-512 46 48, Blvd Anspach 88) is an old brown cafe that's recently been given a new lease of life. Unpolished wooden floors and two charming stained-glass windows attract young, unpretentious types.

Art Nouveau & Grand Cafés

A stalwart of days gone by is *Le Cirio (Map 5; ☎ 02-512 13 95, Rue de la Bourse 18).* This sumptuous *grand café* dates from 1886 and its opulent interior and aproned waiters attract widows with small dogs and tourists galore. Try a *half-en-half,* a champagne and white wine mix.

Falstaff (Map 5; ☎ 02-511 87 89, Rue Henri Maus 17) is an Art Nouveau showpiece that was listed as a protected monument in 2000. It's popular with the fashionable young and eccentric old, and has reasonably priced food and drinks.

Another Brussels gem is *Café Métropole* (Map 5; see Places to Eat – Top End earlier in the chapter).

À la Mort Subite (Map 5; ☎ 02-513 13 18, Rue Montagne aux Herbes Potagères 7) is a long cafe with smoke-yellowed walls

and subtle Art Nouveau tones. One of the country's many brews is named after it (the name means 'instant death' but the beer itself is not that strong). Nonsmokers can breathe (relatively) easy in the nonsmoking section at the front.

The Sablon's Art Nouveau showpiece is the unassuming *Le Perroquet* (Map 6; see Places to Eat – Budget earlier in the chapter for details).

La Porteuse d'Eau (Map 6; ☎ 02-538 83 54, Ave Jean Volders 48, metro Porte de Hal) is a sophisticated Art Nouveau cafe in a scruffy street in St Gilles. Unless you're a real Art Nouveau fan, it's not somewhere you'd make a beeline for.

The auspiciously named *De Ultieme Hallucinatie (Map 4; ☎ 02-217 06 14, Rue Royale 316)* is a famous Art Nouveau cafe and restaurant to the north of town. Built in 1904 by Brussels architect Paul Hamesse, its painted, green facade hides a rich interior.

Belgian Beer Pubs

Brussels has a couple of establishments which specialise in the nation's bevy of brews and where the menu resembles an A-to-Z of beers.

If you want to know something about what you're sinking and don't give a damn about decor then head to *Het Biercircus (Map 4; ☎ 02-218 00 34, Rue de l'Enseignement 89, metro Madou).* This place serves about 200 well-priced brews and the congenial staff can answer most beer queries. There's a nonsmoking room at the back. It opens noon to 2.30 pm and 6 pm to midnight (closed Saturday afternoon and all day Sunday). *Moeder Lambic (Map 6; ☎ 02-539 14 19, Rue de Savoie 68, premetro Horta)* is a smoky little pub in St Gilles with chunky tables and stacks of tattered comic books. It opens from late afternoon until about 4 am daily and is good for those wanting to succumb to the temptation of trying every brew in the book.

Anglophone Pubs & Bars

The bulk of Brussels' many Irish, English and American pubs are dotted around Grand Place and in the EU and Ave Louise areas.

Giant comic-strip murals enliven Brussels' streets.

Manneken Pis models his *au naturel* look.

Dive into Belgium's vats of smooth chocolate.

Belgian chocolates are regarded as everyday essentials by locals, so forget your waistline and indulge.

Climb the Butte du Lion to see where Napoleon's bid for Europe ended at the Battle of Waterloo.

With its delicate statues and fancy stonework Leuven's town hall resembles an overblown wedding cak

One of the oldest is **Rick's** *(Map 6)* – see under Places to Eat – Mid-Range for more details.

The Bank *(Map 6;* ☎ *02-537 52 65, Rue du Bailli 79)* is a congenial Irish pub situated in a former bank. A row of old safe-deposit boxes lines one wall and the cosmopolitan crowd is more arty (and less blinkered by sport on TV) than drinkers at many of the city's other Irish pubs. There's free live music most Saturdays from 10.30 pm.

The Wild Geese *(Map 7;* ☎ *02-230 19 90, Ave Livingstone 2)* is the biggest Irish pub in the city. Within staggering distance of Maelbeek metro station, it's often heaving with Eurocrats and their underlings – small outdoor terraces soak up some of the crowds in summer. There's live jazz on Tuesday (from 9 pm), and a disco at the weekend.

Other Pubs & Bars

Grand Place Area Occupying a guildhall on Grand Place is *Le Roy d'Espagne (Map 5;* ☎ *02-513 08 07, Grand Place 1)*. This big cafe/restaurant affords views of the square and, most notably, uses dried pig's bladders for decoration.

If drinking out of skull-shaped mugs around tables made from coffins is your thing, make a beeline for the *Cerceuil (Map 5;* ☎ *02-512 30 77, Rue des Harengs 10)*. Be prepared for expensive drinks.

Au Soleil *(Map 5;* ☎ *02-513 34 30, Rue du Marché au Charbon 86)* is a corner cafe where drinkers spill out onto a quiet cobbled street in summer. It's a pleasant place to read a paper by day and sample a few beers at night.

St Géry & Ste Catherine New addresses are constantly popping up in these lively areas. Some are chic bistros where the beautiful people congregate to smoke and gossip; others are simply pleasant cafes or down-to-earth wateringholes.

Zebra *(Map 5;* ☎ *02-511 09 01, Place St Géry 33)* was the original bar in this area and is still a popular hangout with alternative types. **Mappa Mundo** *(Map 5;* ☎ *02-514 35 55, Rue du Pont de la Carpe 2–6)* attracts a young clientele (read 18 years old)

while newcomer **Roi des Belges** *(Map 5;* ☎ *02-503 43 00, Rue Van Praet 35)* is arguably the most trendy.

Bizon *(Map 5;* ☎ *02-502 46 99, Rue du Pont de la Carpe 7)* is a happening little grunge bar with live music – piano, jazz, blues or rock – on Sunday to Tuesday night from 8 pm. Admission is free but drink prices are hiked up a bit on nights when there's music.

Café De Markten *(Map 5;* ☎ *02-514 66 04, Rue du Vieux Marché aux Grains 5)* is atypical of cafes in Brussels – it's large and spacious with a minimalist modern interior and a largely Flemish-speaking clientele. Go for a freshly-squeezed fruit or veggie juice (€1.98) or something less healthy.

Marolles The local bar of old, working-class folk from the Marolles is **Brasserie Ploegmans** *(Map 6;* ☎ *02-514 28 84, Rue Haute 148)*. It's typical of the few remaining family-owned pubs on this street and is generally full of smoke and a rich assortment of characters speaking Brussels dialect.

Sablon An ambient cafe on a backstreet in the Sablon is *Le Cercle (Map 6;* ☎ *02-514 03 53, Rue Ste Anne 20)*. Such pubs are rare in this area and it attracts a hip crowd with occasional live music and dance nights.

Porte de Namur Stocking an excellent range of beers at low prices, *L'Ultime Atome* (Map 6; see under Places to Eat – Budget) is a great place to imbibe.

EU Area The *Café de l'Autobus (Map 7;* ☎ *02-230 63 16, Place Jourdan)* is a corner pub popular with students during the week and vendors from the Place Jourdan market on Sunday. It's opposite the city's best *friture* (chip shop) and the owners don't mind if you eat hot chips here while downing a beer.

CLUBS

Most clubs operate Thursday to Saturday from about 10 pm, but the action doesn't really begin until after midnight.

Fuse *(Map 6;* ☎ *02-511 97 89, Rue Blaes 208, metro Porte de Hal)* is in the Marolles

BRUSSELS

and is Brussels' best-known club. It started in 1994 and has one floor devoted to techno, another to house. The club attracts a sound line-up of visiting international DJs and also has a good team of resident locals. It's open every Saturday night and usually goes on until 6 or 7 am. Admission is free between 11 pm and midnight, or €9.91 after. Check its Web site at www.fuse.be for details of the line-up.

The newest club in central Brussels is *Wilde (Map 5; ☎ 02-513 44 59, Blvd Anspach 79)*. This bar-cum-lounge has a free nightclub upstairs on Friday, Saturday and Sunday from 9 pm. Cool guys and chicks are attracted like bees to the bright primary colours and minimal decor.

Celtica (Map 5; ☎ 02-514 22 69, Rue du Marché aux Poulets 55), close to Grand Place, sports a popular disco (free) every Friday and Saturday. Dancing goes on until the wee small hours.

A grungy but longstanding club is *Sonik (Map 5; ☎ 02-511 99 85, Rue du Marché au Charbon 112)*. It's small but has managed to survive and now boasts a new sound system and air-conditioning. House music is favoured. Admission costs €3.71; try it Thursday to Saturday nights.

Tours et Taxi (Map 3; Rue Picard 5, metro Ribaucourt) is a gargantuan 19th-century customs house away to the north of town that turns into a mega dance floor on the first Friday of each month; it plays a range of house, techno and rock. Admission costs €4.95. You can also get there with bus No 14 from Gare du Nord.

Espace de Nuit (Map 5; Rue du Marché aux Fromages 10) is a tourist favourite, playing a mix of 1980s and '90s hits. Located in an old house close to Grand Place, it spans a couple of floors but is relatively small; admission costs €4.95.

Le Salsa (Map 5; Borgval 7) has a tiny dance floor and admission is free. It's good for an hour or two before moving on.

Bazaar (Map 6; ☎ 02-511 26 00, Rue des Capucins 63) is a restaurant-cum-bar and club. The cavernous underground club opens on Friday and Saturday and plays mainly rock and funk; live ethnic music is

staged every Tuesday. Admission costs €7.43 (which includes a drink).

GAY & LESBIAN VENUES

Brussels' gay quarter is situated around Rue du Marché au Charbon, Rue des Pierres and Rue de la Fourche.

The bar at *Tels Quels (Map 5; ☎ 02-512 45 87, Rue du Marché au Charbon 81)* opens from 7 pm and is a good starting point for finding out what's on.

So too is *Le Belgica (Map 5; Rue du Marché au Charbon 32)*. This tatty brown cafe opens 10 pm to 3 am Thursday to Sunday. Despite the unassuming facade and decor, it's one of the city's oldest gay pubs and, if there's a party going on, someone here is sure to know.

The nearby bright pink *L'Incognito (Map 5; ☎ 02-513 37 88, Rue des Pierres 36)* is a funky little bar open from 11 am daily; it features a transvestite show on Sunday evening.

On one Sunday a month the Fuse club becomes *La Démence (Map 6; ☎ 02-511 97 89, Rue Blaes 208)*, a huge gay rave that attracts men from all over Belgium and from neighbouring countries too. There are several dance floors, go-go shows, darkrooms and international DJs. It opens at 11 pm and goes until about midday the following day.

Le Wings (Map 5; ☎ 075-66 09 90, Rue du Cyprès 3) is a lesbian disco that gets going at 10 pm on Saturday. Men are also welcome on Friday.

Another mixed club is *The Gate (Map 5; ☎ 02-223 04 34, Rue Fossé aux Loups 36)*. It's new and polished and welcomes women (only) on Saturday nights. The rest of the week it's mainly for men.

ROCK

Some home-grown bands and singers that you might come across on the Brussels live music circuit include K's Choice, Front 242, dEUS and Venux.

The city's temple for large international gigs and local favourites is *Forest National (Map 3; ☎ 02-340 22 11, Ave du Globe 36)*. It can hold a crowd of about 8000, and tickets generally lie in the €25 to €45 range.

An excellent venue in the heart of the city is the ***Ancienne Belgique*** *(Map 5;* ☎ *02-548 24 24, Blvd Anspach 110)*, known as the 'AB'. Its two auditoriums accommodate international and home-grown bands; the small 1st-floor hall is used for new local bands. Prices generally vary between €7.50 and €23.

The ***Beursschouwburg*** *(Map 5;* ☎ *02-513 82 90, Rue Auguste Orts 20–6)*, close to the Bourse, showcases a diverse mix of contemporary music including rock, jazz, rap and disco; however, at the time of writing, it was expected to temporarily close for restoration.

Flanagans *(Map 5;* ☎ *02-511 80 85, Rue de l'Écuyer 59)* is a small venue three blocks from Grand Place with an upstairs bar and adjoining hall where jam sessions, rock parties and reggae nights are held. Admission costs about €5.

Also central is the ***Rock Classic Bar*** *(Map 5;* ☎ *02-512 15 47, Rue du Marché au Charbon)*. It has occasional live bands, admission is free and it gets going nightly from 9 pm.

Moving away from the centre, there's ***Le Botanique*** *(Map 4;* ☎ *02-226 12 11, Rue Royale 236, metro Botanique)*. This cultural centre for Brussels' French-speaking community also puts on rock, pop, world-music events and theatre. Tickets usually cost between €7.50 and €17.

Continuing north is the ***Halles de Schaerbeek*** *(Map 4;* ☎ *02-218 21 07, Rue Royale Ste Marie 22b)*. This impressive former 19th-century food market is an all-round centre for the performing arts rather than a pure rock venue. Ticket prices range from €8.70 to €22.50. To get there take tram No 92 or 93.

Fool Moon *(Map 4;* ☎ *02-410 10 03, Quai de Mariemont 26)* is a multidisciplinary centre featuring rock, hip-hop and house music as well as theatre and some avant-garde dance. To get there take bus No 63 to Place de la Duchesse de Brabant or tram No 18 to Porte de Ninove.

Magasin 4 *(Map 4;* ☎ *02-223 34 74, Rue du Magasin 4)* has been around for years and is the city's premier venue for alternative bands. Expect anything from noisy experimental rock to electric hip hop. It opens Friday and Saturday from 9 pm; admission costs about €6.20.

The Crow *(Map 3;* ☎ *02-640 41 00, Ave Louise 520)* opened in mid-1998 and hosts live acoustic sets every Thursday plus electric bands on Friday. The ambience is excellent. It's a way out of the centre but easily reached by tram No 93 or 94.

Some of the Anglophone pubs also feature live music – check the earlier Pubs & Bars section for details.

JAZZ

The city's newest and most polished jazz venue is ***The Music Village*** *(Map 5;* ☎ *02-513 13 45, Rue des Pierres 50)*. You can wine and dine here from 7 pm, with concerts (Wednesday to Saturday) beginning at 8.30 pm. There's an €8.67 annual membership fee to get in, and concerts range in price from €7.43 to €9.90.

Those into both Art Deco and live jazz should head to ***L'Archiduc*** *(Map 5;* ☎ *02-512 06 52, Rue Antoine Dansaert 6)*. This exclusive (and expensive) little cafe was built in the 1930s and has live music on Saturday from 5 to 8 pm (there's usually an admission charge for special events). It opens daily from 4 pm until dawn.

The ***Marcus Mingus Jazz Club*** *(Map 5;* ☎ *02-514 16 15, Rue de la Fourche 17)* in the basement of Hôtel Arlequin supports a solid jazz line-up from 9 pm Thursday to Saturday. Admission ranges from free to €7.43.

In Ixelles, ***Sounds Jazz Club*** *(Map 6;* ☎ *02-512 92 50, Rue de la Tulipe 28)* is an unassuming but well-known bar with a small podium out back where local or visiting musicians play every night (except on Sunday). Acts start about 10 pm. Admission varies – from nothing to €12.39. To get there take bus No 54 or 71.

CLASSICAL MUSIC

Classical music buffs will find Brussels offers ample choice and high quality. Besides the big-name concerts (for which admission ranges from €10 to €62), there are often free lunchtime events in small venues dotted around the city – check the What's On supplement of *Bulletin*.

One of the year's highlights is the world-renowned Concours Musical International Reine Elisabeth de Belgique – see under Special Events in the Facts for the Visitor chapter for details.

The *Palais des Beaux-Arts/Het Kunstenpaleis (Map 4; ☎ 02-507 82 15, for bookings call ☎ 02-507 82 00, Rue Ravenstein 23, metro Parc)* is the country's most celebrated classical music venue. It was designed by Horta and opened in 1928, and is home not only to the National Orchestra but also to the Philharmonic Society, which organises much of the capital's classical music program. The Henri Le Bœuf *salle* (hall) is considered to be one of the five best in the world for acoustic quality. Pick up the monthly *Le Journal du Palais des Beaux-Arts* to find out what's on.

The *Conservatoire Royal de Musique (Royal Music Conservatory; Map 6; ☎ 02-511 04 27, Rue de la Régence 30)* is the city's other major venue, though it's considerably smaller than the Palais des Beaux-Arts and hosts a much more modest program.

Among the many smaller venues around town – including churches and the Hôtel de Ville – some worth noting are:

Cathédrale des Sts Michel & Gudule (Map 4; ☎ 02-217 83 45, Parvis Ste Gudule) The cathedral is a popular (if acoustically challenging) setting.
Cirque Royal (Map 4; ☎ 02-218 20 15, Rue de l'Enseignement 81, metro Madou) This converted indoor circus is now a venue for music, operetta and dance.
Église des Minimes (Map 6; ☎ 02-507 82 00, Rue des Minimes 62) This baroque church below the Palais de Justice is an immensely popular venue with a sizeable program.
Musées Royaux des Beaux-Arts (Map 4; ☎ 02-508 32 11, Rue de la Régence 3) A 50-minute lunchtime concert is held here at 12.40 pm every Wednesday; price €4.95.

CINEMAS

Brussels has a good selection of both small and large cinemas. The *Kinepolis (Map 8; ☎ 02-474 26 00, Blvd du Centenaire 20, metro Roi Baudouin)* is a megaplex featur-

Cinema Tips

Cinemas in Brussels screen some films in their original language with subtitles *(ondertiteld/sous-titres)* in French, and sometimes Flemish as well. They also dub many films into French, so check before you go in if you don't want to sit through (to you) incomprehensible gabble. *Bulletin*'s What's On guide has good listings that clearly spell out what's on in what language. Codes you'll come across include 'VO' (original version), 'V fr' (French version), 'V angl' (English version) and 'st' (subtitles). Programs change on Wednesday, and screenings are cheaper at selected cinemas on Monday.

ing 25 screens and an *IMAX theatre*. Tickets cost €6.69 for adults and €4.95 for seniors, students and children.

The *Arenberg Galeries (Map 5; ☎ 02-512 80 63, Galerie de la Reine 26)* is a remodelled Art Deco theatre showing foreign and arty films in its two auditoriums. Cinema tickets cost €6.44 (children, students and seniors €4.95).

The *Musée du Cinéma (Map 4; ☎ 02-507 83 70, Rue Baron Horta 9)*, in a side wing of the Palais des Beaux-Arts, has two screens: one dedicated to showing old *films muets* (silent movies) accompanied by a pianist, the other to classic talkies. Anywhere up to seven films are shown per night. It opens nightly from 5.30 pm and tickets cost €1.48 if reserved at least one day in advance or €2.23 at the door. Come 30 minutes early so you can browse through the museum's collection of old equipment.

On Friday and Saturday nights from 1 July to 30 August a *drive-in cinema* is set up beside the Arcade du Cinquantenaire (Map 7) at Parc du Cinquantenaire. Chairs and headphones are provided for those who don't have a car. The price is €12.39 per car or €3.71 for pedestrians.

Other cinemas include:

Actor's Studio (Map 5; ☎ 02-512 16 96, Petite Rue des Bouchers 16) Art house and foreign films.

Aventure (Map 5; ☎ 02-219 17 48, Galerie du Centre) This place is 40 years old and still the cheapest mainstream cinema in town.

Nova (Map 5; ☎ 02-511 24 77, Rue d'Arenberg 3)

Styx (Map 6; ☎ 02-512 21 02, Rue de l'Arbre Bénit 72) This place is said to be the smallest cinema in Europe.

THEATRE

Brussels is rich with troupes and venues for theatre (*toneel* in Flemish and *théâtre* in French). Most productions are in French or Flemish and a handful are in German; only amateur groups cater for the English-speaking community. Tickets range from €7.45 to €30 (discounted for students).

The mundane-looking **Théâtre National** *(Map 4; ☎ 02-203 41 55, Place Rogier)* is the theatre of the French-speaking community.

Its Flemish counterpart is the **Koninklijke Vlaamse Schouwburg** *(Map 4; ☎ 02-217 69 37, Rue de Laeken 146)*, an ostentatious building dating from the late 1880s. It was built by Jean Baes and is one of the city's finest examples of neo-Renaissance architecture. The building is currently closed for a facelift (expected to be finished in 2002), so the company has temporarily moved to **De Bottelarij** *(Map 4; ☎ 02-412 70 70, Rue Delaunoy 58)* in Molenbeek-St-Jean.

Whether you understand Bruxellois dialect or not, don't miss a performance at the **Théâtre Royal de Toone** *(Map 5; ☎ 02-511 71 37, Impasse Schuddeveld 6 or Petite Rue des Bouchers 21)*. This famous marionette theatre has been staging puppet productions of works such as *The Three Musketeers*, *Faust* and *Hamlet* for well over a century. The first Toone theatre was established in 1830 by Antoine Gente (Toone is a short-ened form of Antoine), and today's Toone VII theatre is the seventh generation. It originated in the Marolles, moving to its present place in 1966. The puppets are made out of wood and papier-mâché. Performances are occasionally in English but usually in Brussels dialect; tickets cost €9.90 (seniors and students €6.20).

Most of the city's amateur theatre groups – including the English Comedy Club, the American Theatre Group and the English

Shakespeare Society – don't have perma-nent venues; check *Bulletin* for details.

OPERA

Brussels' most prestigious cultural venue is the **Théâtre Royal de la Monnaie/Konin-klijke Muntschouwburg** *(Map 5; ☎ 070-23 39 39, Place de la Monnaie)*, better known as simply La Monnaie to French-speakers or De Munt to the Flemish. The revolution of 1830 was sparked during a performance here, and these days it's generally full house. The season runs from September to June and seats cost from €12 to €50. Tickets are hard to get as most seats are snapped up at the start of the season by Belgians with yearly membership.

DANCE

Brussels boasts an array of innovative dance companies and wonderful venues in which to see them. For classical ballet you'll have to go to Antwerp (see under Entertainment in the Antwerp chapter). The **Palais des Beaux-Arts** (see the Classical Music section earlier) and the **Théâtre Royal de la Mon-naie** (see Opera earlier) are the big draws, but there are also performances at **Cirque Royal** (see Classical Music earlier), **Fool Moon** (see Rock earlier Rock) and at the **Kaaitheater-Luna** *(Map 4; ☎ 02-201 59 59, Square Sainctelette 29, metro Yser)*, to name but a few.

SPECTATOR SPORTS

Brussels' most famous football team, RSC Anderlecht, plays at **Vandenstock stadium** *(Map 3; ☎ 02-522 15 39, Ave Théo Ver-beeck 2)* in Anderlecht. To get there take the metro to St Guidon. For more information on football in Belgium see Spectator Sports in the Facts for the Visitor chapter.

Shopping

The focal points of the shopping year are the January and July *solden/soldes* (sales) when prices, particularly for clothes, shoes and jewellery, crash by 30% to 50%.

The main shopping areas are the old centre,

and the Sablon and Ave Louise areas in the Upper Town.

The old centre's most attractive glass-covered shopping arcades are Galeries St Hubert (Map 5), Galerie Bortier near Gare Centrale (Map 5; mainly for second-hand books) and Passage du Nord (Map 5).

In stark contrast to the galleries is the old centre's main shopping thoroughfare – Rue Neuve – a brash consumer's paradise lined with mainstream shops and department stores.

In the Upper Town, Ave Louise and Blvd de Waterloo are the playgrounds of the wealthy – here you'll find international designer clothing and jewellery boutiques, and the Galeries Louise (Map 6). Avenue de la Toison d'Or, with its network of shopping galleries (Map 6), is more mainstream.

Close by, but culturally a world away, is the Galerie d'Ixelles (Map 6). This small gallery is home to shops run by Brussels' Congolese community – colourful African cloth, exotic fruits and hairdressers are the mainstays.

ANTIQUES
The Sablon is the area for antiques. The many private galleries here mostly resemble miniature museums – you'll find ancient artefacts from around the world as well as contemporary art. The streets to head for (all shown on Map 6) are Rue des Minimes, Rue Charles Hanssens, Rue Watteeu, Rue Ernest Allard and, of course, Place du Grand Sablon. The latter is the site of a weekly antique market (see the Markets section for details).

ART
Contemporary art galleries are dotted around town. A good brochure to pick up from the national tourist office is *Art Brussels*. It's published three times a year and lists many of the galleries and their exhibitions.

BEER
De Biertempel (Map 5; ☎ 02-502 19 06, ⒠ info@beertemple.com), Rue du Marché aux Herbes 56b, stocks around 200 brews and matching glasses plus all manner of

beer paraphernalia. Staff here can organise international shipments (but not to the USA). To the UK, a 10kg parcel (roughly 20 33cl bottles) will cost €24.78 for freight; the price of the bottles is extra. Their online shop is at www.beertemple.com.

Beer Mania (Map 6; ☎ 02-512 17 88, fax 02-511 32 42, ⒠ beermania@skynet.be), Chaussée de Wavre 174, is also known as 400 Bière Artisanale as it stocks 400 Belgian beers. It opened in 1983 and was Belgium's first specialist beer shop. The owner Nasser Eftekhari is passionate about the product and sells, among other things, metre-long cases of various beers (€37) and arranges international door-to-door deliveries. As an example of freight prices, it costs US$120/220 for a 30kg parcel (delivered in three days) to the USA/Australia. The shop was expanding at the time of writing and by now should have its own tasting room where beer appreciation evenings will be held. The shop opens 11 am to 7 pm Monday to Saturday, and bus Nos 95 and 96 stop nearby. Its Web site is at www.beermania.be.

BISCUITS
The place in Brussels to buy Belgium's spicy *speculoos*, a cinnamon-flavoured biscuit, is Dandoy (Map 5; ☎ 02-511 03 26), an exquisite little biscuit shop at Rue au Beurre 31.

BOOKS
Comics
Brüsel (Map 5; ☎ 02-502 35 52) Blvd Anspach 100. A chic little comic-book shop named after a book by one of Belgium's best-known contemporary comic artists, François Schuiten. Some English-language translations are available.

Centre Belge de la Bande Dessinée (Map 4; ☎ 02-219 19 80) Rue des Sables 20. The Belgian Centre for Comic Strip Art has an excellent comic shop.

La Boutique de Tintin (Map 5; ☎ 02-514 45 50) Rue de la Colline 13. This shop stocks every Tintin comic you ever wanted and more.

English-Language
Sterling Books (Map 5; ☎/fax 02-223 62 23) Rue du Fossé aux Loups 38. Comfy sofas, a kid's play area and helpful staff make this bookshop

stand out. It opens 10 am to 7 pm Monday to Saturday and noon to 6.30 pm Sunday.

Waterstones (Map 5; ☎ 02-219 27 08) Blvd Adolphe Max 71–5. This is the city's biggest English-language bookshop. It opens 9 am to 7 pm Monday to Saturday and 11.30 am to 6 pm Sunday.

Gay & Lesbian

Artemys (Map 5; ☎/fax 02-512 13 47, e artemys@multimania.com) Galerie Bortier 8. For details on this bookshop for lesbians see Gay & Lesbian Travellers in the Facts for the Visitor chapter.

Darakan (Map 5; ☎ 02-512 20 76) Rue du Midi 9. A tiny gay bookshop.

Second-Hand

De Slegte (Map 5; ☎ 02-511 61 40) Rue des Grandes Carmes 17. A Dutch chain of bookshops specialising in second-hand or remaindered titles. A lot of it is dirt-cheap rubbish but it's possible to pick up some good buys.

Pêle Mêle (Map 4; ☎ 02-548 78 00) Blvd Maurice Lemonnier 55. A cavernous bookshop with a reasonable selection of English-language novels and comics.

Évasions (Map 5; ☎ 02-502 49 56) Rue du Midi 89. This place buys and sells and is totally chaotic.

Travel

Anticyclone des Açores (Map 5; ☎ 02-217 52 46) Rue du Fossé aux Loups 34. Specialist in travel guides, maps and trekking books.

Peuples et Continents (Map 4; ☎ 02-511 27 75) Rue Ravenstein. Good travel bookshop.

Other Bookshops

Art Shop (Map 4; ☎ 02-507 83 33) Rue Ravenstein 23. This bookshop is inside the Palais des Beaux-Arts and has an excellent selection of art books.

FNAC (Map 4; ☎ 02-209 22 11) inside the City 2 shopping centre on Rue Neuve. Large, general bookshop with a good selection of English-language books, travel guides and maps. It opens 10 am to 7 pm Monday to Saturday.

La Librairie de Rome (Map 6; ☎ 02-511 79 37) Ave Louise 50 bis. This small bookshop is best known for its broad range of international magazines and newspapers. It opens 7.30 am to 9 pm daily.

Posada Art Books (Map 5; ☎ 02-511 08 34) Rue de la Madeleine 29. Books on art, both new and second-hand, are stuffed to the ceiling in this little shop.

CHOCOLATE

There's no match for a Belgian chocolate shop. A few to try include:

Galler (Map 5; ☎ 02-502 02 66) Rue au Beurre 44. This shop has an excellent reputation, high prices and a handy location just off Grand Place.

Godiva (Map 5; ☎ 02-511 25 37) Grand Place 37, and another branch (Map 6; ☎ 02-538 13 50) at Chaussée de Charleroi 11. This is the most exclusive of the chain chocolate shops.

Neuhaus (Map 5; ☎ 02-512 63 59) Galerie de la Reine 25. A gorgeous shop with stained-glass windows and sumptuous displays. It was established in 1857 and is now a popular, reasonably priced, national chain.

Pierre Marcolini (Map 6; ☎ 02-514 12 06) Place du Grand Sablon 39. Join the queues at this relative newcomer to the chocolate scene where pralines are packaged in boxes designed by Delvaux (of leather accessories fame).

Planète Chocolat (Map 5; ☎ 02-511 07 55) Rue du Lombard 24. Frank Duval is the force behind this innovative chocolate shop-cum-cafe. You can watch Frank at work at 3 pm on Saturday afternoon, and the €5.45 admission price includes a tasting.

Wittamer (Map 6; ☎ 02-512 37 42) Place du Grand Sablon 6. This is the sister establishment to the nearby patisserie of the same name and one of the city's finest chocolate shops.

CLOTHING & ACCESSORIES
Designer

Ave Louise and Rue Antoine Dansaert are the main stamping grounds for designer boutiques. These include:

Bouvy (Map 6; ☎ 02-513 63 91) Ave de la Toison d'Or 52. There are creations for both sexes by local and international designers here; there's another entrance on Ave Louise.

Delvaux (Map 5; ☎ 02-512 71 98) Galerie de la Reine 31 in Galeries St Hubert. Delvaux is a household name in handbags in Belgium.

Elvis Pompilio (Map 5; ☎ 02-511 11 88). The two Pompilio stores are all about hats – men's are at Rue du Lombard 18 and women's are on the corner of Rue du Lombard and Rue du Midi. All are handmade and prices start at €85.

Kaat Tilley (Map 5; ☎ 02-514 07 63) Galerie du Roi 4. Women's and children's collections.

Lena Lena (Map 5; ☎ 02-502 22 33) Rue Antoine Dansaert 60. This is the outlet for creations by Marina Yee, one of Antwerp's better-known designers.

Nicolas Woit (Map 5; ☎ 02-503 48 32) Rue Antoine Dansaert 80. Woit uses new and second-hand materials for his exotic handmade clothes.

Olivier Strelli There's two branches in Brussels; the main branch is at Ave Louise 72 (Map 6; ☎ 02-512 56 07) and there's a smaller one is at Rue Antoine Dansaert 44 (Map 5; ☎ 02-512 09 42). Strelli is a top-notch Belgian designer of men's and women's collections.

Patrick Pitschon (Map 4; ☎ 02-512 11 76) Rue Antoine Dansaert 88. A young Flemish designer.

Stijl (Map 5; ☎ 02-512 03 13) Rue Antoine Dansaert 74. Home to top Antwerp designers.

Mainstream

Inno is Belgium's only home-grown department store and there are two locations in Brussels – one is at Rue Neuve 111 (Map 5; ☎ 02-211 21 11) and the other is Ave Louise 12 (Map 6; ☎ 02-513 84 94). The Galerie Agora (Map 5) near Grand Place is filled with leather shops.

Second-Hand

SOS Company (Map 5; ☎ 0478 82 29 65), Rue de la Bourse 6, has funky clothes and a good range of jeans. The chic Les Enfants d'Édouard (Map 6; ☎ 02-640 42 45), Ave Louise 175–7, has adjoining shops for men and women containing racks of designer hand-me-downs. Michèle Simon (Map 6; ☎ 02-512 33 89) at Galeries Louise 128 and Boutique 114 (Map 6; ☎ 02-512 40 27) at Rue de Stassart 114 do less expensive women's clothes.

EU MERCHANDISE

Euroline (Map 5; ☎ 02-511 36 30), Rue du Marché aux Herbes 52b, stocks all manner of things bearing the 12 golden stars.

LACE

Manufacture Belge de Dentelles (Map 5; ☎ 02-511 44 77), Galerie de la Reine 6–8, is Brussels' oldest lace shop – in existence since 1810. It has an excellent stock of antique lace, and helpful, knowledgeable staff. Also recommended is F. Rubbrecht (Map 5; ☎ 02-512 02 18), Grand Place 23.

For further advice see the 'Buying Lace' boxed text in the Bruges chapter.

MARKETS

Markets are part of life for many people in Brussels (and Belgium). There are two main types – bric-a-brac *(curiosa/brocante)* and general markets where food, clothing and miscellaneous goods are all sold.

Brussels' biggest general market is held around Gare du Midi (Map 6) every Sunday from 6 am to 1 pm. It sprawls along both sides of the railway lines and has a distinctly North African and Mediterranean feel. Bulbous cheeses, strings of sausages and vendors loudly announcing their wares are all part of it.

For brocante, head to the daily Place du Jeu de Balle fleamarket (Map 6) in the Marolles. It goes from 7 am to early afternoon and is best at the weekend (though prices are higher then). Genuine antiques are few but there's some great junk. Haggling is expected.

Grand Place is home to a small flower market from Tuesday to Sunday, as well as a bird market on Sunday morning.

Antique collectors will inevitably end up at the small market on Place du Grand Sablon (Map 6) each Saturday (from 9 am to 6 pm) and Sunday (9 am to 2 pm).

Excursions

TERVUREN

Tervuren (Map 1) is a picturesque Flemish-speaking town in leafy surroundings, 14km east of Brussels. It's best known for its museum, with its echoes of Belgium's imperial past.

Koninklijk Museum voor Midden-Afrika

The Royal Museum of Central Africa (☎ 02-769 52 11), Leuvensesteenweg 13, has an impressive range of artefacts from the Congo, much of which was acquired during Léopold II's rule (see the boxed text 'Léopold II and the Congo'). Those interested in African wildlife and culture will find it fascinating. The museum is, however, an imperialistic showpiece and there is no mention of the millions of Congolese people

BRUSSELS

Léopold II & the Congo

ALBERT COLE

On coming to the throne in 1865, Léopold II had ambitions of extending his empire. In the 1870s he was assisted in his goal by the Africa explorer Henry Stanley (of 'Dr Livingstone, I presume?' fame) and in 1885, with the consent of the major European powers, he took personal control of the vast Congo region in Central Africa.

During the next two decades, Léopold exploited the area and its people, making vast sums of money through slavery and exporting ivory and rubber. Some of that wealth he poured into monumental projects in Belgium; the rest he kept, becoming one of the country's richest men.

In 1897 he staged an exhibition about the Congo in Brussels and, buoyed by its success, ordered the construction of a huge neoclassical edifice to house his collection of artefacts permanently. The museum at Tervuren opened in 1910. Two years earlier, the Belgian government had stripped Léopold of his personal fiefdom due to international criticism of the exploitation, slavery and atrocities committed under his rule.

The Congo regained its independence from Belgium in 1960.

who died under Léopold's reign (though the Belgians who never returned are remembered on two walls in the museum's Memorial Hall). This imbalance may be addressed in the future as a new director appointed in 2000 has been given the task of breathing new life into the antiquated museum.

Labelling throughout is basic and in French and Flemish only – for more detail you'll need to buy the €2.50 English-language guidebook.

The museum opens 10 am to 5 pm Tuesday to Sunday (until 6 pm at the weekend); admission costs €1.98 (seniors and students €1). The light and airy *Simba Café* inside the museum serves a small range of unexotic meals and snacks.

Park van Tervuren
Tervuren park backs onto the African museum and is a pleasant place for a wander or picnic after touring the museum. Walking paths meander around a series of lakes, past manicured lawns and through forested areas.

Getting There & Away
To get to the museum from Brussels, simply take tram No 44 from Montgomery metro station to its terminus at Tervuren

(€1.23 one way) and then walk 300m. It's a lovely tram ride.

FORÊT DE SOIGNES
This forest (Maps 1 and 3) covers some 43 sq km to the south-east of Brussels and is the largest patch of green in the region. It was originally part of a much greater oak forest that was progressively cut down during the 16th and 17th centuries. The oldest trees today are beech, planted in the 18th century under the Austrian rulers.

The park is one of Belgium's most important state-owned forests and is home to wild boar and deer. It's popular throughout the year but particularly in summer when old trams operated by Brussels' Musée du Transport Urbain trundle through. It includes two arboreta – Tervuren and Groenendaal (both Map 1) – plus the Jean Massart Experimental Garden (Map 3) and the Rouge Cloître (Map 3), a 14th-century abbey with an information centre (☎ 02-629 34 11) open 2 to 6 pm Tuesday to Sunday from May to October (until 5 pm the rest of the year).

Getting There & Away
There are various public transport options to the forest, depending on which part you

wish to access. If you just want to get to any patch of green, take bus No 95 from the Bourse (Map 5) in central Brussels.

LEUVEN

About 25km east of Brussels, Leuven (Louvain in French) is the chief town of the province of Flemish Brabant. It's an ancient capital – the home of the dukes of Brabant since around 1200 – and boasts one of Belgium's most ornate town halls. As Flanders' premier university town (see the boxed text 'The KUL'), it's home to 25,000 students and has a lively, up-to-the-minute air.

The town's main sight is the 15th-century **Stadhuis** (town hall), a flamboyant Gothic structure with terraced turrets and fancy stonework. Across the square is the **St Pieterskerk**, which is another late-Gothic edifice and home to a couple of impressive paintings by Dirk Bouts. Bouts was a 15th-century artist who spent much of his life here.

From Brussels, trains run every half-hour to Leuven (€3.59, 30 minutes).

WATERLOO

Waterloo (Map 1) lies 18km south of Brussels and, with your own car, is easily visited on a day trip from the capital. Once a big tourist pull, these days only 200,000 or so visitors per year come to look out over the plains from the Lion of Waterloo – the site of the 1815 battle that changed the course of European history (see the boxed text 'The Battle of Waterloo').

While Waterloo's image may be grand – it has given its name to more than 100 towns around the world and even Abba sang its praises – the place itself is staid. History and war buffs may find it interesting but many people wonder why they bothered to come. The most important sights are spread over several kilometres, so without your own transport it can be tedious getting around. Plans are afoot to perk the place up for its anniversary in 2015, but that's some time away yet.

Things to See & Do

The best place to start is at the Office du

The KUL

The Katholieke Universiteit van Leuven (KUL) was founded in 1425 and within a century was one of Europe's most highly regarded universities. Its history, however, has been far from smooth, with disputes arising over religion and, later, language. Things came to a head in the late 1960s when Flemish students protested over the absence of lectures in their mother tongue, eventually forcing their French-speaking counterparts to set up a new Francophone university at Louvain-la-Neuve, south-east of Brussels. In one of those typically Belgian scenarios, the university then split its reference library in two – the KUL kept everything from A to L, and Louvain-la-Neuve took M to Z!

Tourisme (☎ 02-354 99 10), Chaussée de Bruxelles 149, in the village of Waterloo. It opens 9.30 am to 6.30 pm daily from 1 April to 30 September, and 10.30 am to 5 pm the rest of the year. The staff sell a combination ticket costing €9.41 (students €7.80, children €6.07) that gives admission to all the major sights and is good value if you plan to make a day of it.

Next to the tourist office is the **Musée Wellington** (☎ 02-354 78 06), Chaussée de Bruxelles 147. Wellington spent the eve of the battle in this old inn, which now contains well laid-out exhibits including battle plans, weapons and personal effects. It's arguably the most interesting museum in the area.

From here proceed to the battlefield, some 5km south of Waterloo centre, where the first stop is generally the large **visitors centre** (☎ 02-385 19 12) at Route du Lion 254.

Behind it rises the **Butte du Lion** (lion's mound; Map 1), a 100m-high monument marking the site where the allies' William, Prince of Orange, was wounded. Women carting baskets of soil took two years to build the impressive mound. You can climb the 226 steps to the massive bronze lion at the top.

Next to the visitors centre is the exceedingly dull **Panorama de la Bataille** (☎ 02-384 31 39) and, opposite, a dreadful **Musée de Cires** (wax museum; ☎ 02-384 67 40).

The last main sight, the **Musée Provincial du Caillou** (☎ 02-384 24 24) at Chaussée de Bruxelles 66, is 4km south of the visitors centre. Napoleon spent the night before the battle at this former farmhouse, which now accommodates some relevant memorabilia such as his camp cot.

Getting There & Away

Bus W from Porte de Hal (Map 6) in Brussels runs every half-hour to Waterloo. It stops at the tourist office/Musée Wellington and then continues to near the visitors centre (you have to walk the last 500m). To reach the Musée Provincial du Caillou you must take bus No 365a from the Gordon

Monument (on Chaussée de Bruxelles, 500m from the visitors centre).

MEISE

The village of Meise (Map 1) is 12km north of central Brussels. Its chief attraction is the fine National Botanical Garden.

Nationale Plantentuin van België

Belgium's National Botanical Garden (☎ 02-260 09 20), known as the Jardin Botanique National in French, is in the Domein van Bouchout on the edge of Meise. It's a beautiful 93-hectare park based around two lakes and the Kasteel van Bouchout (Bouchout castle), which Léopold II gave to his sister, Princess Charlotte, after her castle at Tervuren burnt down in 1879.

The park boasts some 18,000 plant species

The Battle of Waterloo

On 1 March 1815, the legendary French emperor, Napoleon Bonaparte, escaped from the Mediterranean island of Elba where he'd been imprisoned. Rapidly making his way north, he reassembled troops and prepared to fight the two armies that endangered his future – the duke of Wellington's allied force of British, Belgians, Dutch and Germans and a Prussian army commanded by Marshal Blücher. Both armies were in Belgium.

Napoleon initiated a rapid attack on the Prussians on 16 June and deployed 30,000 soldiers to keep Blücher's men occupied while he did battle with Wellington at Waterloo.

At sunrise on Sunday 18 June, the two armies faced each other. Wellington's force of 68,000 were lined up on a high ridge; Napoleon's 72,000 men faced an uphill battle. Only 1500m separated the two armies.

Due to heavy rain overnight, Napoleon delayed the start of the battle in order to allow the ground to dry out. At 11.30 am the French attacked, moving round to the west to a farm at Hougoumont, which was vital for the defence of Wellington's right. The assault failed, and by 1 pm Napoleon had word that the Prussian army was 6km away and moving in fast. Napoleon detached a force to meet them and, at 2 pm, he sent a massive wave of infantry to attack Wellington's left, a confrontation that also proved indecisive.

At 4 pm the French cavalry charged Wellington's centre but were unable to break through the infantry formations. By early evening, with the Prussians starting to arrive to the east, Napoleon ordered his Imperial Guards, the army's best soldiers, to break through Wellington's centre. It was a desperate last-ditch effort – the guards had to slog uphill through mud churned up by the cavalry's previous attempt and were mown down by the opposing infantrymen from their protected high-ground position.

At 8.15 pm Wellington stirred his men into a full-scale advance and the nine-hour battle, which cost the lives of 50,000 men, was over. Napoleon abdicated and spent the rest of his life in exile on St Helena. The emperor's defeat spelt the end of France's military prowess in Europe and of its rule in Belgium.

---

including orchids, carnivorous plants and the famous giant Amazonian water lilies. They are housed in the spectacular Plantenpaleis (plant palace), which is a series of 12 connecting greenhouses that were built in 1966 and have recently been renovated.

Other highlights are the outdoor medicinal garden and, nearby, a small but stunning greenhouse shaped like a king's crown that was built in 1864 by Balat (Horta's teacher and the architect responsible for the magnificent Serres Royales in the capital). The 18th-century orangerie has been converted into a cafe and shop, that sells an English-language guide to the gardens.

The gardens open 10 am to 6 pm daily (until 5 pm from April until 31 October); admission to the Plantenpaleis cost €4 (children €3).

Getting There & Away

By car, take the A12 (Brussels–Antwerp) to the Meise exit and follow the signs to the Nationale Plantentuin van België. By bus from Brussels, take STIB bus L from Gare du Nord to the stop Nationale Plantentuin van België.

Bruges

- postcode 8000
- pop 119,240
- elevation 72m

Bruges (Brugge in Flemish) could be described as the 'perfect' tourist attraction. Suspended in time centuries ago when its lifeline – the Zwin estuary – silted up, it is now one of Europe's best-preserved medieval cities and dreamily evokes a world long since gone. In the middle of summer it teems with tourists; out of season its beauty is a delight to behold. The whole historic centre of Bruges was added to UNESCO's World Heritage List in 2000 and, in 2002, Bruges will take centre stage as European City of Culture.

Bruges was a prosperous cloth manufacturing town and a centre for art between the 12th and 15th centuries. It rose on the strength of its merchant classes, who erected impressive monuments such as the massive market halls and the famous Belfort. This soaring tower can be seen from miles around and was an imposing sight for traders from distant lands as they sailed into the city, their ships laden with cargoes of exotic goods from all over Europe and farther afield. Bruges grew fat, its population outstripped that of London and, under the patronage of the dukes of Burgundy, the arts flourished.

The city's artists, the Flemish Primitives, perfected a style of painting in bold colours that are still vivid today. Pivotal in this scene was Jan Van Eyck, who lived in Bruges for many years. Some of his works, as well as paintings by other noted Flemish Primitive artists such as Roger Van der Weyden, Hans Memling and Gerard David, can be seen in the city's lovely Groeningemuseum.

During the 15th century the Zwin, the waterway linking Bruges to the sea, began to silt up. Ships were no longer able to reach the docks and, despite attempts to build another canal, the city's economic lifeline disappeared. Merchants moved their headquarters to Antwerp, leaving abandoned houses, deserted streets and empty canals.

Bruges, a former hub of Europe, slept for 400 years.

This slumber was captured in the late 19th century by Belgian writer and poet Georges Rodenbach, whose novel *Bruges-la-Morte* (Bruges the Dead) beguilingly described the town's forlorn air and alerted the well-heeled to its preserved charm. At about the same time a major canal, the Boudewijnkanaal, was constructed to link Bruges to the new port of Zeebrugge – sadly best remembered these days for the *Herald of Free Enterprise* ferry tragedy in 1987. Although Zeebrugge suffered extensive damage during both World Wars, Bruges escaped unscathed and now lives largely off tourism.

More than two million tourists inundate Bruges every year. At the height of summer, the mass of people makes it difficult to detect the old-world feel and the sights are overcrowded – you may be hard pressed even to glimpse some of the major works of art or other treasures like the famous relic of Christ's blood in the Heiligbloed-Basiliek.

The positive side to this is that a large number of tourists visit Bruges on day trips and are gone before the sun sets. Stay late on a midsummer evening, when the carillon chimes seep through the cobbled streets and local children (illegally) cast their fishing rods into the willow-lined canals. Alternatively, time your visit for spring when daffodils carpet the tranquil Begijnhof, or autumn when the leaves start to fall – or even winter, when you can sometimes skate on the canals and have the town to yourself. At these times, Bruges readily reveals its age-old beauty.

Getting Around

ORIENTATION

Bruges is neatly encased by an oval-shaped series of canals that follow the city's medieval fortifications; four of the original nine gates still stand. In the centre are two squares, the Markt and the Burg, where the tourist office is situated. Most of the major sights are congregated on these squares as well as in the area to the south of the Markt; they are best visited on foot. Two areas often overlooked by visitors are the quiet streets to the north of the Markt and, to the north-east, the St Anna quarter, which has plenty of less-known but enjoyable attractions. The train station is about 1.5km south of the Markt; buses shuttle regularly between the two.

PUBLIC TRANSPORT

A small network of buses operated by De Lijn covers destinations in and around Bruges. Most depart from the train station, and many also stop at central stops such as the Markt, Wollestraat and Kuipersstraat.

From the train station, bus Nos 1, 3, 4, 6, 8, 11, 13 and 16 head for the centre – take any bus marked 'Centrum' (the last bus departs at 11.10 pm).

A single ticket costs €0.99, a Dagpas Vlaams Stad (day ticket valid for most Flemish cities including Bruges, Ghent and Antwerp) costs €2.85 and a 10-ticket Stadskaart (city card) costs €7.43. Buses run from 6 am until about 11 pm.

The bus information/ticket office outside the train station opens 7.30 am to 6 pm Monday to Saturday (from 9 am on Saturday), and 10 am to 5 pm Sunday. For information call ☎ 059-56 53 53. You can also consult the route and timetable boards at the tourist office.

CAR & MOPED
Car

A medieval city enmeshed by waterways is hardly an ideal place for motorised transport. Although there are several big car parks in town, it's advisable to leave your car on the outskirts. The biggest and cheapest central car park is next to the train station (Map 9). Here you'll pay €0.50 per hour or €2.48 for 24 hours and get a free return bus ticket to the centre for the car's driver and each passenger. Bus tickets are given out at the bus information office in front of the train station (show them your parking ticket).

Alternatively, there are car parks at 't Zand (Map 10) south-west of the city centre, and 't Pandreitje (Map 10) near Koningin Astridpark in the south-east. At any of these more central places you'll pay €1.11 per hour and €8.67 for 24 hours. Entrance signs indicate whether spaces are *vrij* (free) or if the car park is *vol* (full).

Street parking is metered (from 9 am to 7 pm daily). Just buy your ticket from the nearest ticket machine and display it on the dashboard.

For car rental try Europcar (Map 9; ☎ 050-31 45 44) at St Pieterskaai 48.

Moped

In summer, many younger travellers take to the streets on mopeds. They're a convenient (if noisy) way to get around, particularly if you want to explore farther afield. However, we don't recommend them in winter when the cobbled streets can be slippery and dangerous. A driving licence is not required and you can ride with two people on one bike. Helmets are not provided as they are not required by law (providing you ride a 'Class A' moped, which has a maximum speed of 25km/h).

Fietsen Popelier (Map 10; ☎ 050-34 32 62), Mariastraat 26, rents 40cc mopeds for €12.40/24.80/37 for one/three/five hours or €49.60 per day, petrol included.

TAXI

There are taxi ranks on the Markt and in front of the train station. Otherwise phone ☎ 050-33 44 44 or ☎ 050-38 46 60. The fare from the train station to the city centre is €7.43.

BICYCLE

Bikes are a great way to get around town and also to explore nearby sights, such as Damme and parts of the coast. A popular day excursion is the 44km coastal route (the Kustroute) which takes in both Damme and Knokke. A cycling map of this route is available from Fietsen Popelier (see below). Note that strong North Sea winds can make cycling impossible along the polders and the coast on windy days.

Fietsen Popelier (Map 10; ☎ 050-34 32 62), Mariastraat 26, is a good place to hire a bike. The helpful owner charges €2.75/5.60/8 per hour/half-day/day for a normal bike and €6.20/12.40/19.80 for a tandem. Children's seats and baskets are provided free and no deposit is required. It opens 9 am to 7 pm daily (10 am to 6 pm from 1 November to 30 April).

Hotel 't Koffieboontje (see under Places to Stay – Budget later) charges €2.48/4.96 for one/four hours or €8.06/27.89 for a day/week. You'll need to leave a credit card number as a deposit. They have lots of kids' bikes.

The bike shop at the train station (Map 9; ☎ 050-30 23 29) charges €8.55 for a full day or €6.07 from 2 to 8 pm; you'll need to leave a deposit of €12.39. It opens 7 am to 8 pm.

ORGANISED TOURS
Bruges by boat, bike, minibus, foot, Walkman or horse-drawn carriage – you name it and you can almost certainly tour by it. The tourist office has copious details.

Walking Tours
Bruges is an ambler's ultimate dream, its sights sprinkled within leisurely walking distance of its compact centre.

Guided walks can be arranged on an individual basis with prior booking through the tourist office. The price is €37.20 for two hours with a guide. Alternatively, during July and August, a group tour (€3.71) leaves from the tourist office at 3 pm daily.

Themed walking tours, such as the legends of Bruges or Bruges revealed through the eyes of writer Marguerite Yourcenar, can be arranged through an organisation called the Gidsenbond (☎ 050-33 22 33). The interesting Vrouwenwandeling (Women's Walk), which covers sites linked to women of the Middle Ages, should be reserved through SEFA Vrouwencentrum (☎ 050-34 59 00).

A walking tour of Bruges is described in the boxed text 'Walking the Canals' later in the chapter.

Boat Trips
Taking a canal tour is a must for many visitors. Boats depart roughly every 20 min-

utes between 10 am and 6 pm daily (early March to mid-November) from several jetties south of the Burg, including at Rozenhoedkaai (Map 10) and Dijver (Map 10); the tours last 30 minutes. Expect long queues at most jetties in the summer. In winter (15 November until the end of February) there are no services. The price is €4.75 (children €2.35).

For details of the boat trip to Damme see the Excursions section later in the chapter.

Bicycle Tours
A bike tour is a fun way to explore Bruges and its surroundings. Quasimodo (☎ 050-37 04 70 or freecall 0800 97 525, ⓔ info@quasimodo.be) is a small company that runs two highly-recommended mountain-bike tours with English commentary. There's a three-hour (8km) tour of Bruges, or a four-hour (25km) cycle to the Dutch border and back via Damme. Tours run daily from 1 April to 30 September. The cost is €16/14 for those aged over/under 26; booking is essential. Check Quasimodo's Web site at www.quasimodo.be.

Minibus Tours
Quasimodo (see the previous Bicycle Tours section for contact details) offers two sorts of day trip. One takes in Ypres and its famous WWI battlefields; the other promises waffles, beers and chocolates at various establishments around Bruges. Prices are €38/30 for those aged over/under 26, and include all admission charges and a picnic lunch. Pick up is from your hotel and reservations are necessary. Both trips (9 am to 4.30 pm) go three times per week from mid-February to 30 November.

Sightseeing Line (☎ 050-35 50 24) runs a standard 50-minute minibus tour of Bruges, leaving the Markt hourly from 10 am to 4 pm. The tour costs €9.42 (children €6.20).

Horse-Drawn Carriages
Horse-drawn carriages can be boarded on the Markt. Their well-trodden route takes 35 minutes and costs €24.79 for a carriage of five people.

Things to See & Do

THE MARKT & BURG AREA (MAP 10)

The Markt

Exploration of Bruges always starts at the historic Markt. This large open square, now predominantly the domain of pedestrians and horse-drawn carriages, is flanked by medieval-style buildings and, above all, the city's illustrious Belfort (belfry). Standing tall at the centre of the Markt is a **monument** to Pieter De Coninck and Jan Breydel, the leaders of the Brugse Matin (see The Rise of Flanders under History in the Facts about the Cities chapter).

Belfort This massive, 83m-high belfry was built in the 13th century when Bruges was a bustling centre of trade. The 366 steps to the top are an exhausting and usually crowded climb but well worth it, particularly in the afternoon when the view reveals the town's rustic roofs and warm tones. On the way up you'll pass the barred treasury, a triumphal bell, the clock and, farther up, the 18th-century **carillon**. Its 47 bells are still played manually by Aimé Lombaert from 2.15 to 3 pm every Wednesday, Saturday and Sunday from October to June, and 2.15 to 3 pm Sunday and 9 to 10 pm Monday, Wednesday and Saturday the rest of the year.

The grand building from which the Belfort soars is the **Hallen** (halls), a 13th-century (but frequently restored) former marketplace with a massive central courtyard. These days the halls hold temporary art exhibitions.

The Belfort opens 9.30 am to 5 pm daily (closed 12.30 to 1.30 pm October to March); admission costs €2.50 (students and seniors €2, children €1.25). Last tickets are sold at 4.15 pm.

Guildhalls Most of the gabled guildhalls edging the Markt are now restaurants and the domain of tourists. Notable at Markt 16 is **Craenenburg Cafe**; in this building the Hapsburg heir, Maximilian of Austria, was imprisoned by the city's leaders in 1488 after attempting to restrict their privileges. When Maximilian later became emperor, he took revenge by directing trade to Antwerp.

The square's eastern side is dominated by the **Provinciaal Hof**, a neo-Gothic building which formerly housed the West Flanders provincial government (it recently moved to new headquarters outside the city walls). Part of it is now the main post office.

The Burg

The Burg is just as impressive as the Markt. For more than five centuries the former palace on this majestic site was the seat of the counts of Flanders. The St Donatian Cathedral also stood here until 1799, when religious zealots tore it down. These days, the Burg contains the tourist office and the city's most appealing cluster of buildings.

Heiligbloed-Basiliek The recently renovated Basilica of the Holy Blood is squeezed into the south-western corner of the Burg. It takes its name from the relic of Christ's blood that was brought here sometime between 1150 and 1200.

The church has two distinct and highly contrasting sections – the rather subdued and sombre **lower chapel**, built in the 12th century along pure Romanesque lines and almost devoid of decoration, and the much renovated **upper chapel**, accessed by a wide flight of stairs near the entrance to the lower chapel and lavishly embellished.

MARTIN MOOS

MARTIN MOOS

MARTIN MOOS

fe on Bruges' medieval canals can appear suspended in time – once the day-trippers depart, the aterways return to the peace and tranquillity they have enjoyed for the last few hundred years.

If taking to the water is not for you, try clip-clopping around Bruges by horse and carriage.

The lavishly restored Heiligbloed Basiliek, Bruges

St Salvatorskathedraal's ornate interior

In the upper chapel is the silver tabernacle containing the phial that holds a few drops of the holy blood. The relic is still venerated every Friday – from 8.30 to 11 am this ceremony takes place in the lower chapel and from 3 to 4 pm it's in the upper chapel. On Ascension Day it is paraded through the city in the Heilig Bloedprocessie (Holy Blood Procession; see under Special Events in the Facts for the Visitor chapter).

Duck into the pint-sized **treasury** next door to see the jewel-coated reliquary that holds the phial during the procession. Admission to the treasury costs €0.99 (students €0.49).

The church opens 9.30 am to noon and 2 to 6 pm daily in the high season, and 10 am to noon and 2 to 4 pm between October and March (closed Wednesday afternoon). Admission is free.

Stadhuis This is Belgium's oldest, and arguably most beautiful, city hall. Built between 1376 and 1420, its exquisite turreted Gothic stone facade is decorated with replica statues of the counts and countesses of Flanders (the originals were torn down in 1792 by French soldiers). Inside, a few rooms are open to the public but the chief attraction is the 1st-floor **Gotische Zaal** (Gothic hall). The hall's polychromatic ceiling and walls are enlivened with medieval carvings, and murals depicting the town's history add to the room's magnificence. The adjoining exhibition room is interesting for its old maps, which show Bruges through the centuries.

The Gotische Zaal opens 9 am to 5 pm daily (closed 12.30 to 2 pm between October and March). Admission costs €3.73 (students €2.48) and includes entry to the nearby Brugse Vrije.

Brugse Vrije Just one exhibit – an immense 16th-century chimney piece – draws visitors to the **Renaissancezaal** (Renaissance hall) of the Brugse Vrije (literally 'liberty of Bruges'), a medieval administrative body. The Brugse Vrije palace once occupied the entire eastern section of the Burg. Completed in 1531, the chimney's upper section is a detailed oak carving depicting Emperor Charles V alongside an entourage of relatives; black marble and an alabaster frieze adorn the lower part. All in all it's pretty impressive, even without the overblown medieval codpieces worn by some of the men.

Opening hours and admission charges are the same as for the Gotische Zaal in the Stadhuis (see the previous entry).

SOUTH OF THE MARKT
Groeningemuseum (Map 10)

The Groeningemuseum at Dijver 12 is the home of the city's prized collection of art dating from the 14th to the 20th centuries. Most notable is the impressive section on Flemish Primitives, with treasures by all the great names of that period. The museum is relatively small and well laid-out. You'll be given a free audio handset (available in English, Italian, Spanish, French and Flemish) when you enter, which gives details on all of the most important artworks.

Rooms 1 to 5 present the Flemish Primitives and include works by Jan Van Eyck, who is generally considered to be the first great master of this period (see the boxed text 'Jan Van Eyck' in the Facts about the Cities chapter). Room 1 boasts Van Eyck's masterpiece *The Virgin with Canon George Van der Paele* (1436), a radiant portrayal of

Museums in Bruges

Bruges' premier museums – the Groeninge, Arentshuis, Gruuthuse and Memling museums – open daily from 1 April to 30 September; from 1 October to 31 March most museums close for lunch between 12.30 and 2 pm, and some also close on Tuesday.

A €9.92 discount ticket (representing a saving of about €2.70) is available for these four major museums; if one is temporarily closed, another attraction is usually substituted. It can be purchased from the participating museums. Many museums also offer a good-value family ticket.

All the museums can be contacted via one central number – ☎ 050-44 87 11.

the Madonna and the infant Jesus surrounded by three figures: the kneeling canon and, next to him, St George (his patron saint), while a richly clothed St Donatian looks on. The textures and detail are almost photographic – to viewers in the 15th century the portrait must have appeared incredible. Also in this room is Van Eyck's brutally honest portrait of his wife, Margaret.

A highlight in Room 4 is Memling's *Moreel Triptych* from 1484, in which the serious central scene of brown-garbed saints is offset by little details such as the cheeky grin on a nearby child or the priest petting a deer. But it's *The Last Judgement*, a fantastically nightmarish work by Hieronymus Bosch, which mesmerises most people. It depicts the end of time and those who've been condemned to hell, and is filled with fire and mayhem, men and women in scenes of debauchment and strange creatures devouring everything in sight.

Room 5 features the stomach-turning *Judgement of Cambyses* by Gerard David in which a corrupt judge gets his dues.

At the time of writing, Room 6 was temporarily devoted to the works of Hans Memling. These works are usually housed in the Memlingmuseum; however, they have been exhibited here during restoration of that museum (expected to be completed by late 2001).

The Groeninge's collection of paintings from the late 16th and 17th centuries is less captivating, but worth seeking out in Room 7 is Pieter Breughel the Younger's *Boerenadvokaat*, which depicts the chaotic goings-on in the office of a peasant lawyer.

Rooms 12 to 18 are reserved for works from the 18th to 20th centuries and include works by Henry Van de Velde, as well as several dark pieces by Constant Permeke including his brooding charcoal *The Angelus* (1934). A larger-than-life sculpture of *Nel*, the wife of Fauvist artist Rik Wouters, dominates Room 12.

Surrealism gets a look-in in Room 14. The movement's pivotal figure, René Magritte, is represented by *L'Attentat* (The Assault; 1932) and there's also Delvaux's strange 1970 piece *Sérénité*.

The museum opens 9.30 am to 5 pm daily in summer and 9.30 am to 12.30 pm and 2 to 5 pm in winter (closed Tuesday). Admission costs €6.20 (students €3.72).

Arentshuis (Map 10)

This museum at Dijver 16 occupies a stately 18th-century patrician house, which was formerly owned by the Arents family. It contains two collections: the ground-floor **Kantmuseum** (lace museum) and the 1st-floor **Brangwyn Museum**.

The excellent lace collection features both *naaldkant* (needlepoint lace) and *bobijn* (bobbin) lace from Belgium, as well as lace from abroad, all presented in cabinets spread throughout four rooms. Unfortunately, the labels are in Flemish only. In Room 1, case No 7 boasts a fine *strook Brusselse gaskant*, a 19th-century style of lace also known as *point de gaze*. In Room 2 seek out case No 15A with its gorgeous bobbin-lace veil made in 1725.

The upstairs rooms are filled with the powerful and often dark paintings and etchings of Frank Brangwyn (1867–1956), a Bruges-born artist of British parentage. Industrial themes, such as the construction of ships, bridges and monumental buildings, are a strong feature of his work.

Opening hours are the same as for the Groeningemuseum. Admission costs €1.98 (students €0.99).

Gruuthusemuseum (Map 10)

Applied and decorative arts are the theme of this museum at Dijver 17. The collection occupies 22 numbered rooms in a sprawling 15th-century patrician house that adjoins the cathedral. The museum takes its name from the flower and herb mixture – the *gruut* – which was traditionally used for brewing beer. Most of the exhibits are labelled in Flemish only. Still, it's well worth some time as there are superb local tapestries, furniture and sculptures.

Some of the highlights, or more unusual objects to seek out, include the following:

Room 1: polychromatic bust of Emperor Charles V, made in 1520 and still vividly coloured

Room 2: a wooden wall-hanging depicting medieval ways of removing haemorrhoids

Room 5: a 15th-century wooden statue of a rather skeletal-looking Christ

Rooms 8 & 9: wool and silk tapestries from Bruges

Room 17: an exquisite little oak chapel on the 2nd floor from which the high altar of the cathedral can be viewed

Room 21: a small outdoor terrace affording a fine view over the picturesque canal and houses behind the museum

Opening hours are the same as for the Groeningemuseum (see earlier) and admission costs €3.22 (students €1.74).

Memlingmuseum (Map 10)

This small but notable museum is housed in the chapel of the 12th-century St Janshospitaal at Mariastraat 38. Its importance stems from the six masterpieces by Hans Memling (see the boxed text) on display. The museum has been closed for renovations in recent years but is due to re-open in late 2001 (in the meantime, the artworks can be viewed at the Groeningemuseum).

Hans Memling

Hans Memling (c1440–94) was born in Germany but lived for many years in Bruges. He was taught by Rogier Van der Weyden and eventually became one of the city's leading artists.

Memling is noted for the fine quality of the figures in his religious paintings. The Memlingmuseum has several superb examples; at the time of writing they were temporarily displayed in the Groeningemuseum until the renovation of the former is complete (expected late 2001). These include the St John Alterpiece (1479) and the enchanting reliquary of St Ursula. Shaped like a miniature gilded Gothic church, the reliquary's side panels depict the medieval tale of the beautiful St Ursula and the 11,000 virgins that were massacred by the Huns in Germany as they returned from a pilgrimage to Rome. The attention to detail is stunning.

Next to the chapel is a magnificently restored 17th-century **Apotheek** (pharmacy), which originally belonged to the old hospital.

Onze Lieve Vrouwekerk (Map 10)

Located opposite the Memlingmuseum on Mariastraat, the Church of Our Lady is a dark, sober building that dates from the 13th century. It's most noted for its art treasures. Of these, the *Madonna and Child* by Michelangelo is an undisputed gem. This lovely marble statue (1504) was bought in Italy by a Bruges merchant and was the only work of art by Michelangelo to leave Italy in his lifetime. Although pilfered several times by occupying forces, the statue has always been returned.

The church opens 10 to 11.30 am and 2.30 to 4 or 5 pm daily (afternoons only on Sunday). Admission is free.

It's possible to visit the tombs of Charles the Bold (Karel de Stoute) and his daughter, Mary of Burgundy (wife of Maximilian); admission costs €1.73.

Archeologisch Museum (Map 10)

Only true museum buffs are likely to be interested in this small archaeology museum at Mariastraat 36a. Frescoes from the chapel at St Janshospitaal are displayed, as is a cylinder filled with old cow horns and a 13th-century child's shoe. The museum opens 9.30 am to 12.30 pm and 1.30 to 5 pm Tuesday, Thursday, Saturday and Sunday; admission costs €1.49 (students €0.50).

St Salvatorskathedraal (Map 10)

A short detour from the archaeology museum is the 13th-century St Saviour's Cathedral on Steenstraat. It's topped by an unusual tower, 99m high, which incorporates turrets and spires with neo-Romanesque flair.

Inside, the cathedral is very ornate with a massive organ at the rear, beautiful stained-glass windows, huge tapestries and a small chapel where you can see a few murals dating from the 14th century. There's also a museum (admission €1.49) displaying works by Bouts and Pourbus. The cathedral's

opening hours are complicated but generally
it opens 8.30 to 11.45 am and 2 to 5.45 pm.

Diamantmuseum (Map 10)

The slick diamond museum (☎ 050-34 20
56), Katelijnestraat 43, gives lots of gloss
about the global diamond industry and
Bruges' medieval role as the first diamond-
polishing centre. It's home to the world's
two smallest diamond sculptures – tiny pro-
files of King Baudouin and Queen Fabiola,
each valued at US$4000 and no more than
3mm in diameter. Even with the aid of a
magnifying glass, it takes a sizeable imagination to see the resemblance. Admission
costs €4.96. The museum opens 10.30 am
to 5.30 pm daily.

De Halve Maan/Straffe Hendrik (Map 10)

This family brewery (☎ 050-33 26 97) at
Walplein 26 was founded by Henri Maes in
1856. The brewery's real name is De Halve
Maan (The Half Moon); however, it's better known by the beer it produces, Straffe
Hendrik (Strong Henry). Forty-five-minute
guided tours (in English, Flemish and
French all at once) wind their way up and
down the original brewing rooms, finishing
with a beer tasting. Tours run every hour
from 11 am to 4 pm daily during the summer and can include as many as 50 people
(way too many for a place like this). Between October and March there are tours at
11 am and 3 pm, and these are usually uncrowded. The tour price is €3.47.

Begijnhof (Map 10)

This serene *begijnhof* (community of Beguines) dates from the 13th century and was
traditionally the home of Beguines (see the
boxed text 'Begijnen & Begijnhoven' in
the Brussels chapter). Modest but dignified
whitewashed houses, which these days are
home to some 50 single women of all ages,
enclose a grassy square. The large convent
at the rear of the square is inhabited by
Benedictine nuns. In spring a carpet of
daffodils covers the grass.

The Begijnhof is about 800m south of
the Markt. Visiting times are 9 am to 7 pm

Godshuizen of Bruges

One of the delights of wandering around
Bruges is the chance of coming across a
complex of *godshuizen* (almshouses). These
groups of terraced houses were built by
merchant guilds for their members and by
wealthy philanthropists for the poor and elderly. There are still 46 godshuizen complexes
in Bruges – the oldest date from the 14th
century. The complexes are usually surrounded by a protective wall, which encloses
a central garden and chapel.

One of the cutest and most central god-
shuizen is **Godshuis de Vos**, Noordstraat 2–8.
It dates from 1713 but was restored in 1995.
Another is the lovely **Godshuis St Jozef**,
Nieuwe Gentweg 8–32, which you can enter
through its large black doors.

Two of the godshuizen have been turned
into museums (the Museum voor Volkskunde
and the museum at the Kantcentrum), while
the others are still inhabited.

daily in the summer (to 6 pm in winter);
admission is free.

Near the main entrance is **'t Begijnhuisje**,
a typical house which is now a tiny museum
devoted to the life of the women. Admission to the Begijnhuisje costs €2 (seniors,
students and children €1). It opens 10 am
to noon and 1.45 to 5 pm daily.

Minnewater (Map 9)

The Minnewater, also known as the Lake of
Love, was once an inner-city port. For more
details on this area, see the boxed text
'Walking the Canals' later.

ST ANNA QUARTER (MAP 9)

The St Anna quarter, or Verloren Hoek (for-
gotten corner) as it's nicknamed, lies north-
east of the Markt and is an atmospheric
district to explore.

Museum Onze-Lieve-Vrouwe Van de Potterie

This small museum and chapel are up in the
north of the St Anna quarter at Potterierei

79. Originally part of a 14th-century hospital complex, the museum contains many medieval religious paintings. The double-barrelled chapel has a fine baroque interior that has just been renovated.

The museum opens 9.30 am to 12.30 pm and 1.15 to 5 pm daily except Wednesday. Admission costs €1.49 (students €0.50).

Engels Klooster

The English convent, which is at Carmersstraat 85, was founded in 1629 by a community of canonesses (women who belong to a religious order but have not taken a vow) who fled from England and, for many years, offered shelter to other Catholic exiles. Some 30 sisters still reside here and one is on duty each day to give tours of their sumptuous baroque church. It opens 2 to 3.30 pm and 4.15 to 5.15 pm Monday to Saturday; admission is free.

St Janshuismolen

In the 13th century, the great walls around Bruges were dotted with *molens* (wind-mills) where cereals were ground into flour. These days, four mills grace the eastern wall of the city, but only the 18th-century St Janshuismolen at Kruisvest is an original. Its sails are set in motion for the benefit of visitors from 9.30 am to 12.30 pm and 1.15 to 5 pm daily between 1 May and 30 September. Inside the windmill there's a tiny museum. Admission costs €1 (students €0.50).

Guido Gezellemuseum

This museum at Rolweg 64 is devoted to one of Flanders' best-known poets, Guido Gezelle (for more details see the boxed text 'Guido Gezelle'). Occupying the house in which the poet-priest was born, the museum contains books and documents recalling his life and work. It opens 9.30 am to 12.30 pm and 1.15 to 5 pm daily in summer (closed Tuesday in winter). Admission costs €1.49 (students €0.50).

Museum voor Volkskunde

The Folklore Museum at Rolweg 40 occupies a row of restored *godshuizen* (almshouses; see the boxed text 'Godshuizen of Bruges' earlier in the chapter). The exhibits are pretty mundane – an old Flemish kitchen, a hatter's shop and, perhaps best of all, a 1930s-style *snoepwinkel* (sweet shop) in which traditional lollies are made every Thursday afternoon before an audience of school kids. Labels throughout the museum are in Flemish only.

The museum opens 9.30 am to 5 pm daily (in winter it closes at lunchtime and on Tuesday). Admission costs €1.98 (students €0.99).

Kantcentrum & Jeruzalemkerk

This lace centre and adjacent church occupy a complex of buildings at Peperstraat 3.

The Kantcentrum (☎ 050-33 00 72) is best known for its bobbin lace-making demonstrations, an informal gathering of 20 or so women who congregate (afternoons only) in a small room at the rear of the complex (they're joined by school kids on Wednesday afternoons). Nearby, the centre's lace museum displays a modest collection of

---

Guido Gezelle

Born in Bruges in 1830 on the eve of the Belgian revolution, Guido Gezelle is widely considered to be one of Flanders' greatest poets. He studied for the priesthood before turning to writing in a bid to emancipate the Flemish language and its literature from the dominance of French and Dutch. Writing in the old-fashioned dialect spoken by farmers and the poor in western Flanders, his works were not revolutionary but they provoked enemies nonetheless. No-one before had dared to write in anything other than French or, to a lesser extent, Dutch. His efforts were of great consequence to a generation of students, who later turned him into a figurehead of the Flemish nationalist movement. Gezelle's early volumes of romantic and religious poetry were noted for their free style and spiritual expression. A statue of the poet can be seen on Guido Gezelleplein near the Gruuthusemuseum.

BRUGES

Walking the Canals

Bruges' less touristy areas hold some of its most charming features. The walk described below concentrates on water – wandering around the city's picturesque canals is a pleasant way to spend an hour or so once you've seen the main sights. Bear in mind that if you linger, or allow yourself to be lured down sidestreets or into cafes, it can take much longer. The route is marked on the Bruges maps.

The walk starts to the south of town at **Wijngaardplein** (Map 10) which marks the entrance to the **Begijnhof**. Horse-and-carriage teams usually stop for a break here. From Wijngaardplein continue south to **Minnewater** (Map 9; in English known as the Lake of Love), marked by a bridge with a **lockhouse**. In Bruges' medieval heyday, this waterway was a dock where ships from all over Europe and as far afield as Russia came with their cargoes of wool, wine, spices and silk and left loaded with Flemish cloth.

Follow the lake along its western shore until you reach the large stone **tower**. Known as the 'gunpowder tower', it's the sole survivor of two towers built in the early 15th century; its partner was pulled down in 1621 and its base was used to store ice, cut out of the lake, right up until WWI.

Cross the cobbled pedestrian bridge, noting as you go the lovely view back to the city with the cathedral spire and belfry rising in the distance. At the end of the bridge, take the path off to the left which meanders through the Minnewater park before returning to Wijngaardplein. From here, turn left into Walplein, home to a playful little bronze **statue** entitled *Zeus, Leda, Prometheus and Pegasus visit Bruges*, and continue across the square to the stone archway in the north-eastern corner. This archway leads into Stoofstraat, a tiny cobbled passageway reminiscent of medieval times that eventually brings you out onto Mariastraat.

Turn left and follow Mariastraat to the small square, Onze Lieve Vrouwekerkhof, which marks the entrance to the church. Cross the square with its tortuously-trellised trees and enter the small **garden** to the rear of the church. This is one of the most picturesque spots in Bruges, built around a tranquil canal lined with houses boasting beautiful timber facades. The little arched bridge, **Bonifaciusbrug**, though often photographed does not actually date from medieval times. From near the bust of Joan Luis Vivès, a 16th-century Spanish humanist who stayed in Bruges, you get a good view up to a tiny window at the back of the Gruuthusemuseum – it's thought to be the smallest Gothic window in Europe!

traditional lace housed in a complex of godshuizen.

More intriguing is the adjacent, onion-domed Jeruzalemkerk, which was built by the Adorni family in the 15th century as a replica of the Church of the Holy Sepulchre in Jerusalem. It's a rather macabre monument, the dark, split-level church being dominated by a gruesome altarpiece (note the skulls and ladders) and the black marble tomb of Anselm Adorni, whose heart was buried here after he was murdered in Scotland in 1483. To top it all off there's a replica of Christ's tomb, complete with imitation corpse.

The complex opens 10 am to noon and 2 to 6 pm Monday to Friday (to 5 pm on Saturday); admission costs €1.49 (students €0.99).

De Gouden Boom

De Gouden Boom brewery (☎ 050-33 06 99) on Langestraat is not as touristy as its counterpart, Straffe Hendrik, as it opens only to groups of at least 30 people (you'd need to organise a group yourself). However, the associated museum, behind the brewery at Verbrand Nieuwland 10, opens to all from 2 to 6 pm Wednesday to Sunday between 1 May and 30 September.

Admission to the museum costs €2.48 (students €0.99), which includes a taste of the brewery's spicy white beer, Tarwebier (4.8%).

Walking the Canals

Cross the bridge to enter **Hof Arents**, a tree-lined square to the rear of the Arentshuis, which features four sculptures by Rik Poot entitled *De Ruiters van de Apocalyps* (Riders of the Apocalypse). Join up with the Dijver, turn right and follow it along to **Rozenhoedkaai**, which offers the city's best shot of the belfry. It's particularly lovely in the early evening when the belfry's illuminated form is backdropped by a dark azure sky.

Huidenvettersplein is a charming little square to the left off Rozenhoedkaai lined with popular restaurants that leads to the **Vismarkt**, Bruges' morning fish market. From here, Steenhouwersdijk leads into **Groenerei**, a short promenade along a pretty part of the city's canal system. At the corner of Groenerei and Peerdenstraat is a street-corner **statue of the Madonna and Child**; such elevated statues are common in Flanders, though this one is unusual for its modern features.

Groenerei peters out into a pedestrian walkway and curves sharply round to the right, ending at a bridge. Cross the bridge and turn left, following Predikherenrei and the canal back towards the centre of town. Here, at the confluence of the two canals, there's a superb view (at its best in the afternoon) of the city's turreted skyline.

Cross this bridge and then take the first right into Verversdijk and follow it until you reach the first pedestrian bridge. As you cross the canal here, you'll see **St Annakerk** immediately ahead of you; this church was built in the 15th century and lends its name to the St Anna quarter which fans out to the east of here. Once across the canal, turn left and follow St Annarei to the second bridge, which marks the junction of two canals and offers a view of the 15th-century **Poortersloge** (burghers' lodge). With its slender tower, this building was where the city's wealthiest merchants once met. Opposite it is the **Oud Tolhuis**, where tolls were levied on goods being brought into the city until the 18th century.

Cross the canal and follow Genthof to **Woensdagmarkt**, where there's a marble **statue of Hans Memling**, erected in 1874 (Memling is actually buried in St Gilliskerk, or the Church of St Gillis, a few blocks further north). The Woensdagmarkt blends almost imperceptibly into **Jan Van Eyckplein**, which is dominated by a statue of the great Flemish Primitives artist. This square marks the end of a canal that once continued to the Markt and was crammed with boats. These days the streets around here are tranquil and pretty. From here, you're just a few minutes' walk from the Markt.

WHAT'S FREE

Koningin Astridpark (Map 9 and 10) and the grassy lawns at Minnewater (Map 9) are the venues for occasional free live concerts in summer. Silent films are also sometimes screened in Koningin Astridpark. Information about free events is available from the tourist office.

Ice skating on the canals is a delight reserved for really cold winters (the mayor announces when the waterways are properly frozen); you'll need your own skates.

ACTIVITIES

Universal Gym (Map 10; ☎ 050-34 34 46) at Park 6 has weight training equipment. It charges €4.50 for one session or €33.50 for a month. It opens 9.30 am to 9.45 pm weekdays (until 5.45 pm Saturday).

Places to Stay

Bruges' attractiveness has resulted in a wealth of accommodation. There are over 100 hotels, a swarm of B&Bs, a handful of hostels and a burgeoning number of places available for long-term rental. All options are oppressively overbooked in the high season, which starts at Easter and lasts until about 31 October, and also includes the Christmas holiday period (basically from a week before Christmas until the second week in January). Most places don't charge more in the high season; the few that do are indicated.

PLACES TO STAY – BUDGET
Camping

The quietest camp site is *Camping Memling* (*☎/fax 050-35 58 45, Veltemweg 109*) in the suburb St Kruis, about 2.5km east of town. It backs onto the Veltembos forest and opens year round. It charges €2.75/1.60 for adults/children and €3.25/2.50 for a car/small tent. To get there take bus No 11 from the train station to the Vossensteert stop and walk 400m back in the direction of Bruges.

Hostels

For a city of its size, Bruges is well endowed with central hostels.

Gran Kaffee de Passage (*Map 10; ☎ 050-34 02 32, fax 050-34 01 40, Dweersstraat 26–8*) is the city's nicest hostel-cum-hotel. It has fresh, modern dorms (six beds) costing €11.15 per person. The attached hotel has a variety of double rooms with decor ranging from romantic to minimalist to Moroccan. They cost €34.70 with shared bathroom, or €39.66 with private facilities. Bus No 16 from the train station stops nearby.

Bauhaus (*Map 9; ☎ 050-34 10 93, fax 050-33 41 80,* 📧 *info@bauhaus.be, Langestraat 135*) is a big, bustling hostel that also has a budget hotel section next door. It charges €9.41 in an eight-bed dorm, rising to €10.65 in a four-bed dorm. A single room costs €13.63, or there are unexceptional doubles (with a very tiny shower) for €32.22. Take bus No 6 or 16 from the train station.

Snuffel Sleep In (*Map 10; ☎ 050-33 31 33, fax 050-33 32 50,* 📧 *snuffel@flanders coast.be, Ezelstraat 47–9*) is an unpretentious little place that's been going for donkey's years. It's the most 'alternative' of the three private hostels and is a bit grungy. Prices range from €8.67 in a 12-bed dorm to €9.66/12.14 in a six/four-bed dorm. A small kitchen is at the disposal of guests; alternatively, breakfast costs €1.23. From the train station take bus No 3 or 13 and get off at the first stop after the Markt.

The HI-affiliated *Europa Jeugdherberg* (*☎ 050-35 26 79, fax 050-35 37 32, Baron Ruzettelaan 143*) is 500m south of the city walls (Map 9). A dorm bed costs €10.41, or €12.27 in a 'family' room (four beds). Take bus No 2 from the train station to the Wantestraat stop.

B&Bs

Bed and breakfast prices start at €24.80/37.20 for a single/double, but if you can pay a bit more you'll find superb quality.

Cheap but good and friendly is *B&B Degraeve* (*Map 9; ☎/fax 050-34 57 11,* 📧 *wim .vandecappelle@worldonline.be, Kazernevest 32*). It's in a relatively untouristy part of town and is owned by a friendly young couple who have stuffed the two rooms full of curious objects. A single/double/triple costs €29.74/42.14/54.53; bathroom facilities are shared.

B&B Dieltiens (*Map 10; ☎ 050-33 42 94, fax 050-33 52 30,* 📧 *koen.dieltiens @skynet.be, Waalsestraat 40*) is run by a very friendly couple who has been welcoming visitors for well over a decade, and their hospitality still shines. They've recently moved to a mansion which featured on the first map of Bruges (published in the 16th century). Lovingly restored, the house has three guestrooms, all with private facilities, for €45/50 for singles/doubles, or €65/80 for three/four people. The Dieltiens, who own this place, also have a holiday house (minimum three nights) – see Long-Term Rentals at the end of this section for details.

The three lofty rooms at *B&B Gheeraert* (*Map 10; ☎ 050-33 56 27, fax 050-34 52 01,* 📧 *paul.gheeraert@skynet.be, Riddersstraat 9*) are simply gorgeous. Occupying the top floor (up a sweeping spiral staircase) of a mansion just 300m from the Burg, the rooms each have a TV, refrigerator and private bathroom; smoking is not permitted. Singles/doubles/triples cost €45/50/65. The Gheeraerts also have self-catering flats (see Long-Term Rentals later).

Just round the corner is *B&B Setola* (*Map 10; ☎ 050-33 49 77, fax 050-33 25 51,* 📧 *bruno.setola@pi.be, St Walburgastraat*

12). This building dates to 1740 (the foyer is being renovated and is a bit shabby) and has three spacious modern guestrooms, all with private bathroom facilities, on the top floor. It costs €42.14/47.10 for one/two people, or €59.50/71.88 for three/four (an extra €4.95 is charged for stays of one night).

Don't judge a book by its cover – that's the advice needed for *B&B Debruyne (Map 9; ☎ 050-34 76 06, fax 050-34 02 85,* e *marie.debruyne@advalvas.be, Lange Raamstraat 18)*. The plain facade of this house hides an ultra-modern, highly original home, unique furnishings and a fresh, warm welcome! And, quite remarkably for Bruges, there are no stairs to climb! It costs €45/50/65 for a single/double/triple, all with private facilities. Breakfast is taken on a communal table overlooking the garden.

One of the town's most flamboyant B&Bs is *B&B Bruyneel (Map 10; ☎/fax 050-33 35 90,* e *dbruynee@be.packardbell.org, Ezelstraat 24)*. The three big, colourful rooms are well stocked with art and bric-a-brac; two cost €69.41 and the other, with private bathroom, is €74.36. Prices are for one or two people. Breakfast is served in the room.

At the top end of the B&B ladder is *Huyze Die Maene (Map 10; ☎ 050-33 39 59, fax 050-33 44 60,* e *huyzediemaene @pandora.be, Markt 17)*. This place is above a popular brasserie and has three luxurious rooms, two with unbeatable views of the Markt. Prices are €98 for a single or double, and €123/148 for a triple/quad.

Hotels

Hotel 't Koffieboontje (Map 10; ☎ 050-33 80 27, fax 050-34 39 04, e *hotel_koffie boontje@unicall.be, Hallestraat 4)* is a central but unremarkable hotel offering cheap rooms with private bathroom in the low season. A single/double room with a small refrigerator and a stove costs €42/50. Prices include a buffet breakfast. You can find better options in the high season when the price rises to €60/112.

PLACES TO STAY – MID-RANGE

There's a wide selection of hotels in this category.

In the centre of town is the immaculate little *Hotel Malleberg (Map 10; ☎ 050-34 41 11, fax 050-34 67 69, Hoogstraat 7)*. It spans two floors (no elevator) and has eight cosy but spacious rooms with beamed ceilings. A single/double costs €52/71.88; triples/quads cost €86.76/101.

Hotel 't Voermanshuys (Map 10; ☎ 050-34 13 96, fax 050-34 23 90, e *voerman shuys@pophost.eunet.be, Oude Burg 14)* is a quaint hotel in a centuries-old house. An elevator takes you up to 11 decent-sized rooms, each painted in a rich variety of colours and fitted with contemporary and period furniture. Doubles with a private bathroom start at €68; triples cost €92.

Tucked away on a very quiet backstreet, *Hotel Botaniek (Map 10; ☎ 050-34 14 24, fax 050-34 59 39,* e *hotel.botaniek@ping .be, Waalsestraat 23)* is a smart little hotel behind a dignified 18th-century facade. All rooms sport a private bathroom and are accessible by lift. The rooms cost €67/75, or €94 for a triple; prices include a buffet breakfast.

The *Hotel Ter Reien (Map 9; ☎ 050-34 91 00, fax 050-34 40 48,* e *hotel.ter.reien @online.be, Langestraat 1)* has a prime position by a canal. Its 25 rooms are a blend of classical and modern style, and half of them overlook the canal (rooms not on the canal are cheaper but also quite dark). Room No 10 is the most charming. Prices start at €54.53.

Hotel Adornes (Map 10; ☎ 050-34 13 36, fax 050-34 20 85, e *hotel.adornes@proxi media.be, St Annarei 26)* is in the often overlooked St Anna quarter. This charming hotel has a rustic feel, with beamed ceilings and an open fire in the public room. The 20 rooms are all modernly furnished and there's a good buffet breakfast. Prices start from €64.41/74.36 for singles/doubles.

Another area that's often missed by tourists is the quiet quarter around St Gilliskerk. Here you'll find the pleasant *Hotel Jacobs (Map 9; ☎ 050-33 98 31, fax 050-33 56 94,* e *hoteljacobs@glo.be, Baliestraat 1)*, where singles/doubles/triples start at €47 /50/81.

Hotel Salvators (Map 10; ☎ 050-33 19 21,

BRUGES

fax 050-33 94 64, e hotel@hotelsalv
ators.be, St Salvatorskerkhof 17) is a well-
established hotel with a range of rooms. The
cheapest room costs €30.66/44.60 for
one/two people. Otherwise, smallish singles
/doubles with minimalist, modern decor
start at €49.57/74.36. Salvators also has
large, comfortable rooms with kitchenettes
for long-term stays. Prices start at €57/85
for a double/family room.

PLACES TO STAY – TOP END

More than a third of the hotels in Bruges
fall into this category, but many are small
establishments with fewer than 20 rooms. A
buffet breakfast is generally included in the
price.

One of the city's most opulent choices is
*Die Swaene (Map 10; ☎ 050-34 27 98, fax
050-33 66 74, e info@dieswaene-hotel
.com, Steenhouwersdijk 1)*. The 24 lavish
rooms (some with a fireplace or a four-
poster bed) are individually styled. Prices
start at €136/161, and rise to €287 for a
suite. The hotel has an indoor swimming
pool and sauna.

Another hotel catering to lovers of luxury
is the *Romantik Pandhotel (Map 10;
☎ 050-34 06 66, fax 050-34 05 56, e info@
pandhotel.com, Pandreitje 16)*. This so-
called 'boutique' hotel is family-run and a
little pretentious, with antiques and *objets
d'art* used to create a sumptuous, individual
air. Room prices start at €114/136.

For those after something less flamboyant, but nevertheless refined, there's the
19-room *Hotel De Orangerie (Map 10;
☎ 050-34 16 49, fax 050-33 30 16, e info
@orangerie.com, Kartuizerinnenstraat 10)*.
Formerly a 15th-century convent, it boasts
a canal-side position and guests can use the
indoor swimming pool and sauna at its
sister hotel, the nearby Hotel De Tuilerieën.
Prices are the same as De Tuilerieën (see
below for details) except for rooms with
a canal view, which cost €222/247. If possible avoid room No 103 – it's something
of an afterthought. Breakfast costs €18.59
extra. Check out its Web site at www.hotel
orangerie.com.

*Hotel De Tuilerieën (Map 10; ☎ 050-34

36 91, fax 050-34 04 00, e info@hotel
tuilerieen.com, Dijver 7)* is across the canal
from Hotel De Orangerie and has 27 volup-
tuously decorated rooms starting at €172/
197; breakfast costs €18.59. Its Web site is
at www.hoteltuilerieen.com.

The extravagant *Relais Oud-huis Amsterdam (Map 10; ☎ 050-34 18 10, fax 050-
33 88 91, e info@oha.be, Spiegelrei 3)*
occupies an 18th-century mansion overlooking a tranquil canal. The smart rooms,
all different in decor, are furnished with
assorted antiques. Singles/doubles start at
€136/174 in the low season, or €161/198
in the high season.

LONG-TERM RENTALS

Holiday flats are mushrooming in Bruges.
Generally speaking, the longer your reservation, the cheaper the cost per day. Many
places also offer a reduction of about 20%
during the low season (roughly November
to Easter but excluding the Christmas/New
Year season).

The Gheeraerts (see Places to Stay –
Budget earlier) run two *apartments* (maximum six people) and a gorgeous attic *studio flat* (maximum four) in a neoclassical
mansion close to their guesthouse. Bookings are for a minimum of three nights, and
prices range from €55 to €65 per night for
two people in the studio, or €60 to €70
in an apartment. Additional people are
charged €8 per day.

The Dieltiens (see Places to Stay – Budget earlier) also have a lovely old house
which they rent out. It comprises a ground-
floor *studio* and a larger upstairs *apartment*.
The price for the apartment for two people
is €67.50/54.50 per night for three/seven
nights. The studio is €5 per night cheaper.
Each additional person pays €8 per day.

Erik and Marianne Broos run a range of
cheerful, decidedly modern *apartments
(Map 10; ☎ 050-33 44 50, e letsgobruges
@skynet.be, Korte Vuldersstraat 33)*, which
sleep up to eight people, in a renovated
house behind their home. They also operate
the adjoining Lokkedize cafe (see Cafes in
the Places to Eat section later). Prices range
greatly but as an indication, you can expect

to pay about €24.78 per person for short stays (three days) or about €540 for four people for a week.

Places to Eat

From cosy *estaminets* (taverns) to first-class restaurants – Bruges has all bases covered.

PLACES TO EAT – BUDGET
Restaurants
A backpacker's heaven is the hostel *Gran Kaffee de Passage (Map 10; ☎ 050-34 02 32, Dweersstraat 26–8)* where traveller-sized meals such as a *Vlaamse stoofpot* (Flemish stew; €9.17) and vegetarian options are served in intriguing surroundings.

The best option for vegetarians, and anyone into really healthy fare, is the lovely *Lotus (Map 10; ☎ 050-33 10 78, Wapenmakersstraat 5)*. It caters predominantly to local businesspeople, and the food is excellent. You can choose a *kleine maaltijd* (small meal) for €7.18, or there's the *grote* (big) version for €7.68. It opens for lunch only from 11.45 am to 2 pm – it's closed Sunday).

Soul Food (Map 9; ☎ 050-33 41 13, Langestraat 15) is an earthy-toned eatery that's popular with 20- and 30-somethings. World cuisine, particularly Thai, Cambodian and Indian flavours, are the go and vegetarians are catered for. Meals cost around €9.91. The food and service are good. It opens Tuesday to Saturday.

No-nonsense food served in intimate surroundings is the drawing card of *In den Wittenkop (Map 10; ☎ 050-33 20 59, St Jakobsstraat 14)*. This little restaurant has been around for years and the simple menu (mains between €9.41 and €14.74) is complemented by an extensive selection of regional beers. It's closed on Sunday and Monday.

Het Ander Idee (Map 9; ☎ 050-34 17 89, Hauwerstraat 9) is an Italian bistro located away from the tourist bustle. The neighbourhood is nothing special but the food, atmosphere and service more than compensate, and it is well priced (mains range

from €6.69 to €9.66). It opens for lunch and dinner (closed Monday and Tuesday).

Tearooms
De Belegde Boterham (Map 10; ☎ 050-34 91 31, Kleine St Amandsstraat 5) is convenient and convivial. Tucked away in a tiny pedestrianised alley, it offers a range of salads (€8.55) and sandwiches (€4.21). It opens noon to 5 pm Monday to Saturday.

Het Dagelijks Brood (Map 10; ☎ 050-33 60 50, Philipstockstraat 21) is part of a national bakery/tearoom chain. It has one big table plus a few little side tables where you can eat lunch staples such as salads, *boterhammen* (sandwiches) or savoury tarts. It opens 7 am to 6 pm daily (except Tuesday), and from 8 am on Sunday.

As its name foretells, the city's top tearoom is *Prestige (Map 10; ☎ 050-34 31 67, Vlamingstraat 12)*. Bruges' elderly set love this place, with its big glass windows, decadent patisserie counter and refined service. It opens 7.30 am to 6.30 pm Tuesday to Sunday.

Cafes
Like everywhere in Belgium, Bruges has an enviable selection of cafes where you can while away an hour or three over a drink or something more substantial.

Lokkedize (Map 10; ☎ 050-33 44 50, Korte Vuldersstraat 33) is one of the city's most *gezellig* (convivial) cafes. An open fire, moody music and tables decked with fresh flowers and oil lamps ensure its popularity with locals and tourists. Meals, typically Mediterranean fare such as meze or moussaka, cost from €6 to €9.80 and are served until 1 am. It opens at 7 pm (except Monday).

Close to the Burg is *De Kluiver (Map 10; ☎ 050-33 89 27, Hoogstraat 12)*, a little *kroeg* (cafe) with maritime overtones and decent snacks and meals. It's closed on Tuesday.

De Bottelier (Map 10; ☎ 050-33 18 60, St Jakobsstraat 50) is a rustic *eetkaffee* (eating cafe) where tables are flanked by alarm clocks and piano-playing mannequins. The bistro-style menu has something for everyone

– steaks, vegetarian dishes, seafood and pasta – and nothing costs over €14.74. It's closed on Sunday and Monday.

Across from Koningin Astridpark, *L'Est-aminet (Map 10; ☎ 050-33 09 16, Park 5)* has been enticing an eclectic crowd for almost a century. Its intimate atmosphere is perfect on cold days; in summer a large terrace fans out towards the park. There's a decent snack menu and it opens at 11.30 am (closed Monday night and all day Thursday).

In the St Anna quarter, *'t Gezelleke (Map 9; ☎ 050-33 81 02, Carmersstraat 15)* is an unpretentious brown cafe named after the town's favourite poet. If it's closed, another good option in this area is *De Windmolen (Map 9; ☎ 050-33 97 39, Carmersstraat 135)*, a colourful corner cafe overlooking St Janshuismolen.

In the north of town is *Herberg du Phare (Map 9; ☎ 050-34 35 90, Sasplein 2)*. Although the menu is unimaginative – spaghetti, pizza and scampi – the generous servings and reasonable prices ensure its popularity in this otherwise often unvisited quarter. The kitchen opens for lunch and dinner and vegetarian options are available. It is closed on Sunday.

Fast Food

The golden arches have thankfully not yet risen above central Bruges. Instead, for hamburgers there's *Quick (Map 10; ☎ 050-33 19 79, Markt 14)*, open 9 am to 11 pm daily.

For a hamburger with a bit more individuality try *Pickles (Map 10; ☎ 050-33 79 57, St Jakobsstraat 1)*. This dine-in or takeaway place also sells a variety of fried snacks such as *frites* and *frikadel* (a minced meatball).

Takeaway frites and hotdogs can be bought from the two *frietkotjes* in front of the Belfort on the Markt.

Those into seafood should head to the little *fish shops* opposite the Vismarkt (Map 10), where snacks such as *maatjes* (herring fillets) and seafood pastries cost between €1.23 and €1.98.

A cheap place for a quick snack or meal while shopping is the self-service restaurant on the 1st floor of the *Hema* store *(Map*

10; ☎ 050-34 96 56, Steenstraat 75). It opens till 6 pm Monday to Saturday.

If you just want a sandwich on the go, try *Panos (Map 10; ☎ 050-33 83 38, Geldmunstraat 14)*.

Self-Catering

The *Profi* supermarket *(Map 9; ☎ 050-33 82 36, Langestraat 55)* opens from 9 am to 12.30 pm and 1.30 to 6 pm Monday to Saturday. The *Nopri* supermarket *(Map 10; ☎ 050-34 16 12, Noordzandstraat 4)* opens 9 am to 6.30 pm Monday to Saturday.

For other food options, don't forget the *markets* (see under Shopping later in the chapter).

PLACES TO EAT – MID-RANGE

The restaurants lining the Markt all specialise in traditional Belgian food and, predictably, tourists are their main target. Popular with locals and visitors is *Huyze Die Maene (Map 10; ☎ 050-33 39 59, Markt 17)*, a proficient brasserie that offers a variety of seasonal Flemish meals, such as *gebakken fazanthaan met witloof* (baked pheasant with chicory). Three-course set *menus* (from €14.74 to €24.16) are served at both lunch and dinner.

All the restaurants on the Markt dish up the ubiquitous mussels and frites, but the ambience in some of these places is trite and the service can be lacking. If you want both good mussels (cooked in a creamy beer sauce) and attentive service, follow the locals to *De Koetse (Map 10; ☎ 050-33 76 80, Oude Burg 31)*. This cosy corner restaurant is also noted for its succulent *paling in 't groen* (eel in spinach sauce), another local speciality. Mains cost around €17.35.

Tom's Diner (Map 9; ☎ 050-33 33 82, West Gistelhof) is a little away from the centre but well worth the wander. The two young guys who run this place dish up Flemish cuisine with superb presentation – the sort of stuff you'd expect to receive in a restaurant with multiple stars. Mains are in the €9.91 to €17.35 range. It opens for dinner only (closed Tuesday); reservations are needed at the weekend.

Bistro De Eetkamer (Map 10; ☎ 050-33

78 86, Eekhoutstraat 6) is a sober and quite refined little restaurant (just seven or so tables) serving excellent seasonal Flemish food. Main courses all cost under €19.33, and there's a *menu*, including wine and coffee, for €23.55 at lunchtime.

A zany team of chefs and staff is one of the main attractions of ***The Cafedraal*** *(Map 10; ☎ 050-34 08 45, Zilverstraat 38)*. Excellent local cuisine and a Middle Ages ambience are the other enticements. Expect mains around the €19.85 mark.

For an evening of Burgundian-style revelry and indulgence head to ***Den Dyver*** *(Map 10; ☎ 050-33 60 69, Dijver 5)*. This large, well-established restaurant uses the nation's priceless range of beer as a base for much of its traditional-style cuisine. The €37.20 *menu* (including drinks) is great value. It's closed on Wednesday (and Tuesday in winter).

The antique frame of ***Bistro De Schaar*** *(Map 9; ☎ 050-33 59 79, Hooistraat 2)* holds a pristine little eatery with an intimate atmosphere. Australian rib-eye fillets (€15.50) are grilled on the open fire, and there are slightly cheaper seasonal Flemish dishes.

PLACES TO EAT – TOP END

Foodies consider Bruges to be second only to Brussels for fine dining in Belgium.

At the top of the ladder is ***De Karmeliet*** *(Map 9; ☎ 050-33 82 59, Langestraat 19)*, serving French *haute cuisine*. Its three-star Michelin greatness means it's known to food lovers throughout Belgium. Chef Geert Van Hecke is responsible for all this fuss. *Menus* range from €66 to €105, and for weekends you'll need to book a week ahead. It's closed Sunday evening and Monday.

Die Swaene *(Map 10; ☎ 050-34 27 98, Steenhouwersdijk 1)* is a lavish restaurant in the hotel of the same name. The cuisine is French/Belgian, and *menus* start at €50.

Den Braamberg *(Map 10; ☎ 050-33 73 70, 't Pandreitje 11)* occupies a 17th-century patrician's house on a quiet backstreet close to the Dijver. The *spécialité de la maison* is *homard* (lobster) costing

around €27.25 per person. It's closed Thursday and Sunday.

The charming ***De Stove*** *(Map 10; ☎ 050-33 78 35, Kleine St Amandsstraat 4)* is tucked away on a pedestrianised lane not far from the Markt. Arranged around an old stove, this refined little place (just eight tables) is run by a husband-and-wife team and is intimate and personable. The food – largely fish specialities – is excellent. The four-course *menu* costs €35; alternatively, mains cost about €18.60. It's closed on Wednesday and Thursday.

There's no shortage of cellar restaurants in Bruges – the best is ***'t Voermanshuys*** *(Map 10; ☎ 050-33 71 72, Oude Burg 14)* at the hotel of the same name. An intimate atmosphere coupled with innovative French/Belgian cuisine and an award-winning young chef have made this a respected family-run restaurant. Mains cost from €18.60 to €25, or there are *menus* from €34.70 up to €62. It's closed on Monday and Tuesday.

Entertainment

There are two free entertainment publications worth picking up while you're at the tourist office. *Events@Brugge* is a handy, bimonthly what's-on guide which lists classical and contemporary music events, theatre, markets and festival programs. The other, *Bruges Around the Clock*, is a pamphlet, published annually, listing some of the city's most happening pubs and their opening hours.

A good place to find out what's on in the way of hip dance clubs in nearby towns or cities is Doctor Vinyl (Map 10; ☎ 050-33 53 64), Hoogstraat 32, a music shop.

PUBS & BARS

't Brugs Beertje *(Map 10; ☎ 050-33 96 16, Kemelstraat 5)* is probably the most famous pub in Belgium. More than 300 different beers are on offer in this reasonably priced little cafe, which is owned by Jan De Bruyne, a man well known in Belgian beer circles. It opens 4 pm to 1 am nightly (closed Wednesday). Jan's love of beer has

Bruges' Top 5 Bars

- 't Brugs Beertje
- 't Dreupelhuisje
- Vino Vino
- Retsin's Lucifernum
- Herberg Vlissinghe

led him to open a new cafe, *De Brugse Bierkaai (Map 10;* ☎ *050-34 38 00, Nieuwstraat 9)*, which comes complete with its own brewery. It's a relatively large place and from the cafe you can see the brewing room.

Those into exploring Belgian *jenever* (gin) can head to *'t Dreupelhuisje (Map 10;* ☎ *050-34 24 21, Kemelstraat 9)*. This refined but cosy place offers 100 types of gin.

Bruges' oldest cafe is *Herberg Vlissinghe (Map 10;* ☎ *050-34 37 37, Blekerstraat 2)*. Someone has been pouring beer here since 1515 – mindblowing really. It opens at 11 am (closed Tuesday).

Vino Vino (Map 10; ☎ *050-34 51 15, Grauwwerkersstraat 15)* is an immensely popular, two-storey bar on a corner in the backstreets north of the Markt. It's busiest from 10 pm, Thursday to Saturday.

De Garre (Map 10; ☎ *050-34 10 29, Garre 1)* bills itself as 'a traditional alehouse for people with (beer) culture'. Hidden away in a tiny cobbled cul-de-sac between the Markt and the Burg, this old *estaminet* (tavern) has over 100 beers and opens from noon to midnight or 1 am daily.

One of Belgium's oddest places to drink is *Retsin's Lucifernum (Map 10;* ☎ *050-34 16 50, Twijnstraat 8)*. A huge mansion strewn with moody paintings, it's frequented by those who love a shot of hot rum (that's about all you can order) and weird art. It opens at 9 pm on Friday and Saturday and the €2.50 admission charge includes a drink.

All the hostels (see Places to Stay earlier) sport cafes or bars, some more popular than others, but all are inevitably good meeting places.

For a few lively late-night bars attracting a young, hip clientele it's best to head to 't Zand (Map 9), Eiermarkt or Langestraat (Map 9). *The Top (Map 10;* ☎ *050-33 03 51, St Salvatorskerkhof 5)* is a tiny pub that opens late and moves until morning.

De Kleine Nachtmuziek (Map 10; ☎ *050-33 50 84, St Jakobsstraat 60)* is simply a good pub with good music. It opens evenings only (closed Wednesday).

Another ambient little pub, especially for those into world/folk music, is *Kwassa Kwassa (Map 9;* ☎ *050-34 52 93, West Gistelhof 13)*. It's closed on Sunday.

If you want a drink at the quaintest terrace cafe you're ever likely to see, head to *Terrastje (Map 10;* ☎ *050-33 09 19, Genthof 45)*. In spring it's covered in a mass of delicate clematis flowers.

CLUBS

Bruges is not a raging metropolis as far as clubs and discos are concerned. If you want to dance, head to 't Zand, where many of the bars and cafes turn into impromptu clubs as the night livens up. The most popular and long-standing is *L'Obcédé (Map 10;* ☎ *050-34 71 71, 't Zand 11)*, which generally gets going around 11 pm. Admission is free.

GAY & LESBIAN VENUES

Gay and lesbian nightlife in Bruges is nonexistent – most people head to Antwerp, Brussels or Ghent for a night out. To find out what's happening in the way of parties in Brussels and elsewhere around Flanders, contact Holebifoon (☎ 09-238 26 26), the Ghent-based information hotline.

LIVE MUSIC

The city's premier venue for contemporary and world music – either live or DJ parties – is the *Cactus Club (Map 10;* ☎ *050-33 20 14, St Jakobsstraat 33)*. Live performances usually rate a €8.67 admission.

As in other cities in Belgium, jazz is a firm favourite in Bruges. *De Versteende Nacht (Map 9;* ☎ *050-34 32 93, Langestraat 11)* is a cafe with live jazz, including jam sessions, every Wednesday from 9 pm; admission is free.

De Werf (Map 9; ☎ *050-33 05 29, Werf-*

straat 108) features the occasional jazz evening. There's usually a cover charge of up to €13.60/11.15 for those aged over /under 26, or €4.95 for under 21s.

The Duke *(Map 10; ☎ 050-34 05 61, St Jakobsstraat 41)*, a bar inside the four-star Hotel Navarra, features a solid jazz line-up from 9 pm every Friday. Admission is free.

Two Irish pubs, **Celtic Ireland** *(Map 10; ☎ 050-34 45 02, Burgstraat 8)* and **Celtica** *(Map 9; ☎ 050-34 47 86, Langestraat 121)* offer pints of draught Guinness and live music, be it rock, jazz or traditional, most Friday and/or Saturday nights from about 9 pm. Admission at both is free.

Herberg du Phare *(Map 9; ☎ 050-34 35 90, Sasplein 2)* stages blues concerts from 9 pm every second Sunday. The cover charge is usually €2.50 to €6.20.

CINEMAS
Mainstream films are screened at **Cinema Liberty** *(Map 10; ☎ 050-33 20 11, Kuipersstraat 23)*. **Cinema Lumière** *(Map 10; ☎ 050-33 48 57, St Jakobsstraat 36a)* has two auditoriums and shows foreign and mainstream films and, occasionally, a classic.

PERFORMING ARTS
Bruges' new *concertgebouw* (concert hall /theatre) was under construction at the time of writing. It should be finished by 2002 for the city's fling as European City of Culture. The design was chosen from an international competition and the hall will be used for classical music, theatre and dance. It will include a large auditorium with 1200 seats and a smaller music chamber with a capacity for 250 people.

The city's other major venue is the **Stadsschouwburg** *(Map 10; ☎ 050-44 30 60, Vlamingstraat 29)*.

SPECTATOR SPORTS
Bruges' major sporting venue is the **Jan Breydel Stadium** *(☎ 050-40 21 21, Olympialaan 74)*, 3km west of town. It's home to Club Brugge, one of the country's best soccer teams, and you can often see matches here. Tickets, available from the stadium, cost from €10 to €25.

Shopping

Steenstraat, the main shopping thoroughfare, is lined with big-name shops and department stores. The nearby Geldmuntstraat and Noordzandstraat are home to boutiques. Between the two is Zilverpand, a shopping gallery.

BEER
The Woolstreet Company (Map 10; ☎ 050-34 83 83), Wollestraat 31a, stocks 200 beers plus their accompanying glasses. It opens 9 am to 9 pm daily (6 pm in winter).

Just up the road at No 13 is the Bottle Shop (Map 10; ☎ 050-34 99 80). This big, slick place claims to stock more than 500 types of Belgian beers and 200 varieties of gin. It opens 9.30 am to 7 pm daily.

BOOKS
De Reyghere Boekhandel (Map 10; ☎ 050-33 34 03), Markt 12, is one of the oldest bookshop in Flanders. It stocks a selection of English-language novels (known as *pockets* in Flemish), travel guides, maps and international newspapers. It opens 8.30 am to 6 pm, Monday to Saturday.

The Brugse Boekhandel (Map 10; ☎ 050-33 29 52), Dijver 2, stocks a similar range and opens Monday to Saturday (daily between April and December).

CHOCOLATE
Neuhaus (Map 10; ☎ 050-33 88 55), 't Zand 4, occupies a little brick building and has lovely praline displays.

Pralinette (Map 10; ☎ 050-34 84 44), Wollestraat 31b, has a good reputation for handmade chocolates, and you can watch pralines being made from the swirling chocolate in the three vats at the rear of the shop. A single praline costs €0.60.

CLOTHING
Belgium's best-known designer, Olivier Strelli (Map 10; ☎ 050-34 38 37), is at Eiermarkt 3. For home-grown handbags head to Delvaux (Map 10; ☎ 050-49 01 31), Breidelstraat 2. Second-hand Delvaux bags (in

BRUGES

very good nick) can be bought at Secondo (Map 10; ☎ 050-33 07 88), a chic little shop at Mallebergplein 3. Another good hunting ground for second-hand shops is Langestraat. Here you'll find De Kobbe (Map 9; ☎ 050-34 44 88), Langestraat 12, a tatty little outlet good for unearthing vintage and club clothes as well as coats, shoes and bags.

DIAMONDS
The Brugs Diamanthuis (Map 10; ☎ 050-33 64 33) at Katelijnestaat 43 has an opulent showroom attached to the Diamantmuseum.

LACE & TAPESTRIES
It's not finding lace that's the problem in Bruges – it's getting away from it. About 80 lace shops operate here, many tucked away in nooks and crannies in the town centre or concentrated along Wollestraat and Breidelstraat. Well away from all of these and with a good reputation is 't Apostolientje (Map 9; ☎ 050-33 78 60) at Balstraat 11. About 70% of its stock is antique lace and most is handmade in Belgium. Just round the corner and also recommended is the

Buying Lace

The bulk of lace sold in shops throughout Belgium these days is handmade in Taiwan and China, or machine-made in France. If you want handmade lace from Belgium you must say so. Even reputable shops generally do not advertise which of their stock is made outside Belgium – it's up to you to ask.

You must also be prepared to pay a high price for the real thing. As one lace-maker in Bruges put it: 'The average hourly rate for workers in Belgium is about €7.50 to €10. It takes 12 hours to make the lace trim on a standard handkerchief – if we were to charge those same rates it would be a very expensive cloth on which to wipe your nose!'

Antique lace is generally considered to be lace made before 1930. Renaissance lace is made half by hand and half by machine. For more on lace, see Traditional Textiles under Arts in the Facts about the Cities chapter.

shop at the Kantcentrum (see under Kantcentrum & Jeruzalemkerk earlier in the chapter). For more advice, see the boxed text 'Buying Lace'.

Mille-Fleurs (Map 10; ☎ 050-34 54 54), Wollestraat 33, is a specialised shop dealing in tapestries made in Flanders.

MARKETS
The biggest market is Saturday's food and general-goods market on 't Zand; stalls bustle from 8 am to 1 pm. More picturesque is Wednesday morning's food market on the Markt.

Fishmongers have been selling their produce at the old Vismarkt for centuries. These days a few vendors still set up on the cold stone slabs from 7 am to 1 pm, Tuesday to Saturday.

The canal-side Dijver is taken over by antique and bric-a-brac stalls every Saturday and Sunday afternoon from April to October.

TINTIN MEMORABILIA
The Tintin Shop (Map 10; ☎/fax 050-33 42 92), Steenstraat 3, stocks everything any Tintin buff could ever want, and more. It opens daily.

Excursions

DAMME
postcode 8340 • pop 11,000
The former fishing village of Damme is just 5km north-east of Bruges and is an immensely popular destination for day-trippers. A long time ago, Damme nestled on the edge of the Zwin, a waterway connected to the sea. A canal was built between Damme and Bruges and, by the 13th century, Damme was the region's bustling port. But along with Bruges, its fate was sealed when the Zwin silted up.

Things to See & Do
The village has a sprinkling of buildings, most devoted to the inordinate tourist trade in one way or another. Central to everything is the Gothic **Stadhuis** (town house), where one of the nation's 15th-century rulers,

The view of the gabled houses lining Bruges' Markt is worth the 366-step climb up the huge Belfort.

he 13th-century Belfort towers over Bruges.

The warm tones of Bruges' medieval centre

MARTIN MOOS

St Salvatorskathedraal's unusual 99m-high tower

MARTIN MOOS

St Janshuismolen's sails fly when the wind's high

LEANNE LOGAN

Sombre reminders of WWI are many in the Ypres Salient, where more than 300,000 soldiers were killed

Charles the Bold (Karel de Stoute), and Margaret of York wed in lavish style in 1468. Directly in front of the Stadhuis is a **statue of Jacob Van Maerlant**, a 13th-century Flemish poet who lived and died in Damme. He's buried in **Onze Lieve Vrouwekerk** (Our Lady's Church) on Kerkstraat. The church dates to the 12th century and was vastly expanded in the village's heyday, only to be abandoned and partially torn down when the village declined. You can climb the robust tower for good views in summer.

Opposite the Stadhuis, in a restored patrician's house, is the tourist office (☎ 050-35 33 19), Jacob Van Maerlantstraat 3. Next to the tourist office is ***Brasserie De Spieghel*** *(☎ 050-37 11 30, Jacob van Maerlantstraat 10)*, a rustic eatery serving great snacks and typical Flemish fare. Try an Uilenspiegelbier, the local brown beer (8%).

Getting There & Away
A river barge, *Lamme Goedzak*, plies between Bruges and Damme (35 minutes one way). From Bruges it leaves from Noorweegse Kaai 31, a good 45-minute walk north-east from the Markt (or take bus No 4 from the Markt, or the special bus from the Markt or the train station). A one-way /return journey costs €4.70/6.19 (children €3.47/4.46). It operates five times daily between Easter and 30 September.

THE BELGIAN COAST
The Belgian coast is not a great pull for visitors but it does have a few interesting nooks and crannies. Much of the 66km coastline underwent unsightly development in the 20th century and is now draped with ugly high-rise apartment blocks. Amongst these, though, are windswept dunes, interesting towns and villages such as Ostend, De Haan or Knokke, and small nature reserves such as Het Zwin. A great way to explore the Belgian coast is to ride the Kusttram (coast tram) – see Getting There & Around at the end of this section for details.

Things to See & Do
The main coastal town is **Ostend** (Map 1; Oostende in Flemish, Ostende in French)

which was one of Europe's most stylish 19th-century seaside resorts. These days it's more down to earth and is a convenient starting point for exploration. In good weather, it's well worth wandering along the Visserskaai (fishermen's quay), the town's famed seafood quayside. Ostend was home to Ensor, Belgium's best-known 19th-century artist, and the Ensorhuis (☎ 059-80 53 35), Vlaanderenstraat 27, where he lived and painted from 1875 to 1916 can still be visited. The Ostend tourist office (☎ 059-70 11 99), Monacoplein 2, is 1.25km from the train station, adjacent to the landmark Casino-Kursaal. Trams stop close to the tourist office.

Heading south from Ostend, the Kusttram stops at **St Idesbald** (Map 1) where the Paul Delvaux Museum (☎ 058-52 12 29), Delvauxlaan 42 (1km from the tram stop), delves into the life of one of the nation's most famous Surrealist artists.

Alternatively, go north from Ostend to arrive at **De Haan** (Map 1), arguably the coast's most picturesque village with a lovely little Art Nouveau tram station.

Continue farther north and you'll reach **Knokke** (Map 1), an urbane resort town and the preferred summer destination for Belgium's bourgeois. The Knokke tourist office (☎ 050-63 03 80), at Zeedijk 660 on the beachfront in the heart of Knokke, is some 2km from the train and tram stations.

About 5km east of Knokke is the tiny nature reserve of **Het Zwin** (Map 1; ☎ 050-60 70 86), Graaf Leon Lippensdreef 8. It's a tranquil region of polders and mudflats and is an important destination for migrating swans, ducks and geese – some 20,000 reed geese flock here each year. Europe's largest owl, the *oehoe* (eagle owl), lives here as do many storks, the result of a highly successful breeding program that started in 1956. The salty landscape hides rare species of beetle and spider, as well as the *zwinnebloem* (sea lavender), which coats much of the area in purple in summer. A third of the reserve opens to the public, and there are paths for hikers (rubber boots are essential for much of the year). No public transport goes to Het Zwin – access is limited to car, bike or foot.

Getting There & Around

You can easily reach Ostend or Knokke by train from Bruges (€2.72, 15 minutes). Knokke is also a feasible ride for cyclists.

From either town you can pick up one the Kusttram (coast tram), which trundles between De Panne, in the south-west, and Knokke in the north-east. There are 70 stops en route, with a tram roughly every half-hour; it takes just over two hours to traverse the whole coastal strip. A single ticket for a short journey costs €1, or you can purchase a one-day ticket for unlimited travel for €7.50.

YPRES

postcode 8900 • pop 35,280

Stories have long been told about the WWI battlefields of Flanders. There were the tall red poppies that rose over the flat, flat fields; the soldiers who disappeared forever in the quagmire of battle; and the little town of Ypres (Ieper in Flemish) that was wiped off the map.

Sitting in the country's south-western corner, Ypres and the surrounding area were the last bastion of Belgian territory unoccupied by the Germans in WWI. As such, the region was a barrier to the German advance towards the French coastal ports around Calais. More than 300,000 Allied soldiers were killed on the Ypres Salient during four years of fighting that left the medieval town flattened. Convincingly rebuilt, its outlying farmlands are today dotted with cemeteries, and in early summer the poppies still flower.

The town's hub is the Grote Markt, a five-minute walk from the train station.

Information

The Ypres Visitors Centre (☎ 057-22 85 84, fax 057-22 85 89) is in the Lakenhalle on the Grote Markt. It opens 9 am to 6 pm daily (from 10 am Sunday) from 1 April to 30 September, and until 5 pm during the rest of the year.

Things to See & Do

In medieval times, Ypres ranked alongside Bruges and Ghent as an important cloth town and its postwar reconstruction holds true to its former prosperity. The southern part of the town is flanked by a wide moat and steep stone **ramparts** that are topped by pleasant gardens and walking paths.

Lakenhalle & Stadhuis The enormous Lakenhalle (cloth hall) with its 70m-high belfry dominates the Grote Markt. The original version was completed in 1304 beside the Ypreslee river, which is now under-

Ypres' Cat Festival

Ypres' main folkloric event is the annual Kattenfestival, or Festival of the Cats. Though cat-lovers around the world will be enraged by the idea, the festival has its roots in the 12th-century tradition of throwing live cats from the Lakenhalle's belfry. Cats, it was believed, personified evil spirits and this ritual, which continued until 1817, was their undoing. Today's version – which sees toy cats hurled on the second Sunday in May – was revived in the 1930s. The celebration has its climax every three years when the town hosts the Kattenstoet, a parade of giant cats – the next will be in May 2003.

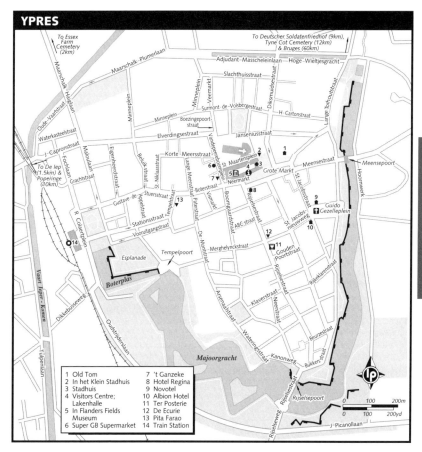

YPRES

To Essex Farm Cemetery (2km)

To Deutscher Soldatenfriedhof (9km), Tyne Cot Cemetery (12km) & Bruges (60km)

Adjudant-Masscheleinlaan — Hoge-Wieltjesgracht

Maarschalk-Plumerlaan
Slachthuisstraat

Minneplein — Veemarkt
Surmont-de-Volsbergestraat
Diksmuidestraat
H-Cartonstraat

Minneplein
Boezingepoort-straat
Elverdingsestraat
Janseniusstraat

Korte-Meersstraat
St Maartensplein
Meensestraat — Meensepoort

Grote Markt
Hoornwerk

Neermarkt

Boterstraat

Guido Gezelleplein

St Jacobs-nieuwweg

Gouden Poortstraat

Merghelynckstraat

Klaverstraat

Majoorgracht

Rijselsepoort

0   100   200m
0   100   200yd

1 Old Tom	7 't Ganzeke
2 In het Klein Stadhuis	8 Hotel Regina
3 Stadhuis	9 Novotel
4 Visitors Centre; Lakenhalle	10 Albion Hotel
5 In Flanders Fields Museum	11 Ter Posterie
6 Super GB Supermarket	12 De Ecurie
	13 Pita Farao
	14 Train Station

BRUGES

ground. In those times, ships could sail into the Lakenhalle to unload their cargoes of wool, which were stored on the 1st floor and sold from the halls at street level.

The Renaissance-style Stadhuis is attached to the eastern end of the Lakenhalle. It's noted for the lovely arcade gallery that runs along the front and, inside, for a huge and impressive stained-glass window.

In Flanders Fields Museum This outstanding museum (☎ 057-22 85 84), Grote Markt 34, occupies the 1st floor of the Lakenhalle. It is devoted to the promotion of

peace as much as the remembrance of war, and is a moving testament to the wartime horrors experienced by ordinary people – it tells the stories of soldiers, nurses, fugitives and children. It opens 10 am to 6 pm daily from 1 April to 30 September, and 10 am to 5 pm Tuesday to Sunday from 1 October to 31 March. Admission costs €6.20 (children €3.10). Its Web site is www.inflandersfields.be.

Meensepoort The Menin Gate stands at the end of Meensestraat, about 300m from the tourist office, and is one of the saddest reminders of the town's past. It is inscribed with the names of 54,896 British and Commonwealth troops who were lost in the quagmire of the trenches and who have no graves. A bugler sounds the last post here at 8 pm every evening.

The Ypres Salient The Ypres Salient is a portion of land that stretches for about 25km from Langemark north of Ypres to near Menen close to the border with France. The Salient was actually a bulge in the frontline between the opposing armies, a line which extended from the North Sea at Nieuwpoort in Belgium all the way to Switzerland.

The wartime reminders of the Ypres Salient are many and they're scattered over a large area. Organised tours are the easiest way to see the main sights, such as **Tyne Cot Cemetery** (the largest British Commonwealth war cemetery in the world), the **Deutscher Soldatenfriedhof** (German cemetery), and the **Essex Farm Cemetery** where Canadian John McCrae wrote the famous poem: 'In Flanders Fields the poppies blow, between the crosses, row on row…'

Two good tour companies are Salient Tours (☎ 075-91 02 23), which does 2½/4-hour tours for €16.10/23.50; or Quasimodo (☎ 050-37 04 70), which runs tours of Ypres from Bruges for €45 (those aged under 26 €38).

Places to Stay

The closest hostel is *De Iep* (*☎/fax 057-20 88 11, Poperingseweg 34)*, about 2km west of town. It charges €13.40/12.65 for adults /students.

One of the most affordable central hotels is the friendly *Old Tom* (*☎ 057-20 15 41, fax 057-21 91 20,* [e] *old.tom@pandora.be, Grote Markt 8)*. It has nine old-fashioned single/double rooms for €48/57.

The new *Albion Hotel* (*☎ 057-20 02 20, fax 057-20 02 15,* [e] *info@albionhotel.be, St Jacobsstraat 28)* has stylish rooms for €69.50/86.80.

Hotel Regina (*☎ 057-21 88 88, fax 057-*
21 90 20, [e] *info@hotelregina.be, Grote Markt 45)* overlooks the Lakenhalle and has old, very ordinary rooms for €74.50, or new, large and beautifully rustic rooms for €99. Check its Web site at www.hotel regina.be.

A new *Novotel* (*☎ 057-42 96 00, fax 057-18 07 55, Guido Gezelleplein 7)* was due to open in September 2001.

Places to Eat

The *Pita Farao* (*☎ 057-21 94 31, Tempelstraat 7)* does excellent stuffed *pitas* (pitta-bread sandwiches) from €3.50/5.50 and vegetarian felafel.

't Ganzeke (*☎ 057-20 00 09, Vandepeereboomplein 5)* is a no-nonsense brasserie (with a nonsmoking section) that's good for a snack or light meal.

In het Klein Stadhuis (*☎ 057-21 55 42, Grote Markt 32)* is a smooth, split-level cafe tucked away next to the Stadhuis and offers good-value meals throughout the day and night.

Arguably the best restaurant in town is *De Ecurie* (*☎ 057-21 73 78, Merghelynckstraat 1a)*. This renovated stable is charmingly rustic and the versatile menu offers old favourites with a modern twist. Mains all cost under €15. It's closed Monday and Wednesday evening. The attached cafe is good for a pre or post-dinner drink.

The *Super GB* (*☎ 057-20 17 90, Vandepeereboomplein 15)* supermarket opens from 9 am to 7 pm Monday to Saturday.

Beer devotees should head to *Ter Posterie* (*☎ 057-20 05 80, Rijselsestraat 57)*, a cellar pub serving snacks and 250 national brews (closed Wednesday). Try the regional Hommelbier – a moderately strong beer brewed at the nearby town of Poperinge.

Getting There & Away

There are hourly trains direct to Kortrijk (€3.71, 30 minutes) and Ghent (€7.93, one hour). For Brussels (€12.27, 1¾ hours) and Bruges (€8.42, 1¾ hours) you have to change in Kortrijk. For train information call ☎ 057-20 00 70.

Antwerp

- postcode 2000
- pop 456,700
- elevation 14m

Second in size only to Brussels and in some ways more likeable, Antwerp (Antwerpen in Flemish, Anvers in French) is Belgium's most underrated city. Bold, proud and beautiful, it basks in its role as the capital of the province of the same name and positively brims with self-confidence. Strangely enough this bravado is seldom extolled beyond the city limits, and even less so abroad. As a result, many people from outside Europe would be hard-pressed to pinpoint Antwerp on a world map, and even Europeans tend to think of it as the city they missed en route from Brussels to Bruges.

Antwerp came to the fore as Western Europe's greatest economic centre in the 15th and early 16th centuries. Although much has befallen it since those heady days, it's once again at the centre of Belgium's economic might – its confidence is a result of this. With a prime spot on the River Scheldt (Schelde in Flemish), the city has grown from a thriving medieval harbour to the world's third-largest port, with a multitude of associated industries securing its standing. Although this massive harbour stretches from the Dutch border to near the old city centre, it's possible to visit Antwerp and hardly realise the port exists.

No single thing draws people to Antwerp – its lures are manifold. The old city centre, built around the country's most impressive cathedral, is as beautiful and intimate as it was centuries ago. Cobbled lanes lead to open squares with beguiling names such as Handschoenmarkt, the glove-makers' market. Tucked away in alleys and backstreets are enough restaurants and bars to rival Brussels and, in between, are antique shops, art galleries, designer boutiques and diamond shops where the elite of Antwerp enjoy spending their money.

The city is distinctive for its bold Gothic and baroque architecture; it was the home of Pieter Paul Rubens, northern Europe's greatest baroque artist. Rubens created most of his masterpieces at his home and studio in the centre of the city – a building that showcases his life and can still be visited today. Museums and churches around the city display some of his most acclaimed works, including *The Descent from the Cross*, one of four monumental canvases that hang in the mighty Onze Lieve Vrouwkathedraal (Cathedral of Our Lady) in the old centre.

If all this sounds a bit too yesteryear, you're in for a shock. Antwerp is fast gaining a reputation as a humdinger of a party city and it's not just the city's fashionable young things who are raving all night. Every weekend the largest gay club in this corner of Europe attracts clubbers from near and far – Antwerp is, after all, only two hours by fast train from both Amsterdam and Paris, and just over three hours from London. Thousands of cafes and bars, each one different from the next and many of them right in the heart of the city, amount to one of the best nights on the town you're ever likely to have.

There are other surprises for those not in the know. Designers from Antwerp are at the cutting edge of fashion, and the city's boutiques are a treat for anyone into avant-garde. The world's largest diamond-cutting industry operates behind discreet facades in the Jewish neighbourhood. In the old sailors' quarter, just north of the centre, bored women sit framed in red lights, while in the famous Zurenborg area the architects simply ran riot.

Cosmopolitan, full of contrasts, confident and fun…Antwerp in a nutshell.

Getting Around

ORIENTATION

Antwerp flanks the River Scheldt and is bordered by the Ring, a motorway that skirts three-quarters of the city. The old centre, based around the Grote Markt on the right bank of the river, is a brisk 20-minute walk from the impressive Centraal Station. The two are linked together by the pedestrianised Meir (pronounced 'mare'), a bustling shopping thoroughfare.

Many of the city's major sights are concentrated between Centraal Station and the old centre, an area easily covered on foot, although the attractions outside the old centre should not be overlooked.

The neighbourhood on everyone's lips at present is Het Zuid (the south), commonly abbreviated as 't Zuid. This area to the south of the city centre was first developed as a dockland in the second half of the 19th century. It now sports a diverse mix of museums, art galleries, restaurants and clubs, all spread over a considerable area. Focal points are the Koninklijk Museum voor Schone Kunsten (for more information see Things to See & Do later), and the nearby Waalsekaai and Vlaamsekaai, two former quays separated by an enormous (and desolate) square.

North of the Grote Markt is the Schipperskwartier, or sailors' quarter, best known for its red-light district and clubs. A little farther north, an area of 19th-century docks, today referred to as somewhat poetically as 't Eilandje (little island), is fast becoming one of the city's trendiest quarters.

Immediately south of Centraal Station is the diamond quarter and adjoining Jewish neighbourhood. Antwerp has been home to a sizeable Jewish community since the Middle Ages and it's common here to see Orthodox Jewish men in their distinctive black coats and hats.

Farther south-east is Zurenborg, a district settled a century ago and today considered one of the city's finest neighbourhoods. The area is cut by the railway line and has two distinct quarters – the rich *belle-époque* Cogels-Osylei area, and the middle-class quarter around Dageraadplaats.

From the Ring, Antwerp fans out into suburbs such as Berchem, Deurne, Hoboken and Wilrijk. The city also extends to Linkeroever (the left bank), which is easily accessible via the pedestrianised St Anna-tunnel under the Scheldt.

THE AIRPORT

Antwerp's airport, known as Luchthaven Deurne, is 4km south-east of the centre in the suburb of Deurne. The airport services a very limited number of flights to/from the UK (see the Getting There & Away chapter). For general airport enquiries call ☎ 03-285 65 00.

TO/FROM THE AIRPORT

Bus No 16 connects the airport with Quellinstraat, two blocks west of Centraal Station (20 minutes). Taxis cost about €9.90 one way.

PUBLIC TRANSPORT

A good network of buses, trams and a premetro (a tram that runs underground for part of its journey) is run by De Lijn (☎ 03-218 14 06). Public transport maps covering the city centre (free) or greater Antwerp (€1.98) are available from De Lijn's ticket and information kiosks around the city – the most useful are located at the premetro stations Diamant (below Centraal Station) and Groenplaats, and on Franklin Rooseveltplaats (Map 12).

These kiosks open 8 am to 4 pm weekdays (also 9 am to noon on Saturday at Groenplaats).

Stad (city) and *streek* (regional) buses leave from various places around the city including the main bus hub at Franklin Rooseveltplaats. Make sure you know which direction you're heading in – as many bus (and tram) routes start at one side of the city and finish on the other, it's possible to be on the right-numbered bus (or tram) but travelling in the wrong direction.

The tram network is well established with routes as far out as Hoboken, Deurne and Mortsel.

The tiny, two-line premetro simply consists of above-ground trams that dive underground. Tram Nos 2 and 15 traverse the main drag from Centraal Station to Groenplaats and continue under the Scheldt to surface on the Linkeroever. The signs in the premetro stations can be confusing; you'll need to know your tram's end destination in order to choose the right platform.

The same tickets can be used for buses, trams and premetro. Single tickets (valid for one hour) cost €0.99, 10-journey cards are €7.43, or there's a 24-hour *Dagpas Vlaams Stad* (day ticket for Flemish cities) for €2.85. The latter ticket is valid for use in Antwerp, Bruges, Ghent and Mechelen but not Brussels or Ypres. Single tickets and the Dagpas can be bought from drivers; the 10-journey card must be purchased from a ticket kiosk.

Public transport generally runs from about 6 am to midnight. There's also a *nachtlijn* (night bus) service at the weekend (€1.48 per ticket), although it's very limited.

CAR & MOTORCYCLE

Driving in Antwerp is easier than in Brussels but parking is the usual problem. Street parking is scarce and metered (9 am to 6 pm Monday to Saturday; €0.74 to €1.48 per hour for a maximum of two hours). Buy your ticket from the nearest machine and display it on the dashboard.

One of the best places to park (free) is on the covered riverside quays (in the Zuiderterras hanger to be exact) near the heart of town. The northern section of this hanger is paid parking, but the southern end (and all of the open-air parking next to it) is free. The entrance is opposite Fortuinstraat (Map 12). If it's full there's also free parking in 't Zuid on the Gedempte Zuiderdokken (Map 11), the big square found between Vlaamsekaai and Waalsekaai. From here, bus Nos 6 and 34 will take you to Steenplein near the Grote Markt, and bus No 23 runs to Franklin Rooseveltplaats.

The easiest central parking garage to access is the 24-hour underground car park at Groenplaats (Map 12). Day/night rates are €1.73/0.99 for one hour, €5.20/2.47 for three hours and €12.39 for 24 hours.

Car rental companies include Budget (Map 12; ☎ 03-232 35 00), at Ankerrui 20, and also at Deurne airport (☎ 03-218 12 82); Europcar (Map 11; ☎ 03-206 74 44) at Plantin-Moretuslei 35; and Avis (Map 11; ☎ 03-218 94 96) at Plantin-Moretuslei 62.

TAXI

Taxis wait at Groenplaats, outside Centraal Station and nearby Koningin Astridplein. Otherwise call Antwerp Taxi (☎ 03-238 98 25). An extra €2.50 is added to taxi fares between 10 pm and 6 am.

BICYCLE

In summer, bikes can be hired from De Windroos (Map 12; ☎ 03-480 93 88), Steenplein 1a; they cost €1.85 for one hour or €7.43 per day.

As bicycle theft is common, the city council has set up *gratis bewaakte fietsenstallingen* – free, guarded parking areas for bikes. There's one on Koningin Astridplein and another at Groenplaats. Bikes can be left here from 10 am to 6 pm Monday to Saturday.

WALKING

Antwerp is a delight to discover on foot. A good number of streets in the old centre are pedestrianised – just watch out for irregular cobblestone paving and dog poo.

Also, keep off cycle paths, which are generally marked with a bicycle symbol and often paved red. These paths are reserved for cyclists who rightfully get annoyed when pedestrians are blocking the way.

ORGANISED TOURS

Horse-drawn carriages, and motorised and horse-drawn trams all make their way around the old centre; ask at the tourist office (Map 12), Grote Markt 13, for details.

Boat Trips

Flandria (Map 12; ☎ 03-231 31 00), on Steenplein, offers cruises from Easter to October. The 50-minute Scheldt trip departs from Steenplein and affords great views of the city skyline. It costs €6.45 (seniors and children €3.71). The 2½-hour harbour cruise departs from *kaai* (quay) No 13 (Map 11) in 't Eilandje district, 1km north of the Grote Markt; the cost is €11.15 (seniors and children €6.20).

ANTWERP

Things to See & Do

Antwerp boasts a varied selection of excellent museums. The majority are sprinkled throughout the old city centre, but don't overlook the museums in 't Zuid. All the museums listed in this section, unless otherwise stated, open 10 am to 5 pm Tuesday to Sunday. The major museums mostly charge €2.50 for admission (seniors and students €1.25); any exceptions are noted in the text.

OLD CITY CENTRE (MAP 12)
The Grote Markt

The heart of Antwerp is the Grote Markt, a vast, pedestrianised, triangular market square, which is dominated by the impressive Stadhuis (city hall) and the much-loved Brabo Fountain.

The Grote Markt is lined on two sides by Renaissance-style **guildhalls**, most of which were reconstructed in the 19th century. The tallest and most impressive is No 7, topped by a gilded statue of St George astride a rearing horse as he spears a dragon. Nos 38 and 40 – De Oude Waag and Rodenborg – are original and were the headquarters of the cloth-makers and tanners, respectively.

The voluptuous, baroque **Brabo Fountain** rises from a rough pile of rocks in the centre of the Grote Markt. Crafted in 1887 by Jef Lambeaux (who lived at Grote Markt 44), it depicts the legend of how Antwerp got its name (see the boxed text 'The Legend of Brabo').

The Renaissance-style **Stadhuis** (☎ 03-221 13 33) was designed by Cornelius Floris De Vriendt and was completed in 1565. The palatial facade is a blend of Flemish and Italian styles, an innovative departure from the standard Gothic architecture prevalent at the time of construction. The commanding gable is topped by a fine gilded eagle and flanked by statues representing Wisdom and Justice. The interior was renovated in the 19th century; a marble staircase now covers what was once an open-air courtyard. The entrance is on Suikerrui. Guided tours (€0.75, 40 minutes) are conducted at 2 and 3 pm daily (except Thursday and Sunday).

Before entering the Stadhuis you'll see the proud 19th-century bronze statue the **Bag Bearer**, by Constantin Meunier, which pays tribute to the city's dock workers and was crafted by Belgium's most famous sculptor.

Next to the Stadhuis entrance is the **Etnografisch Museum** (Ethnographic Museum; ☎ 03-220 86 00), Suikerrui 19. It contains a highly respected collection of traditional artefacts from around the world and is spacious and well set out. Lounge chairs and reading corners are provided and, although labelling is exclusively in Flemish, an English booklet (free but must be returned) is available. The museum's prize piece is the *Voorouderbeeld*, a black wooden statue of an African ancestor made by the Hemba, one of the Luba tribes in Congo. It's on the ground floor. Nearby is another treasure, the *Voorouder-herdenkingspaal*, a 5.5m-high memorial pole from Irian Jaya made in 1957. For opening hours and admission, see the start of the Things to See & Do section.

Onze Lieve Vrouwkathedraal

The splendid Cathedral of Our Lady, one block from the Grote Markt, is the largest and finest Gothic cathedral in Belgium. It was 169 years in the making (1352–1521) and the work of several architects (Appelmans, Domien and Keldermans). Its graceful 123m-high spire was a mighty landmark in early times and is still visible from miles around today.

The Legend of Brabo

ALBERT COLE

Two stories are told about the origins of the name Antwerp.

The not so popular, but more likely, explanation lies with archaeological remains found near the Steen. The findings proved that a Gallo-Roman settlement existed on a mound (aanwerp) that partly vanished when the quays were straightened in the 1880s.

The legend – depicted in the Brabo Fountain – is much more colourful. It tells of a giant, Druon Antigoon, who lived at the bend of the Scheldt and forced shipmasters to pay a toll whenever they passed. Those who refused lost a hand. Along came Silvius Brabo, a Roman warrior, who killed the giant, chopped off his hand and chucked it in the river. Hand werpen (hand throwing) subsequently evolved into Antwerpen, the city's name in Flemish.

The entrance is on Handschoenmarkt. A fire in the Middle Ages, the Iconoclastic Fury and plundering during the French occupation mean that little of what you see inside today is original Gothic. Instead, baroque decorations – notably four early canvases by Rubens – adorn its light but imposing interior.

From the centre of the seven-aisled nave you can look straight down to the high altar and Rubens' *Assumption* (1625). Although impossible to view up close, this painting's radiance is profound. To the left of the central crossing is *The Raising of the Cross* (1610), while the much smaller *Resurrection* (1612) hangs in a small chapel to the right of the high altar. The most celebrated of Rubens' four paintings is *The Descent from the Cross* (1612) immediately to the right of the central crossing. In this sensitive triptych, the deathly-grey Christ is lowered by mourners while the Virgin, whose face was painted by Van Dyck, reaches to touch her son.

The cathedral opens 10 am to 5 pm Monday to Friday, to 3 pm on Saturday and 1 to 4 pm Sunday. Admission costs €1.75 (students and seniors €1). There are free summer carillon concerts held at 8 pm on Monday.

Handschoenmarkt

Snuggled between the Grote Markt and Groenplaats, this tiny, picturesque square takes its name from the glove market that once thrived here. It's lined with gabled houses and terrace cafes, all dwarfed by the Onze Lieve Vrouwkathedraal on one side.

In a corner stands a **well** with decorative wrought-iron work attributed to a 16th-century painter, Quinten Matsijs. So the story goes, Matsijs (from a blacksmith family) became an artist simply to marry the daughter of a painter as, in those days, marriage between families of different guilds was frowned upon.

Just off Handschoenmarkt, at Oude Koornmarkt 16, is the entrance to **Vlaeykensgang**, one of the few 16th-century alleys that have survived in Antwerp. Originally these tiny streets were the domain of the city's most impoverished citizens (in this case cobblers); nowadays Vlaeykensgang is synonymous with one of the most expensive restaurants in town, the Sir Anthony Van Dyck, named after the well-known baroque artist (for more information see the Places to Eat section).

ANTWERP

Groenplaats

This large square was the town's graveyard until the 18th century. A much photographed **statue of Rubens**, sculpted in 1840, commands centre stage here; popular terrace cafes flank the square's northern side.

ModeMuseum

A short walk from Groenplaats is the new ModeMuseum (Fashion Museum), better known as MoMu, on the corner of Nationalestraat and Drukkerijstraat in the heart of the city's fashion district. It is due to open on 7 October 2001 as part of the closing celebrations for Antwerp Fashion 2001, an event devoted to the city's designers. For more on Antwerp fashion, see the boxed text 'At the Cutting Edge'.

Museum Plantin-Moretus

Two blocks west of the ModeMuseum is Vrijdagmarkt, home to a Friday auction and market that has been going for centuries. Here too, behind a modest 18th-century facade, is the fascinating Museum Plantin-Moretus (☎ 03-221 14 50), Vrijdagmarkt 22.

The museum deals with the world of a prosperous 16th- and 17th-century printing family headed by Christoffel Plantin. Plantin moved from France to Antwerp where he set up as a bookbinder in 1548. Eight years later he started a printing business that was eventually to become the largest printing and publishing concern in the Low Countries. It also became a magnet for intellectuals, scientists and humanists. On Plantin's death, the business passed to his son-in-law, Jan Moretus, and later it passed to Jan's son, Balthasar, who expanded it greatly. Balthasar was a contemporary and friend of Rubens, and some of the family portraits exhibited inside this museum are the master's works.

Built around a central courtyard, the museum is worth visiting for the mansion alone, but also for the insight it gives into old typesetting, proofreading and printing processes. The rooms are filled with ancient presses, copper plates, old globes, Flemish tapestries and, of course, splendid old books and manuscripts, including a rare copy of the Gutenberg Bible. In an age of email and paper recycling, it's hard not to admire the painstaking effort and dedication that was then needed to produce a 'simple' book.

St Jansvliet to Steenplein

Head to the waterfront from Vrijdagmarkt and you'll arrive at **St Jansvliet**, a small, tree-

At the Cutting Edge

Mention Flanders in the right circles and the immediate word association will be 'fashion'. Designers from Antwerp have been avant-garde leaders since the early 1980s when a handful of graduates from the city's Koninklijke Academie voor Schone Kunsten (Royal Academy of Fine Arts) loaded a truck with their designs and sped over to a showing in London.

Their ideas were collectively daring, provocative and extreme, but markedly different from each other, and they were soon labelled the 'Antwerp Six' – Anne Demeulemeester, Dries Van Noten, Walter Van Beirendonck, Dirk Van Saene, Dirk Bikkembergs and Martin Margiela. Marina Lee is another well-known Antwerp designer who grew out of this time.

The talent didn't end there. The academy continues to spawn new designers who are making names for themselves – Raf Simons and Véronique Branquinho are just two.

Such is the optimism in Antwerp these days that a new Flanders Fashion Institute and fashion museum, ModeMuseum, is expected to open in Drukkerijstraat (Map 12) in October 2001 as part of Antwerp Fashion 2001 – a series of events celebrating the city's designers. The same building will also become home to the Fashion Department of the Koninklijke Academie voor Schone Kunsten. In mid-September every year the city hosts a fashion week that draws an international crowd, and on a daily level there's no shortage of shops handling designer gear.

lined square best known as the entrance to the **St Annatunnel**, a 572m-long pedestrian tunnel under the Scheldt linking the city centre with the **Linkeroever**, or left bank, from where there's an excellent panorama of the city's riverfront. The tiled tunnel was built in the 1930s and is reached by wooden escalators or a big Art Deco elevator.

From St Jansvliet, follow **Hoogstraat**, a popular pedestrianised shopping street, to Reyndersstraat where at No 4 you'll find the **Jordaenshuis** (Jordaens' House). This former home of one of the city's three eminent baroque artists is now an art centre – pop in to see the facade and inner courtyard.

Alternatively, from St Jansvliet you can climb stairs to the raised **promenades**, known as *wandelterrassen*, built 70 years ago alongside the river and the city's main dock so that townsfolk could view the exotic cargoes brought from the former Belgian Congo. Wandering along these promenades is still an immensely popular pastime for families and lovers at the weekend, and from the **Zuiderterras** (south terrace) you get a great view of the city's skyline.

The Zuiderterras ends at **Steenplein**, another tree-lined square and home to the city's oldest building, the **Steen**. This castle, dating from 1200, has been much restored; it is also a vestige of the 9th-century fortifications that once stood here. At its entrance is a **statue of Lange Wapper**, a tall and mischievous folklore figure who was nothing short of a Peeping Tom.

Nationaal Scheepvaartmuseum

Located inside the Steen is the charming National Maritime Museum (☎ 03-232 08 50), at Steenplein 1. Model ships, of all ages and types, and maritime maps and instruments are exhibited in a clearly labelled series of rooms that wind through the gatehouse and front section (which is all that remains) of the 13th-century castle.

Highlights of the museum include an intriguing nautical totem shaped like a snake's head (Room 3), intricate model fishing boats (Room 6) and boats from around the world, including an 18th-century coracle or skin boat (Room 9). The €2.50 booklet

on sale at reception pinpoints other highlights.

Next to the museum, in one of the big iron hangars beneath the raised promenade, is the museum's open-air collection of river barges, canal boats and *De Schelde P905*, a 1950's Belgian navy patrol ship.

Vleeshuis

Due east of the Steen, and visible from there, is the striking Butchers' Hall (☎ 03-233 64 04), Vleeshouwersstraat 38–40. The 14th-century headquarters of the butchers' guild was the only place in the city where meat could be sold at one time. Its red-and-white layered stonework is reminiscent of rashers of bacon, appropriately enough for this most influential group of merchants.

Inside, the huge halls house a collection of applied arts, much of which pertains to Antwerp and its surrounding villages. Unfortunately, all labels are in Flemish only and there's no English-language guidebook. At the rear of the ground floor, look out for the retable from Averbode Abbey, a superbly delicate, religious woodcarving from 1514. The 1st floor, accessed by a narrow spiral staircase (or a lift), houses weapons, jewellery and period rooms with gilded, leather wallpaper. Worth trying to pinpoint in the coin cabinet are two *Protestantse spotpenningen* (Protestant joke coins) from 1550. From one side the coins feature the head of the pope and a cardinal; viewed upside down, they become the face of the devil and an evil joker.

Oude Beurs

Continue east from the Vleeshuis for two blocks to arrive at the Oude Beurs (old stock exchange), Hofstraat 15. It dates from the 14th century, although the current building, with its picturesque stone pillars and Gothic arcades, was built in 1515. Note the fine 1616 corner tower, known as a *pagadder* (from the Spanish *pagador*, meaning paymaster).

Rockoxhuis

Just outside the old city centre, across St Katelijnevest, is the Rockox House (☎ 03-231 47 10), Keizerstraat 10–12. Like the famous Rubenshuis, it is a well-restored,

17th-century mansion, this time belonging
to Nicolaas Rockox, a former mayor of the
city and friend and patron of Rubens. It's
built around a central courtyard and is furnished in classical Flemish style. Its small
but esteemed collection of paintings includes works by Rubens, Jordaens and Van
Dyck. Admission is free.

Paintings to note include Quinten Mat-
sijs' golden-toned *Holy Virgin and Child*
(Room 1); Van Dyck's *Two Studies of a
Man's Head*; two works by Rubens, *The
Virgin in Adoration Before the Sleeping
Child* and the small work *Christ on the
Cross* (Room 2); and Pieter Breughel the
Younger's *Proverbs* in Room 6.

The latter painting, called *De Spreekwo-
orden* in Flemish, is no run-of-the-mill village scene. It depicts 108 Flemish proverbs
and is a wonderfully engaging work of art.
It's well worth asking a museum attendant
for a moment of their time to explain a few
of the proverbs.

Some are obvious (like the man bashing
his head against a brick wall, ie stupidity, or
the two dogs fighting over a bone, ie a bone
of contention), but others are more cryptic
(such as a guy peeing on the moon, ie trying to do the impossible). The museum sells
a card (€1.25) with explanations of each
proverb, but unfortunately it's not published
in English.

Hendrik Conscienceplein

This secluded square, reached via a cluster of
cobbled lanes, is arguably the most handsome square in the city. It's named after the
revered 19th-century Flemish writer Hendrik
Conscience, whose **statue** graces the square.

More commanding, however, is the stunning facade of **St Carolus-Borromeuskerk**, a
beautiful, baroque church at Hendrik Conscienceplein 6. Built by the Jesuits in 1621,
much of it, including the facade and tower,
was designed by Rubens. Unfortunately,
most of the marble interior and 39 ceiling
paintings by Rubens and his colleagues
were destroyed by fire in 1718. However,
baroque art at its prime can be seen in the
small Onze Lieve Vrouwkapel (Chapel of
Our Lady), inside to the right of the entrance, which was spared by the flames.
Opening hours vary but the church is generally accessible 10 am to 12.30 pm and 2
to 5 pm Monday to Saturday.

MEIR AREA (MAP 12)
The Meir

The pedestrianised Meir is the city's stately
main artery and hive of shopping activity.
Gilded, allegorical statues top many of the
classical and rococo-style buildings that
line this thoroughfare.

The **Torengebouw** marks the western end
of the Meir. This stocky, Art Deco building,
completed in 1932, was Europe's first sky-
scraper. However, it is better known by its
nickname 'Boerentoren' (Farmers' Tower),
a snide reference to its rather blunt appearance. It rises at the junction of Eiermarkt
and Schoenmarkt.

Heading east towards Centraal Station,
look out for the **Koninklijk Paleis**, Meir 50,
a palatial building used at various times by
Napoleon and the Belgian royal family.

Also keep an eye out for the **'bobkes'**.
These shin-high stone blocks were erected
in 1992 to prevent cars parking illegally,
but they also obstruct pedestrians and a
good number of people have sued the council for injuries after banging into them. The
blocks are jokingly referred to as 'bobkes',
named after Bob Cools, mayor of Antwerp
when they were installed.

The Meir terminates at the **statue of Antoon Van Dyck**, one of Antwerp's three most celebrated baroque artists. Here it imperceptibly changes into Leysstraat, which paves the way to Centraal Station.

Rubenshuis

Just off the Meir, on a rather nondescript square known as Wapper, is the prestigious Rubenshuis (☎ 03-201 15 55), Wapper 9–11. The home and studio of the city's most celebrated painter, Pieter Paul Rubens (see the boxed text), it was little more than a ruin when the city acquired the building in 1937. Superbly restored along original lines, it's now the city's chief attraction, despite the fact that only a handful of Rubens' lesser works are exhibited here.

Rubens built this beautiful baroque mansion in 1611 when he was 34 years old; he died here 29 years later. The building is divided in two: on the left are the living quarters and an elaborate art gallery where Rubens displayed sculptures and paintings by artists he admired; to the right you'll see the master's studio where he taught and worked. Near the entrance is a baroque portico, and beyond this lies a formal garden. Much of the furniture inside the house dates from Rubens' era but was not part of the original decor.

Admission costs €5 (students €2.05).

St Jacobskerk

One block north of the Meir is the Church of St James, Lange Nieuwstraat 73. It was the aristocracy's place of worship and is a showcase of their wealth, with more than 100 types of marble used in its construction, paintings by the leading artists of the time, and no less than 23 chapels where the gentry vied to be buried. Started in 1491, it took nearly 150 years to build and the result is

---

Pieter Paul Rubens

Pieter Paul Rubens (1577–1640) was Belgium's most influential artist in the early 17th century. His paintings fused Flemish and Italian influences and his enormous canvases, with their glowing colours and animated forms, are baroque masterpieces.

Rubens was born in Siegen (in Germany) in 1577 after his parents fled Antwerp due to religious turmoil. When his father died a decade later, the family returned to Antwerp where Rubens started painting – by the age of 21 he was a master in the Antwerp Guild of St Lukas. In 1600 he journeyed to Italy and was soon appointed court painter to the Duke of Mantua. For the next eight years he travelled extensively in Italy and also to Spain, all the while painting for the wealthy and soaking up the rich Renaissance art and architecture.

When his mother died in 1608, Rubens returned to Antwerp and, in 1610, completed *The Descent from the Cross*, a huge canvas filled with saints, muscular soldiers and distraught women that earned him immediate success. Today it's displayed in the Onze Lieve Vrouwkathedraal, the city's cathedral. With commissions pouring in, he established a studio in his house in the city centre from where he proceeded to paint portraits of Europe's royalty and a series of grand religious canvases. Joined by contemporaries such as Antoon Van Dyck and Jacob Jordaens, the studio's output was staggering.

In the 1620s Rubens broadened his painting repertoire and also took on diplomatic missions, including a visit to England where he was commissioned to paint part of the ceiling of the Banqueting House in London's Whitehall Palace and was knighted by Charles I.

During his last decade he married Hélèna Fourment, his second wife, whom he used as a model for some of his later, largely allegorical, paintings.

ALBERT COLE

ANTWERP

---

a Gothic facade cloaking mainly baroque embellishments inside.

Most visitors come to see the tomb of Rubens and his family, located in a small chapel behind the high altar. It's adorned with a painting, *Our Lady Surrounded by Saints*, which Rubens executed specifically for his tomb and which is actually a family portrait, with the master as St George and his wives and father the other figures.

St Jacobskerk opens noon to 5 pm Monday to Saturday between April and October, and 9 am to noon the rest of the year. Admission costs €2 (students and children €1.50).

Museum Mayer Van den Bergh

This museum (☎ 03-232 42 37), at Lange Gasthuisstraat 19, is a short walk south of the western end of the Meir. It occupies a simulated 16th-century townhouse, built in 1904 by the mother of Fritz Mayer Van den Bergh, a prosperous art connoisseur who died in 1901 at the age of 41. His highly prized collection of sculptures and paintings, including works by Quinten Matsijs and Cornelius De Vos, form the core of the museum. Other wonderful examples of applied arts, including furniture, tapestries, ceramics and illuminated manuscripts, are spread over the three floors.

The collection's most famous piece is Pieter Breugel the Elder's *Dulle Griet* (Mad Meg), an allegorical painting in which a demented woman roams a grotesque war-torn landscape which is marked by demons and monsters. This is one of Breugel's most Bosch-like paintings and interpretations of its meaning vary – some say it's an allegory of misogyny, others of human madness.

Maagdenhuis

Just down the road from Museum Mayer Van den Bergh is the Maidens' House (☎ 03-223 56 20), Lange Gasthuisstraat 33. The building takes its name from its original purpose – in the 16th and 17th centuries it was an orphanage and refuge for girls of poor families. These days it's home to the city's social welfare organisation and a small collection of art.

As you enter, note the delicate sandstone

carvings of young girls above the archway. The museum then splits in two: to the left is the reception and a handful of rooms, in one of which you'll find Cornelius De Vos' moving *Portrait of an Orphan Girl*; to the right is a small chapel containing, among other things, Belgium's largest collection of medieval porridge bowls (60 in all) and a cabinet displaying a collection of identification tokens – playing cards or religious pictures that were cut in half when girls were brought into the refuge; one piece was retained by the parent and the other kept with the child. Unfortunately there's little explanation (in any language) throughout the museum.

It opens 10 am to 5 pm weekdays (except Tuesday) and 1 to 5 pm at the weekend.

Kruidtuin

The only place to sit among trees in this part of town is the tiny Kruidtuin, or botanical garden, on Leopoldstraat, immediately south-east of the Maagdenhuis. It's actually the original herb garden of the St Elisabeth-gasthuis, a hospital that dates back to medieval times. This relatively informal garden is home to some 2000 plant species and, despite its diminutive size, is a lovely getaway from crowds and vehicles.

CENTRAAL STATION QUARTER (MAP 12)
Centraal Station

Most visitors to Antwerp arrive at Centraal Station, the country's most attractive railway station and one of Antwerp's premier landmarks. It was designed by Louis Delacenserie at the start of the 20th century in a harmonious blend of styles. Steps lead from the main hall with its enormous dome to the glass-covered train platforms above. At the time of research the station was undergoing massive and disruptive expansion which is expected to last until 2005 (see under Train in the Getting There & Away chapter for details).

Diamond District

Immediately south-west of Centraal Station is the diamond district (see the boxed text 'Diamonds'). The first thing most people see of this quarter is the **gold containers**, a long line of pre-fab diamond and gold shops that have recently been erected along Pelikaanstraat. Prior to the containers, traders operated out of decrepit little hole-in-the-wall shops which were demolished as part of the expansion of Centraal Station. Take note, some of the trade going on in this area is run by illegal immigrants and some shopkeepers vocally oppose anyone trying to take a photo of their premises.

Those who'd like to explore Antwerp's diamond history can head to the **Provinciaal Diamantmuseum** (☎ 03-202 48 90), newly relocated at Koningin Astridplein 19, next to Centraal Station. Its aim is to be the world's largest and most modern diamond museum – judge for yourself when it reopens in early 2002. Normally, opening hours are 10 am to 5 pm daily. At the time of writing, the new admission price was expected to be €5.

Antwerp Zoo

Antwerp Zoo (☎ 03-202 45 40), Koningin Astridplein 26 right next to Centraal Station, ranks among the world's oldest. It was opened in 1843 during Belgium's colonial heyday and originally covered an area much larger than the current 10-hectare park. Located immediately behind Centraal Station, it's home to an extremely diverse range of animals; some (such as the penguins) live in state-of-the-art enclosures, but many are still in cages you could weep about. The zoo has a good reputation for its captive-breeding program. It opens 9 am to 4.30 or 6 pm daily; admission costs €11.40 (seniors and children €7.31).

Stadspark

The Stadspark is Antwerp's largest inner-city park. It's located between the railway lines and Frankrijklei and has paths that meander around a series of ponds. It's popular with families and joggers.

'T ZUID (MAP 11)
Koninklijk Museum voor Schone Kunsten

The Royal Museum of Fine Arts (☎ 03-238 78 09), at Leopold De Waelplaats 1–9, is a

Diamonds

ASA ANDERSSON

Diamonds have been processed in Flanders since the 15th century when rough stones from India were crafted in Bruges. The decline of Bruges meant the rise of Antwerp, which, despite various slumps over the centuries, is now the diamond capital of the world.

The industry directly employs some 30,000 people and is largely run by Orthodox Jews who arrived here in the late 19th century from Eastern Europe.

To get a glimpse of the amount of diamonds (and gold) being traded, just wander along Pelikaanstraat or Hoveniersstraat at any time during the day (except on Saturday when Sabbath, the Jewish holy day, closes many shops down). The new gold containers that line Pelikaanstraat provide the area with a bit of glitz, but otherwise much of the trade goes on behind discreet, sometimes shabby, facades and in the four *beurzen voor diamanthandel* (diamond exchanges) dotted around the quarter.

monumental, neoclassical edifice built at the end of the 19th century. Its stately rooms house an impressive collection of paintings dating from the 14th century to contemporary times, which includes works by some of the great Flemish masters.

The size of the museum's collection

means that paintings are sometimes rotated. To find the highlights you'll need to pick up a museum plan and audio headset (both free) from reception.

The Flemish Primitives are represented by Jan Van Eyck, Hans Memling, Rogier Van der Weyden and Gerard David. Highlights include Van Eyck's unusual, almost monotone *Saint Barbara* (1437), Memling's rich *Christ Among Angels Singing and Playing Instruments* and Van der Weyden's portrait of *Filips Van Croy*.

Sixteenth-century works to seek out include Quinten Matsijs' profound triptych *The Lamentation of Christ* (also called the *Triptych of the Joiners' Guild*). There are no original works by Pieter Breugel the Elder; however, paintings by his followers detail the enchanting peasant scenes for which Breugel was famous.

The museum's best section is undoubtedly the 17th-century Flemish baroque masters display. There are several enormous canvases by Rubens including his famous *Adoration of the Magi* (1624), a hugely expressive and animated work, as well as a selection of smaller, preparatory paintings and oil sketches. The other major local players of that time, Jacob Jordaens and Antoon Van Dyck, are also well represented. Watch out for Jordaens' *As the Old Sing, the Young Play Pipes* (1638), in which senior citizens are shown setting a good example to the young. Van Dyck was best known for his portraiture, a fine example of which is *Portrait of Maarten Pepijn* (1632).

Moving on to modern art, the museum has a diverse collection of paintings by James Ensor that traces his conservative beginnings – such as the *Woman Eating Oysters* (1882) – to his disturbing later works, exemplified here by *Masks Fighting over a Hanged Man* (1891).

Other Belgian artists of note whose works are exhibited include Constant Permeke and Rik Wouters, as well as surrealists René Magritte and Paul Delvaux.

The museum opens 10 am to 5 pm Tuesday to Sunday. Admission costs €3.75 (seniors and students €3), except on Friday when it's free but when the audio headset

costs €1.25. Take tram No 8 from Groenplaats, or bus No 23 (direction Zuid) from Franklin Rooseveltplaats.

Museum voor Hedendaagse Kunst van Antwerp

The Museum for Contemporary Arts of Antwerp (MUHKA; ☎ 03-238 59 60), Leuvenstraat 23, contains a permanent collection of Belgian and international art, dating from the 1970s onwards. For those into modern art it's likely to thrill; others might be left a bit cold. The best place to start is the elevator (a work of art in itself); take it to the 6th floor and make your way down through the airy, whitewashed rooms. The few explanations that exist are in Flemish only.

MUHKA opens 10 am to 5 pm Tuesday to Sunday; admission costs €3.72 (seniors and students €2.40). Bus No 23 (direction Zuid) from Franklin Rooseveltplaats stops nearby.

Museum voor Fotografie

Five blocks south of MUHKA and with an excellent reputation is the Photography Museum (☎ 03-216 22 11), Waalsekaai 47. Housed in a renovated warehouse, this museum traces the evolution of photography and film-making and has a huge collection of black-and-white photographs, old portraits and ancient cameras. One of its highlights is the Keizerspanorama, a huge, motorised, slide-viewing contraption built in 1905 for Antwerp Zoo.

The museum is closed until spring 2002 while it undergoes a large scale expansion. When it reopens, it will also house the city's Filmmuseum (see under Cinema in the Entertainment section), which will have two cinemas devoted to screening golden oldies.

At the time of writing, the new admission prices and opening hours were not known – ask at the tourist office for up-to-date details. Bus No 23 (direction Zuid) from Franklin Rooseveltplaats will get you to the museum.

Art Nouveau Architecture

Although Zurenborg (see the Zurenborg section later in the chapter) has the city's most dense concentration of Art Nouveau

ANTWERP

LEANNE LOGAN

Antwerp's Grote Markt is lined by elaborate guildhalls – once the true seat of power in Belgium's cities.

MARTIN MOOS

The elongated statue of mischievous Lange Wapper stands in front of Antwerp's 13th-century Steen.

The Brabo Fountain, standing before the grand city hall, tells the story of how Antwerp got its name.

Antwerp's skyline is dominated by its cathedral.

St Annatunnel runs deep under the River Scheld

architecture, two other fine examples can be seen in 't Zuid and both are just short walks from the Koninklijk Museum voor Schone Kunsten.

't Bootje, at the corner of Schildersstraat and Plaatsnijdersstraat, has a little ship-shaped balcony that is part of a 1901 townhouse called De Vijf Continenten (The Five Continents).

Help U Zelve, Volkstraat 40, is arguably the most beautiful and harmonious Art Nouveau facade in Antwerp. Built in 1901 by the architects Van Asperen and Van Averbeke, it features mosaics and strongly geometric wrought-iron work. It's now used as a Steiner school.

SCHIPPERSKWARTIER (MAP 12)
St Pauluskerk

St Paul's Church at Veemarkt marks the start of the sailors' quarter, or Schipperskwartier. The proud, white Gothic church was built for the Dominicans and dates from 1517. It has suffered much damage over the years due to fires, the latest in 1968 when locals rallied to save the art treasures inside. The baroque interior is resplendent with a stunning procession of wooden confessionals and carvings, altars, a (partly) ancient organ and marble embellishments, as well as paintings by the 17th-century masters and lesser artists. The church opens 2 to 5 pm daily Easter to September; admission is free.

Red-Light District

Antwerp's red-light district is the largest in Belgium, but it's still small fry compared with neighbouring Amsterdam. It's based between St Paulusplaats and Verversrui and includes the appropriately named Oude Manstraat (Old Man Street). Much of the quarter has a seedy, dog-eared feel and the fanfare and crass consumerism that makes its counterpart in the Netherlands so famous is noticeably absent here.

ZURENBORG (MAP 11)

This area, about 2km south-east of Centraal Station, is famed for the strikingly eclectic architecture found in a handful of streets here. The showcase is **Cogels-Osylei**, a

street where the city's affluent citizens went wild a century ago, creating competing and highly contrasting facades ranging in style from Art Nouveau and baroque to neoclassical and neo-Renaissance. Roofs and towers spiked with onion tops or witches' hats, wrought-iron balconies, bay windows, slate tiles, stained glass and mosaics…you name it and this street probably has it.

Most of the buildings were constructed between 1894 and 1914 and involved many architects. In the 1960s, the houses faced demolition and were only saved thanks to protests by groups of artists and hippies.

The area's focal point is the small roundabout on Cogels-Osylei, which is flanked by the **Witte Paleizen** (white palaces), grand facades resembling chateaux in France's Loire Valley. Three exquisite Art Nouveau examples on Cogels-Osylei are the **Huize Zonnebloem** (Sunflower House) at No 50, built by Jules Hofman in 1900, **De Morgenster** (The Morning Star; built 1904) at No 55 and **Quinten Matsys** (built 1904) at No 80.

More Art Nouveau swirls and mosaic facades can be found on Waterloostraat, including **Les Mouettes** (The Dumb; built 1905 by J. De Weerdt) at No 39. Mosaics are at their best at **De Vier Seizoenen** (The Four Seasons), designed in 1899 by the architect Bascourt and located at the intersection of Waterloostraat and Generaal Van Merlenstraat. The **Euterpia house** (built 1906), at Generaal Capiaumontstraat 2, follows Greek neoclassical lines (the main door handle even resembles an Olympic torch). The **Twaalf Duivels** (built 1896 by Jules Hofman), at Transvaalstraat Nos 59 and 61, has a timber facade which gives way to 12 wooden devils that leer at passers-by.

The area is a little way from the centre, but easily reached and well worth a wander. Tram No 11 (direction Eksterlaar) runs right along Cogels-Osylei.

GREATER ANTWERP (MAP 11)
Openluchtmuseum voor Beeldhouwkunst Middelheim

The Middelheim Open-Air Statuary Museum (☎ 03-828 13 50), Middelheimlaan 61, is a large, landscaped park 4km south of

ANTWERP

the city centre. It contains more than 300 works by sculptors including notable nationals (such as Rik Wouters) and influential internationals (including the likes of Auguste Rodin and Henry Moore).

Opening hours vary seasonally: 10 am to 7 or 9 pm Tuesday to Sunday between April and September, until 5 pm the rest of the year. Admission is free. To get there take bus No 17 (direction Wilrijk Universitair Ziekenhuis) from in front of Centraal Station, get off at Beukenlaan and walk 500m east.

WHAT'S FREE
The following museums do not charge for admission: Rockoxhuis; Openluchtmuseum voor Beeldhouwkunst Middelheim; and the open-air section of the Nationaal Scheepvaartmuseum. The excellent Koninklijk Museum voor Schone Kunsten is free on Friday.

Some churches are also free to enter. During the summer the cathedral's carillon concerts at 8 pm on Monday are free. Viewing the city's Art Nouveau monuments also costs nothing.

ACTIVITIES
The most central public swimming pool is the Olympisch Zwembad Wezenberg (Map 11; ☎ 03-259 23 11), on the corner of Binnensingel and Gerard Legrellelaan. Admission costs €1.75 (children €1); take tram No 2 (direction Hoboken) from Groenplaats.

The Action Club (Map 12; ☎ 03-203 18 80), on the 1st floor of the Astrid Park Plaza Hotel at Koningin Astridplein 1, has a swimming pool (12m) plus cardiovascular and weight-training machines, a solarium and a sauna. A day pass (which does not include the solarium) costs €19.85. Hotel guests can use the facilities free of charge.

Moving (Map 12; ☎ 234 03 79), Oudaan 15, is a semi-private gym with an elitist door policy. If you can get in, a workout will cost €9, or a 10-session card costs €62.

Places to Stay

Many hotels are located within the old city centre. However, there are also good B&Bs

in 't Zuid. At weekends some hotels reduce prices by up to 60%, but these rates are usually only available if you book through the tourist office.

PLACES TO STAY – BUDGET
Camping
There are two camp sites in Antwerp, both open April to September and charging €1.85 per adult or child, plus €1 for a tent, caravan or car.

De Molen (Map 11; ☎ 03-219 81 79, St Annastrand) is on the left bank of the Scheldt; take bus No 81 or 82 (direction Linkeroever).

Vogelzang (Map 11; ☎ 03-238 57 17, Vogelzanglaan) is sandwiched between noisy roads near the Bouwcentrum (a complex of exhibition halls); take tram No 2 (direction Hoboken).

Hostels
Antwerp's hostel scene has nose-dived in recent times.

The HI-affiliated *Op Sinjoorke* (Map 11; ☎ 03-238 02 73, fax 03-248 19 32, Eric Sasselaan 2) is nearly 3km from the centre and beds cost €10.65 per person. To get there take tram No 2, direction Hoboken.

The only other alternative is a dorm room at the New International Youth Hotel (see the following Hotel section for details).

Guesthouses
The Guild of Antwerp Guestrooms is an organisation overseeing some 20 B&Bs in Antwerp. It has a Web site at www.bb-antwerp.com.

Smack in the centre is *B&B Peetermans* (Map 12; ☎ 03-231 37 92, fax 03-231 00 45, @ enichanders@antwerpen.be, Leeuwenstraat 12), a stone-sculptor's home and studio. It's popular with independent types – if you don't mind organising your own breakfast from a bag of goodies hung on your door handle the night before, this is your place. Each room has a small kitchenette. Prices start at €32.22 for one person; each extra person (up to four) pays €12.39.

In 't Zuid you'll find the friendly *B&B Lenaerts* (Map 11; ☎/fax 03-248 09 13, *e* *dirk.lenaerts@pandora.be, Verschans-ingstraat 55)*. It has two attic rooms that share a combined kitchen and shower. Rooms cost €19.85/34.70 for one/two people. Take bus No 23 (direction Zuid) from Koningin Astridplein.

Just outside 't Zuid and very popular is *B&B Stevens (Map 11;* ☎ *03-259 15 90, fax 03-259 15 99,* *e* *greta.stevens@pandora .be, Molenstraat 35)*. This place is run by a friendly and dynamic woman and has three immaculate rooms (each with a private bathroom). The single/double rooms cost €35.95/47 on weekdays or €60 at the weekend; triples/quads cost €63/74. To get there take bus No 290 (direction Hoboken) from Franklin Rooseveltplaats and get off at the 'Gerechtshof' stop.

Close by is the wonderfully spacious *B&B Ribbens (Map 11;* ☎ *03-248 15 39, Justitiestraat 43)*. Wooden floors and old-fashioned furniture lend this a charming air. Single/double rooms with huge private bathrooms cost €37/47. To get there follow the directions for B&B Stevens.

Hotels

The budget hotel scene in Antwerp is as varied as the city itself. Unless mentioned otherwise, breakfast is included in the rate.

The *Scoutel (Map 11;* ☎ *03-226 46 06, fax 03-232 63 92,* *e* *scoutel@vvksm.be, Stoomstraat 3)* is a modern scouts' residence that also welcomes travellers. It's close to Centraal Station (train noise might bother light sleepers) and offers spartan rooms, all with private bathrooms. Singles cost €26/28.50 for those aged under/over 25, doubles cost €32.50/45 and there are also triples and quads.

The *New International Youth Hotel (Map 11;* ☎ *03-230 05 22, fax 03-281 09 33,* *e* *niyh@pandora.be, Provinciestraat 256)* is a hotel-cum-hostel, some 10 minutes' walk from Centraal Station through the Jewish neighbourhood. It's a rabbit warren of neat rooms. Singles/doubles/quads with communal bathrooms cost €25.28/38.67 /63.46; doubles with private bathrooms are €45.58. Beds in eight-bed dormitories cost €11.65. It has a Web site at www.niyh.com.

The *Internationaal Zeemanshuis (Map 12;* ☎ *03-227 54 33, 03-234 26 03,* *e* *recep tie@zeemanshuis.be, Falconrui 21)* is a large hotel for seamen in the heart of the old sailors' quarter. This efficiently run complex also welcomes women and landlubbing men; spick-and-span rooms with private bathroom cost €27.27/48.09. Breakfast is €2.73 extra; parking is free.

Rubenshof (Map 11; ☎ *03-237 07 89, fax 03-248 25 94,* *e* *rubenshf@xsa4all.be, Amerikalei 115)* is on a boulevard near 't Zuid. No two rooms are alike and all are clean and comfortable. The cheaper rooms mainly occupy the 3rd floor, which is only accessible via a narrow staircase. Singles /doubles/triples with communal bathroom cost €25/37/49.50; those with private bathrooms are €49.50/62/74.50. Take tram No 24 (direction Zuidstation) from Franklin Rooseveltplaats as far as the Brederodestraat stop.

PLACES TO STAY – MID-RANGE
Old City Centre

The *Hotel Scheldezicht (Map 12;* ☎ *03-231 66 02, fax 03-231 90 02, St Jansvliet 12)* is a relatively new hotel with a great location in the heart of town near the river. The spacious, old-style rooms have private shower cubicles (the toilets are shared) and are well-priced at €31/45.85.

Hotel Postiljon (Map 12; ☎ *03-231 75 75, fax 03-226 84 50, Blauwmoezelstraat 6)* is as central as it gets. Located on a pedestrian lane next to Onze Lieve Vrouwkathedraal, it has 23 tastefully furnished but very small rooms. The downside of the location is the considerable street noise from late-night revellers. Singles/doubles with communal facilities start at €30/50; doubles with private bathrooms cost €65. Breakfast is €4.95 extra.

Tucked away on a quiet street in the fashion quarter is *Pension Cammerpoorte (Map 12;* ☎ *03-231 28 36, fax 03-226 28 43,* *e* *jactoe@net4all.be, Steenhouwersvest 55)*. It has 16 bright rooms, some with kitchenette, from €48.35/60.75 to €65.70/78.

On the riverfront to the north of the centre is the pleasant *Antigone Hotel (Map 12;* ☎ *03-231 66 77, fax 03-231 37 74, Jordaenskaai 11–12)*. Some of the rooms are

ANTWERP

triangular in shape and not overly large, but the pick of the crop are spacious and have pleasant views over the river. Soothing pale tones have been used throughout, and the hotel has a personal atmosphere. The rooms are very good value at €76.84/89.24. The rate includes a buffet breakfast, and there's free parking.

Centraal Station Quarter
Hotel Eden (Map 12; ☎ 03-233 06 08, fax 03-233 12 28, Lange Herentalsestraat 25–7), in the heart of the diamond district, is an efficient, somewhat old-fashioned hotel catering largely to businesspeople and tourists from the Netherlands at the weekend. Rooms cost from €73.12/85.52 during the week, or €64.45/71.88 at the weekend. There's a buffet breakfast and private parking.

't Zuid
Hotel Industrie (Map 11; ☎ 03-238 66 00, fax 03-238 86 88, e hotelindustrie@pandora.be, Emiel Banningstraat 52) is a chic little hotel on the edge of 't Zuid, popular with businesspeople. Single/double rooms with private bathrooms, safes, mini-bars and TVs are good value at €59.50/71.88. To get there take tram No 8 (direction Lambermontplaats) from Groenplaats.

Beyond the Old City Centre
The **Hotel-Pension Granducale** (Map 11; ☎/fax 03-239 37 24, St Vincentiusstraat 3), about 1.5km south of the centre, is a well-ordered family-run hotel with 11 rooms. Singles/doubles with shared facilities cost €37.18/57; those with private bathrooms cost €49.57/74.36. Tram No 8 from Berchem train station stops close by, or take tram No 15 (direction Mortsel) from Centraal Station to the stop near Lange Leemstraat.

PLACES TO STAY – TOP END
Old City Centre
One of the top addresses in Antwerp is **De Witte Lelie** (Map 12; ☎ 03-226 19 66, fax 03-234 00 19, e hotel@dewittelelie.be, Keizerstraat 16–18). Occupying a renovated 16th-century mansion on a quiet backstreet, it has 10 luxurious rooms, each individually

furnished with an outstanding mix of the modern and antique. Rates start at €166/215 for singles/doubles; bookings are essential. There's a private garage (€12.40).

Hotel Rubens (Map 12; ☎ 03-222 48 48, fax 03-225 19 40, e hotel.rubens@glo.be, Oude Beurs 29) is a charmingly discreet hotel with 36 rooms, very close to the Grote Markt. Elegant, mellow-toned rooms with floral prints and classical furniture start at €112/123 during the week and €112/118 at the weekend.

The **Hilton** (Map 12; ☎ 03-201 12 12, fax 03-204 12 13, Groenplaats) has more than 200 rooms overlooking the city's largest square. Prices start at €166/191 during the week (€151 at the weekend for a single or double; breakfast costs €21).

Centraal Station Quarter
The relatively new **Astrid Park Plaza Hotel** (Map 12; ☎ 03-203 12 34, fax 03-203 12 51, e appres@parkplazahotels.be, Koningin Astridplein 7) is a megalithic pile of Lego-like blocks with 229 rooms starting at €198.31/223.10 (discounted to €109.07/128.90 at the weekend). Breakfast costs €19.70. It's very handy for the train station, and there's a swimming pool, sauna, ballroom and business centre.

Beyond the Old City Centre
The small **Hotel Firean** (Map 11; ☎ 03-237 02 60, fax 03-238 11 68, e hotel.firean@skynet.be, Karel Oomsstraat 6) is another exclusive hotel. Owned by the Iserbyt family, the 15 rooms occupy a 1929 Art Deco building that is resplendent with a mix of antique furniture and contemporary stained glass. Rates start at €114/136; bookings are essential. It's 2.5km south of the old centre.

LONG-TERM RENTALS
Antwerp does not have much in the way of long-term holiday rentals.

B&B Ribbens (see the earlier B&Bs section) has a studio and an apartment available for monthly rental at €545.

Pension Cammerpoorte (see Places to Stay – Mid-Range earlier) also has rooms with kitchenettes, as do **B&B Peetermans**

and **B&B Lenaerts** (see Places to Stay – Budget earlier). Discounts may be negotiated for longer stays.

For something a little more upmarket, the most central option is **Hotel Euro** *(Map 12; ☎ 03-233 00 75, fax 03-226 08 13, e info@ hoteleuro-antwerp.com, St Jacobsmarkt 91)* where small single/double rooms with kitchenette cost €73/94 per day.

A more upmarket 'apart hotel' is **Arass** *(Map 11; ☎ 03-206 71 00, fax 03-206 72 21, e mail@arasshotel.be, Plantin-Moretuslei 111)*. It has a large range of rooms with kitchenettes – prices start at €79.50/104 per day.

Places to Eat

Antwerp is a food city. Locals here simply love to eat out, and as a result there is a staggering number of restaurants.

The old city centre is well endowed with places to eat in all price categories: Suikerrui is the street for mussels, Oude Koornmarkt is for those into funky settings or a cheap *pita* (stuffed pitta bread), Grote Pieter Potstraat has trendy cafes and bistros, Pelgrimstraat is popular with tourists and the cobbled streets around Hendrik Conscienceplein are dotted with intimate eateries. In between all of these are quiet side streets, dimly lit alleys and cobbled lanes where restaurants of all descriptions thrive. You're bound to discover your own favourites.

PLACES TO EAT – BUDGET
Old City Centre
Round the corner from the Grote Markt and guaranteed to cheer up any grey day is **Sjalot en Schanul** *(Map 12; ☎ 03-233 88 75, Oude Beurs 11)*. This cheerful little eatery is great for a snack or light meal, with tables mingled in among crates of exotically colourful fruit and veggies. A *boterham* (sandwich) costs €4.21, salads go for €9.79, or there are mains for €11.52. The kitchen opens 9 am to 8 pm daily.

For authentic Flemish *stoemp* (mashed potatoes), go no farther than **Eethuisje De Stoemppot** *(Map 12; ☎ 03-231 36 86, Vlasmarkt 12)*. This down-to-earth little restaurant serves the types of dishes you might expect in a Belgian home – big portions of stoemp accompanied by a *boerenworst* (sausage) or a *spiegelei* (fried egg). Prices range from €5 to €9 (€2 extra for a second helping of stoemp). It opens for dinner only and is closed on Wednesday.

The **Domus Eethuisje** *(Map 12; ☎ 03-225 15 06, Wolstraat 11)* is a little eatery frequented by local businesspeople. It's nothing special but is honest and affordable – expect pasta (€6.50) and salads (€6.20 to €9.40).

Lenny's *(Map 12; ☎ 03-233 90 57, Wolstraat 47)* is a tiny, relaxed place where you can eat well for around €10. Sandwiches and sumptuous salads are the main offerings; it fills up quickly at lunchtime (it's closed Sunday and Monday).

A cosy little place in winter and with a nice terrace in summer is the **Gulden Swaene** *(Map 12; ☎ 03-233 12 59, Hendrik Conscienceplein 15)*. It sports a simple menu, the meals (around €8.50) are large and the staff are friendly. It opens 10 am to 10 pm daily.

Ilha Formosa *(Map 12; ☎ 03-290 47 30, Grote Pieter Potstraat 20)* is a cellar *eethuis* (eating house) specialising in oriental cuisine, with an emphasis on meals using tofu and other soya-bean products. Mains hover around €11.15 to €12.39, or there's a good-value two-course *menu* for €14.74. It opens for dinner only (closed Monday).

In the heart of the fashion quarter is **Het Dagelijks Brood** *(Map 12; ☎ 02-226 76 13, Steenhouwersvest 48)*. This bakery-cum-tearoom is part of a successful chain. The house speciality is *boterhammen*, slices of bread with exotic toppings (€4.40). It opens 7 am to 7 pm daily.

A great place to nurse your hangover is **Pitten & Bonen** *(Map 12; ☎ 03-213 28 88, Lombaardvest 310)*. Fruit/veggie juices, milk/yogurt shakes and a mouth-watering range of panini and focaccia (all for between €2.75 and €3.75) are served at this austere but popular little eatery. The juicer runs from 11.30 am to 5 pm.

For waffles with class there's **Désiré de Lille** *(Map 12; ☎ 03-233 62 26, Schrijnwerkersstraat 14)*. Take time out with elite shoppers in the quaint courtyard section.

ANTWERP

Frituurs (chip shops) and pita places abound along Oude Koornmarkt. One of the most popular for pita is *Mama's Garden* *(Map 12; ☎ 03-233 06 18, Oude Koornmarkt 41)* where you can dine at a big bar counter or, in summer, on a raised outdoor terrace.

Self-caterers will find a *GB* supermarket *(Map 12; ☎ 03-221 36 11)* in the basement of the Grand Bazar shopping centre at Groenplaats.

Goossens (Map 12; ☎ 03-226 07 91, Korte Gasthuisstraat 31) is one of the city's top bakeries; try its rye-and-raisin bread (€1.90) or a *suikerbrood* (sugarbread). It opens 7 am to 7 pm (closed Sunday).

Centraal Station Quarter

Lamalo Grill (Map 12; ☎ 03-213 22 00, Appelmansstraat 28) is a casual little Israeli eatery serving quality food. It's a dream for vegetarians and carnivores alike, with yummy brochettes (€5.45), felafel (€7.18) and a range of delicious salads – everything from smooth houmus (a chickpea dip) to pickled vegetables. A mix of 12 salads costs €13.64 and is plenty for two hearty appetites. On Sunday there's lamb or chicken couscous (€11.15). It's closed on Friday night and all of Saturday.

There is absolutely no shortage of fast-food places in this area. For *pita* and *frites*, head to Statiestraat, close to Centraal Station. Here too you'll find *Rolmops (Map 12; ☎ 03-232 31 24, Statiestraat 13)*, which offers a huge choice of *belegde broodjes* (filled sandwiches) starting at €1.85. Hamburger places are also abundant – try *Quick (Map 12; ☎ 03-226 85 22, Meir 14)*.

Self-caterers have an expensive *Spar* supermarket *(Map 12; ☎ 03-226 44 13)* at Jezusstraat 22.

't Zuid

Although many of the restaurants in this area are trendy mid-range places, there's a clutch of cheap *pide* (Turkish pizza) joints on and around Gillisplein. Near here too is *Finjan (Map 11; ☎ 03-248 77 14, Graaf van Hoornestraat 1)*, one of the best pita places in Antwerp.

The *Zuiderpershuis (Map 11; ☎ 03-248 20 42, Waalsekaai 14)* is a cafe attached to a world cultural centre (see the Other Live Music Venues under Entertainment later in the chapter for details) and is housed in the foyer of a former 19th-century power station. It has a cool, industrial feel and is popular with students, artists and chess players. Standard bistro-style food is the order of the day. It's closed on Monday.

Self-caterers will find a *Delhaize* supermarket *(Map 11; ☎ 03-248 31 52)* at Museumstraat 38.

Schipperskwartier

The self-service restaurant at the *Internationaal Zeemanshuis (Map 12; ☎ 03-227 54 33, Falconrui 21)* has considerably more charm than the average cafeteria and offers the cheapest *dagschotel* (plate of the day; €5.20) in town. Steak meals cost €9.17 and small/large servings from the salad bar are €2.23/3.71. It opens for lunch and dinner daily.

PLACES TO EAT – MID-RANGE
Old City Centre

Come with a *grote honger* (huge appetite) and expect to leave stuffed – that's the advice needed for *De Gouden Ecu (Map 12; ☎ 03-232 71 25, St Michielsstraat 11)*. This modest restaurant serves gargantuan portions of traditional Flemish food, such as rabbit baked in *gueuze* (a well-known Brussels beer) or *rijstpap* (rice pudding), prepared by chef Bert De Bruyne. A small selection of main courses (€12.50) is offered on weekdays but it's Saturday when the true feast occurs – the three course *menu* (€24) will make you explode. On Sunday Bert rests (ie the restaurant's closed). It opens for dinner only.

Another authentic Flemish eatery is *De Vagant (Map 12; ☎ 03-233 15 38, Reyndersstraat 25)*. This pub/restaurant specialises in *jenever* (Belgian gin) and laces its cuisine with gin to produce unique flavours. It's popular with small groups, and mains hover between €11.55 to €16.73.

One of the best mid-range seafood restaurants is *Het Nieuwe Palinghuis (Map 12; ☎ 03-231 74 45, St Jansvliet 14)*. This quiet

ANTWERP

restaurant is on a slightly grungy square but is well known for its attentive service and seasonal seafood. Mussels served in *look* (garlic) cost €11.40, but most other main courses are in the €17.85 to €21 bracket.

Pottenbrug (Map 12; ☎ 03-231 51 47, Minderbroedersrui 38) has changed little over the years and gets perennial rave reviews. This wonderful old bistro-style place – tables close together, antique posters and a terrace in summer – has main courses in the €13 to €20 bracket, as well as an excellent dagschotel for €8.70. It opens for lunch and dinner (closed Monday evening).

Dock's Cafe (Map 12; ☎ 03-226 63 30, Jordaenskaai 7) is a fashionable, split-level restaurant serving good French/Italian cuisine. Ask for a table upstairs to really enjoy its convivial atmosphere. The meals are relatively small (mains from €17.35 to €22.31). It's closed Saturday lunchtime.

De Peerdestal (Map 12; ☎ 03-231 95 03, Wijngaardstraat 8) caters for splurging foreigners keen to sample the house speciality – horse (*paard* in Flemish). A *filet van 't paard* costs €16.75 while a regular horse steak is a bit cheaper.

Folies d'Anvers (Map 12; ☎ 03-231 71 15, Reyndersstraat 13) is perfect for a reasonably priced romantic tryst. The modern Belgian cuisine (mains €14.25 to €19.21) is served in understated surroundings and attracts many bright young things. In summer, reserve a table on the *dakterras* (rooftop terrace), a tiny, open-air area with a view of the cathedral spire and an intimate atmosphere.

Café de la Gare (Map 12; ☎ 03-226 49 27, Haarstraat 3) is a slick, sunken restaurant pandering to Antwerp's artistic elite. Writers and artists favour it for the modern, minimalist decor and versatile cuisine. Expect mains in the region of €20.

Centraal Station Quarter

The *Full Sing (Map 12; ☎ 03-225 06 54, Van Arteveldestraat 65)* is a Chinese dim sum restaurant on a dog-eared street in Antwerp's small Chinatown quarter. Some 300 dishes (from €2.23 to €6.19) are listed on the menu; like everyone else, you'll leave here feeling well and truly satisfied.

Meet George Jetson…you'd expect to at *Sushi Express (Map 12; ☎ 03-226 67 88, Appelmansstraat 21)*. Flying saucers topped with sushi delights (€2.47 to €4.95) rotate around the long counter of this giga-modern, electric-blue eatery. Study the colour-coded price list before you start devouring.

Hoffy's (Map 11; ☎ 03-234 35 35, Lange Kievitstraat 52) is a stylish kosher restaurant and takeaway on a scruffy backstreet in the Jewish district. Specialities include sweet carp, stuffed aubergines and big crisp potato patties; most main courses cost around €18.50. First-time kosher eaters can sample a variety of flavours by trying the mixed platter (€21). Hoffy's opens 11 am to 9.30 pm daily except Saturday.

't Zuid

The first cafe-cum-bistro to open in 't Zuid was *L'Entrepot du Congo (Map 11; ☎ 03-238 92 32, Vlaamsekaai 42)*. It occupies an old, stylishly renovated warehouse and is noticeably less pretentious than some of the other eateries in this area. Drinks are reasonably priced and the bistro-style food is a cut above the average. It opens 8 am to 3 or 4 am daily, although the kitchen closes at 10.30 pm.

Cargo (Map 11; ☎ 03-260 60 10, Leopold De Waelplaats 24b) is one of Antwerp's hottest new addresses. The interior of this big bar/brasserie is so minimal that you have little to do but eyeball everyone else. The food is French, Belgian and Italian inspired, and there's a wide choice of wines available by the glass. It opens for lunch and dinner daily, and mains range from €12.65 to €22.80, but there's also cheaper snack fare.

De Wok en 't Tafeldier (Map 11; ☎ 03-248 95 95, Gentplaats 1) specialises in dim sum and Asian food. It's a huge, trendy place, open from 6 pm to midnight daily. The 'Late Wok Special' (€9.90, available after 10 pm Monday to Thursday) is good value for those who love to eat late in the evening.

The modern *Eiland (Map 11; ☎ 03-230 16 60, Isabellalei 1)*, in a prominent corner location between 't Zuid and the Jewish quarter, is a haven for the health-conscious, preparing reasonably priced meals (around

ANTWERP

€9.40) using organic veggies and hormone-free meats. For once there's a nonsmoking section, and what's more it's bigger than the smoking area! It opens for lunch and dinner Tuesday to Saturday.

Schipperskwartier
Amadeus (Map 12; ☎ 03-232 25 87, St Paulusplaats 20) is a big place with an old-world atmosphere smack in the red-light district. Diners sit along mirrored walls while starched waiters march up and down bringing the house speciality – spare ribs *à volonté* (as much as you can eat) for €11.55. It's good value and opens daily for dinner.

't Eilandje
Model aeroplanes and futuristic spacemen set the scene at *Fly Inn (Map 11; ☎ 03-231 84 17, Bordeauxstraat 7c)*, a spacious brasserie in a renovated warehouse. It's popular with yuppies and weekday businesspeople and even the Belgian prime minister, Guy Verhofstadt, has been seen here. Mains average about €17.50.

Zurenborg
The heart of Zurenborg is Dageraadplaats, a tree-lined square framed by a few trendy bistros and cafes, and good for a bite after you've explored the nearby Cogels-Osylei area.

Overvloed (Map 11; ☎ 03-235 52 41, Dageraadplaats 8) is a 1st-floor bistro overlooking Dageraadplaats. It offers an eclectic mix of dishes including vegetarian, meat and seafood at good prices (from €8) and opens daily for lunch and dinner (closed for lunch at the weekend).

PLACES TO EAT – TOP END
Antwerp has an enviable number of first-rate restaurants right in the city centre.

As would be expected, seafood reigns supreme in this port city and *De Matelote (Map 12; ☎ 03-231 32 07, Haarstraat 9)* is where you'll find it at its best. This exclusive restaurant is on a quiet, pedestrian lane and has an ancient interior and just six tables. Main courses cost from €25 to €40. Reservations are essential; it's closed on Sunday and at lunchtime on Saturday and Monday.

Innovative Flemish cuisine and a secretive location have ensured the reputation of *Sir Anthony Van Dyck (Map 12; ☎ 03-231 61 70, Oude Koornmarkt 16)* as one of the city's finest restaurants. Situated in a nook in the Vlaeykensgang (a tiny cobbled 16th-century alley), it offers four-course *menus* for €40 or a la carte main courses from €18 to €23. Booking is necessary.

Of the many mussel restaurants lining Suikerrui, *Preud'Homme (Map 12; ☎ 03-233 42 00, Suikerrui 28)* holds centre stage. It's generally considered to be the best place in Antwerp to eat bivalves and the prices reflect it. The decor – petite black lampshades and grey suede seats – is decidedly modern.

For excellent French/Italian cuisine head for *'t Fornuis (Map 12; ☎ 03-233 62 70, Reyndersstraat 24)*. This deservedly popular restaurant is on a quiet backstreet and serves set *menus* for €99 including wine. It's closed Saturday and Sunday.

Entertainment

Antwerp is fast establishing itself as a party city. What with some 4000 bars and cafes, a lively music scene, notable clubs, fashionable discos, a small red-light district and a good dose of high culture, there's little lacking.

Several free entertainment guides list what's happening. The most concise for non-Flemish speakers is *Week Up*, which comes out each Wednesday, and has cinema and rock and jazz listings. For classical music, theatre, dance and *tentoonstellingen* (art exhibitions), the most comprehensive listings are in the monthly (Flemish language) *Cultuurkrant Antwerpen*. Both publications are free and can be picked up from the tourist office.

Tickets for concerts, opera, theatre and dance performances can be bought from two major locations: FNAC (Map 12; ☎ 03-213 56 55), on Groenplaats, located inside the Grand Bazar shopping centre and open 10 am to 6.30 pm Monday to Saturday; or the Stadswinkel (Map 12; ☎ 02-220 81 80) at Grote Markt 40.

PUBS & BARS

About the only thing better in Antwerp than eating is drinking. The city boasts a plethora of pubs, mostly small friendly places, as well as some wonderful terrace cafes scattered around Handschoenmarkt and Groenplaats.

One of the most *gezellig* (convivial) brown cafes in the city is *De Ware Jacob* *(Map 12; ☎ 03-213 37 89, Vlasmarkt 19).* Typical of cafes of this type, it has marble tables and a wood and mirror-panelled interior.

Den Engel (The Angel; Map 12; ☎ 03-233 12 52, Grote Markt 3) is located in a guildhall and is one of the city's oldest watering holes. It opens from 9 am daily and is seemingly always packed with men and smoke.

A real tourist trap (expensive beers) but nevertheless worth a look for its angel-adorned interior is *'t Elfde Gebod (The 11th Commandment; Map 12; ☎ 03-232 36 11, Torfbrug 10).* It opens from noon daily.

Nearby and good for sampling a beer or two is *Paeters Vaetje (Map 12; ☎ 03-231 84 76, Blauwmoezelstraat 1),* a brown cafe with 100 brews on the menu and a great atmosphere.

Those into gin should make a beeline for *De Vagant (Map 12; ☎ 03-233 15 38, Reyndersstraat 21).* More than 200 types of gin are served in this humble little cafe/restaurant, which opens from noon daily. The house cocktail – a potent mix of white and lemon gin plus a few other liqueurs and fruit juice (€3.96) – is well worth braving.

Pelgrom (Map 12; ☎ 03-234 08 09, Pelgrimstraat 15) hides in 15th-century brick-vaulted cellars. Long tables and benches add to the historic feel.

The new *Horta Grand Café (Map 12; ☎ 03-232 28 15, Hopland 2)* is the city's top-notch address for a coffee or light bite. It opened in 2000 and the stunning architecture incorporates iron girders salvaged from Victor Horta's ill-fated Maison du Peuple. The sheer glass panelling makes it a prime place to 'be seen' (if you're lucky enough to get your foot in the door), and the prices are suitably inflated.

Directly opposite in location and atmosphere is the *Oud Arsenaal (Map 12; ☎ 03-232 97 54, Pijpelincxstraat 4).* This pint -sized pub with nicotine-stained walls is popular with stallholders from the weekend Vogelmarkt and elderly locals during the week. Beers are among the cheapest in town (just €1.75 for a Duvel). It's closed on Thursday.

In winter, warm your toes by an open fire at *Babylon (Map 12; Jeruzalemstraat 16).* The patron, Eddy, plays old vinyl albums at this long-time rock and blues stronghold, and the beers (and soup) are cheap.

Next to De Koninck (Map 11), the city's main brewery, are two unassuming neighbourhood pubs where a *bolleke* (little bowl) of the city's most popular beer (simply named De Koninck after the brewery) is the drink on everyone's lips. The larger of the two is *De Pelgrim (Map 11; ☎ 03-218 91 30, Boomgaardstraat 8).* Here, clients in need of a shot of vitamin B down a *gistje*, a sour-tasting yeast extract served in a schnapps glass, along with their beers. The liquid is a by-product of the brewing process next door and, not surprisingly, is free.

The place in town to sink a host of Belgian beers is *Bierhuis Kulminator (Map 12; ☎ 03-232 45 38, Vleminckveld 32).* This place has been around for years and boasts more than 600 types of beer, many of them stacked up behind the counter (don't bother with the beer list – just point at what you want). Opening hours are a bit irregular – from 11 am most days, but from 5 pm on Saturday and 8 pm on Monday (it is closed on Sunday).

De Foyer (Map 12; ☎ 03-233 55 17,

ANTWERP

Antwerp's Top 5 Bars

• Horta Grand Café
• Oud Arsenaal
• The Bar Room
• De Vagant
• Bierhuis Kulminator

Komedieplaats 18) is a highly civilised bistro on the 1st floor of the neoclassical Bourlaschouwburg theatre. Chic *madammekes* and their poodles come here to enjoy expensive gateaux while businesspeople partake of an extensive range of world wines. In the middle of the afternoon it's a pleasant spot to read a paper or flick through a magazine while idling over a drink (closed Sunday evening).

Those into coffee culture need go no further than *Jacqmotte (Map 12; ☎ 03-231 52 97, Hoogstraat 37)*. This trendy coffee house is part of a growing chain aimed at affluent trendies with money to burn.

Talk of the town is *The Bar Room (Map 11; ☎ 03-257 57 40, Leopold de Waelplaats 30)* in 't Zuid. A hybrid between a lounge bar and club, it's a tiny but exceedingly cool place.

CLUBS
Old City Centre
Kafé Marqué (Map 12; ☎ 03-232 24 28, Grote Pieter Potstraat 3) is a basement club catering largely to tourists. The DJs play rock and Britpop from about 11.30 pm on Friday and Saturday. It's free before midnight; otherwise admission costs €5.

't Zuid
A couple of years old and still going strong, that's *Zillion (Map 11; ☎ 03-248 15 16, Jan Van Gentstraat 4)*. This huge club spans three floors and has nearly a dozen bars. It also generally has sizeable queues. Top international DJs set the scene on Friday and Saturday nights; on Thursday night it's house and techno. The clientele is young and fashionable, and things get moving around midnight. Admission costs €7.45.

Club Geluk (Map 11; Luikstraat 6) is a cellar nightclub with an underground vibe. It gets busy from about 11 pm on Thursday, Friday and Saturday nights; admission costs €6.20.

Just around the corner is another favourite, *Café Local (Map 11; ☎ 03-238 50 04, Waalsekaai)*. It was previously known for techno parties but these days prefers the sounds of salsa and global grooves. It starts at about 10 pm on Friday, Saturday and Sunday; admission costs €8.70.

Schipperskwartier
Like 't Zuid, this area is a nightlife hub, with clubs mingled among the red-light district.

The *Fill Collins Club (Map 12; ☎ 03-213 05 55, Lange Schipperskapelstraat 11)* is a mixed gay and gay-friendly disco held at *Red & Blue* (see the following Gay & Lesbian Venues section for details) on Friday nights.

Nearby is *Café d'Anvers (Map 12; ☎ 03-226 38 70, Verversrui 15)*. This club is really for the fashion conscious and every so often it holds *mode* parties complete with clothes stalls and hairdressers! Admission costs €8.70 and it opens Friday to Sunday.

Le Beau Zoo (Map 11; ☎ 03-213 14 00, Godefriduskaai 50) is one of the city's newer dance clubs. It occupies a big old building overlooking Willemdok and boasts a large open terrace for partying on over fine weekends. Admission costs €7.45.

GAY & LESBIAN VENUES
For information on Het Roze Huis, the city's new gay and lesbian community centre, see Gay & Lesbian Travellers in the Facts for the Visitor chapter.

Popi Café (Map 11; ☎ 03-238 15 30, Riemstraat 22) is a funky day-and-night *eetkaffee* (eating cafe) catering to gays, lesbians and the gay-friendly community. It has reasonably priced bistro food as well as cocktails and, on Saturday from 10 pm, there's a DJ and a small dance floor (admission free).

Café Hessenhuis (Map 12; ☎ 03-231 13 56, Falconrui 53) is a popular cafe in the old Hessenhuis building, a historic 16th-century warehouse that was rediscovered by a group of artists in the 1950s and given a total makeover. The cafe's cool, modern interior attracts a trendy, mixed clientele during the day, but in the evening it tends to be almost exclusively gay men; it opens from 10 am daily.

Oi! Food & Booze (Map 12; ☎ 03-231 06 71, Kleine Kraaiwijk 10) is a relatively

ANTWERP

new gay cafe/restaurant in the Schippers-kwartier. Live piano music, excellent food (mains between €12.39 and €14.87) and a tranquil courtyard ensure its popularity. It's closed on Tuesday.

Red & Blue (Map 12; ☎ 03-213 05 55, Lange Schipperskapelstraat 11) bills itself as 'the biggest gay dance club in Benelux (Belgium, the Netherlands and Luxembourg). True or not, it's the city's hottest gay club and is capable of drawing over 1000 punters from miles around. It operates on Saturday and is for gay men only. Admission costs €6.20 after midnight. On Friday night, Red & Blue changes its name to the *Fill Collins Club* when it draws a mixed crowd from 11 pm; admission costs €7.45. It pumps until about 7 am with house, techno, rap and soul.

The Boots (Map 11; ☎ 03-231 34 83, Van Aerdtstraat 22) has the distinction of being the country's most disreputable nightclub, with rooms devoted to fulfilling almost every imaginable sexual fantasy. It opens on Friday and Saturday from 10.30 pm to 5 am.

Atthis (Map 11; ☎ 03-216 37 37, Geuzen-straat 27) is the meeting place-cum-bar of Belgium's longest running lesbian group.

ROCK

Unassuming *Muziekdoos (Map 11; Verschansingstraat 63)* hangs on to its formula of giving buskers a free platform.

Swingcafé (Map 12; ☎ 03-233 14 78, Suikerrui 13–15) is known for its informal program of surprisingly decent bands and crowds that spill out onto the street.

JAZZ

One of the city's most popular jazz venues is *Café Hopper (Map 11; ☎ 03-248 49 33, Leopold De Waelstraat 2)* in 't Zuid. It supports (almost) nightly sessions including some well-known international names. It's small, so come early if you want to get in. Admission (€6.20) may be charged, depending on who's on.

In the mid-1970s, *De Muze (Map 12; ☎ 03-226 01 26, Melkmarkt 15)* was *the* meeting place for the city's free-thinking

youth. That radical edge is now gone but it's still an immensely popular cafe spanning three floors with a spectacular interior. It's also a bastion of live jazz – free nightly sessions start from 10 pm.

BLUES

The unpretentious *Crossroads Café (Map 11; ☎ 03-231 52 66, Mechelsesteenweg 8)* is the city's chief exponent of the blues. Live concerts featuring local or visiting bands take place at 4.30 to 8 pm most Sundays; admission costs between €4.95 and €7.45. It's about a 15-minute walk from the Grote Markt; tram No 7 (direction Mortsel) stops outside.

OTHER LIVE MUSIC VENUES

Right in the heart of town, near the Grote Markt, is *Café Buster (Map 12; ☎ 03-232 51 53, Kaasrui 1)*. This little place stages live concerts (funk, rock and roll or crooners) most Fridays and Saturdays, and does jazz on Wednesday. Occasionally there's also stand-up comedy and cabaret. However, it's at its best during Thursday's Open Jam (from 10 pm) when anyone can take to the podium.

Just down the street is *The Irish Times (Map 12; ☎ 03-227 43 60, Grote Markt 52)*, a heavy-duty drinking pub with live bands (no cover charge) from 8 pm most Friday and Saturday nights.

Zuiderpershuis (Map 11; ☎ 03-248 01 00, Waalsekaai 14) is a cultural centre that specialises in music, dance, theatre and workshops from non-western cultures. Its calendar of events is impressive, with at least three artists or groups performing per week. Tickets are generally in the €8.70 to €16 bracket. There's also a popular cafe attached to the venue.

The *Sportpaleis (Map 11; ☎ 03-326 11 07, Schijnpoortweg 113)* in the suburb of Merksem, north-east of Antwerp, is the main stage for big-name concerts.

CLASSICAL MUSIC

Antwerp has two major venues for classical music. The most popular is *deSingel (Map 11; ☎ 03-248 28 28, Desguinlei 25)*, a modern, arguably ugly building dating to 1980

ANTWERP

and sporting two concert halls – the Rode Zaal and Blauwe Zaal. Tickets are usually about €19. Modern experimental dance and theatre is also sometimes staged here – expect to pay between €8.68 to €14.87.

The other main venue is the **Koningin Elisabethzaal** *(Queen Elisabeth Concert Hall; Map 12; ☎ 0900-00311, Koningin Astridplein 23–4)* next to Centraal Station.

From early October to late March, you can catch lunchtime concerts and recitals at the **Vlaamse Opera** (see the following Opera section). They're held every Wednesday at 12.30 pm and cost €3.72/2.48 for adults/students.

The lovely **Bourlaschouwburg** (see the Theatre section later) is the occasional venue for performances by the Koninklijk Filharmonisch Orkest van Vlaanderen (Flanders Royal Philharmonic Orchestra).

CINEMAS

The **UGC** *(Map 12; ☎ 0900-10440, Van Ertbornstraat 17)* is a 17-screen state-of-the-art complex near Centraal Station that dishes up all the latest releases. Tickets cost €6.70 (seniors and students €5.50), or €5.50 for noon screenings. A tad bigger is the huge 24-screen **Metropolis** *(☎ 0900-00555, Groenendaallaan 394)*, way to the north of town.

Cartoons *(Map 12; ☎ 03-232 96 32, Kaasstraat 4–6)* is the place to get away from the general release Hollywood pulp. Arthouse movies and quality foreign films are screened in its three auditoria. Tickets cost €6.20 (seniors and students €5.45), or €4.45 on Monday.

The **Filmmuseum** *(Map 12; ☎ 03-233 85 71, Meir 50)* screens one or two films – everything from silent films to golden oldies or recent releases – nightly. On Saturday at 2.30 pm it offers *jeugdmatinees*, American and local films popular with young people. It will move to the Museum voor Fotografie (see under 't Zuid in the Things to See & Do section) in early 2002.

THEATRE

There are several venues around town, although much of the theatre on offer is in Flemish.

The mecca for international theatre performances is **deSingel** (for details see the Classical Music section). A highly innovative program is offered throughout the year at this modern concrete complex.

The **Stadsschouwburg** *(Map 12; ☎ 03-227 03 06, Theaterplein 1)* is an ugly cement eyesore built in 1980 and still largely unpopular: it's commonly referred to as 'the bunker'. It houses one of the country's largest theatrical stages and a children's theatre company.

The **Bourlaschouwburg** *(Map 12; ☎ 03-231 07 50, Komedieplaats 18)* is a grand old theatre with a distinct rounded facade topped by statues of nine muses, composers and writers. Built in the 1830s for the city's French-speaking elite by architect Pierre Bourla, it eventually fell into disuse and was on the brink of demolition a decade or so ago. It's now the city's most dignified theatre and is the home of Het Toneelhuis theatre company.

OPERA

The **Vlaamse Opera** *(Flemish Opera House; Map 12; ☎ 03-233 66 85, Frankrijklei 3)* is a fitting place to hear a performance by the highly regarded Koninklijke Vlaamse Opera (Royal Flemish Opera). Built in 1907, the building's majestic facade is unfortunately diminished by the mirrored monstrosity built next to it. Still, the marbled interior is sumptuous and the quality of the performances superb. Tickets generally cost from €7.43 to €61.97.

DANCE

Theatre 't Eilandje *(Map 11; ☎ 03-234 34 38, Westkaai 16)* is the relatively new home of the Koninklijk Ballet van Vlaanderen (Royal Flanders Ballet), the nation's only classical ballet company. The company moved to Theatre 't Eilandje in 1999; the palatial grey building perfectly harmonises with the area's maritime architecture. You can see the ballet perform here or occasionally catch a performance at the Vlaamse Opera.

The usual venue for modern dance is ***deSingel*** (for details see the Classical Music section earlier in the chapter).

SPECTATOR SPORTS

Antwerp traditionally had two top competing soccer clubs, Antwerp and Beerschot. Both are now so degraded that Beerschot amalgamated with a suburban soccer club to become Germinal Beerschot; Antwerp kicks along on its own. Going to watch a match is unlikely to be a highlight of your visit to Belgium.

Shopping

The big three in Antwerp are up-to-the-minute fashion, diamonds and antiques. The Meir is Antwerp's main shopping precinct. It offers department stores such as Inno as well as many smaller shops.

For more intimate shopping, head to the cluster of small streets on either side of Huidevettersstraat. This so-called Quartier Latin is home to some of the city's most exclusive shops; Schuttershofstraat and Korte Gasthuisstraat are the best places to start.

ANTIQUES

Komedieplaats, Leopoldstraat and Sint Jorisspoort, near St Elisabethgasthuis, are the streets for antiques. Many of the shops here

resemble private museums more closely than trading stores; the aura of aloofness is positively forbidding to anyone not wearing a fur coat or Olivier Strelli attire. If that's you, time your visit for the last weekend in November when antique dealers throw open their shops to all visitors, moneyed or not, during an open-door weekend.

BEER & GIN

The best selection of brews (280 at the last count) is at Belgium Beers (Map 12; ☎ 03-226 68 53), Reyndersstraat 2. This shop has been around for years and opens 11 am to 7 pm daily.

Bierparadijs (Map 12; ☎ 03-231 05 17), Handschoenmarkt 9, has less choice but is more centrally located.

De Vagant (Map 12; ☎ 03-233 15 38, Reyndersstraat 25) is a pub/restaurant specialising in gin. It operates a *slijterij* (a shop selling strong alcohol) across the street from the pub and in this shop 400 types of gin are sold (in bottles ranging from 30mL to 8L).

BOOKS
Comics

Mekanik Strip (Map 12; ☎ 03-234 23 47), St Jacobsmarkt 73, is the city's largest comic-strip shop. The collection is vast and includes a small selection in English. It also has a little gallery devoted to the 'ninth art' upstairs. It opens 10 am to 6 pm Monday to Saturday.

English-Language

Jenny Hannivers (Map 12; ☎ 0495-74 03 27), at Melkmarkt 30, is the city's only English-language bookshop. It's tiny and has mainly second-hand books. You can buy, sell or exchange, and there's a small bar for sipping coffee while browsing. It opens 10.30 am to 6.30 pm daily.

Another good source of second-hand novels in English is De Slegte (see the Second-Hand section later).

Gay & Lesbian

Boekhandel 't Verschil (Map 12; ☎ 03-226 08 04), at Minderbroedersrui 42, has gay information, novels and magazines and a cafe that is especially popular for Sunday brunch. It opens noon to 6 pm Friday to Sunday and until 8 pm on Saturday.

Second-Hand

De Slegte (Map 12; ☎ 03-231 66 27), Wapper 5, is a big shop and stocks books on many subjects, from novels to art and history. Quite a lot of books are in English.

Travel

Travel guides and maps can be found in FNAC (see the following section), but for a specialist store head to VTB Reisboekhandel (Map 12; ☎ 02-220 33 66), St Jacobsmarkt 45–7. It opens 9 am to 6 pm on weekdays and 9.30 am to 4.30 pm on Saturday (until noon in the summer).

Other Bookshops

FNAC (Map 12; ☎ 03-231 20 56), in the Grand Bazar shopping centre on Groenplaats, stocks a wide selection of Flemish, French and English-language literature. It opens 10 am to 6.30 pm daily.

The International Magazine Store (Map 12; ☎ 03-233 16 68), at Melkmarkt 17, is the place for foreign newspapers and top-selling magazines. It's usually packed full of people and opens until 6.30 pm daily.

CHOCOLATE & SWEETS

Del Rey (Map 12; ☎ 03-233 29 37), Appelmansstraat 5–9, is the city's best *chocolatier*. An assortment of 80 different pralines, as well as exquisite biscuits, beckon from sumptuous displays. Sampling is done at the neighbouring *dégustation* salon, where an espresso, plus one praline and a biscuit, costs €2.72.

Another excellent chocolatier is Burie (Map 12; ☎ 03-232 36 88), Korte Gasthuisstraat 3, in the old centre. Those after some diamond-shaped chocolates or *Antwerpse handjes* (chocolates designed like a hand) will find them here.

Philip's Biscuits (☎ 03-231 26 60), Korte Gasthuisstraat 11, specialises in *speculoos*, cinnamon-flavoured biscuits (€13/kg) and *peperkoek*, a type of honey cake.

CLOTHING
Designer

The fashion quarter, south of Groenplaats, is based around Nationalestraat, Lombaardvest, Huidevettersstraat and Schuttershofstraat. Top local and international designers have outlets alongside the new talent from the Koninklijke Academie voor Schone Kunsten (Royal Academy of Fine Arts). Most of the shops are closed on Sunday. For more information on Antwerp designers, see the boxed text 'At the Cutting Edge' earlier in the chapter.

Louis (Map 12; ☎ 03-232 98 72), Lombaardstraat 4, is one of the best-known boutiques for collections by local designers including Martin Margiela, Jurgi Persoons, Véronique Branquinho and Raf Simons.

Walter (Map 12; ☎ 03-213 26 44), St Antoniusstraat 12, is the Van Beirendonck outlet, although it looks more like an ultramodern art gallery than somewhere to buy clothes.

The distinct, 19th-century, domed Het Modepaleis (Map 12; ☎ 03-233 94 37), Nationalestraat 16, is the headquarters and shop of Dries Van Noten.

Ann Demeulemeester (Map 11; ☎ 03-216 01 33), Verlatstraat 38, opened her own shop in 1999 in 't Zuid. It stocks her complete line of women's and men's clothing.

Mainstream

The Meir is the street for 'regular' clothes although it is also worth checking out Meir Square (Map 12), a covered shopping gallery connecting the Meir with Huidevettersstraat.

Second-Hand

Pardaf (Map 12; ☎ 03-232 60 40), Gemeentestraat 8, is arguably the best second-hand clothing shop in Belgium. It spans four floors and sells pre-worn clothing and shoes to suit most tastes. Designer cast-offs are often found on the racks. It opens 11 am to 6 pm (closed on Sunday).

DIAMONDS & GOLD

Diamond and gold traders are thick as thieves on Pelikaanstraat, Hoveniersstraat,

Vestingstraat and Appelmansstraat. At Diamondland (Map 12; ☎ 03-234 36 12), Appelmansstraat 33a, you can see workers cutting diamonds; there is a huge range of stones for sale. For more information on the history of diamond trading in Antwerp, see the boxed text 'Diamonds' earlier in the chapter.

MARKETS
The principal market is the Vogelmarkt (bird market), held 6 am to 3 pm every weekend on Theaterplein (Map 12). On Saturday it's a lively food market; on Sunday general stuff is added.

Other markets include Sunday's *rommelmarkt* (bric-a-brac market) held on St Jansvliet (Map 12) between 7 am and 3 pm; the auction of second-hand goods (mainly clothes and furniture) every Friday morning at Vrijdagmarkt (Map 12); and an antique market held at the side of Onze Lieve Vrouwkathedraal on Lijnwaadmarkt every Saturday morning.

Bric-a-brac traders selling odds and ends of all descriptions have taken over Kloosterstraat and Oever (south of St Jansvliet) in recent years. These shops are great for unearthing old rubbish.

Excursions

PORT OF ANTWERP
Pick up any tourist map of Antwerp and in the north-western corner you'll note some blue patches. Most visitors think of this area as the port of Antwerp. It is, in fact, just the tip of the iceberg. With 127km of quays, the world's largest sea lock, **Berendrechtsluis** (Map 1), and the capacity to store 110 million tonnes of goods per year, the port of Antwerp is the third largest in the world.

It wasn't all that long ago that the city's port did cover a relatively small area. But massive transformation of the surrounding farmlands and polders in the 20th century (including the annihilation of whole villages) has seen the port grow from a prosperous medieval harbour based around waterways (now filled in) in the heart of the old town to a giant that stretches to the Dutch border.

Napoleon initiated this expansion with the creation of two (at that time) huge docks – Bonapartedok and Willemdok. Towards the end of the 19th century, the nearby Kattendijkdok was constructed and from there it has soared.

A tour through this area is like entering a surreal world – a maze of cranes and loading yards, docks and warehouses, railway lines and industrial estates, the latter belonging to petroleum refineries, car assembly plants and petrochemical industries. More picturesque is the polder village of Lillo (Map 1), one of the lucky survivors and home to a little museum devoted to life before the great transformation.

Unless you've got your own car and don't mind getting very lost, the only way to visit the port is on a Flandria boat trip – see Organised Tours in the Getting Around section earlier in the chapter for details.

LIER
postcode 2500 • pop 32,000
The town of Lier, or Pallieterstad as it's also known, sits 17km south-east of Antwerp near the confluence of two rivers – the big and little Nete. Its nickname comes from Pallieter, the name of a popular character invented by Felix Timmermans, a 20th-century writer who lived here for many years.

Lier is a tranquil and typically Flemish provincial town. It has a smattering of interesting sights but is most noted for its **Begijnhof**, a charming cluster of cottages and one of the oldest and best-kept *begijnhoven* in Belgium. Not far away is another curiosity, the **Zimmertoren**, a tower that was once part of the town's ramparts and now boasts a quite amazing astronomical clock built in 1930 by the prosperous local Lodewijk Zimmer. Another of Zimmer's timepieces is inside the neighbouring pavilion.

Worth tasting while you're here is a *Liers vlaaike*, a small, sweet tart sold in bakeries.

Getting There & Away
From Antwerp to Lier (€1.98, 15 minutes), there are trains every half hour. The train

ANTWERP

station is 1km from the tourist office (☎ 03-488 38 88) located on the Grote Markt.

MECHELEN
postcode 2800 • pop 75,500

The town of Mechelen (Malines in French, Mechlin in English) sits roughly equidistant from Antwerp and Brussels and is, of course, overshadowed by them both. Its history is, however, rich – it was the short-lived capital of the Low Countries in the early 16th century, during which time many of its most elaborate buildings were constructed.

The town's most impressive feature is **St Romboutskathedraal**, on the Grote Markt. This robust cathedral features a gigantic, 97m-high tower that was completed in the middle of the 16th century and in fine weather can be seen from Brussels. It's topped by the country's heaviest carillon – appropriately enough considering Mechelen boasts a world famous school of campanology – bell-ringing – and students come from far and wide to learn the art.

Getting There & Away

There are trains every half hour to Antwerp (€2.72, 15 minutes) and Brussels (€3.09, 15 minutes). Mechelen's train station is 1.25km from the town's Grote Markt where you'll find the tourist office (☎ 015-29 76 55).

GHENT
postcode 9000 • pop 225,000

Medieval Europe's largest city outside Paris was Ghent (known as Gent in Flemish and Gand in French). Its glory lies in its industrious and rebellious past. Sitting on the junction of the Leie and Scheldt rivers, by the mid-14th century it had become Europe's largest cloth producer, importing wool from England and employing thousands of people. The townsfolk were well known for their armed battles, for civil liberties and against the heavy taxes imposed on them.

Today, Ghent is home to many university students who give the city a cheerful, innovative air. Its location makes it an almost effortless visit from Antwerp, Bruges or Brussels.

Maneblussers of Mechelen

ASA ANDERSSON

'Maneblussers' is the popular nickname for the citizens of Mechelen. It comes from a local legend in which a late-night, 17th-century reveller had one too many beers and thought that the tower of St Romboutskathedraal was on fire. The man raised the alarm and townsfolk from all around rallied to put out the blaze. It soon became apparent that the so-called fire was simply the light of the moon casting an unusual reddish glow around the tower. Hence their nickname 'extinguishers of the moon'.

Orientation

Unlike many Flemish cities, Ghent does not have one central square. Instead, the medieval core is a series of large open areas, separated by two imposing churches and a belfry whose line of towers has long been the trademark of Ghent's skyline. The Korenmarkt is the westernmost square, and is technically the city's centre – it's a 25-minute walk from the main train station, St Pietersstation, but is regularly connected with it by tram Nos 1, 10, 11 and 12 (which depart from the tunnel next to the train station).

Halfway between Ghent's two centres is the university quarter, spread along St Pietersnieuwstraat.

MARTIN MOOS

Antwerp's imposing Onze Lieve Vrouwkathedraal is home to four of Rubens' vast canvases.

LEANNE LOGAN

DOUG McKINLAY

en street-corner shrines are gilded in Antwerp.   Classical Flemish style in Antwerp's Rockoxhuis

EDWARD SNIJDERS

Let Lier's 14th-century astronomical clock worry about the time as you relax in its bustling cafes.

MARTIN MOOS

Mechelen's joyous town mascot – Op-Signoorke – flies through the air outside its tourist office.

MARTIN MOOS

The innovative university town of Ghent attracts a diverse range of special events and big-name DJ

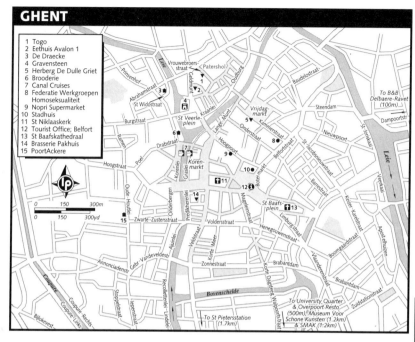

GHENT

1 Togo
2 Eethuis Avalon 1
3 De Draecke
4 Gravensteen
5 Herberg De Dulle Griet
6 Brooderie
7 Canal Cruises
8 Federatie Werkgroepen Homoseksualiteit
9 Nopri Supermarket
10 Stadhuis
11 St Niklaaskerk
12 Tourist Office; Belfort
13 St Baafskathedraal
14 Brasserie Pakhuis
15 PoortAckere

Information

The tourist office (☎ 09-266 52 32, fax 09-225 62 88, **e** voorlichting@gent.be) is at Botermarkt 17 under the belfry and opens 9 am to 8 pm daily from April to early November, and 9.30 am to 6 pm the rest of the year.

Things to See & Do

Ghent's attractions are largely medieval and, with the exception of the main museums, are centrally located.

St Baafskathedraal Though St Baaf's Cathedral (☎ 09-225 16 26), St Baafsplein, is unimpressive from the outside, crowds line up to see *De Aanbidding van het Lams God* (Adoration of the Mystic Lamb) – a lavish representation of medieval religious thinking and one of the earliest-known oil paintings. It was painted by Jan Van Eyck as an altarpiece in 1432 and has 20 panels – originally the interior panels were designed to be displayed

only on important religious occasions though these days they're always open for viewers to see. The work represents an allegorical glorification of Christ's death: on the upper tier sits God the Father flanked by the Virgin and John the Baptist and on the outer panels are Adam and Eve. The lower tier centres on the Lamb, symbolising the sacrifice made by Christ, surrounded by all manner of religious figures and a landscape dotted with local church towers. The luminous colours and the rich, detailed crowd scenes are stunning.

The entrance to the cathedral is on St Baafsplein; it opens 8.30 am to 6 pm daily. The crypt with the *Mystic Lamb* opens 9.30 am to 5 pm Monday to Saturday and 1 to 5 pm on Sunday (in winter it opens 10.30 am to noon and 2.30 to 4 pm daily, and 2 to 5 pm on Sunday). Admission to the cathedral is free but it costs €2.50 to see the *Mystic Lamb*.

Belfort This 14th-century belfry rises from the old Lakenhalle (cloth hall) on the

ANTWERP

Botermarkt and affords spectacular views of the city. The top can be reached either by a lift or stairs. It opens 10 am to 12.30 pm and 2 to 5.30 pm daily from mid-April to mid-November; admission costs €2.50.

Gravensteen With moat, turrets and arrow slits, this fearsome 12th-century castle (☎ 09-222 93 06) belonged to the counts of Flanders and is the quintessential castle, built to protect the townsfolk as well as to intimidate them into law-abiding submission. It's at St Veerleplein, north of the Korenmarkt, and opens 9 am to 6 pm daily (until 5 pm from October to 31 March); admission costs €5.

Museum voor Schone Kunsten The Museum of Fine Arts (☎ 09-222 17 03), Citadelpark, is well worth a couple of hours, particularly when combined with a visit to SMAK (see the following section). The Flemish Primitives are well represented, as are Rubens, Jordaens, Van Dyck, Ensor and Delvaux. The museum opens 9.30 am to 5 pm Tuesday to Sunday and admission costs €2.50.

Stedelijk Museum voor Actuele Kunst (SMAK) The Museum of Contemporary Art (☎ 09-221 17 03), better known by its acronym SMAK, is opposite the Museum of Fine Arts in the Citadelpark. Look out for works by Belgian Pierre Alechinsky, as well as artworks by international celebrities such as Christo, Warhol and Hockney. The museum opens 10 am to 6 pm (closed Monday); admission costs €2.50.

Places to Stay
Ghent has a smattering of accommodation to suit all budgets. The attractive hostel *De Draecke* (☎ 09-233 70 50, fax 09-233 80 01, [e] *youthhostel.gent@skynet.be, St Wido-straat 11)* occupies a renovated warehouse ideally located close to the heart of town. A bunk in a six-bed room with private facilities costs €12.64, or there are singles/doubles for €20.32/29.79. There's no curfew. From the train station, take tram No 1, 10, 11 or 12 to St Veerleplein.

The Gilde der Gentse Gastenkamers (GGG; ☎ 09-233 30 99), Tentoonstellingslaan 69, B-9000 Ghent, is a guild organising the city's thriving B&Bs. It publishes a free booklet (in English) detailing guesthouses in and around the city.

One excellent option is ***B&B Delbaere-Ravet*** (☎/fax 09-233 43 52, [e] *sderavet @worldonline.be, Hagelandkaai 38)*, which has four fantastically spacious rooms in a 19th-century townhouse for €24.80/39.70, or €52/64.50 for three/four people. The closest train station is Gent-Dampoort, or take bus No 70 from St Pietersstation.

Brooderie (☎ 09-225 06 23, Jan Breydelstraat 8) is principally a bakery-cum-tearoom, but it also has three lovely rooms located upstairs. The rooms have unpolished wooden floors and earthy furniture; bathroom facilities are shared. Prices are €37.17/56.99.

The new ***PoortAckere*** (☎ 09-269 22 10, fax 09-269 22 30, [e] *reservations@poort ackere.com, Oude Houtlei 50–8)* is a converted convent that now houses a hotel and *gastenverblijf* (guesthouse). The ground-floor hotel is quite luxurious with rooms from €62/111. The 1st-floor gastenverblijf occupies the former nuns' rooms – they're smaller, sober and cheaper, starting at €37.20/86.80.

Places to Eat
The student ghetto, a 10-minute walk southeast of the Korenmarkt, is the best area for inexpensive meals. Here on St Pietersnieuwstraat and its continuation, Overpoortstraat, you'll find plenty of cafes and pubs.

The cheapest eatery is the self-service student cafeteria known as ***Overpoort Resto*** (☎ 09-264 72 51, Overpoortstraat 49). A *menu* will set you back about €5; it opens weekdays for lunch and dinner.

In the centre, ***Eethuis Avalon 1*** (☎ 09-224 37 24, Geldmunt 32) is a vegetarian restaurant with a rabbit warren of rooms and a small outdoor terrace. The dagschotel costs €7.45 or there's a *menu* for €9.91; it's closed on Sunday.

Brooderie (see under Places to Stay) is a rustic eatery serving soup, savoury pies and sandwiches and is full most lunchtimes.

The cluster of cobbled lanes just north of the Leie is called the Patershol quarter. The choice of restaurants here is ample. *Togo* *(☎ 09-223 65 51, Vrouwebroersstraat 21)* specialises in African cuisine and is recommended; expect mains around €12.40. *Brasserie Pakhuis (☎ 09-223 55 55, Schuurkenstraat 4)* is arguably Ghent's hottest dining address. This huge brasserie-cum-restaurant occupies a beautifully restored textile warehouse on a quiet backstreet and draws young and old alike. The cuisine is eclectic and mains cost from €15 to €25. It's closed Sunday.

The *Nopri* supermarket *(☎ 09-225 05 92, Hoogpoort 42)* opens 9 am to 6 pm Monday to Saturday.

To the south-east, across the bridge on the Vrijdagmarkt (once the city's forum for public meetings and executions), are many restaurants and pubs. Here you'll find *Herberg De Dulle Griet (☎ 09-224 24 55, Vrijdagmarkt 50)*, one of Ghent's best-known beer pubs. Beware of all the scary local brews – Guillotine (9.3%), Delirium Tremens (9.5%) and Piraat (10.5%).

Getting There & Away

The train station information office (☎ 09-222 44 44) opens 5 am to 9 pm daily. There are IC trains to Antwerp (€6.69, 45 minutes), Bruges (€4.58, 20 minutes), Brussels (€6.19, 45 minutes) and Ypres (€7.93, one hour).

ANTWERP

Language

FLEMISH

It's important to note that Flemish uses two forms for the English 'you': polite *(U/Uw)* and informal *(jij/je/jou)*. Always use the polite form when addressing an adult who is not a personal friend. In this language guide we have included both forms, separated by a slash.

Pronunciation

Vowels Single vowels are pretty straightforward, with long and short sounds for each. If they come at the end of a syllable, their pronunciation is long. Combined vowels are more unusual:

a	short, as the 'a' in 'apple'
aa	long, as the 'a' in 'father'
au, ou	somewhere between the 'ow' in 'how' and the 'ow' in 'glow'
e	short, as in 'bet', or as the 'e' in 'fern'
e, ee	long, as the 'ay' in 'day'
ei, ij	as the 'ey' in 'they'
eu	like the German 'ö', or an exaggerated 'o' in 'over'
ë	separates 'e' from the preceding vowel, for example *Australië* (pronounced 'os-tra-lee-a')
i	short and clipped, as in 'it'
i, ie	as the 'ee' in 'meet'
o	short, as in 'pot'
o, oo	long, as in 'note'
oe	as the 'oo' in 'zoo'
u	short, similar to the 'u' in 'urn'
u, uu	long, as in the German *über*
ui	no equivalent sound in English; in French, the 'eui' in *fauteuil* is close (if you leave out the slide towards the 'l')

Consonants These, too, are pretty straightforward:

ch, g	a soft, lisping sound
j	as the 'y' in 'yes'
r	a trilled sound
s	as in 'safe'; sometimes as the 's' in 'pleasure'
w	as English 'w'

Greetings

Hello.	*Goeiendag/Hallo.*
Good morning.	*Goedemorgen.*
Good evening.	*Goedenavond.*
Good night.	*Goedenacht.*
Goodbye.	*Dag* or *Tot ziens.*

Basics

Yes.	*Ja.*
No.	*Nee.*
Please.	*Alstublieft/Alsjeblieft.*
Thank you.	*Dank U/je wel* or *Bedankt.*
You're welcome.	*Zonder dank.*
Excuse me.	*Pardon/Excuseert.*
Sorry.	*Sorry.*
Maybe.	*Misschien.*

Small Talk

How are you?	*Hoe gaat het met U/jou?*
I'm fine, thanks.	*Goed, bedankt.*
What's your name?	*Hoe heet U/je?*
My name is ...	*Ik heet ...*
Where are you from?	*Vanwaar zijt U/ben je?*

I'm from ...	*Ik kom uit ...*
Australia	*Australië*
Canada	*Canada*
England	*Engeland*
Germany	*Duitsland*
Ireland	*Ierland*
New Zealand	*Nieuw Zeeland*
Scotland	*Schotland*
the USA	*de Verenigde Staten*
Wales	*Wales*

Language Difficulties

Do you speak English?	*Spreekt U/spreek je Engels?*
I understand.	*Ik begrijp het.*

196

Signs – Flemish

Ingang	**Entrance**
Uitgang	**Exit**
Open	**Open**
Gesloten	**Closed**
Informatie/	**Information**
Inlichtingen	
Politiebureau	**Police Station**
Verboden	**Prohibited**
Kamers Vrij	**Rooms Available**
Vol	**No Vacancies**
WC/Toiletten	**Toilets**
Heren	**Men**
Dames	**Women**

I don't understand. *Ik begrijp het niet.*
Please write it *Schrijf het alstublieft/*
  down. *alsjeblieft op.*

Getting Around

What time does *Hoe laat vertrekt/*
the ... leave/arrive? *arriveert de ...?*
  (next) *(volgende)*
  airplane *vliegtuig*
  boat *boot*
  bus *bus*
  train *trein*
  tram *tram*

I'd like a ... ticket. *Ik wil graag een ...*
  one-way *enkele reis*
  return *heen en terug*
  1st class *eerste klas*
  2nd class *tweede klas*

Where is (the) ...? *Waar is ...?*
  bus stop *de bushalte*
  ferry terminal *de veerhaven*
  luggage locker *de bagagekluis*
  metro station *het metrostation*
  ticket office *het kaartjeskantoor*
  train station *het treinstation*
  tram stop *de tramhalte*

The train is ... *De trein is ...*
  delayed *met vertraging*
  early *te vroeg*
  on time *op tijd*

I'd like to hire ... *Ik wil graag ... huren.*
  a bicycle *een fiets*
  a car *een auto*
  a guide *een gids*

Directions

What street/road *Welke straat/weg*
  is this? *is dit?*
(Go) straight ahead. *(Ga) rechtdoor.*
Turn left/right. *Ga linksaf/rechtsaf.*

at the traffic lights *bij het stoplicht*
at the next corner *bij de volgende hoek*
far/near *ver/dichtbij*
behind *achter*
in front of *voor*
opposite *tegenover*
north *noord*
south *zuid*
east *oost*
west *west*

Around Town

Where is (a/the) ...? *Waar is ...?*
  bank *de bank*
  ... embassy *de ... ambassade*
  exchange office *het wisselkantoor*
  (nearby) hotel *een hotel (dichtbij)*
  post office *het postkantoor*
  public toilet *een openbaar toilet*
  telephone centre *het telefoonkantoor*
  tourist office *het toeristenbureau*

What time does it *Hoe laat opent/*
  open/close? *sluit het?*
I'd like to change *Ik zou graag geld*
  some money. *willen wisselen.*

How do I get to ...? *Hoe kom ik bij/aan ...?*
  the cathedral *de kathedraal*
  the city centre *het stadscentrum*
  the church *de kerk*
  the main square *het hoofdplein*

Accommodation

camp site *camping*
guesthouse *gastenkamer*
hotel *hotel*
youth hostel *jeugdherberg*

Do you have any rooms available?	Heeft U kamers vrij?

How much is it ...?	Hoeveel is het ...?
per night	per nacht
per person	per persoon

Is breakfast included?	Is het ontbijt erbij inbegrepen?

Can I see the room?	Kan ik de kamer zien?

single room	eenpersoonskamer
double room	tweepersoonskamer
shower	douche
one night	een nacht
two nights	twee nachten
day/days	dag/dagen
week/weeks	week/weken

Shopping

How much is it?	Hoeveel is het?
Can I look at it?	Kan ik het zien?
It's too expensive.	Het is mij te duur.
That's cheap.	Dat is goedkoop.

bookshop	boekenwinkel
chemist/pharmacy	drogist/apotheek
clothes shop	kledingzaak
laundrette	wassalon
market	markt
newsagent's	krantenwinkel
supermarket	supermarkt

big/small	groot/klein
more/less	meer/minder

Do you accept credit cards?	Neemt U krediet-kaarten aan?

Time & Dates

What time is it?	Hoe laat is het?
It's two o'clock.	Het is twee uur.

When?	Wanneer?
today	vandaag
tonight	vanavond
tomorrow	morgen
the day after tomorrow	overmorgen
yesterday	gisteren

Emergencies– Flemish

Help!	Help!
Call a doctor!	Haal een dokter!
Call the police!	Haal de politie!
Call an ambulance!	Haal een ziekenauto!
There's been an accident!	Er is een ongeluk gebeurd!
I'm lost.	Ik ben de weg kwijt.
Go away!	Ga weg!

all day	de hele dag
in the morning	's-morgens
in the afternoon	's-middags
in the evening	's-avonds

Monday	maandag
Tuesday	dinsdag
Wednesday	woensdag
Thursday	donderdag
Friday	vrijdag
Saturday	zaterdag
Sunday	zondag

January	januari
February	februari
March	maart
April	april
May	mei
June	juni
July	juli
August	augustus
September	september
October	oktober
November	november
December	december

Numbers

0	nul
1	een
2	twee
3	drie
4	vier
5	vijf
6	zes
7	zeven
8	acht
9	negen
10	tien

11	*elf*
12	*twaalf*
13	*dertien*
14	*veertien*
15	*vijftien*
16	*zestien*
17	*zeventien*
18	*achttien*
19	*negentien*
20	*twintig*
21	*eenentwintig*
22	*tweeëntwintig*
30	*dertig*
40	*veertig*
50	*vijftig*
60	*zestig*
70	*zeventig*
80	*tachtig*
90	*negentig*
100	*honderd*
1000	*duizend*

| one million | *een miljoen* |
| one billion | *een miljard* |

Health

I'm sick.	*Ik ben ziek.*
I need a doctor.	*Ik heb een dokter nodig.*
Where is the hospital?	*Waar is het ziekenhuis?*
I'm ...	*Ik ben ...*
asthmatic	*astmatisch*
diabetic	*suikerziek*
epileptic	*epileptisch*
pregnant	*in verwachting*
I'm allergic to ...	*Ik ben allergisch voor ...*
antibiotics	*antibiotica*
penicillin	*penicilline*
antiseptic	*ontsmettingsmiddel*
aspirin	*aspirine*
condoms	*condooms*
contraceptive	*voorbehoedsmiddel*
medicine	*geneesmiddel*
nausea	*misselijkheid*
sunblock cream	*zonnecrême*
tampons	*tampons*

FRENCH

Like Flemish, French uses two forms for the English 'you': polite *(vous)* and informal *(tu)*. *Tu* is only used when addressing people you know well, children or animals. When addressing an adult who is not a personal friend, *vous* should be used unless the person invites you to use *tu*. The polite form is used in this guide unless otherwise indicated.

Pronunciation

Most letters in French are pronounced more or less the same as their English equivalents. A few that may cause confusion are:

é	as the 'ay' in 'may'
è	slightly longer than the 'e' in 'very'
ê	as the 'e' in 'met'
u	short, similar to the 'u' in 'urn'
c	before **e** and **i**, as the 's' in 'sit'; before **a**, **o** and **u** it's pronounced as the English 'k'. When underscored with a 'cedilla' (ç) it's always pronounced as the 's' in 'sit'.
j	as the 's' in 'leisure'

Greetings

Hello/Good morning.	*Bonjour.*
Good evening.	*Bonsoir.*
Good night.	*Bonne nuit.*
Goodbye.	*Au revoir.*

Basics

Yes.	*Oui.*
No.	*Non.*
Please.	*S'il vous plaît.*
Thank you.	*Merci.*
You're welcome.	*Je vous en prie.*
Excuse me.	*Excusez-moi.*
Sorry/Forgive me.	*Pardon.*
Maybe.	*Peut-être.*

Small Talk

How are you?	*Comment allez-vous?* (polite)
	Comment vas-tu?/ Comment ça va? (informal)
Fine, thanks.	*Bien, merci.*

Signs – French

Entrée	**Entrance**
Sortie	**Exit**
Ouvert	**Open**
Fermé	**Closed**
Renseignements	**Information**
Interdit	**Prohibited**
(Commissariat de) Police	**Police Station**
Chambres Libres	**Rooms Available**
Complet	**No Vacancies**
WC/Toilettes	**Toilets**
Hommes	**Men**
Femmes	**Women**

What's your name?	*Comment appelez-vous?*
My name is ...	*Je m'appelle ...*
Where are you from?	*De quel pays êtes-vous?*

I'm from ...	*Je viens ...*
Australia	*d'Australie*
Canada	*du Canada*
England	*d'Angleterre*
Germany	*d'Allemagne*
Ireland	*d'Irlande*
New Zealand	*de Nouvelle Zélande*
Scotland	*d'Écosse*
the USA	*des États-Unis*
Wales	*du Pays de Galle*

Language Difficulties

Do you speak English?	*Parlez-vous anglais?*
I understand.	*Je comprends.*
I don't understand.	*Je ne comprends pas.*
Could you please write it down?	*Est-ce que vous pouvez l'écrire?*

Getting Around

What time does the ... leave/arrive?	*À quelle heure part/arrive ...?*
(next)	*(prochain/e)*
airplane	*l'avion*
bus (city)	*l'autobus*
ferry	*le ferry(-boat)*
train	*le train*
tram	*le tram*

I'd like a ... ticket.	*Je voudrais un billet ...*
one-way	*aller-simple*
return	*aller-retour*
1st class	*première classe*
2nd class	*deuxième classe*

Where is (the) ...?	*Où est ...?*
bus stop	*l'arrêt d'autobus*
luggage locker	*coffre de bagage*
metro station	*la station de métro*
train station	*la gare*
tram stop	*l'arrêt de tramway*
ticket office	*le guichet*

The train is ...	*Le train est ...*
delayed	*en retard*
early	*en avance*
on time	*à l'heure*

I'd like to hire ...	*Je voudrais louer ...*
a bicycle	*un vélo*
a car	*une voiture*
a guide	*un guide*

Directions

How do I get to ...?	*Comment est-ce que je dois aller pour arriver à ...?*
Is it near/far?	*Est-ce près/loin?*
Can you show me on ...?	*Est-ce que vous pouvez me montrer sur ...?*
the map	*la carte*
the city map	*le plan*
Go straight ahead.	*Continuez tout droit.*
Turn left.	*Tournez à gauche.*
Turn right.	*Tournez à droite.*

at the traffic lights	*aux feux*
at the next corner	*au prochain coin*
behind	*derrière*
in front of	*devant*
opposite	*en face de*
north	*nord*
south	*sud*
east	*est*
west	*ouest*

Around Town

I'm looking for ...	*Je cherche ...*
a bank/	*une banque/*
exchange office	*un bureau de change*
the city centre	*le centre-ville*
the ... embassy	*l'ambassade de ...*
my hotel	*mon hôtel*
the post office	*le bureau de poste/ la poste*
a public phone	*une cabine téléphonique*
a public toilet	*les toilettes*
the tourist office	*l'office de tourisme*
Where is (the) ...?	*Où est ...?*
cathedral	*la cathédrale*
church	*l'église*
main square	*la place centrale*
What time does it open/close?	*Quelle est l'heure d'ouverture/ de fermeture?*
I'd like to change ...	*Je voudrais changer ...*
some money	*de l'argent*
travellers cheques	*chèques de voyage*

Accommodation

camp site	*camping*
guesthouse	*pension*
hotel	*hôtel*
youth hostel	*auberge de jeunesse*
Do you have any rooms available?	*Est-ce que vous avez des chambres libres?*
I'd like to book ...	*Je voudrais réserver ...*
a bed	*un lit*
a single room	*une chambre pour une personne*
a double room	*une chambre pour deux personnes*
a room with a shower and toilet	*une chambre avec douche et WC*
How much is it ...?	*Quel est le prix ...?*
per night	*par nuit*
per person	*par personne*

Is breakfast included?	*Est-ce que le petit déjeuner est compris?*
Can I see the room?	*Est-ce que je peux voir la chambre?*
I'm going to stay ...	*Je resterai ...*
one day	*un jour*
one week	*une semaine*

Shopping

How much is it?	*C'est combien?*
Can I look at it?	*Est-ce que je peux le/la voir?* (m/f)
It's too expensive for me.	*C'est trop cher pour moi.*
That's cheap.	*C'est bon marché.*
Do you accept credit cards?	*Est-ce que vous acceptez des cartes de crédit?*
It's too big/small.	*C'est trop grand/petit.*
more/less	*plus/moins*
bookshop	*la librairie*
chemist/pharmacy	*la pharmacie*
laundrette	*la laverie*
market	*le marché*
newsagent's	*l'agence de presse*
supermarket	*le supermarché*

Time & Dates

What time is it?	*Quelle heure est-il?*
It's (two) o'clock.	*Il est (deux) heures.*
When?	*Quand?*
today	*aujourd'hui*
tonight	*ce soir*
tomorrow	*demain*
day after tomorrow	*après-demain*
yesterday	*hier*
all day	*toute la journée*
in the morning	*le matin*
in the afternoon	*l'après-midi*
in the evening	*le soir*
Monday	*lundi*
Tuesday	*mardi*
Wednesday	*mercredi*
Thursday	*jeudi*
Friday	*vendredi*
Saturday	*samedi*
Sunday	*dimanche*

Emergencies – French

Help!	Au secours!
Call a doctor!	Appelez un médecin!
Call the police!	Appelez la police!
Call an ambulance!	Appelez une ambulance!
There's been an accident!	Il y avait une accident!
I've been robbed.	On m'a volé.
I've been raped.	On m'a violée.
I'm lost.	Je me suis perdu.
Go away!	Laissez-moi tranquille!

January	janvier
February	février
March	mars
April	avril
May	mai
June	juin
July	juillet
August	août
September	septembre
October	octobre
November	novembre
December	décembre

Numbers

0	zéro
1	un
2	deux
3	trois
4	quatre
5	cinq
6	six
7	sept
8	huit
9	neuf
10	dix
11	onze
12	douze
13	treize
14	quatorze
15	quinze
16	seize
17	dix-sept
18	dix-huit
19	dix-neuf
20	vingt
21	vingt-et-un
22	vingt-deux
30	trente
40	quarante
50	cinquante
60	soixante
70	soixante-dix
80	quatre-vingt
90	quatre-vingt-dix
100	cent
1000	mille

one million	un million
one billion	un milliard

Health

I'm sick.	Je suis malade.
I need a doctor.	Il me faut un médecin.
Where is the hospital?	Où est l'hôpital?

I'm ...	Je suis ...
asthmatic	asthmatique
diabetic	diabétique
epileptic	épileptique
pregnant	enceinte

I'm allergic ...	Je suis allergique ...
to antibiotics	aux antibiotiques
to penicillin	à la pénicilline

antiseptic	antiseptique
aspirin	aspirine
condoms	préservatifs
contraceptive	contraceptif
medicine	médicament
nausea	nausée
sunblock cream	crème solaire de haute protection
tampons	tampons hygiéniques

FOOD – FLEMISH
Basics

breakfast	het ontbijt
lunch	het middagmaal
dinner	het avondmaal
vegetable	groente
fish	vis
meat	vlees

poultry	*gevogelte*
game	*wild*
dessert	*nagerecht*
grocery store	*de kruidenier*
chip shop	*frituur*

I'd like the set menu.
  Ik neem het dagmenu.
I'm a vegetarian.
  Ik ben vegetarisch.
I don't eat meat.
  Ik eet geen vlees.

Menu
Starters, Soups & Snacks

belegd broodje	filled sandwich
boterham	slice of bread
frieten	chips/French fries
koude voor-	cold starter
gerechten	
pide	Turkish pizza
pita	pitta bread sandwich
soep	soup
warme voor-	warm starter
gerechten	

Meat

bloedworst	black pudding
eend	duck
everzwijn	boar
fazant	pheasant
hammetje	ham on the bone
hersenen	brains
hert	venison
hesp	ham
kalf	veal
kalkoen	turkey
kip	chicken
konijn	rabbit
lam	lamb
lever	liver
paard	horse
parelhoen	guinea fowl
ribstuk	rib steak
rund	beef
schaap	mutton
slak	snail
spek	bacon
tong	tongue
varken	pork
vleeswaren	cooked/prepared meats
worst	large sausage

Fish & Seafood

ansjovis	anchovy
baars	bream
forel	trout
garnaal	shrimp
haring	herring
inktvis	squid
kabeljauw	cod
krab	crab
kreeft	lobster
maatjes	herring fillets
mossel	mussel
oester	oyster
paling	eel
rivierkreeft	crayfish
rog	ray
roodbaars	red mullet
steurgarnaal	prawn
St Jacobsschelp	scallop
tong	sole
tonijn	tuna
waterzooi	cream-based fish stew
zalm	salmon
zeebaars	sea bream

Vegetables

aardappel	potato
ajuin	onion
artisjok	artichoke
asperge	asparagus
avocado	avocado
boon	bean
champignon	mushroom
courgette	courgette/zucchini
eierplant	aubergine/eggplant
erwtjes	peas
groene/rode	green/red pepper
peper	(capsicum)
komkommer	cucumber
kool	cabbage
look	garlic
maïs	sweet corn
olijf	olive
peterselie	parsley
pompoen	pumpkin
porei	leek
selder	celery
sjalot	shallot
spinazie	spinach
spruitjes	Brussels sprouts

stoemp	Flemish-style mashed potatoes
truffel	truffle
witloof	chicory
wortel	carrot

Desserts

ijskreem	ice cream
koek	cake
pannekoek	pancake
speculoos	cinnamon-flavoured biscuit
taart	tart (pie)
wafel	waffle

Drinks

bier	beer
jenever	Belgian gin
lambiek	Brussels beer
wijn	wine

Miscellaneous

azijn	vinegar
boter	butter
brood	bread
ei	egg
geitenkaas	goat's cheese
kaas	cheese
konfituur	jam
melk	milk
peper	pepper
rijst	rice
suiker	sugar
water	water
zout	salt

Cooking Methods

aan 't spit	spit-roasted
gebakken	baked
gegratineerd	browned on top with cheese
gegrild	grilled
gepaneerd	coated in breadcrumbs
gerookt	smoked
geroosterd	roasted
gesauteerd	sautéed
gestoomd	steamed
gevuld	stuffed
op het houtvuur	cooked over a wood stove

FOOD – FRENCH
Basics

breakfast	*le petit déjeuner*
lunch	*le déjeuner*
dinner	*le dîner*
vegetable	*légume*
fish	*poisson*
meat	*viande*
poultry	*volaille*
game	*gibier*
dessert	*dessert*
grocery store	*l'épicerie*
chip shop	*friture*

I'd like the set menu.
  Je prends le menu.
I'm a vegetarian.
  Je suis végétarien/végétarienne. (m/f)
I don't eat meat.
  Je ne mange pas de viande.

Menu
Starters, Soups & Snacks

croque monsieur	grilled ham and cheese sandwich
entrées chaudes	warm starter
entrées froides	cold starter
frites	chips/French fries
potage	soup
sandwich garni	filled sandwich
tartine	slice of bread

Meat

agneau	lamb
bœuf	beef
boudin noir	black pudding
brochette	kebab
canard	duck
cerf	venison
cervelle	brains
charcuterie	cooked/prepared meats
cheval	horse
dinde	turkey
entrecôte	rib steak
escargot	snail
faisan	pheasant
foie	liver
jambon	ham
jambonneau	ham on the bone
langue	tongue
lapin	rabbit

marcassin	boar
mouton	mutton
pintade	guinea fowl
porc	pork
poulet	chicken
saucisson	large sausage
veau	veal

Fish & Seafood

anchois	anchovy
anguille	eel
brème	bream
cabillaud	cod
calmar	squid
coquille St-Jacques	scallop
crabe	crab
crevette	shrimp
dorade	sea bream
hareng	herring
homard	lobster
huître	oyster
langouste	crayfish
moule	mussel
raie	ray
rouget	red mullet
saumon	salmon
scampi	prawn
sole	sole
thon	tuna
truite	trout

Vegetables

ail	garlic
artichaut	artichoke
asperge	asparagus
aubergine	aubergine/eggplant
avocat	avocado
carotte	carrot
celeri	celery
champignon	mushroom
chicon	chicory
chou	cabbage
choux de Bruxelles	Brussels sprouts
citrouille	pumpkin
concombre	cucumber
courgette	courgette/zucchini
échalote	shallot
épinards	spinach
haricot	bean
maïs	sweet corn
oignon	onion

olive	olive
persil	parsley
petit pois	peas
poireau	leek
poivron rouge/ vert	red/green pepper (capsicum)
pomme de terre	potato
truffe	truffle

Desserts

crêpe	pancake
gâteau	cake
gaufre	waffle
glace	ice cream
tarte	tart (pie)

Drinks

bière	beer
genièvre	Belgian gin
lambic	Brussels beer
vin	wine

Miscellaneous

beurre	butter
confiture	jam
eau	water
fromage	cheese
fromage de chèvre	goat's cheese
lait	milk
œuf	egg
pain	bread
poivre	pepper
riz	rice
sel	salt
sucre	sugar
vinaigre	vinegar

Cooking Methods

à la broche	spit-roasted
à la vapeur	steamed
au feu de bois	cooked over a wood stove
au four	baked
farci	stuffed
fumé	smoked
gratiné	browned on top with cheese
grillé	grilled
pané	coated in breadcrumbs
rôti	roasted
sauté	sautéed

Glossary

See the Food section in the Language chapter for a list of culinary terms.

FLEMISH
apotheek – pharmacy

bakker/bakkerij – baker/bakery
beeldverhalen – comic strips
begijn, begijnen (pl) – Beguine; member of a Catholic order of women
begijnhof – community of *begijnen*
Belasting Toegevoegde Waarde (BTW) – value-added tax (VAT)
Belgische Spoorwegen – Belgian National Railways
benzine met lood – leaded petrol
benzine zonder lood – unleaded petrol
betalend parkeren – paid street parking
brouwerij – brewery
bruine kroeg – brown cafe (small pub)
Brusselaar – inhabitant of Brussels

centrum – centre
concertgebouw – concert hall
curiosa – bric-a-brac

dagmenu – fixed-price, multi-course meal of the day
dagschotel – dish of the day
dakterras – roof-top terrace

eethuis – eating house
eetkaffee – eating cafe
eetkroeg – eating cafe/pub
Europese Instellingen – EU Institutions

fiets – bicycle
fuif – list of upcoming parties

galerij – covered shopping centre/arcade
gastenkamer – B&B/guesthouse
gastenverbliff – guesthouse
gebak – cakes and pastries
gemeente – municipality
gezellig – cosy convivial atmosphere
godshuis – almshouse
gratis – free

half pond – 250g
hallen – covered market
herberg – old-style pub
hof – garden

ingang – entry

jenever – gin
jeugdherberg – youth hostel
jeugdmatinees – American and local films popular with young people

kaai – quay
kaartje – ticket
kamer – room
kant – lace
kasteel – castle
kerk – church
kroeg – cafe

loodvrije benzine – lead-free petrol

markt – market
menu – fixed-price meal with two or more courses
molen – windmill

nachtlijn – night bus

ondertitels – subtitles
oude stad – old town or city
o.v. (originele versie) – nondubbed film (shown in its original language)

paard – horse
PB postbus – post box
plein – square
pond – 500g
poort – gate in city wall

rommelmarkt – flea market
rond punt – roundabout

slijterij – shop selling strong alcohol
snoepwinkel – sweet shop
spijskaart – menu
stad – city

stadhuis – town or city hall
streek – regional

tentoonstellingen – art exhibitions
toneel – theatre
toren – tower
treinstation – train station
tuin – garden

uitgang – exit

vijver – pond
voorrang van rechts – priority-to-the-right traffic rule

wandelterrassen – promenades
wassalon – laundrette
wisselkantoor – foreign-exchange bureau

ziekenhuis – hospital

FRENCH
ARAU – Atelier de Recherche et d'Action Urbaine; Urban Research and Action Group
auberge de jeunesse – youth hostel

bandes dessinées – comic strips
béguinage – community of *béguines*
béguine – Beguine; member of a Catholic order of women
billet – ticket
boulangerie – bakery
BP (boîte postale) – post office box
brasserie – brewery; cafe/restaurant serving food all day
brocante – bric-a-brac
Bruxellois – inhabitant of Brussels and the name of the city's old dialect
bureau de change – foreign-exchange bureau

carte – menu
centre – centre
chambre – room
chambre d'hôte – B&B/guesthouse
château – castle
chocolatier – chocolate-maker
commune – municipality
confiserie – chocolate/sweet shop

dentelle – lace

église – church
entrée – entry
essence avec plomb – leaded petrol
essence sans plomb – lead-free petrol
estaminet – tavern
étang – pond

galerie – covered shopping centre/arcade
gare – train station
genièvre – gin
glacier – ice-cream seller
gratuit – free

halles – covered market
hôpital – hospital
hôtel de ville – town or city hall

Institutions Européennes – EU Institutions

jardin – garden

laverie – laundrette

marché – market
marché aux puces – flea market
menu/menu du jour – fixed-price, multi-course meal of the day
musée – museum

pâtisserie – cakes and pastries; shop selling them
pharmacie – pharmacy
place – square
plat du jour – dish of the day
porte – gate of city wall
pralines – filled chocolates
priorité à droite – priority-to-the-right traffic rule

rond point – roundabout

Société National des Chemins de Fer Belges – Belgian National Railways
sortie – exit
sous-titres – subtitles
stationnement payant – paid parking
STIB – Société des Transports Intercomnaux de Bruxelles; Brussels public transport company

taxe de séjour – visitors tax
Taxe sur la Valeur Ajoutée (TVA) – value-added tax (VAT)
théâtre – theatre
TIB – Tourist Information Brussels
tour – tower

ULB – Université Libre de Bruxelles

vélo – bicycle
vieille ville – old town or city
v.o. (version originale) – nondubbed film

GENERAL
ATM – automated teller machine
brown cafes – small, old-fashioned pubs, noted for their interiors
EU – European Union
gyros – stuffed pita bread
ISIC – International Student Identity Card
polder – land reclaimed from the sea
premetro – trams (found in Brussels and Antwerp) that go underground for part of their journey
sgraffito – type of ceramic decoration

Appendix – Alternative Place Names

COUNTRY & COAST

English	Flemish	French
Belgium	België	Belgique
Flanders	Vlaanderen	Flandres
Wallonia	Wallonië	La Wallonie
Ardennes	Ardennen	Ardennes
North Sea	Noordzee	Mer du Nord

CITIES, TOWNS & RIVERS

English	Flemish	French
Antwerp	Antwerpen	Anvers
Bruges	Brugge	Bruges
Brussels	Brussel	Bruxelles
Courtrai	Kortrijk	Courtrai
Ghent	Gent	Gand
Liège	Luik	Liège
Lier	Lier	Lierre
Louvain	Leuven	Louvain
Mechlin	Mechelen	Malines
Meuse	Maas	Meuse
Mons	Bergen	Mons
Namur	Namen	Namur
Ostend	Oostende	Ostende
Scheldt	Schelde	Escaut
Senne	Zenne	Senne
Veurne	Veurne	Furnes
Tournai	Doornik	Tournai
Ypres	Ieper	Ypres

COMMUNES OF BRUSSELS

Flemish	French
Oudergem	Auderghem
St-Agatha-Berchem	Berchem-Ste-Agathe
Vorst	Forest
Elsene	Ixelles
Laken	Laeken
Marollen	Marolles
St-Jans-Molenbeek	Molenbeek-St-Jean
St Gillis	St Gilles
St Joost	St Josse
Schaarbeek	Schaerbeek
Ukkel	Uccle
St-Lambrechts-Woluwe	Woluwé-St-Lambert
St-Pieters-Woluwe	Woluwé-St-Pierre
Watermaal-Bosvoorde	Watermael-Boitsfort

PLACES IN BRUSSELS

Flemish	French
Terkamerenbos	Bois de la Cambre
Zoniënwoud	Forêt de Soignes
Centraal Station	Gare Centrale
Zuidstation	Gare du Midi
Noordstation	Gare du Nord
Heizel	Heysel
Zavel	Sablon

LONELY PLANET

You already know that Lonely Planet produces more than this one guidebook, but you might not be aware of the other products we have on this region. Here is a selection of titles that you may want to check out as well:

Belgium & Luxembourg
ISBN 1 86450 245 2
US$17.99 • UK£11.99

French phrasebook
ISBN 0 86442 450 7
US$5.95 • UK£3.99

Western Europe
ISBN 1 86450 163 4
US$27.99 • UK£15.99

Europe phrasebook
ISBN 1 86450 224 X
US$8.99 • UK£4.99

Read This First: Europe
ISBN 1 86450 136 7
US$14.95 • UK£8.99

Europe on a shoestring
ISBN 1 86450 150 2
US$24.99 • UK£14.99

Brussels City Map
ISBN 1 86450 256 8
US$5.99 • UK£3.99

Available wherever books are sold

LONELY PLANET

ON THE ROAD

Travel Guides explore cities, regions and countries, and supply information on transport, restaurants and accommodation, covering all budgets. They come with reliable, easy-to-use maps, practical advice, cultural and historical facts and a rundown on attractions both on and off the beaten track. There are over 200 titles in this classic series, covering nearly every country in the world.

 Lonely Planet Upgrades extend the shelf life of existing travel guides by detailing any changes that may affect travel in a region since a book has been published. Upgrades can be downloaded for free from **www.lonelyplanet.com/upgrades**

For travellers with more time than money, **Shoestring** guides offer dependable, first-hand information with hundreds of detailed maps, plus insider tips for stretching money as far as possible. Covering entire continents in most cases, the six-volume shoestring guides are known around the world as 'backpackers bibles'.

For the discerning short-term visitor, **Condensed** guides highlight the best a destination has to offer in a full-colour, pocket-sized format designed for quick access. They include everything from top sights and walking tours to opinionated reviews of where to eat, stay, shop and have fun.

CitySync lets travellers use their Palm™ or Visor™ hand-held computers to guide them through a city with handy tips on transport, history, cultural life, major sights, and shopping and entertainment options. It can also quickly search and sort hundreds of reviews of hotels, restaurants and attractions, and pinpoint their location on scrollable street maps. CitySync can be downloaded from **www.citysync.com**

MAPS & ATLASES

Lonely Planet's **City Maps** feature downtown and metropolitan maps, as well as transit routes and walking tours. The maps come complete with an index of streets, a listing of sights and a plastic coat for extra durability.

Road Atlases are an essential navigation tool for serious travellers. Cross-referenced with the guidebooks, they also feature distance and climate charts and a complete site index.

LONELY PLANET

ESSENTIALS

Read This First books help new travellers to hit the road with confidence. These invaluable predeparture guides give step-by-step advice on preparing for a trip, budgeting, arranging a visa, planning an itinerary and staying safe while still getting off the beaten track.

Healthy Travel pocket guides offer a regional rundown on disease hot spots and practical advice on predeparture health measures, staying well on the road and what to do in emergencies. The guides come with a user-friendly design and helpful diagrams and tables.

Lonely Planet's **Phrasebooks** cover the essential words and phrases travellers need when they're strangers in a strange land. They come in a pocket-sized format with colour tabs for quick reference, extensive vocabulary lists, easy-to-follow pronunciation keys and two-way dictionaries.

Miffed by blurry photos of the Taj Mahal? Tired of the classic 'top of the head cut off' shot? **Travel Photography: A Guide to Taking Better Pictures** will help you turn ordinary holiday snaps into striking images and give you the know-how to capture every scene, from frenetic festivals to peaceful beach sunrises.

Lonely Planet's **Travel Journal** is a lightweight but sturdy travel diary for jotting down all those on-the-road observations and significant travel moments. It comes with a handy time-zone wheel, a world map and useful travel information.

Lonely Planet's eKno is an all-in-one communication service developed especially for travellers. It offers low-cost international calls and free email and voicemail so that you can keep in touch while on the road. Check it out on **www.ekno.lonelyplanet.com**

FOOD & RESTAURANT GUIDES

Lonely Planet's **Out to Eat** guides recommend the brightest and best places to eat and drink in top international cities. These gourmet companions are arranged by neighbourhood, packed with dependable maps, garnished with scene-setting photos and served with quirky features.

For people who live to eat, drink and travel, **World Food** guides explore the culinary culture of each country. Entertaining and adventurous, each guide is packed with detail on staples and specialities, regional cuisine and local markets, as well as sumptuous recipes, comprehensive culinary dictionaries and lavish photos good enough to eat.

OUTDOOR GUIDES

For those who believe the best way to see the world is on foot, Lonely Planet's **Walking Guides** detail everything from family strolls to difficult treks, with 'when to go and how to do it' advice supplemented by reliable maps and essential travel information.

Cycling Guides map a destination's best bike tours, long and short, in day-by-day detail. They contain all the information a cyclist needs, including advice on bike maintenance, places to eat and stay, innovative maps with detailed cues to the rides, and elevation charts.

The **Watching Wildlife** series is perfect for travellers who want authoritative information but don't want to tote a heavy field guide. Packed with advice on where, when and how to view a region's wildlife, each title features photos of over 300 species and contains engaging comments on the local flora and fauna.

With underwater colour photos throughout, **Pisces Books** explore the world's best diving and snorkelling areas. Each book contains listings of diving services and dive resorts, detailed information on depth, visibility and difficulty of dives, and a roundup of the marine life you're likely to see through your mask.

LONELY PLANET

OFF THE ROAD

Journeys, the travel literature series written by renowned travel authors, capture the spirit of a place or illuminate a culture with a journalist's attention to detail and a novelist's flair for words. These are tales to soak up while you're actually on the road or dip into as an at-home armchair indulgence.

The range of lavishly illustrated **Pictorial** books is just the ticket for both travellers and dreamers. Off-beat tales and vivid photographs bring the adventure of travel to your doorstep long before the journey begins and long after it is over.

Lonely Planet **Videos** encourage the same independent, tough-minded approach as the guidebooks. Currently airing throughout the world, this award-winning series features innovative footage and an original soundtrack.

Yes, we know, work is tough, so do a little bit of deskside dreaming with the spiral-bound Lonely Planet **Diary** or a Lonely Planet **Wall Calendar**, filled with great photos from around the world.

TRAVELLERS NETWORK

Lonely Planet Online. Lonely Planet's award-winning Web site has insider information on hundreds of destinations, from Amsterdam to Zimbabwe, complete with interactive maps and relevant links. The site also offers the latest travel news, recent reports from travellers on the road, guidebook upgrades, a travel links site, an online book-buying option and a lively traveller's bulletin board. It can be viewed at **www.lonelyplanet.com** or AOL keyword: lp.

Planet Talk is a quarterly print newsletter, full of gossip, advice, anecdotes and author articles. It provides an antidote to the being-at-home blues and lets you plan and dream for the next trip. Contact the nearest Lonely Planet office for your free copy.

Comet, the free Lonely Planet newsletter, comes via email once a month. It's loaded with travel news, advice, dispatches from authors, travel competitions and letters from readers. To subscribe, click on the Comet subscription link on the front page of the Web site.

Lonely Planet Guides by Region

L onely Planet is known worldwide for publishing practical, reliable and no-nonsense travel information in our guides and on our Web site. The Lonely Planet list covers just about every accessible part of the world. Currently there are 16 series: Travel guides, Shoestring guides, Condensed guides, Phrasebooks, Read This First, Healthy Travel, Walking guides, Cycling guides, Watching Wildlife guides, Pisces Diving & Snorkeling guides, City Maps, Road Atlases, Out to Eat, World Food, Journeys travel literature and Pictorials.

AFRICA Africa on a shoestring • Botswana • Cairo • Cairo City Map • Cape Town • Cape Town City Map • East Africa • Egypt • Egyptian Arabic phrasebook • Ethiopia, Eritrea & Djibouti • Ethiopian Amharic phrasebook • The Gambia & Senegal • Healthy Travel Africa • Kenya • Malawi • Morocco • Moroccan Arabic phrasebook • Mozambique • Namibia • Read This First: Africa • South Africa, Lesotho & Swaziland • Southern Africa • Southern Africa Road Atlas • Swahili phrasebook • Tanzania, Zanzibar & Pemba • Trekking in East Africa • Tunisia • Watching Wildlife East Africa • Watching Wildlife Southern Africa • West Africa • World Food Morocco • Zambia • Zimbabwe, Botswana & Namibia
Travel Literature: Mali Blues: Traveling to an African Beat • The Rainbird: A Central African Journey • Songs to an African Sunset: A Zimbabwean Story

AUSTRALIA & THE PACIFIC Aboriginal Australia & the Torres Strait Islands •Auckland • Australia • Australian phrasebook • Australia Road Atlas • Cycling Australia • Cycling New Zealand • Fiji • Fijian phrasebook • Healthy Travel Australia, NZ & the Pacific • Islands of Australia's Great Barrier Reef • Melbourne • Melbourne City Map • Micronesia • New Caledonia • New South Wales • New Zealand • Northern Territory • Outback Australia • Out to Eat – Melbourne • Out to Eat – Sydney • Papua New Guinea • Pidgin phrasebook • Queensland • Rarotonga & the Cook Islands • Samoa • Solomon Islands • South Australia • South Pacific • South Pacific phrasebook • Sydney • Sydney City Map • Sydney Condensed • Tahiti & French Polynesia • Tasmania • Tonga • Tramping in New Zealand • Vanuatu • Victoria • Walking in Australia • Watching Wildlife Australia • Western Australia
Travel Literature: Islands in the Clouds: Travels in the Highlands of New Guinea • Kiwi Tracks: A New Zealand Journey • Sean & David's Long Drive

CENTRAL AMERICA & THE CARIBBEAN Bahamas, Turks & Caicos • Baja California • Belize, Guatemala & Yucatán • Bermuda • Central America on a shoestring • Costa Rica • Costa Rica Spanish phrasebook • Cuba • Cycling Cuba • Dominican Republic & Haiti • Eastern Caribbean • Guatemala • Havana • Healthy Travel Central & South America • Jamaica • Mexico • Mexico City • Panama • Puerto Rico • Read This First: Central & South America • Virgin Islands • World Food Caribbean • World Food Mexico • Yucatán
Travel Literature: Green Dreams: Travels in Central America

EUROPE Amsterdam • Amsterdam City Map • Amsterdam Condensed • Andalucía • Athens • Austria • Baltic States phrasebook • Barcelona • Barcelona City Map • Belgium & Luxembourg • Berlin • Berlin City Map • Britain • British phrasebook • Brussels, Bruges & Antwerp • Brussels City Map • Budapest • Budapest City Map • Canary Islands • Catalunya & the Costa Brava • Central Europe • Central Europe phrasebook • Copenhagen • Corfu & the Ionians • Corsica • Crete • Crete Condensed • Croatia • Cycling Britain • Cycling France • Cyprus • Czech & Slovak Republics • Czech phrasebook • Denmark • Dublin • Dublin City Map • Dublin Condensed • Eastern Europe • Eastern Europe phrasebook • Edinburgh • Edinburgh City Map • England • Estonia, Latvia & Lithuania • Europe on a shoestring • Europe phrasebook • Finland • Florence • Florence City Map • France • Frankfurt City Map • Frankfurt Condensed • French phrasebook • Georgia, Armenia & Azerbaijan • Germany • German phrasebook • Greece • Greek Islands • Greek phrasebook • Hungary • Iceland, Greenland & the Faroe Islands • Ireland • Italian phrasebook • Italy • Kraków • Lisbon • The Loire • London • London City Map • London Condensed • Madrid • Madrid City Map • Malta • Mediterranean Europe • Milan, Turin & Genoa • Moscow • Munich • Netherlands • Normandy • Norway • Out to Eat – London • Out to Eat – Paris • Paris • Paris City Map • Paris Condensed • Poland • Polish phrasebook • Portugal • Portuguese phrasebook • Prague • Prague City Map • Provence & the Côte d'Azur • Read This First: Europe • Rhodes & the Dodecanese • Romania & Moldova • Rome • Rome City Map • Rome Condensed • Russia, Ukraine & Belarus • Russian phrasebook • Scandinavian & Baltic Europe • Scandinavian phrasebook • Scotland • Sicily • Slovenia • South-West France • Spain • Spanish phrasebook • Stockholm • St Petersburg • St Petersburg City Map • Sweden • Switzerland • Tuscany • Ukrainian phrasebook • Venice • Vienna • Wales • Walking in Britain • Walking in France • Walking in Ireland • Walking in Italy • Walking in Scotland • Walking in Spain • Walking in Switzerland • Western Europe • World Food France • World Food Greece • World Food Ireland • World Food Italy • World Food Spain **Travel Literature:** After Yugoslavia • Love and War in the Apennines • The Olive Grove: Travels in Greece • On the Shores of the Mediterranean • Round Ireland in Low Gear • A Small Place in Italy

Lonely Planet Mail Order

Lonely Planet products are distributed worldwide. They are also available by mail order from Lonely Planet, so if you have difficulty finding a title please write to us. North and South American residents should write to 150 Linden St, Oakland, CA 94607, USA; European and African residents should write to 10a Spring Place, London NW5 3BH, UK; and residents of other countries to Locked Bag 1, Footscray, Victoria 3011, Australia.

INDIAN SUBCONTINENT & THE INDIAN OCEAN Bangladesh • Bengali phrasebook • Bhutan • Delhi • Goa • Healthy Travel Asia & India • Hindi & Urdu phrasebook • India • India & Bangladesh City Map • Indian Himalaya • Karakoram Highway • Kathmandu City Map • Kerala • Madagascar • Maldives • Mauritius, Réunion & Seychelles • Mumbai (Bombay) • Nepal • Nepali phrasebook • North India • Pakistan • Rajasthan • Read This First: Asia & India • South India • Sri Lanka • Sri Lanka phrasebook • Tibet • Tibetan phrasebook • Trekking in the Indian Himalaya • Trekking in the Karakoram & Hindukush • Trekking in the Nepal Himalaya • World Food India **Travel Literature:** The Age of Kali: Indian Travels and Encounters • Hello Goodnight: A Life of Goa • In Rajasthan • Maverick in Madagascar • A Season in Heaven: True Tales from the Road to Kathmandu • Shopping for Buddhas • A Short Walk in the Hindu Kush • Slowly Down the Ganges

MIDDLE EAST & CENTRAL ASIA Bahrain, Kuwait & Qatar • Central Asia • Central Asia phrasebook • Dubai • Farsi (Persian) phrasebook • Hebrew phrasebook • Iran • Israel & the Palestinian Territories • Istanbul • Istanbul City Map • Istanbul to Cairo • Istanbul to Kathmandu • Jerusalem • Jerusalem City Map • Jordan • Lebanon • Middle East • Oman & the United Arab Emirates • Syria • Turkey • Turkish phrasebook • World Food Turkey • Yemen **Travel Literature:** Black on Black: Iran Revisited • Breaking Ranks: Turbulent Travels in the Promised Land • The Gates of Damascus • Kingdom of the Film Stars: Journey into Jordan

NORTH AMERICA Alaska • Boston • Boston City Map • Boston Condensed • British Columbia • California & Nevada • California Condensed • Canada • Chicago • Chicago City Map • Chicago Condensed • Florida • Georgia & the Carolinas • Great Lakes • Hawaii • Hiking in Alaska • Hiking in the USA • Honolulu & Oahu City Map • Las Vegas • Los Angeles • Los Angeles City Map • Louisiana & the Deep South • Miami • Miami City Map • Montreal • New England • New Orleans • New Orleans City Map • New York City • New York City City Map • New York City Condensed • New York, New Jersey & Pennsylvania • Oahu • Out to Eat – San Francisco • Pacific Northwest • Rocky Mountains • San Diego & Tijuana • San Francisco • San Francisco City Map • Seattle • Seattle City Map • Southwest • Texas • Toronto • USA • USA phrasebook • Vancouver • Vancouver City Map • Virginia & the Capital Region • Washington, DC • Washington, DC City Map • World Food New Orleans **Travel Literature**: Caught Inside: A Surfer's Year on the California Coast • Drive Thru America

NORTH-EAST ASIA Beijing • Beijing City Map • Cantonese phrasebook • China • Hiking in Japan • Hong Kong & Macau • Hong Kong City Map • Hong Kong Condensed • Japan • Japanese phrasebook • Korea • Korean phrasebook • Kyoto • Mandarin phrasebook • Mongolia • Mongolian phrasebook • Seoul • Shanghai • South-West China • Taiwan • Tokyo • Tokyo Condensed • World Food Hong Kong • World Food Japan **Travel Literature:** In Xanadu: A Quest • Lost Japan

SOUTH AMERICA Argentina, Uruguay & Paraguay • Bolivia • Brazil • Brazilian phrasebook • Buenos Aires • Buenos Aires City Map • Chile & Easter Island • Colombia • Ecuador & the Galapagos Islands • Healthy Travel Central & South America • Latin American Spanish phrasebook • Peru • Quechua phrasebook • Read This First: Central & South America • Rio de Janeiro • Rio de Janeiro City Map • Santiago de Chile • South America on a shoestring • Trekking in the Patagonian Andes • Venezuela **Travel Literature**: Full Circle: A South American Journey

SOUTH-EAST ASIA Bali & Lombok • Bangkok • Bangkok City Map • Burmese phrasebook • Cambodia • Cycling Vietnam, Laos & Cambodia • East Timor phrasebook • Hanoi • Healthy Travel Asia & India • Hill Tribes phrasebook • Ho Chi Minh City (Saigon) • Indonesia • Indonesian phrasebook • Indonesia's Eastern Islands • Java • Lao phrasebook • Laos • Malay phrasebook • Malaysia, Singapore & Brunei • Myanmar (Burma) • Philippines • Pilipino (Tagalog) phrasebook • Read This First: Asia & India • Singapore • Singapore City Map • South-East Asia on a shoestring • South-East Asia phrasebook • Thailand • Thailand's Islands & Beaches • Thailand, Vietnam, Laos & Cambodia Road Atlas • Thai phrasebook • Vietnam • Vietnamese phrasebook • World Food Indonesia • World Food Thailand • World Food Vietnam

ALSO AVAILABLE: Antarctica • The Arctic • The Blue Man: Tales of Travel, Love and Coffee • Brief Encounters: Stories of Love, Sex & Travel • Buddhist Stupas in Asia: The Shape of Perfection • Chasing Rickshaws • The Last Grain Race • Lonely Planet ... On the Edge: Adventurous Escapades from Around the World • Lonely Planet Unpacked • Lonely Planet Unpacked Again • Not the Only Planet: Science Fiction Travel Stories • Ports of Call: A Journey by Sea • Sacred India • Travel Photography: A Guide to Taking Better Pictures • Travel with Children • Tuvalu: Portrait of an Island Nation

Index

Abbreviations

Ant – Antwerp

Brg – Bruges

Brs – Brussels

Text

Bold indicates maps.

Places to Stay

Places to Eat

Boxed Text

MAP 2 BRUSSELS METRO

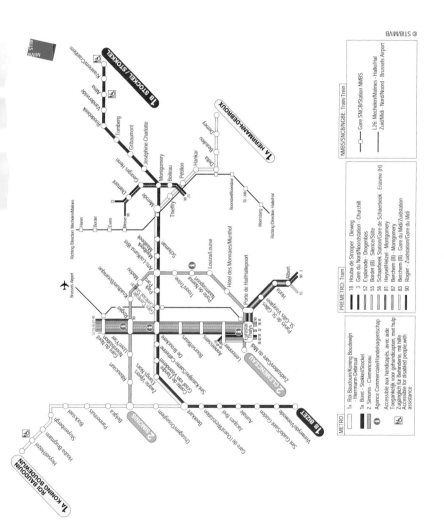

© STIB/MIVB

NMBS/SNCB/NGBE: Train/Trein

━┿━ Gare SNCB/Station NMBS

──── L76: Mechelen/Malines - Halle/Hal
Zuid/Midi - Nord/Noord - Brussels Airport

PREMETRO: Tram

━━ 18   Houba-de Strooper - Dieweg
━━ 3   Gare du Nord/Noordstation - Churchill
━━ 52   Esplanade - Drogenbos
━━ 55   Bordet (B) - Silence/Stilte
━━ 56   Schaerbeek Station/Gare de Schaerbeek - Erasme (H)
━━ 81   Heysel/Heizel - Montgomery
━━ 82   Berchem (B) - Montgomery
━━ 83   Berchem (B) - Gare du Midi/Zuidstation
━━ 90   Roger - Zuidstation/Gare du Midi

METRO:

━━ 1a   Roi Baudouin/Koning Boudewijn - Hermann-Debroux
━━ 1b   Bizet - Stokkel/Stockel
━━ 2   Simonis - Clemenceau

①   Agence Commerciale/Handelsagentschap

⬛   Accessible aux handicapés, avec aide
Toegankelijk voor gehandicapten, met hulp
Zugänglich für Behinderte, mit Hilfe
Accessible for disabled people, with assistance

MAP 3 GREATER BRUSSELS

PLACES TO STAY
2 Sheraton Brussels Airport

PLACES TO EAT
22 La Petite Planète
23 Le Doux Wazoo

OTHER
1 Zaventem (Brussels National) Airport
3 NATO Headquarters

4 Musée Magritte
5 Basilique Nationale de Sacré-Coeur
6 Tours et Taxi
7 Baele-Schmitz
8 Alliance Française
9 Musée du Béguinage
10 Vandenstock Stadium
11 Maison d'Erasme
12 Canadian Embassy

13 German Embassy
14 Mellaerts Ponds
15 Centre Sportif de la Woluwé-St-Pierre
16 British & Commonwealth Women's Club
17 Rouge Cloître
18 Jean Massart Experimental Garden
19 Netherlands Embassy
20 American Express

OTHER Contd.
21 Vrije Universiteit Brussel
24 ULB Library
25 Université Libre de Bruxelles
26 Institut Géographique National; Abbaye de la Cambre
27 Musée Constantin Meunier
28 The Crow
29 Musée David et Alice Van Buuren
30 La Selle à Deux Roues
31 Villa Bloemenwerf
32 Forest National; Ice-Skating Rink
33 Yeti Ski
34 Royal Amicale Golf Club

MAP 3 GREATER BRUSSELS

To Mechelen (14km)
& Antwerp (40km)

Ring

❌ 1

2

Zaventem

R0

Chaussée de Vilvorde

Avenue de Vilvorde

Canal de Willebroek

Chaussée de Haecht

Ave Léopold III

Blvd Lambermont

3

Evere

Schaerbeek

7 Leuvensesteenweg

To Leuven
(15km)

A3 E40

Kraainem

Chaussée de Louvain

Ave de
l'Émeraude

MAP 7

8

Blvd Auguste Reyers

Roodebeek Vandervelde

Alma Kraainem

Ave Émile Vandervelde

-belbeek

Schuman

Tomberg Woluwé-
St-Lambert

Gribaumont

12
Montgomery
Place
Mérode Josephine-Charlotte

Stockel

Wezembeek-
Oppem

Ave de 13
Montgomery Rue du Duc

Tervuren

Etterbeek

Parc
de
Woluwé

Woluwé-
St-Pierre

Rue au Bois

Ave Salomé

Ave Orban

15

Ave de la Couronne

Jacques

Blvd de Triomphe

Général
Blvd de la Plaine

21

Chaussée de la Plaine

14

Blvd du Souverain

Chaussée de Wavre

R0

To Tervurenlaan
(3km)

Rue au Bois

16

Tervurenlaan

Ave Adolphe Buyl

22▼

23▼

Chaussée de Boondael

25

24

Chaussée de Tervuren

19 18
Herrmann-
Debroux

17
Ave Herrmann-Debroux

Forêt
de Soignes

Bois de
Cambre

Ave F. Roosevelt

20

Blvd du Souverain

Auderghem

A4

E411

Ave du Vivier d'Oie

Chaussée de la Hulpe

d'Oie

To
Waterloo
(8km)

Watermael-
Boitsfort

Forêt
de Soignes

Forêt
de Soignes

R0

To Groenendaal
Arboretum (3km)
& Waterloo (8km)

To Louvain-la-Neuve (15km)
& Namur (50km)

UP

0   1   2km

0   0.5   1mi

MAP 4 CENTRAL BRUSSELS

PLACES TO STAY
3 Hôtel Albert
12 Art Hotel Siru
15 Sleep Well Hostel
17 Centre Vincent Van Gogh Hostel
19 Jacques Brel Hostel; Les Auberges de Jeunesse
23 Hôtel Sabina
35 Hôtel Marie José
48 Bruegel
50 Hôtel à la Grande Cloche
65 Génération Europe Hostel

PLACES TO EAT
5 Metin
46 Toute & n'Importe Quoi
51 Comme Chez Soi
54 L'Étoile d'Or
59 Den Teepot
60 In 't Spinnekopke

PUBS & BARS
6 De Ultieme Hallucinatie
9 Magasin 4
25 Het Biercircus
49 La Fleur en Papier Doré

OTHER
1 Gare du Nord
2 Halles de Schaerbeek
4 Église Ste Marie
7 Eurolines Bus Station/ Main Office
8 Kaaitheater-Luna
10 Randy Wash-matic
11 Koninklijke Vlaamse Schouwburg
13 Théâtre National
14 City 2 Shopping Centre; FNAC; Post Office Branch; GB Supermarket
16 Le Botanique; Centre Culturel de la Communauté Française
18 Amazone
20 Musée de Jouet
21 Centre Belge de la Bande Dessinée; Grand Magasin Waucquez
22 Colonne du Congrès
24 Nederlands Taalinstituut
26 Cirque Royal

OTHER Contd.
27 Hankar Shop (Florist)
28 Cathédrale des Sts Michel & Gudule
29 Palais de la Nation
30 French Embassy
31 Musée Charlier
32 Touring Club de Belgique
33 Australian Embassy
34 USA Embassy
36 Musée du Cinéma
37 Palais des Beaux-Arts; Art Shop
38 Peuples et Continents
39 Bibliotheque Royale Albert I
40 Musée des Instruments de Musique; Old England
41 Godefroid de Bouillon Statue
42 Musée de la Dynastie
43 Palais Royal
44 Église St Jacques sur Coudenberg
45 Musées Royaux des Beaux-Arts
47 Salon Lavoir de la Chapelle
52 Palais du Midi; Fitness La Salle; Cercle Royal de Billard
53 Musée Bruxellois de la Gueuze
55 Pêle Mêle
56 Mural Isabelle
57 Mural La Marque Jaune
58 Mural Lucky Luke
61 Mural Cori Le Moussaillon
62 Mural The Dreams of Nic
63 Patrick Pitschon
64 Flanders Gate Squash Club
66 De Bottelarij
67 Fool Moon

MAP 5

MAP 6

Ribaucourt
Rue Houteau
Rue de l'Ourthe
Blvd Léopold II
Av. du Port
Quai des Matelots
Quai des Péniches
Rue Fernand
Rue des Commerçants
Rue de Ribaucourt
Rue du Jardinier
Rue de Molenbeek
Rue Demaerteloère
Rue de l'Adolphe Lavalée
Place Sainctelette
Square Sainctelette
Rue Vanderstichelen
Rue Dupré
Rue Descampheieere
Rue de Comte de Flandre
Rue du Choeur
Rue des Courtois
Rue des Ateliers
Blvd de P. Dixmude
Q. du Commerce
Rue Piers
Rue de la Place de l'Avenir
Rue de la Foret d'Houthulst
Q. aux Barques
Rue St-Joseph
Rue Bonnevie
Comte de Flandre
Rue Ste-Marie
Rue de Witte de Haelen
Chaussée de Merchtem
Rue de la Perle
Mais et Communale Place
Rue Vandermaelen
Rue Locquenghien
Chaussée du Prado
Porte de Flandre
Rue de Flandre
Rue Antoine Dansaert
Ste Catherine
Chaussée de Gand
Rue de l'Éléphant
Rue Rempart
Rue Fin
Rue du Brontraut
Quai du Hainaut
Blvd Barthélemy
Houblon
Rue Delaunoy
Rue St-Martin
Rue Evariste Pierron
Chaussée de Ninove
Porte et Place de Ninove
Rue des Fabriques
Rue Notre-Dame de Sommer
Rue du Serment
Rue du Boulet
Rue Van Artevelde
St Géry
Quai de Mariemont
Square A Smets
Place du Jardin aux Fleurs
R. de l'Abattoir
Rue Anneessens
Rue Cuerens
Rue 't Kint
Anneessens
Place Anneessens
Rue Van Artevelde
Rue d'Anderlecht
Rue de Cureghem
Rue de la Senne
Rue Camusel
Rue de la Buanderie
Rue des Tanneurs
Rue Pierre
Rue Plattesteen
Rue du Vautour
Rue Terre-Neuve
Verdure
Place Rouppe
Rue Biognez
Blvd de l'Abattoir
Blvd du Midi
Blvd Poincaré
Rue des Foulons
Rue d'Artois
Rue Roger Van der Weyden
Rue de la Caserne
Place Rouppe
Rue Gheude
53

0   125   250m
0   125   250yd

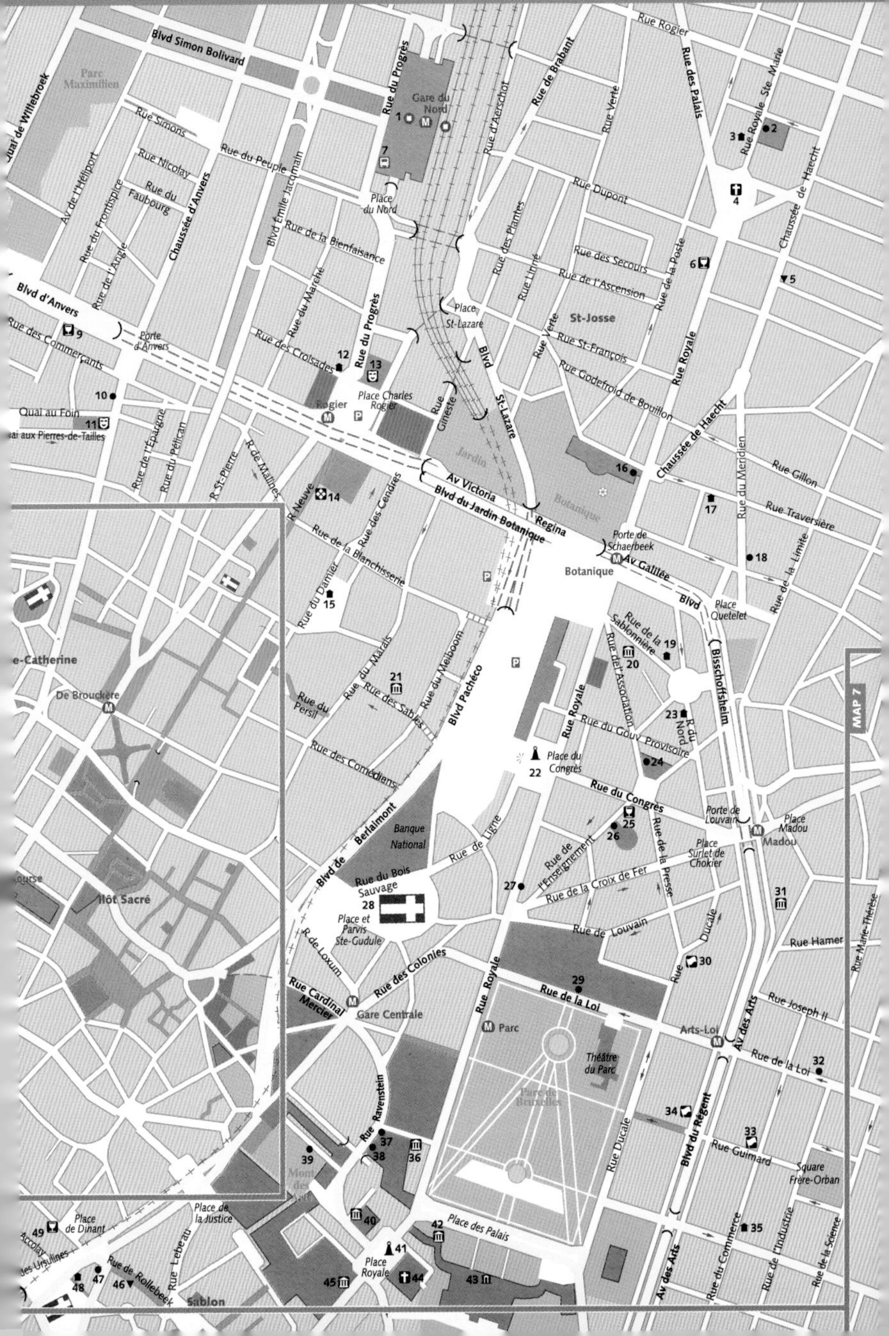

MAP 4 CENTRAL BRUSSELS

Blvd Simon Bolivard

Parc Maximilien

Quai de Willebroek

Rue Simons

Rue du Peuple

Rue Nicolay

Chaussée d'Anvers

Rue du Faubourg

Rue Émile Jacqmain

Rue du Progrès

Gare du Nord

Rue d'Aerschot

Rue de Brabant

Rue Rogier

Rue des Palais

Rue Royale Ste-Marie

1 M

7

Place du Nord

Rue Dupont

Rue Verte

3

2

4

Av du Port

Av de l'Héliport

Rue des Commerçants

Blvd d'Anvers

Porte d'Anvers

Rue du Marais

Rue de la Bienfaisance

Rue des Croisades

Rue des Plantes

Rue Limite

Rue des Secours

Rue de l'Ascension

Chaussée de Haecht

Rue de la Poste

St-Josse

6

5

9

10

Quai au Foin

11

Rue de l'Épargne

Rue du Pélican

R.-St-Pierre

Rue du Progrès

12

13

Place Charles Rogier

Rogier

P

Rue St-François

Rue Godefroid de Bouillon

Rue St-Lazare

Blvd St-Lazare

Place St-Lazare

Rue Verte

Rue Royale

16

Chaussée de Haecht

Rue Gillon

Rue du Méridien

17

Rue Traversière

e-Catherine

De Brouckère

M

14

Rue des Cendres

Rue de la Blanchisserie

Rue du Damier

15

Rue du Marais

Av Victoria

Blvd du Jardin Botanique

Regina

Jardin

Botanique

Porte de Schaerbeek

M Av Galilée

Botanique

Blvd

Place Quetelet

18

Rue de la Limite

MAP 7

Rue du Persil

21

Rue des Sables

Blvd Pacheco

Rue du Marais

Rue des Comédiens

Rue de la Sablonnière

19

20

Rue de l'Association

Rue Royale

Rue du Gouv. Provisoire

23

R. du Nord

Bischoffsheim

24

Bourse

Îlot Sacré

Berlaimont

Blvd de

Rue du Bois Sauvage

28

Place et Parvis Ste-Gudule

R. de Loxum

Rue des Colonies

Rue Cardinal Mercier

Gare Centrale

Place du Congrès

22

Rue du Congrès

25

26

Rue de l'Enseignement

27

Rue de la Croix de Fer

Rue de la Ligne

Rue de la Presse

Porte de Louvain

Place Madou

Madou

Place Surlet de Chokier

31

Rue Ducale

Rue de Louvain

30

Rue Hamer

Rue Marie-Thérèse

29

Rue de la Loi

M Parc

Parc

M Parc

Théâtre du Parc

Parc de Bruxelles

Arts-Loi

M

Av des Arts

Rue de la Loi

32

34

Blvd du Régent

33

Rue Guimard

Square Frère-Orban

Ravenstein

37

38

36

39

Mont des

40

Place de Dinant

Place de la Justice

42

41

Place des Palais

43

49

Place de Dinant

Rue Lebeau

48

47

46

45

Place Royale

44

Sablon

Rue de Rollebeek

Rue des Minimes

Accolay

Rue aux Laines

Rue Ducale

35

Rue de Commerce

Rue de l'Industrie

Av des Arts

Rue de la Science

MAP 5 LOWER TOWN

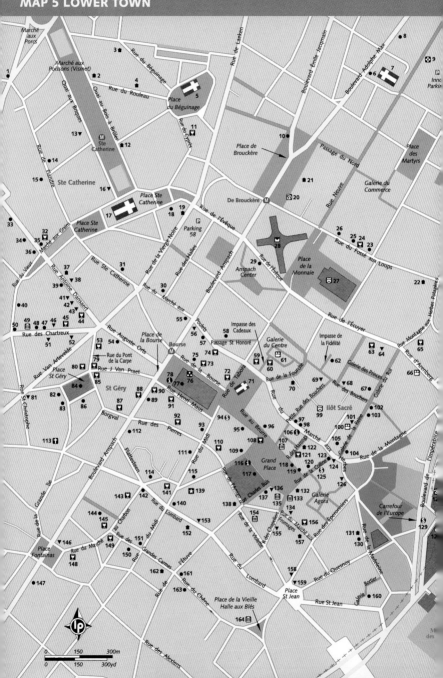

Marché aux Porcs

Marché aux Poissons (Vismet)

8

9 ☒

Inno Parki

Boulevard Émile Jacqmain

Boulevard Adolphe Max

3 ♦ Rue du Béguinage

6 ● 7 ✚

2 ●

Rue du Rouleau

4 ●

Place du Béguinage

5 ✚

Quai aux Briques

Quai au Bois à Brûler

Rue de Laeken

13▼

M Ste Catherine

Rue du Cyprès

11 ✚

Place de Brouckère

Passage du Nord

Place des Martyrs

12 ●

●14

15 ●

Ste Catherine

Rue de Flandre

16 ▼

Place Ste Catherine

10 ●

Rue Neuve

Galerie du Commerce

Rue de l'Évêque

17 ✚

18 ● 19 ●

De Brouckère M

21 ▶

20 ▣

33 ●

Place Ste Catherine

Rue Antoine Dansaert

Rue de la Vierge Noire

Rue de Laeken

Parking 58 P

26 ●

25 ● 24 ☒

23 ☒

Rue du Fossé aux Loups

34 ●

32 ●

35 ●

Marché aux Grain

Rue Ste Catherine

29 ●

Anspach Center

Place de la Monnaie

22 ☒

36 ●

31 ●

Rue de l'Écuyer

37 ▼

38 ▼

Rue du Marché aux

Boulevard Anspach

Rue de Hêve

28

27 ▣

39 ●

Rue du Vieux

41▼

42▼

43▼

44

Rue du Marché aux Poulets

55 ●

56 ●

58 ●

Impasse des Cadeaux

Galerie du Centre

Impasse de la Fidélité

Rue Montagne aux Herbes Potagères

49 ● 48 ● 47 ● 45 ●

46 ●

40 ●

50 ●

Rue des Chartreux

51 ●

52 ●

53 ● 54 ●

Place de la Bourse

57 ●

Passage St Honoré

59 ●

60 ●

61 ●

62 ●

63 ☒ 64 ☒

65 ●

Galerie des Princes

Rue d'Arenberg

66 ●

Rue Auguste Orts

Bourse M

74 ▼

75 ●

73 ▼

72 ●

Rue de Tabora

71 ✚

69 ▼

70 ●

Rue des Bouchers

67 ●

Galerie du Roi

Rue Van Artevelde

79 ●

80 ▼

Rue du Pont de la Carpe

Rue J Van Praet

85 ●

78 ▼

77 ●

76 ●

Rue de la Bourse

Rue de la Fourche

Ilôt Sacré

101 ●

102 ●

Place St Géry

84 ●

St Géry

88 ▼

90 ●

Rue Henri Maus

99 ●

100 ☐

103 ●

81 ▼

82 ●

83 ●

86 ●

87 ●

89 ●

91 ●

92 ●

94 ●

95 ●

96 ●

97 ●

98 ●

106 ●

105 ●

104 ●

Rue de la Montagne

Borgval

Rue des Pierres

93 ●

108 ●

109 ●

Rue au Beurre

Marché aux Herbes

122 ●

121 ●

123 ●

120 ●

124 ●

113 🏛

112 ●

111 ●

110 ●

115 ●

116 ●

117 ●

Grand Place

118 ●

119 ●

125 ●

126 ●

114 ●

141 ●

139 ☒

140 ●

143 ☒

142 ▼

Rue du Lombard

153 ▼

152 ●

154 🏛

155 ●

Rue Chapeliers Fromages

156 ▼

Rue des Éperonniers

132 ●

133 ●

Galerie Agora

134 ●

135 ●

136 ●

137 ●

138 ▲

Rue Charles Buls

Rue au Beurre

157 ●

Carrefour de l'Europe

129 ●

131 ▲

130 ●

144 ▼

145 ☒

146 ▼

Rue du Marché

149 ●

150 ●

151 ●

Rue des Grandes Carmes

162 ▲

161 ●

163 ●

Rue du Chêne

Place de la Vieille Halle aux Blés

164 🏛

158 ▼

159 ▼

Place St Jean

160 ●

Rue St Jean

147 ●

148 ●

Place Fontainas

Rue de l'Étuve

Rue du Lombard

Rue du Quesnoy

Rue de la Madeleine

Boulevard de l'Impératrice

LP

0   150   300m
0   150   300yd

Rue des Alexiens

MAP 5

PLACES TO STAY
2 Citadines Apart'Hotel
3 Hôtel Noga
4 Résidence Les Écrins
12 Hôtel Welcome
19 Novotel Tour Noire
21 Hôtel Métropole; Café Métropole
22 Radisson SAS;John Harris Fitness Centre
37 Pacific Sleeping Hôtel
70 Hôtel Arlequin; Actor's StudioCinema; Marcus Mingus Jazz Spot
122 Hôtel Sema
131 Hôtel Le Dixseptième
132 Hôtel St Michel
138 Hôtel Amigo
152 Hôtel La Légende
157 Hôtel Mozart
162 Hôtel La Vieille Lanterne

PLACES TO EAT
13 Jacques
16 Le Vistro
38 La Papaye Verte
41 Bonsoir Clara
42 Kasbash
43 Le Pain Quotidien/Het-Dagelijks Brood
46 Fin de Siècle
51 Arteaspoon
52 AM Sweet
56 Crock'In
64 Centre Hémisphère
68 Chez Léon
69 Aux Armes de Bruxelles
81 Mamesse
101 Taverne du Passage
124 Panos
126 Quick
134 Pita Places
136 La Maison du Cygne
146 Rugantino
153 Planète Chocolat
155 Brasserie de la Roue d'Or
158 Al Barmaki
159 Waka Moon

PUBS, BARS & CLUBS
11 Le Wings
24 The Gate
32 Café De Markten
44 L'Archiduc
45 Le Greenwich
53 Bizon
59 À l'Imaige de Nostre Dame
60 Au Bon Vieux Temps
63 Flanagans
65 À la Mort Subite
72 À la Bécasse
73 Le Cirio
74 Celtica

79 Roi des Belges
80 Mappa Mundo
85 Zebra
87 La Salsa
88 Wilde
90 El Metteko
91 Falstaff
92 L'Incognito
108 Le Roy d'Espagne
110 The Music Village
121 Cerceuil
141 Le Belgica
143 Rock Classic Bar
145 Tels Quels
148 Sonik
149 Au Soleil
156 Espace de Nuit

OTHER
1 Mural Dommel
5 Église St Jean Baptiste au Béguinage
6 ARAU
7 Église Notre Dame du Finistère
8 Waterstones
9 Inno Department Store; Lunch Garden
10 Eurolines Office
14 Ipsomat
15 Maison la Bellone
17 Église Ste Catherine
18 Tour Noire
20 easyEverything
23 Sterling Books
25 Anticyclone des Açores
26 AirStop/TaxiStop
27 Théâtre Royal de la Monnaie/De Munt
28 Main Post Office; Centre Monnaie;Belgacom Téléboutique
29 STIB/MIVB Office
30 GB Supermarket
31 Infor Jeunes
33 Nicolas Woit
34 Stijl
35 Art Deco Building
36 Lena Lena
39 Olivier Strelli
40 Stained-Glass Windows
47 Belle Fitness
48 Mural L'Archange
49 Album
50 Zinneke
54 Beursschouwburg
55 Ad Delhaize Supermarket
57 Multipharma
58 Caroline Music
61 Aventure Cinema
62 Jeanneke Pis
66 Nova Cinema
67 Kaat Tilley

71 Église St Nicolas
75 SOS Company
76 Bruxelaa 1238
77 Bourse
78 STIB kiosk
82 Mural Nero
83 Courtyard Entrance
84 Halles St Géry
86 Wash Club
89 Brüsel
93 Darakan
94 Basle
95 Dandoy
96 Galler
97 Euroline
98 De Biertempel
99 Théâtre Royal de Toone; Toone Bar
100 Arenberg Galeries
102 Delvaux
103 Neuhaus
104 Galeries St Hubert
105 Manufacture Belge de Dentelles
106 Flemish & Walloon Tourist Authorities
107 Musée de la Villede Bruxelles
109 Thomas Cook
111 usit Connections
112 Ancienne Belgique
113 Église Notre Dame des Riches Claires
114 Mural Broussaille
115 Mural Le Passage
116 Tourist Information Brussels (TIB)
117 Hôtel de Ville
118 F. Rubbrecht
119 Godiva
120 La Boutique de Tintin
123 De Boeck
125 Fortis Banque
127 Belgacom Téléboutique
128 Gare Centrale
129 Citibank
130 Posada Art Books
133 Musée du Cacao et du Chocolat
135 Musée de la Brasserie
137 Art Nouveau Plaque
139 Police Station
140 Elvis Pompilio
142 Mural Victor Sackville
144 Mural Ric Hochet
147 Hertz
150 De Slegte
151 Évasions
154 Musée du Costume et de la Dentelle
160 Artemys
161 Manneken Pis
163 Mural Olivier Rameau
164 Fondation Jacques Brel

MAP 6 MAROLLES, SABLON & IXELLES

PLACES TO STAY
1 Hôtel Ustel
11 Hôtel Stanhope
22 Hôtel Galia
37 B&B Guilmin
38 Résidence Parnasse
65 Hôtel Rembrandt
67 Conrad International
70 Hôtel Manos Stéphanie
71 Hôtel De Boeck's

PLACES TO EAT
2 La Grande Écluse
7 Wittamer
8 La Pirogue; Le Cercle
10 Sotto Ripa
14 Le Pain Quotidien/
   Het Dagelijks Brood
16 Le Perroquet
20 Bazaar Restaurant & Club
21 Brasserie La Clef d'Or
25 Le Cheval de Troie
30 Eetcafé Het Warm Water
32 Ici Même
34 La Canardière; Spaghetteria
35 Hector Chicken
40 L'Ultime Atome
41 Table d'Hôte Bio
42 Yamato
49 Au Stekerlapatte
54 Il Rinascimento
55 La Crêmerie de
   la Vache
63 L'Amour Fou
72 L'Amadeus
73 Trave Negra
79 La Tsampa
81 Le Framboisier
83 Touch & Go
84 Notos
86 L'Atelier de la Truffe Noire
90 Rick's Restaurant/Bar
95 La Quincaillerie
96 Le Fils de Jules

PUBS, BARS & CLUBS
19 Brasserie Ploegmans
51 Fuse; La Démence
53 La Porteuse d'Eau
61 Sounds Jazz Club
98 The Bank
101 Moeder Lambic

OTHER
3 Église Notre Dame
   de la Chapelle
4 Lavoir Friza
5 Pierre Marcolini
6 Sablon Shopping Gallery
9 New Zealand Embassy
12 Monument to Counts
   Egmont & Hoorn
13 Église Notre Dame
   du Sablon
15 Conservatoire Royal
   de Musique
17 Église des Minimes
18 Musée Breugel
23 Mural Bollie & Billie
24 Mural The Cat
26 Post Office
27 Gare du Midi; GB Express
28 Eurolines Office
29 Fleamarket
31 Palais de Justice
33 Galeriés de la Toison d'Or
36 CyberTheatre
39 Beer Mania
43 Galerie d'Ixelles
44 Eurospeak
45 Bouvy

46 Inno Department Store;
   Lunch Garden
47 BBL Bank
48 Service for Foreign
   Students
50 Hôpital St Pierre
52 Porte de Hal
56 Godiva
57 La Librairie de Rome
58 Galeriés Louise
59 Michèle Simon
60 Boutique 114
62 Musée Communal d'Ixelles
64 Styx Cinema
66 Olivier Strelli
68 Regus
69 Post Office
74 Piscine Victor Boin
75 Maison Hankar
76 Maison Camberlaini
77 Hôtel Tassel
78 Les Enfants d'Édouard
80 Art Nouveau House
82 Nopri Supermarket
85 Hôtel Solvay
87 Art Nouveau House
88 Art Nouveau Houses
89 Art Nouveau Houses
91 Hôtel Hallet
92 Budget
93 Bed & Brussels
94 Avis
97 Église des Augustins
99 Art Nouveau House
100 Musée Horta
102 Clinique Van
   Neck
103 Hôtel Hannon

MAP 6 MAROLLES, SABLON & IXELLES

MAP 4

MAP 2

Rue Montoyer

Place de la Chapelle

3

4

7

8

Place du Grand Sablon

5

6

Sablon

13

Rue Bréderode

Place du Trône

Av des Arts

Rue du Commerce

Square de Meeûs

Rue Marie de Bourgogne

9

Rue du Luxembourg

10

Rue Blaes

Rue Haute

Rue du Temple

Rue des Minimes

Rue Ernest Allard

Rue de la Régence

16

14

12

15

Place du Petit Sablon

Rue de Namur

Upper Town

Place du Champ de Mars

Rue du Trône

11

Place du Luxembourg

17

18

19

Square P Breughel

Palais d'Egmont

Porte de Namur

R du Champ de Mars

Rue de Dublin

37

Place de Londres

38

Rue d'Italie

Place Poelaert

Jardin d'Egmont

Square du Bastion

35

36

Rue d'Edimbourg

34

32

Blvd de Waterloo

33

Rue de Stassart

43

Chaussée de Wavre

39

Av de la Toison d'Or

Rue du Grand Cerf

Rue des Drapiers

44

Rue des Chevaliers

Rue du Berger

41

Rue Longue

42

40

Rue St Boniface

R.

Rue de la Paix

Rue de Longue Vie

45

Place Louise

Louise

47

46

Rue Cap Crespel

Rue de la Pépinière

9

Place Jacobs

48

Waterloo

Av de la Toison d'Or

R De Joncker

54

55

Rue Jean Stas

58

57

59

56

Place Stéphanie

60

Rue de Stassart

Rue du Prince Royal

Rue Keyenveld

Rue du Prince Royal

Chaussée d'Ixelles

61

Rue de Tulipe

Rue Sans-Souci

Rue du Viaduc

Rue Sans-Souci

Rue Bosquet

Rue Jourdan

Rue de l'Écosse

Rue de Suisse

Capouillet

Rue Berckmans

Place Loix

Chaussée de Charleroi

68

69

66

67

70

65

Rue de la Concorde

Rue du Président

Rue Jean d'Ardenne

Rue de Livourne

Petit

Rue de l'Arbre

64

Rue Souverains

Place Fernand Cocq

Rue Mercelis

63

Rue du Collège

Rue de Venise

Rue Van Aa

R. Van Volxem

62

Place Conscience

Rue de la Source

Av Louise

Rue de la Longue Haie

Ixelles

Rue de la Croix

Chaussée d'Ixelles

Rue Blanche

Rue de Livourne

Rue de Bordeaux

Rue de la Victoire

Rue Veydt

71

72

Rue du Beau Site

Rue de l'Ermitage

Rue Defacqz

76

Rue Faider

Rue Paul Émile-Janson

77

78

Rue Lesbroussart

75

79

80

Rue du Mont-Blanc

Rue St-Bernard

81

84

83

82

85

Rue du Châtelain

86

Rue Gachard

Chaussée de Vleurgat

Lake Ebangs

98

97

99

Rue du Bailli

Chaussée de Charleroi

Rue de l'Aqueduc

100

Rue Américaine

96

95

Rue du Page

Rue Washington

Rue de Tenbosch

93

94

87

88

89

Av du Général de Gaulle

Av de la Cambre

Rue Vilain XIV

Rue du Lac

91

92

90

Av Louise

102

103

de la Jonction

Chaussée de Waterloo

Rue Henri Wafelaerts

MAP 7 EU AREA

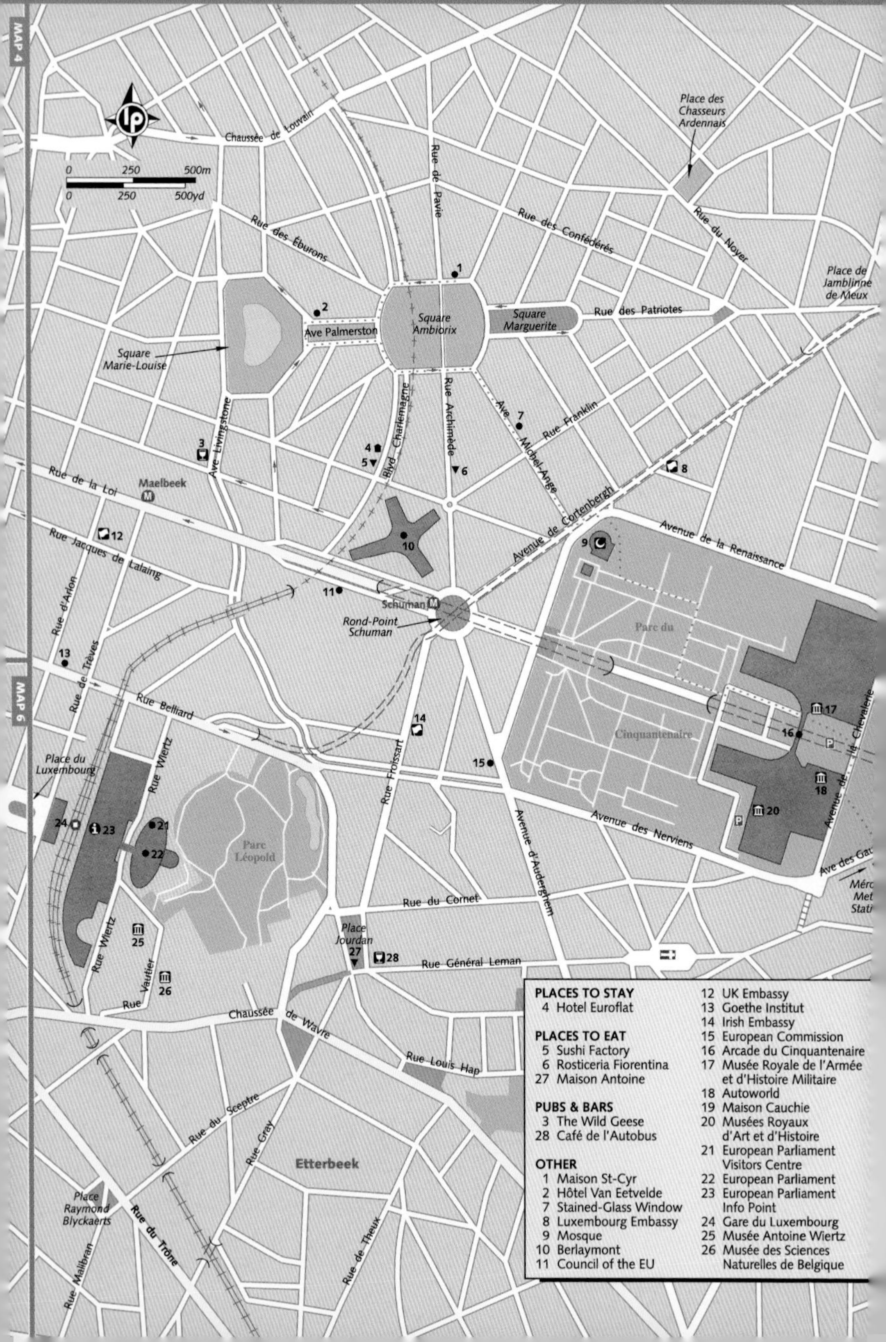

MAP 4

MAP 6

0 250 500m
0 250 500yd

Chaussée de Louvain

Place des
Chasseurs
Ardennais

Rue de Pavie

Rue des Confédérés

Rue du Noyer

Place de
Jamblinne
de Meux

Rue des Eburons

Square
Marie-Louise

Ave Palmerston

Square
Ambiorix

Square
Marguerite

Rue des Patriotes

Rue Franklin

Blvd Charlemagne

Rue Archimède

Ave Michel-Ange

Ave Livingstone

Rue de la Loi

Maelbeek
M

Rue Jacques de Lalaing

Rue d'Arlon

Avenue de Cortenbergh

Avenue de la Renaissance

Parc du
Cinquantenaire

Rue de Trèves

Rue Belliard

Schuman M
Rond-Point
Schuman

Rue Froissart

Place du
Luxembourg

Rue Wiertz

Rue Wiertz

Rue Vautier

Parc
Léopold

Avenue d'Auderghem

Avenue des Nerviens

Ave des Gat

Mérc
Met
Stati

Place
Jourdan

Rue du Cornet

Rue Général Leman

Chaussée de Wavre

Rue Louis Hap

Etterbeek

Place
Raymond
Blyckaerts

Rue du Trône

Rue du Sceptre

Rue Gray

Rue des Theux

Rue Malibran

PLACES TO STAY	12 UK Embassy
4 Hotel Euroflat	13 Goethe Institut
	14 Irish Embassy
PLACES TO EAT	15 European Commission
5 Sushi Factory	16 Arcade du Cinquantenaire
6 Rosticeria Fiorentina	17 Musée Royale de l'Armée
27 Maison Antoine	et d'Histoire Militaire
	18 Autoworld
PUBS & BARS	19 Maison Cauchie
3 The Wild Geese	20 Musées Royaux
28 Café de l'Autobus	d'Art et d'Histoire
	21 European Parliament
OTHER	Visitors Centre
1 Maison St-Cyr	22 European Parliament
2 Hôtel Van Eetvelde	23 European Parliament
7 Stained-Glass Window	Info Point
8 Luxembourg Embassy	24 Gare du Luxembourg
9 Mosque	25 Musée Antoine Wiertz
10 Berlaymont	26 Musée des Sciences
11 Council of the EU	Naturelles de Belgique

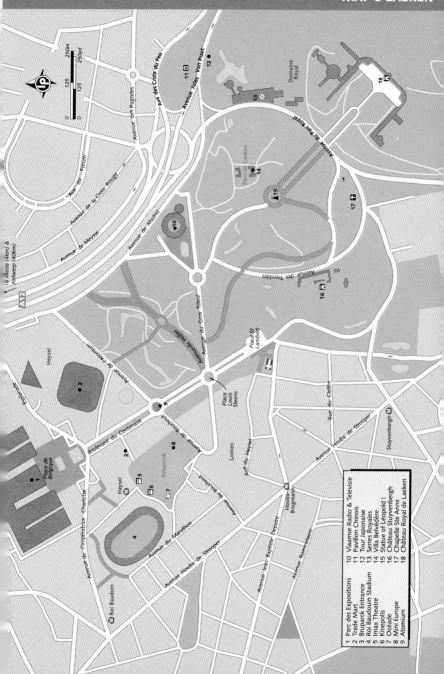

MAP 8 LAEKEN

250m
250yd
125
125
0
0

A12

To Meise (4km) &
Antwerp (40km)

Avenue des Pagodes
Avenue du Forum
Ave des Croix du Feu
Avenue Jules Van Praat
Avenue de la Croix-Rouge
Avenue de Meysse
Avenue de Madrid

Domaine Royal

Parc Laeken

Avenue du Parc Royal

Avenue des Trembles

Avenue du Gros Tilleul
Avenue Hallet

Place St-
Lambert

Heysel

Avenue de l'Atomium

Place Louis
Steens

Boulevard du Centenaire

Brupark

Avenue de Bouchout

Laeken

Rue du Heysel

Rue du Cloître

Avenue Houba de Strooper

Stuyvenbergh

Houba-
Brugmann

Place de
Belgique

Heysel

Avenue de l'Impératrice Charlotte

Avenue du Marathon

Avenue Houba de Strooper

Avenue Jean-Baptiste Depaire

Avenue Romineère

Roi Baudoin

1	Parc des Expositions	10	Vlaamse Radio & Televisie
2	Trade Mart	11	Pavillon Chinois
3	Bruparck Entrance	12	Tour Japonaise
4	Roi Baudouin Stadium	13	Serres Royales
5	Imax Theatre	14	Villa Belvédère
6	Kinepolis	15	Statue of Léopold I
7	Océade	16	Château Stuyvenbergh
8	Mini Europe	17	Chapelle Ste Anne
9	Atomium	18	Château Royal de Laeken

MAP 9 BRUGES (BRUGGE)

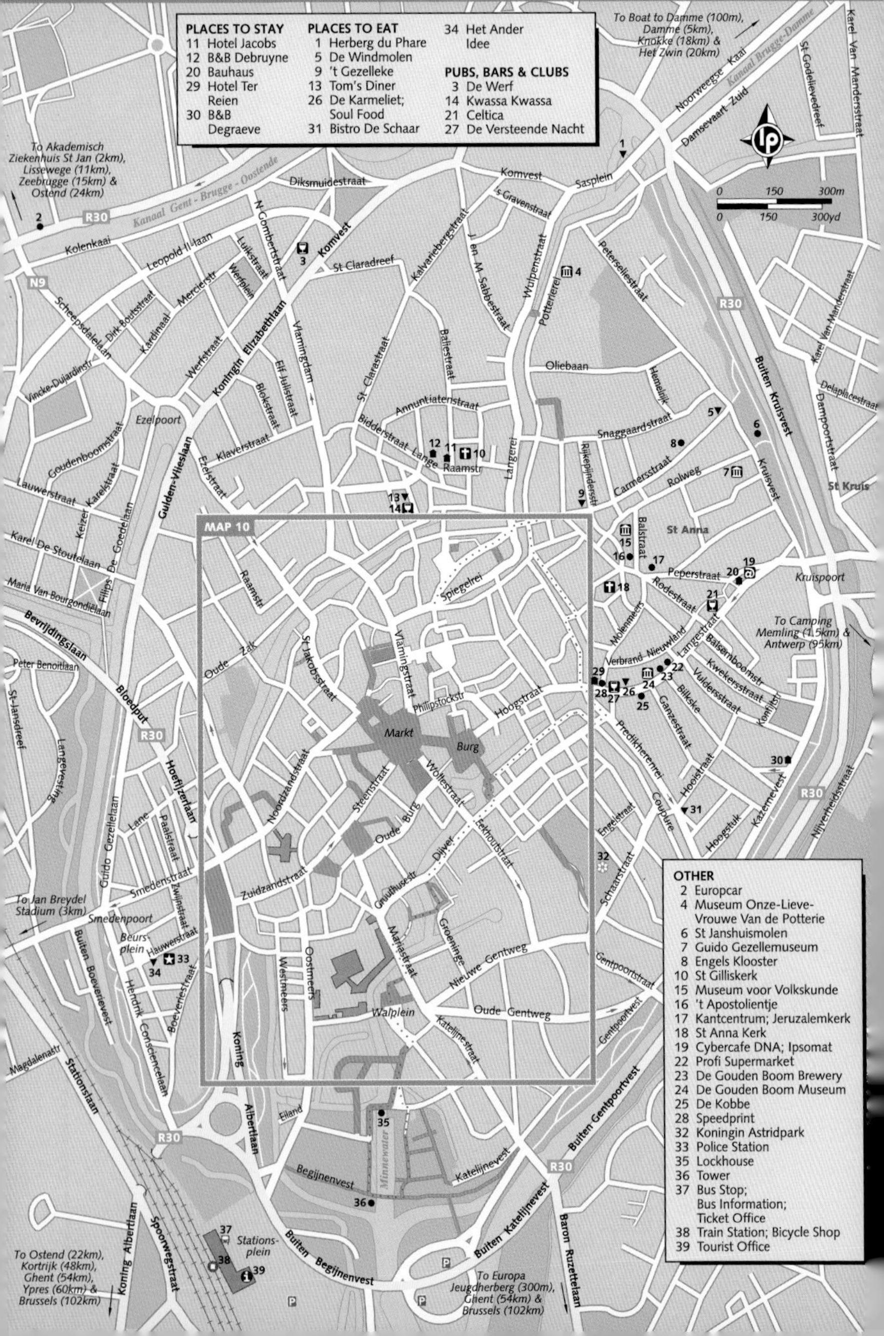
PLACES TO STAY
11 Hotel Jacobs
12 B&B Debruyne
20 Bauhaus
29 Hotel Ter Reien
30 B&B Degraeve
PLACES TO EAT
1 Herberg du Phare
5 De Windmolen
9 't Gezelleke
13 Tom's Diner
26 De Karmeliet; Soul Food
31 Bistro De Schaar
34 Het Ander Idee
PUBS, BARS & CLUBS
3 De Werf
14 Kwassa Kwassa
21 Celtica
27 De Versteende Nacht
OTHER
2 Europcar
4 Museum Onze-Lieve-Vrouwe Van de Potterie
6 St Janshuismolen
7 Guido Gezellemuseum
8 Engels Klooster
10 St Gilliskerk
15 Museum voor Volkskunde
16 't Apostolientje
17 Kantcentrum; Jeruzalemkerk
18 St Anna Kerk
19 Cybercafe DNA; Ipsomat
22 Profi Supermarket
23 De Gouden Boom Brewery
24 De Gouden Boom Museum
25 De Kobbe
28 Speedprint
32 Koningin Astridpark
33 Police Station
35 Lockhouse
36 Tower
37 Bus Stop; Bus Information; Ticket Office
38 Train Station; Bicycle Shop
39 Tourist Office
To Boat to Damme (100m), Damme (5km), Knokke (18km) & Het Zwin (20km)
To Akademisch Ziekenhuis St Jan (2km), Lissewege (11km), Zeebrugge (15km) & Ostend (24km)
To Camping Memling (1.5km) & Antwerp (95km)
To Jan Breydel Stadium (3km)
To Ostend (22km), Kortrijk (48km), Ghent (54km), Ypres (60km) & Brussels (102km)
To Europa Jeugdherberg (300m), Ghent (54km) & Brussels (102km)
0 150 300m
0 150 300yd
MAP 10
Markt
Burg
St Anna
St Kruis
Kanaal Gent - Brugge - Oostende
Kanaal Brugge-Damme
Minnewater
Stationsplein
Walplein
Komvest
Kruispoort
Smedenpoort
Ezelpoort
R30
N9

Bruges, one of Europe's best-preserved medieval cities, dreamily evokes a world long since gone.

The guildhalls on Bruges' Markt are still lively centres of debate – but over a relaxing coffee and waffle.

MAP 10 BRUGES (BRUGGE) CENTRE

Sledestr 1
Jan Boninstraat
Ezelstraat 2
Raamstraat
Zakke
Oude Zak
Rozendal
St Jorisstraat
Jan Miraelstraat
Pottenmakerstraat
Augustijnenrei
Korteweinkel
Peter Pourbusstr
Vlamingstraat
Kipgras
Spaanseplein
Spaansestraat
Gouden Handrei
Krom Genthof
Genthof
Oosterling-plein 4
Woensdag-markt
Spiegelrei 8
Gouden Handrei 5
6
Biekorfstraat 7
Strostraat
St Annarei
Verversdijk

3 Adjjestraat
Pottenmakerstraat
Grauwwerkersstraat
Academiestraat
Rode Haanstr
Jan Van Eyckplein 9
Biskajersplein 10
B Ostenstr
St Jansstraat
Kraanplein
Spinolarei
Engelstraat
Koningstraat
Hoornstraat
Maartens-plein
Boomgaardstraat
Kandelaarstraat

St Jakobs-plein
Boterhuis
14
15
11
13
A Willaertstr
J Van Ooststr
12
Kraanplein
St Jan-plein
St Walburgstr 29
Twinstraat 28
30
31

16 18
17 19
Palmstraat
St Jakobsstraat
Naaldenstraat
Kuiperstraat
20
Niklaus Desparsstraat
Vlamingstraat
Jozefstraat
Vlamingdam
St Walburgstraat
Ridderstraat
Kraken
Kuipenstraat
Hoogstraat
27
32
33
Hertsbergestr
34
Groenerei

Geerwijnstraat
Moerstraat
21
22
Eiermarkt
Geernaart-straat
23
Philipstockstraat
Burgstraat
26
35
Meestraat
Peerdenstraat

Muntplein
42
40 41
Markt 37
24
25
Breidelstraat
36
Burg
60
Predikherenstraat

43
44
St Amandsstraat
Korte Zilverstr
Klein St Amandsstr
39 38
48
49
53 54 55 56 57
Cala
58 59
63
Braambergstraat
Freren Fonteinstraat
65

Steenhouwersstraat
Prinsenhof
Oude Zilverstr
45
46 47
50
52
51
Wollestraat
Vismarkt
62
61
70
66
67
Park
Waalsestraat

Hallestraat
Wulfhagestraat
Glasstraat
Noordzandstraat
Steenstraat
St Niklaasstraat
Kartuizerinnestraat
80
79
78
81
Huiden-vetters-plein
69
68
Genthof
Kraanlei
Koningin Astridpark

92
91
Zilverstraat
Kuselstraat
88
87
86
Loppemstraat
Simon Stevin-plein
Oude Burg
82
76 77
75
74 73
71 72
Eekhoutstraat
Geerolfstraat
Stalijzerstraat
Gevangenisstraat

90
89
85
Dweersstraat
Zuidzandstraat
Steenstraat
Nieuwstraat
Mariastraat
83
84
Guido Gezelle-plein
100 101
102
103
105
104
Eekhoutpoort
Groenerei
Gentmerk

93
94
95
't Zand
96
St Anna-kerkhof
97
98
99
Heilige Geeststraat
Grauthusestraat
Guido Gezelleplein
107
108
106
O.L.V. Kerkhof
Groenerei
Nieuwe Gentweg

Korte Vulderstr
Hoogste van Brugge
Geestraat
St Jan in de Meers
Bakkersstr
Oostmeers
109
110
O.L.V. Kerkhof Zuid
Kastanjeboomstraat
Nieuwe Gentweg

Koolbrandersstraat
Westmeers
St Janshospitaal
111
Stoofstraat
Mariastraat
Walstraat
112
Oude Gentweg
113

Walplein
Zonnekemeers
114
115
116
117 118
Wijngaardstraat
Noordstraat

0   100   200m
0   100   200yd

MAP 10

A boat trip along the canals is a highlight of many people's stay in Bruges.

PATRICK SYDER

MAP 11 ANTWERP (ANTWERPEN)

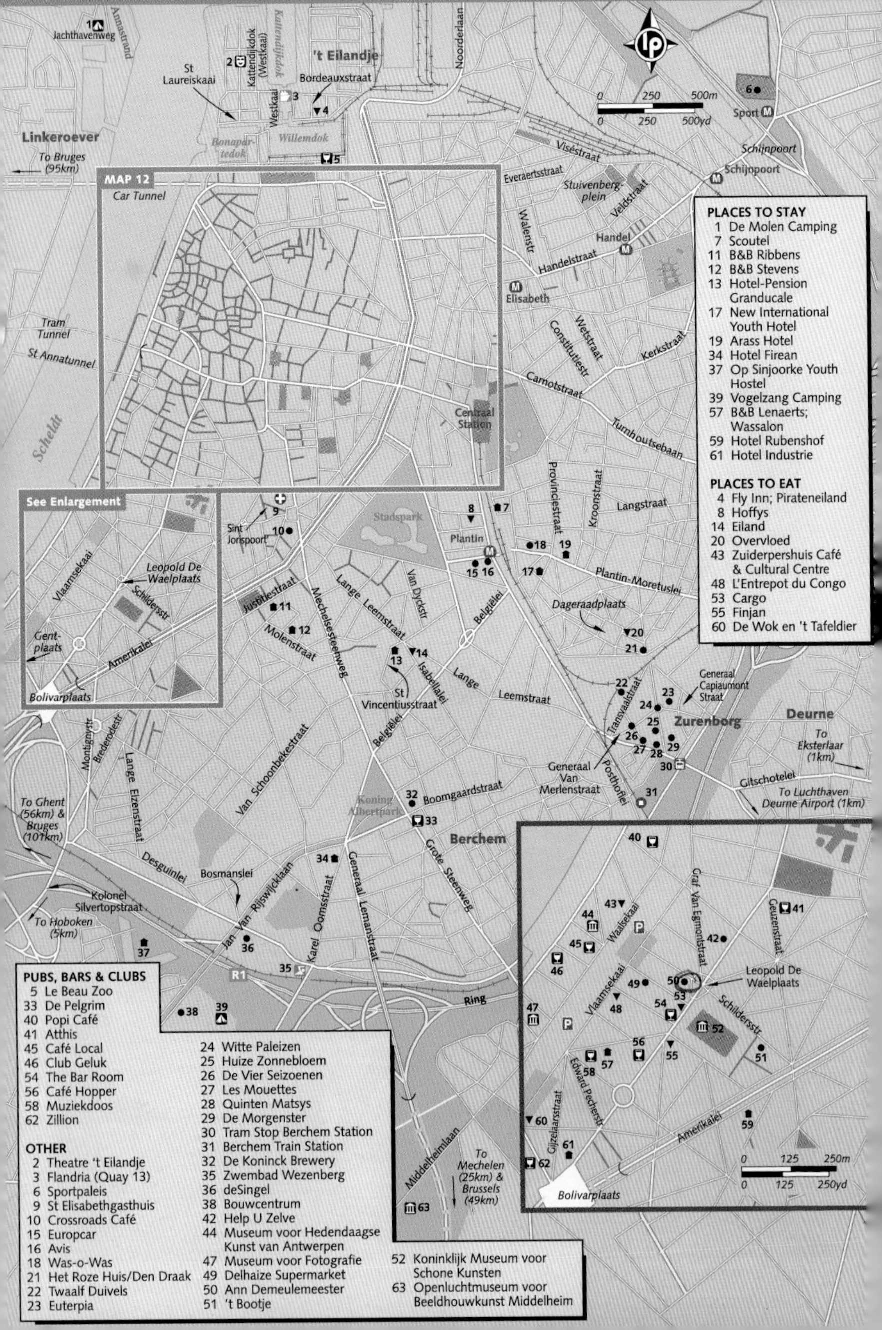

Jachthavenweg
Annastrand
Kattendijkdok (Westkaai)
Kattendijkdok
't Eilandje
Noorderlaan
St Laureiskaai
Bordeauxstraat
Westkaai
Linkeroever
To Bruges (95km)
Bonapartedok
Willemdok
MAP 12
Car Tunnel
Everaertsstraat
Viséstraat
Stuivenberg-plein
Veldstraat
Schijnpoort
Sport
0 250 500m
0 250 500yd
Walenstr
Handel
Handelstraat
Elisabeth
Constitutiestr
Wetstraat
Kerkstraat
Carnotstraat
Centraal Station
Turnhoutsebaan
Tram Tunnel
St Annatunnel
Scheldt
See Enlargement
Sint Jorispoort
Stadspark
Provinciestraat
Kroonstraat
Langstraat
Plantin
Plantin-Moretuslei
Dageraadplaats
Vlaamsekaai
Leopold De Waelplaats
Schildersstr
Gentplaats
Amerikalei
Bolivarplaats
Justitiestraat
Molenstraat
Mechelsesteenweg
Lange Leemstraat
Van Dyckstr
Belgiëlei
Isabellalei
St Vincentiusstraat
Lange Leemstraat
Transvaalstraat
Generaal Capiaumont Straat
Zurenborg
Deurne
To Eksterlaar (1km)
Generaal Van Merlenstraat
Posthoflei
Gitschotelei
To Luchthaven Deurne Airport (1km)
Montignystr
Brederodestr
Lange Elzenstraat
Van Schoonbekestraat
Koning Albertpark
Boomgaardstraat
Berchem
To Ghent (56km) & Bruges (101km)
Desguinlei
Bosmanslei
Jan Van Rijswijcklaan
Karel Oomsstraat
Generaal Lemanstraat
Grote Steenweg
Kolonel Silvertopstraat
To Hoboken (5km)
R1
Ring
Middelheimlaan
To Mechelen (25km) & Brussels (49km)
Graaf Van Egmontstraat
Geuzenstraat
Waalsekaai
Vlaamsekaai
Schildersstr
Edward Pecherstr
Cijzelaarsstraat
Amerikalei
Bolivarplaats
0 125 250m
0 125 250yd

PLACES TO STAY
1 De Molen Camping
7 Scoutel
11 B&B Ribbens
12 B&B Stevens
13 Hotel-Pension Granducale
17 New International Youth Hotel
19 Arass Hotel
34 Hotel Firean
37 Op Sinjoorke Youth Hostel
39 Vogelzang Camping
57 B&B Lenaerts; Wassalon
59 Hotel Rubenshof
61 Hotel Industrie

PLACES TO EAT
4 Fly Inn; Pirateneiland
8 Hoffys
14 Eiland
20 Overvloed
43 Zuiderpershuis Café & Cultural Centre
48 L'Entrepot du Congo
53 Cargo
55 Finjan
60 De Wok en 't Tafeldier

PUBS, BARS & CLUBS
5 Le Beau Zoo
33 De Pelgrim
40 Popi Café
41 Atthis
45 Café Local
46 Club Geluk
54 The Bar Room
56 Café Hopper
58 Muziekdoos
62 Zillion

OTHER
2 Theatre 't Eilandje
3 Flandria (Quay 13)
6 Sportpaleis
9 St Elisabethgasthuis
10 Crossroads Café
15 Europcar
16 Avis
18 Was-o-Was
21 Het Roze Huis/Den Draak
22 Twaalf Duivels
23 Euterpia
24 Witte Paleizen
25 Huize Zonnebloem
26 De Vier Seizoenen
27 Les Mouettes
28 Quinten Matsys
29 De Morgenster
30 Tram Stop Berchem Station
31 Berchem Train Station
32 De Koninck Brewery
35 Zwembad Wezenberg
36 deSingel
38 Bouwcentrum
42 Help U Zelve
44 Museum voor Hedendaagse Kunst van Antwerpen
47 Museum voor Fotografie
49 Delhaize Supermarket
50 Ann Demeulemeester
51 't Bootje
52 Koninklijk Museum voor Schone Kunsten
63 Openluchtmuseum voor Beeldhouwkunst Middelheim

MAP 12

PLACES TO STAY
4 International Zeemanshuis
12 Antigone Hotel
16 Hotel Rubens
24 De Witte Lelie
32 Hotel Euro
58 Hotel Postiljon
85 Hilton
100 Astrid Park Plaza Hotel;
Regus; Action Club
127 B&B Peetermans
130 Hotel Scheldezicht
131 Pension Cammerpoorte
142 Hotel Eden

PLACES TO EAT
8 Amadeus
11 Dock's Cafe
18 Domus Eethuisje
20 Lenny's
21 Pottenbrug
27 Full Sing
39 Gulden Swaene
41 De Peerdestal
47 Sjalot en Schanul
68 Preud'Homme
69 De Matelote
70 Café de la Gare
72 Ilha Formosa
73 Eethuisje De Stoemppot
78 Folies d'Anvers
79 Sir Anthony Van Dyck
83 Mama's Garden
93 Quick
99 Rolmops
110 Sushi Express
112 Lamalo Grill
118 Goossens
121 Désiré de Lille
123 Pitten & Bonen
126 't Fornuis
129 Het Nieuwe Palinghuis
132 Het Dagelijks Brood
135 De Gouden Ecu

PUBS, BARS & CLUBS
1 The Boots
3 Café Hessenhuis
5 Café d'Anvers
7 Red & Blue; Fill
Collins Club
9 Oil Food & Booze
17 Babylon
42 Café Buster

44 The Irish Times
48 Den Engel
52 Swingcafé
57 Paeters Vaetje
59 't Elfde Gebod
60 De Muze
71 Kafé Marqué
74 De Ware Jacob
75 Jacqmotte
81 De Vagant
82 Pelgrom
113 Horta Grand Café
114 Oud Arsenaal
138 Bierhuis Kulminator

OTHER
2 Budget
6 Red-Light District
10 St Pauluskerk
13 The Steen; Nationaal
Scheepvaartmuseum
14 Vleeshuis
15 Oude Beurs
19 2Zones
22 Boekhandel 't Verschil
23 Rockoxhuis
25 Universitaire Faculteiten St
Ignatius (UFSIA)
26 GOC
28 Vlaamse Jeugdherbergcentrale
29 Eurolines
30 Pardaf
31 Info Kiosk De Lijn
33 Mekanik Strip
34 Airstop/Taxistop
35 VTB Reisboekhandel
36 Centrale Openbare Bibliotheek
37 St Jacobskerk
38 St Carolus-Borromeuskerk
40 Stadsbibliotheek
43 Apotheek Lotry
45 ATM Dexia Bank
46 Tourist Office
49 Flandria
50 Cartoons Cinema & Café
51 De Windroos
53 Etnografisch Museum
54 Stadhuis
55 Brabo Fountain
56 Stadswinkel
61 International Magazine Store
62 usit Connections

63 Jenny Hannivers
64 Onze Lieve Vrouwkathedraal
65 Bierparadijs
66 Goffin
67 Bag Bearer Statue
76 Belgium Beers
77 Jordaenshuis
80 De Vagant
84 Rubens Statue
86 FNAC Bookshop & Ticket
Service
87 Grand Bazar Shopping
Centre; GB Supermarket
88 Torengebouw (Boerentoren);
KBC Bank
89 Meir Square; Lancelot & Co
90 Filmmuseum; Koninklijk
Paleis
91 Rubenshuis
92 De Slegte
94 Van Dyck Statue
95 Spar Supermarket
96 Post Office
97 Vlaamse Opera
98 UGC Cinema
101 Koningin Elisabethzaal
102 Provinciaal Diamantmuseum
103 Antwerpen Zoo; Tourist
Office Kiosk
104 Thomas Cook
105 Centraal Station
106 Post Office
107 Leo Stevens Exchange
108 easyEverything
109 Del Rey
111 Diamondland
115 Bourlaschouwburg; De Foyer
116 Museum Mayer Van den
Bergh
117 Moving
119 Philip's Biscuits
120 Burie
122 Louis
124 Main Post Office
125 Het Modepaleis
128 Museum Plantin-Moretus
133 Wassalon
134 ModeMuseum
136 Walter
137 Police Station
139 Maagdenhuis
140 Kruidtuin
141 Stadsschouwburg
143 Provinciaal Diamantmuseum

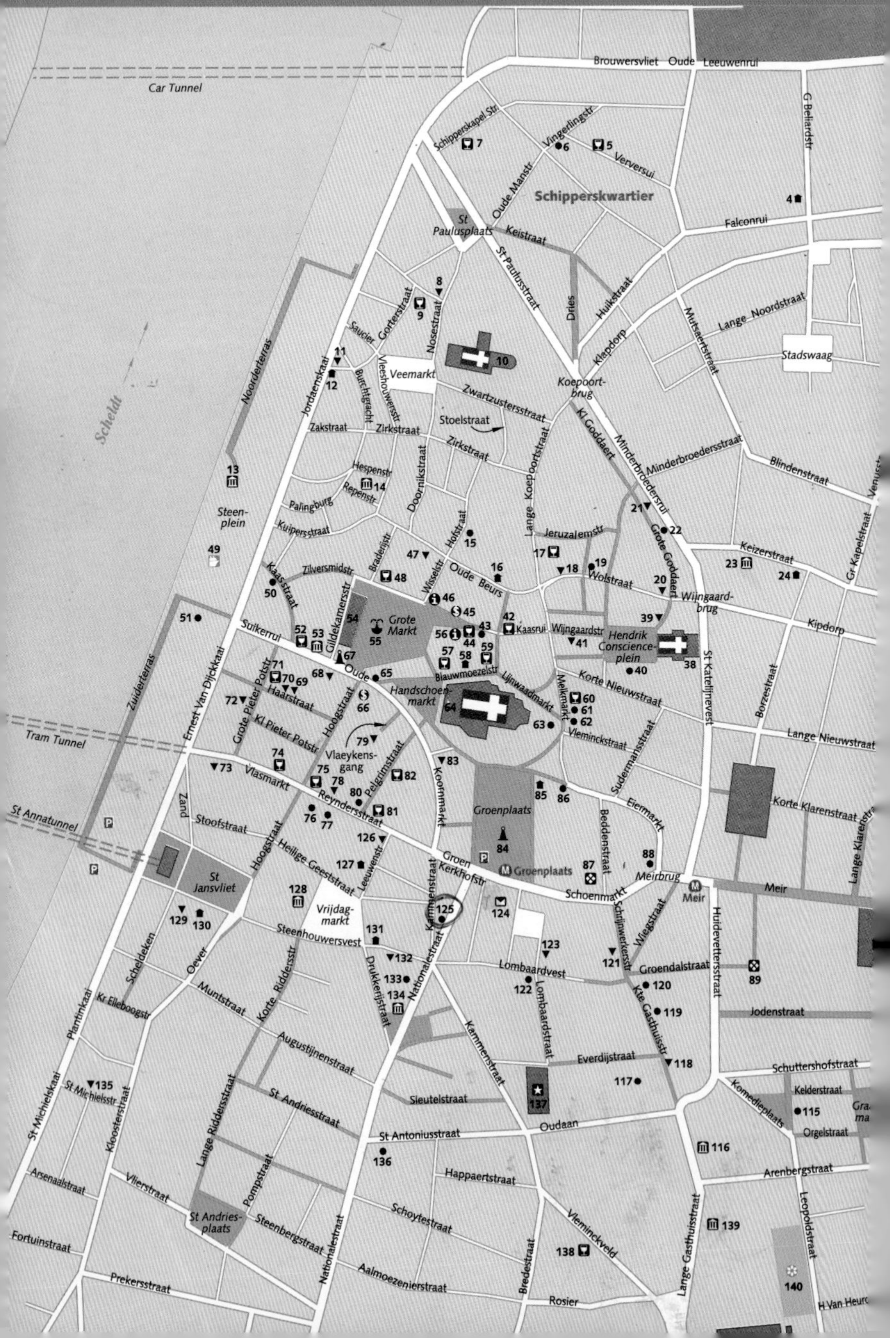

MAP 12 ANTWERP (ANTWERPEN) CENTRE

Car Tunnel

Brouwersvliet Oude Leeuwenrui

G Beliardstr

Schipperskwartier

Schipperskapel Str 7

Vingerlingstr 6 5 Verversui

4

Falconrui

Lange Noordstraat

Oude Manste

St Paulusplaats

Keistraat

St Paulusstraat

Dries

Huikstraat

Kipdorp

Stadswaag

8

Sauder Gortenstraat

Noesstraat

9

Vleeshouwersstr

Veemarkt

10

Zwartzusterstraat

Koepoort-brug

Kl Goddaart

Minderbroedersrui Minderbroedersstraat

Blindenstraat

Jordaenstraat 11 12

Butchersstr

Zakstraat

Zirkstraat

Zirkstraat

Lange Koepoortstr

21

Cte Goddaart 22

Keizerstraat 23 24

Gr Kapelstraat

Verulst

Hespenstr Repenstr 14

Doeenstraat

Stoelstraat

Jeruzalemstr

17

Wolstraat 18 19

20

Wijngaard-brug

Kipdorp

Steen-plein

13

Palingburg

Kuiperstraat

Oude Beurs

15

16

Kaasrui 42 Wijngaardstr

39

Hendrik Conscience-plein 38

Lange Nieuwstraat

49

Zilversmidstr

47 48

Woestr 46 45 43 44

56 57 58 59

40

Korte Nieuwstraat

Borzestraat

Scheldt

50

Suikerrui

Gildekamerstr 52 53 54 55 67

Grote Markt

Blauwmoezelstr

Lijnwaadmkt

60 61 62

Vleminckstraat

Suderminderstraat

51

71 70 69 68 65 66

Oude

Handschoen-markt

54

63

Korte Klarenstraat

Lange Klarenstr

Tram Tunnel

Zuiderterras

Ernest Van Dijckkaai

Grote Pieter Potstr Haarstraat

Hoogstraat

79 Vlaeykens-gang

83

Koornmarkt

85 86

Eiermarkt

72 73 Vlasmarkt

74

75 78 80

Reyndersstraat

82

Groenplaats

88

St Annatunnel

Zand

Stoofstraat

76 77

81

126

84

Groenplaats 87 Meirbrug Meir

Meir

St Jansvliet

129 130

Oever

Hoogstr Heilige Geeststraat

127

128

Leeuwenstr

Groen Kerkhofstr

124

Schoenmarkt 123 121

Huidevettersstraat

Jodenstraat

89

Vrijdag-markt

131

125

Kr Eliboogstr

Muntstraat

Korte Riddersstr

Steenhouwersvest

132

133 134

Lombaardvest

122

Lombaardstraat

Kte Gasthuisstr 120 119

Everdijstraat 118

Schuttershofstraat

Keiderstraat Grama

Pieterstraat

135

St Michielsstr

Kloosterstraat

Augustijnenstraat

St Andriesstraat

Sleutelstraat

Oudaan

137

117

115 Orgelstraat

Kammenstraat

Arenbergstraat

Arsenaalstraat

Vlierstraat

Lange Riddersstr Pompstraat

St Andries-plaats

136

St Antoniusstraat

Happaertstraat

116

139

Fortuinstraat

Prekerstraat

Steenbergstraat

Nationalestraat

Schoytestraat

Vlemin ckveld

138

140

Aalmoezenierstraat

Rosier

Breėdestraat

Lange Gasthuisstr

Leopoldstraat

H Van Heur